WITHDRAWN

The Shaping of a Community

St Andrews Studies in Reformation History

Editorial Board:

Andrew Pettegree, Bruce Gordon and John Guy

Forthcoming titles in this series include:

*The Shaping of a Community: The Rise and Reformation
of the English Parish c. 1400–1560*
Beat Kümin

*Seminary or University? The Genevan Academy and
Reformed Higher Education, 1560–1620*
Karin Maag

Protestant Identity and History in Reformation Europe
edited by Bruce Gordon

Marian Protestantism: Six Studies
Andrew Pettegree

The Shaping of a Community

The Rise and Reformation of the English Parish
c. 1400–1560

BEAT A. KÜMIN

SCOLAR
PRESS

© Beat Kümin, 1996

All rights reserved. No part of this publication may be reproduced, stored in a retrieval system, or transmitted in any form or by any means, electronic, mechanical, photocopying, recording, or otherwise without the prior permission of the publisher.

Published by
SCOLAR PRESS
Gower House
Croft Road
Aldershot
Hants GU11 3HR
England

Ashgate Publishing Company
Old Post Road
Brookfield
Vermont 05036
USA

British Library Cataloguing in Publication Data

Kümin, Beat A.
    Shaping of a Community: Rise and
    Reformation of the English Parish,
    c. 1400–1560.
    (St Andrews Studies in Reformation History)
    I. Title II. Series
    942

Library of Congress Cataloging-in-Publication Data

Kümin, Beat.
    The shaping of a community: the rise and reformation of the
    English parish, c. 1400–1560/Beat A. Kümin.
        p.   cm. Includes bibliographical references
    ISBN 1–85928–164–8
    1. Great Britain—History—Lancaster and York, 1399–1485.
    2. Great Britain—Politics and government—1399–1485.   3. Great
    Britain—Politics and government—1485–1603.   4. Great Britain—
    History—Tudors, 1485–1603.   5. Community life—England—History.
    6. Parishes—England—History.   7. England—History, Local.
    I. Title.
    DA245.K85   1995   95–8752
    942'.04—dc20   CIP

ISBN 1 85928 164 8

Typeset in Sabon by Bournemouth Colour Press and printed in Great Britain by Biddles Ltd, Guildford.

DA
245
.K85
1996

032096-6596H5

Contents

List of tables, figures, and maps

Tables

Figures

Maps

Preface

It is perhaps not immediately obvious why a foreign author should want to address the 'shaping' of the English parish, and a word or two of explanation may be appropriate. As it happens, this can be easily done, for the book owes its existence largely to the direction and encouragement of my two principal academic teachers. Peter Blickle set my mind firmly on the study of local communities from day one of my undergraduate course at Berne, and, come the time of selecting a dissertation topic, pointed me towards the copious English parish archives. Patrick Collinson agreed to act as my supervisor at Cambridge, listened patiently to my questions, and prevented me from making many a premature judgement. The influence of two different approaches and historiographical traditions proved an extremely stimulating experience, and I can only hope that the resulting study, whatever its merits or shortcomings, manages to reflect something of the fortunate circumstances under which it was written.

Naturally, I have accumulated a great many debts to the scholars who supported me in this project. Heinrich R. Schmidt provided absolutely invaluable help at the early stages, particularly in matters of methodology and quantitative analysis, while later on in England, I benefited greatly from the critical advice of Clive Burgess, John Craig, Katherine French and from both my examiners, Eamon Duffy and Richard M. Smith. Virginia Bainbridge, Caroline Barron, Christopher Brooke, Patrick Carter, Barrie Dobson, Christopher Dyer, Ken Farnhill, Rosi Fuhrmann, Gary Gibbs, John Hatcher, Ronald Hutton, Neil Jones, Caroline Litzenberger, Diarmaid MacCulloch, Mark Ormrod, Susan Reynolds, Gervase Rosser, Miri Rubin, Peter Spufford, and Irene Zadnik have all readily contributed comments or allowed me to read some of their unpublished manuscripts. Seminar groups at Birmingham, Cambridge, London, Norwich, Oxford, St Andrews, and particularly Peter Blickle's *Doktorandenkolloquium* at Berne provided many important suggestions, while the termly 'parish meeting' at the Institute of Historical Research has been an excellent opportunity for a general exchange of ideas. Among the many people who made my work easier in one way or another were Bob Scribner, Jim Oeppen, J. S. Johnston, the vicar of Prescot, and the staff at Cambridge University Library, as well as the record offices at Bristol and Taunton. Andrew Pettegree's initiative and enthusiasm were instrumental for me and no doubt for many other members of the 'European Reformation Research Group'. Scolar Press, and Alec McAulay in particular, deserve a special mention for their energetic support of new historical research. I am also very grateful to my father, who read the proofs of the thesis as competently as if he were a native English speaker, and to Michelle Webster for quite a lot besides. For too many reasons to be listed, this book is dedicated to my parents.

Ever since I crossed the Channel, Cambridge has offered a social and intellectual atmosphere which must be difficult to match. The president and members of the Leckhampton community have made my stay as a postgraduate student a most enjoyable experience, and so have CFC, KFC, JP, SW, the odd football game, and many an Italian restaurant. I am grateful for the generous financial support of the Swiss National Science Foundation, the Bridges Scholarship of Corpus Christi College, the Overseas Research Student Awards Scheme, and the Archbishop Cranmer, Lightfoot, and Prince Consort and Thirlwall Funds of the Faculty of History at Cambridge, which made this project possible. And, last but not least, my thanks must go to Magdalene for providing me with a very privileged platform from which to continue my research.

Notes and abbreviations

1. The dates are those found in the manuscripts, but the year is taken to begin on 1 January.
2. The original spelling has been retained, except in the case of Christian names, standard abbreviations, and obsolete letters.
3. In the interest of consistency (not all the manuscripts are foliated) and in accordance with the structure of the database files, all references to churchwardens' accounts take the following form: [parish] CWA, [year].

All Saints CWA	BRO, P/AS/ChW/1: 1406–7 to 1481–2 3: 1485–6 to 1559–60
Andrew Hubbard CWA	GL, MS 1279/1: 1454–6 to 1522–3 2: 1524–5 to 1558–60
Ashburton CWA	A. Hanham (ed.), *The CWA of Ashburton 1479–1580*, Devon and Cornwall RS, NS xv (Torquay, 1970)
Botolph Aldersgate CWA	GL, MS 1454, rolls 1 (1466–8) to 65 (1559–60)
Boxford CWA	P. Northeast (ed.), *Boxford CWA 1530–61*, Suffolk RS xxiii (Woodbridge, 1982)
BRO	Bristol Record Office
CW(s)	Churchwarden(s)
CWA	Churchwardens' accounts
EcHR	Economic History Review
Edmund CWA	H. J. F. Swayne (ed.), *The CWA of St Edmund and St Thomas, Sarum 1443–1702*, Wiltshire RS (Salisbury, 1896)
EHR	English Historical Review
f./fos	folio(s)

ff.	and following pages
fn.	Footnote
GL	London: Guildhall Library
Halesowen CWA	F. Somers (ed.), *Halesowen CWA 1487–1582*, Worcestershire Historical Society xl (London, 1952–7)
JEH	Journal of Ecclesiastical History
Mary–at–Hill CWA	H. Littlehales (ed.), *The Medieval Records of a London City Church, St Mary at Hill 1420–1559*, Early English Text Society cxxv and cxxviii (London, 1904–5)
MS(S)	Manuscript(s)
NS/OS	New Series/Old (or Original) Series
PaP	Past and Present
Peterborough CWA	W. T. Mellows (ed.), *Peterborough Local Administration: Parochial Government before the Reformation: CWA 1467–1573*, Publications of the Northamptonshire RS ix (Kettering, 1939)
Prescot CWA	F. A. Bailey (ed.), *The CWA of Prescot, Lancashire 1523–1607*, The RS for the Publication of Original Documents Relating to Lancashire and Cheshire civ (Preston, 1953)
PRO	London: Public Record Office
PSIA	Proceedings of the Suffolk Institute of Archaeology
RS	Record Society
SCH	Studies in Church History
SRO	Taunton: Somerset Record Office
St Ewen's CWA	B. R. Masters and E. Ralph (eds), *The Church Book of St Ewen's, Bristol 1454–1584*, Publications of the Bristol

and Gloucestershire Archaeological
Society, Records Section vi (Bristol,
1967)

TBGAS   Transactions of the Bristol and
                       Gloucestershire Archaeological Society

TRHS   Transactions of the Royal Historical
                       Society

VCH   The Victoria History of the Counties of
                       England

Yatton CWA   SRO, D/P/yat/4/1/1: 1445–6 to 1521–2
                                         2: 1523–4 to 1539–40
                                         3: 1540–1 to 1559–60

Mine Eltere

CHAPTER ONE

Introduction

Compared to the title pages of early printed books, with their meticulous description of subject matter, source material, and methodology, those of contemporary historical studies tend to be rather less elaborate. The present one is a case in point, and a closer definition of the basis and scope of the inquiry must be the first priority of these opening passages. Three notions in particular should be addressed. First, to associate the 'rise' of the English parish with the years between 1400 and 1560 does not imply that the subject can be understood without a closer look at previous centuries. On the contrary, the creation of the parochial network was an achievement of the high Middle Ages, and both the formulation of canonical duties and the emergence of the main parochial institutions date from before the fifteenth century. By 1400, the rise of the parish was well under way, but the vagaries of source survival prohibit any comparative or quantitative analysis of the process for the early stages. And yet, there are more than just documentary reasons to suggest that the process continued and arguably intensified during the following century and a half. As will be shown in more detail below, this period witnessed the commitment of increasing resources to the parish, the development of new liturgical and social customs, a growth in secular and voluntary communal activities, and, famously, the 'great age of parish church rebuilding'. From the mid-sixteenth century, Tudor legislation added the finishing touches to the shaping of the community by turning it into a local government unit. This, however, amounted to a fundamental redefinition of its role, and the start of the Elizabethan reign can serve as a convenient cut-off point for our purposes. Due to the gradual emergence of other types of parochial records, the expansion of statutory communal responsibilities, and the definitive break with the old religious ways too many parameters changed, and any further analysis would have to adopt radically different approaches. 'Reformation', to clarify the second notion, should thus be taken to refer only to the early and repeatedly reversed changes under Henry VIII, Edward VI, and Mary Tudor.

Third, the use of the term 'community' may have to be justified. Due to its recent proliferation and indiscriminate application to all sorts of social groups it has become rather meaningless to some observers.[1] Here, however, 'parish community' appears not as an anachronistic transfer of anthropological terminology or as part of a sinister plot to obscure the potential for conflict in local society, but as a common-sense acknowledgement of the existence of a geographically defined religious and social unit with certain collective responsibilities and the capability to act, sue, and be represented as a quasi-corporate body.[2] It reflects the fact that it could nurture 'pride' and 'intense loyalty' among its members,[3] as well as the observation that much of late medieval worship was of a distinctly 'corporate' nature.[4] These three points, I hope, will help to put the following argument in perspective.

The scientific interest in the religious life of the later Middle Ages is of course no recent phenomenon. Historians of all denominations have studied a wide variety of aspects, focusing on idiosyncratic beliefs of individuals as well as attempting to come to an understanding of popular piety.[5] In the late 1960s, the emphasis shifted noticeably towards the unorthodox and pagan, based on the assumption of a significant gap between the teachings of the official Church and the religious feelings of the population at large. Rather than as an age of faith, Jean Delumeau interpreted the Middle Ages as only superficially Christianized, and Keith Thomas's influential work unearthed an impressive amount of magical elements in contemporary religious practice.[6] There was also a strong interest in minorities and heretical movements, of which England possessed one of the foremost examples. Much valuable and interesting

---

[1] M. Rubin, 'Small groups: identity and solidarity in the late Middle Ages' in J. Kermode (ed.), *Enterprise and Individuals in Fifteenth-Century England* (Stroud, 1991), pp. 133–4. For Christine Carpenter, 'there is now a strong case for banning the word "community" from all academic writing' ('Gentry and community in medieval England', *Journal of British Studies*, 33 (1994), 340).

[2] 'Community' in its more pragmatic sense as a concept 'negotiated and renegotiated to suit the self-interests of its participants' rather than a synonym for harmony and unity continues to be useful to medieval historians: M. Kowaleski, 'Introduction' (to 'Vill, gild, and gentry: forces of community in later medieval England'), ibid., 339.

[3] P. Marshall, *The Catholic Priesthood and the English Reformation* (Oxford, 1994), p. 200; similar J. A. F. Thomson, *The Early Tudor Church and Society 1485-1529* (London/New York, 1993), p. 265.

[4] E. Duffy, *The Stripping of the Altars* (New Haven/London, 1992), Chapter 4.

[5] J. van Engen, 'The Christian Middle Ages as an historiographical problem', *American Historical Review*, 91 (1986), 519–52, provides a convenient survey of English and Continental historiography on the subject.

[6] J. Delumeau, *Catholicism between Luther and Voltaire* (London, 1977), and K. Thomas, *Religion and the Decline of Magic* (2nd edn, London, 1971).

work has since been done on the Lollards, their geographical spread, writings, and social background.[7]

However, such approaches can be criticized for adopting a somewhat reductionist and selective view of the later Middle Ages. Orthodox, everyday religious activities are much more difficult to trace in historical sources, simply because neither chronicler nor ecclesiastical judge found them worth recording. Any attempt to arrive at a general assessment valid for as large a section of society as possible must therefore resist the temptation to extrapolate from the extravagant or exceptional. At the very least, existing sources of ordinary religious life have to be incorporated alongside other evidence. Naturally, these do rarely answer the sort of questions that present-day historians would like to ask, and, given that their *raison d'être* was often administrative and practical, they can be repetitive, tedious, and confusing. Yet means and ways have to be found to make them accessible and manageable. This is the process that this study seeks to contribute to.

In the sphere of English Reformation history, A. G. Dickens's pioneering work displayed some of the methodological bias described above.[8] To this day, he focuses on early signs of religious discontent, anticlericalism, and heretical doctrines, in spite of the challenges of his revisionist critics and their blunt statement that the English people 'did not want the Reformation'.[9] The historiographical debate has become rather inflexible, with Dickens trying to provide more and more cases of committed Protestants, and the revisionists pointing out how divided a nation England remained deep into the reign of Elizabeth.[10] At present, the problem does not seem to lend itself to a satisfactory solution, and the choice of an appropriate approach to reassess developments at the grass-roots level is far from obvious.[11] For a long time, wills were

---

[7] J. A. F. Thomson, *The Later Lollards 1414-1520* (Oxford, 1965), K. B. McFarlane, *John Wycliffe and the Beginnings of English Nonconformity* (3rd edn, London, 1972), D. Plumb, 'The social and economic spread of rural Lollardy: a reappraisal' in W. J. Sheils and D. Wood (eds), *Voluntary Religion* (Oxford, 1986), pp. 111–29, and the works of Ann Hudson and Margaret Aston, to name but a few.

[8] *The English Reformation* (London, 1964; revised edn, 1989). For a somewhat partisan, but valuable introduction to the relevant recent literature: C. Haigh, 'The recent historiography of the English Reformation', *Historical Journal*, 25 (1982), 995–1007.

[9] J. J. Scarisbrick, *The Reformation and the English People* (Oxford, 1984), p. 1.

[10] A. G. Dickens, 'The early expansion of protestantism in England 1520–58', *Archive for Reformation History*, 78 (1987), 187-222; C. Haigh, *English Reformations* (Oxford, 1993), pp. 285–95.

[11] A. J. Slavin, 'Upstairs, downstairs: or the roots of Reformation', *Huntington Library Quarterly*, 49 (1986), 252, discusses theological and legal treatises of writers such as St German and assures us that 'it is in dialogue with such texts … that we must seek parochial realities'. The methodological problems of such an approach are evident, and it is not a road which this study will seek to explore.

considered to be the way forward. Countless local studies have focused on the interpretation and quantitative analysis of preambles, charting slower or faster progress of reformed ideas, but recently the voices urging methodological caution have become more and more prominent.[12] The source should not be discarded of course, but for a balanced analysis of the pre- and early Reformation periods, it has to be supplemented by the records of collective and communal institutions. The revisionists have led the way by exploring fraternity registers and (very selectively) churchwardens' accounts.[13] Here we can hope for some insight into the elusive processes of negotiation, conflict management, elections, and everyday administration which involved more than just individuals or selected social groups. Given the lack of a sharp contemporary distinction between the secular and ecclesiastical, they should also allow us a glimpse at both of these spheres.

In the former, the study of local communities is nothing new. In line with their economic and cultural importance, townspeople have always attracted a great deal of interest, and as early as 1922, Joan Wake stressed that an analysis of village life demanded more than a look at seigneurial sources.[14] A quick glance at recent work suggests that this advice has now been heeded.[15] Robert Goheen may have gone furthest when he called for a revision of the historical convention that peasants cannot understand political issues, that they are mere objects and unworthy of special analysis. A new definition of consciousness, he argued with reference to Gilbert Ryle and Jean Paul Sartre, should reflect that 'the mind is now understood to include the ability to act intelligently, and not just to theorize action'.[16]

In the realm of religious history, the equivalent social unit is the parish, which has now clearly emerged as the main point of reference for the

---

[12] See for example Duffy, *Stripping of the Altars*, pp. 504–23, and C. Burgess, 'Late medieval wills and pious convention: testamentary evidence reconsidered' in M. A. Hicks (ed.), *Profit, Piety and the Professions in Later Medieval England* (Gloucester, 1990), pp. 14–33.

[13] Scarisbrick, *Reformation*, pp. 19–39 (lay fraternities), and R. Hutton, 'The local impact of the Tudor Reformations' in C. Haigh, *The English Reformation Revised* (Cambridge, 1987), pp. 114–38.

[14] J. Wake, 'Communitas villae', *EHR*, 37 (1922), 409.

[15] R. M. Smith, ' "Modernization" and the corporate village community: some sceptical reflections' in A. Baker and D. Gregory (eds), *Explorations in Historical Geography* (Cambridge, 1984), pp. 150–61, discusses the main 'schools' of village historiography. For other long-term surveys on the English and European countryside see C. Dyer, 'Power and conflict in the medieval village' in D. Hooke (ed.), *Medieval Villages* (Oxford, 1985), pp. 27–32, *Communautés rurales* (Paris, 1984), and L. Genicot, *Rural Communities in the Medieval West* (Baltimore/London, 1990).

[16] 'Peasant politics? Village communities and the crown in fifteenth-century England', *American Historical Review*, 96 (1991), 61.

analysis of everyday devotional and social life.[17] This is an astonishing development: it is not that long ago since John Bossy asserted 'that the Church of the last medieval centuries was not in actual fact a parochially grounded institution',[18] and as recently as 1988, it was still appropriate to regret that hardly anything had been written on this local 'focus of loyalty as well as of administration, or on the unique blend of secular and ecclesiastical that underpinned it'.[19] In the same year, however, there were signs of change even in as unlikely a field as the study of 'popular culture', when one of its protagonists conceded that the parish was 'perhaps the most essential organizational form of social exchange'.[20] And by 1995, an impressive amount of conference papers, essays, and monographs have been written which tackle the subject from a variety of different angles.[21] Furthermore, much valuable research has been undertaken in neighbouring areas. There are now up-to-date accounts of the complex relationships between clergymen and their communities,[22] revisionist summaries of the political progress of the Reformation,[23] reconstructions of the origin and development of communal customs and rituals,[24] and new approaches to the liturgical and devotional life of late medieval and early Tudor parishioners.[25] At the same time, the whole image of the late Middle Ages as a period of stagnation or decline has been markedly revised. Summarizing accounts of church institutions, undistracted by the long shadow of the Reformation, can nowadays use

---

[17] According to Thomson, *The Early Tudor Church*, p. 265, the parish commanded the 'main attention' in people's religious life.

[18] 'The Counter-Reformation and the people of catholic Europe', *PaP*, **47** (1970), 53.

[19] D. Palliser, 'Introduction: the parish in perspective' in S. Wright (ed.), *Parish, Church and People* (London, 1988), p. 6. Previously, lay parochial organization tended to be discussed from an architectural and art-historical perspective. See for example C. Platt, *The Parish Churches of Medieval England* (London, 1981), which includes a chapter on the 'Community of the parish'. Demographers, of course, had made extensive use of parish registers, culminating in E. A. Wrigley and R. S. Schofield, *The Population History of England 1541–1871* (London, 1981).

[20] A. Gurevich, *Medieval Popular Culture* (Cambridge, 1988), p. 79.

[21] Susan Wright edited a pioneering collection of essays entitled *Parish, Church and People* in 1988, and the medieval congresses at Kalamazoo 1993 and Leeds 1994 both featured sessions on the topic. As for the sources, the Bishop's Stortford CWA have recently been (re-)published (ed. S. Doree) and several other sets will follow shortly.

[22] In addition to the classic studies of Peter Heath and Margaret Bowker: Marshall, *The Catholic Priesthood*, and M. Skeeters, *Community and Clergy: Bristol and the Reformation c.1530-c.1570* (Oxford, 1993).

[23] Haigh, *English Reformations*.

[24] R. Hutton, *The Rise and Fall of Merry England: The Ritual Year 1400–1700* (Oxford, 1994).

[25] Duffy, *The Stripping of the Altars*.

positive terms to describe the state of diocesan administration, ecclesiastical courts, or the parish clergy.[26]

It goes without saying that this book cannot attempt to do justice to all of these new developments in equal measure. Its scope and perspective is more adequately defined by a few juxtapositions: community rather than individual, social rather than theological, orthodox rather than unorthodox, laity rather than clergy, horizontal rather than vertical, and long-term rather than short-term. To put it briefly: it looks at a period of English history through the eyes and sources of parishioners in their collective capacity, or, more precisely, through the records of their wardens. It cannot pretend to cover each and every aspect of parochial life, not even all those of a collective nature, but it assesses the principal communal office. The political and religious influence of princes or bishops, in contrast, appears only indirectly. This is not to deny their impact on parochial life, be it by means of injunctions, visitations, legislation or jurisdiction, but the priority here is to assess how these signals were received, modified, or resisted by people whose experiences went beyond contacts with their social betters, and who in turn embarked on their own independent initiatives. In villages as well as towns, everyday life was dominated as much by local issues and internal problems as seigneurial influence.

It is fair to ask, though, whether the renewed interest in parish religion has left scope for another detailed study. Furthermore, is there anything to add to the new interpretation of the later Middle Ages? Three particular reasons seem to justify a fresh inquiry.

First, English churchwardens' accounts are unique in their broad pre-Reformation survival and the minute covering of parish income and expenses. Late medieval parish accounts in France are 'assez rares',[27] and historians in, say, the Netherlands or Germany have found it equally difficult to find a comparable body of records to assess communal

---

[26] C. Harper-Bill, *The Pre-Reformation Church in England 1400–1530* (London/New York, 1989), pp. 22 (courts), 24ff (bishops) and 44 (parish clergy).

[27] G. Constant, 'Une source trop négligée de l'histoire paroissiale: les registres de marguilliers', *Revue d'Histoire de l'Eglise de France*, 24 (1938), 172. In some dioceses (for example Mans) the survival is better: G. Huard, 'Considérations sur l'histoire de la paroisse rurale des origines à la fin du moyen âge', ibid., 17. Later on, the situation improves generally, and Andrew Spicer and Penny Roberts have made me aware of the sixteenth-century *comptes de la fabrique* discussed by E. Soil de Mariané, *L'Eglise Saint-Brice* (Tournai, 1908): Tournai; A. N. Galpern, *The Religions of the People in Sixteenth-Century Champagne* (Cambridge Mass., 1976): Troyes; and P. Benedict, *Rouen during the French Wars of Religion* (Cambridge, 1981).

religious life.[28] Scholarly interest in the source may of course increase, and new archival discoveries should never be ruled out, but they are unlikely to occur in large numbers. The favourable English record survival in this field seems to correspond to the pattern identified for other ecclesiastical sources.[29] Churchwardens' accounts thus form the empirical basis for this study, supplemented by visitation records, and a fresh reading of secondary literature. Many people have looked at parish accounts before, and the most interesting sets have been printed. However, they have never been taken as a whole. Historians have seen them as a quarry, as a basis for rather impressionistic interpretations. The main focus was often on extraordinary 'specimen entries',[30] on the printing of extracts 'to represent the whole',[31] or on the collection of empirical evidence to prove a particular point,[32] and the complete editions, too, deserve more attention than they have received. Even in France, where starting conditions are much less favourable, religious and social historians have repeatedly called for a wider use of parish accounts, particularly because 'tant à l'étranger qu'en France, un bon historien ... trouve, en des livres de comptes, que conservent les paroisses ou les archives, nombre de choses utiles ... à l'histoire générale de l'Eglise'.[33] To explore this potential by means of a comprehensive analysis of both published and manuscript sources, will be the first priority of the argument presented below.

---

[28] I am grateful to A. J. A. Bijsterveld and Peter Dykema for this information. Occasional evidence does survive: Jürgen Beyer for example, provided me with a reference to a pre-1550 *Kirchenrechnungsbuch* from Germany (H. J. Freytag, 'Zur Geschichte der Reformation in Plön', *Jahrbuch Plön*, **20** (1990), 32-5).

[29] 'The richness of English medieval material is perhaps unusual': D. Hay, *The Church in Italy in the Fifteenth Century* (Cambridge, 1977), p. 5.

[30] J. C. Cox, *CWA from the Fourteenth Century to the Close of the Seventeenth Century* (London, 1913), pp. 53ff (St Edmund, Sarum).

[31] C. B. Pearson (ed.), 'The CWA of St Michael, Bath', *Somersetshire Archaeological and Natural History Society Proceedings*, **23** (1877), xix.

[32] Recently above all the attempt to measure the amount of acquiescence in or resistance to the Reformation: R. Whiting, *The Blind Devotion of the People* (Cambridge, 1989), and Hutton, 'Local impact'. The same is true for Hutton, *Merry England*, which uses accounts primarily for the identification and (methodologically delicate) dating of religious rituals and secular ceremonies. J. Morrill, 'The Church in England, 1642-9' in his *Reactions to the English Civil War 1642-9* (London, 1982), pp. 89–114, scrutinized a nationwide sample of CWA for evidence of Anglican survival in the religious turmoil of the 1640s.

[33] G. Constant, 'Une source négligée de l'histoire ecclésiastique locale: les registres anciens de marguilliers. Etude d'un de ces registres du XVIᵉ siècle', *Revue d'Histoire Ecclésiastique*, **34** (1938), 541. See also his 'Une source trop négligée de l'histoire paroissiale', and, very recently, the renewed plea by P. Goujard, 'Les fonds de fabriques paroissiales: une source d'histoire religieuse méconnue', *Revue d'Histoire de l'Eglise de France*, **68** (1982), 99–111.

Second, the various waves of scholarly interest have not yet produced a homogeneous analysis of the available evidence on a nationwide scale. Nineteenth- and early twentieth-century studies adopted a predominantly local and antiquarian perspective,[34] or presented a more or less eclectic survey of the sources.[35] More recent studies either had a broader overall theme,[36] a topographic–architectural bias,[37] or an interest in the origin and early development of the parish.[38] Yet others shed much useful light on communal life by means of their analysis of subparochial institutions such as chantries[39] and fraternities,[40] while a range of recent work has relied heavily on parochial sources for in-depth local, regional, or county surveys.[41] This study, however, attempts a wider comparative

[34] J. Staples, *Notes on St Botolph without Aldersgate* (London, 1881), and T. S. Henrey, *St Botolph without Aldersgate* (London, 1895) on one of the parishes featured here, J. F. Nicholls and J. Taylor, *Bristol Past and Present* (vol. ii, Bristol, 1881) on parish life in one of the leading provincial cities, as well as countless articles in local record societies and introductions to published accounts.

[35] A. Jessopp, 'Parish life in England before the great pillage', *Nineteenth Century*, **43** (1898), 47–60, 431–47, and Cox, *CWA*.

[36] R. N. Swanson, *Church and Society in Late Medieval England* (Oxford, 1989), pp. 209–51, and Thomson, *The Early Tudor Church*, pp. 264–300, provide the best general surveys of the topic. S. Reynolds, *Kingdoms and Communities in Western Europe 900-1300* (Oxford, 1984), has a valuable chapter on the early history of the parish, and Genicot, *Rural Communities*, ch. 'parochia', offers a survey for rural Europe.

[37] G. H. Cook, *The English Medieval Parish Church* (London, 1954), Platt, *Parish Churches*, and R. Morris, *Churches in the Landscape* (London, 1989).

[38] C. E. S. Drew, *Early Parochial Organisation in England: The Origins of the Office of Churchwarden* (London, 1954), remains the classic study on the period from the thirteenth to the fifteenth century. For earlier stages see G. W. O. Addleshaw, *The Development of the Parochial System from Charlemagne to Urban II* (London, 1954) and his *Rectors, Vicars and Patrons in Twelfth and early Thirteenth-Century Canon Law* (York, 1956). C. N. L. Brooke and G. Keir, *London 800–1216* (London, 1975), ch. 6, discuss the origins of the parish system in the capital, J. Blair (ed.), *Minsters and Parish Churches* (Oxford, 1988), the situation in the country at large. See also the collection of essays the latter co-edited with R. Sharpe, *Pastoral Care Before the Parish* (Leicester, 1992), in which nos 6–11 deal with the Anglo-Saxon church.

[39] K. L. Wood-Legh, *Perpetual Chantries in Britain* (Cambridge, 1965), A. Kreider, *English Chantries: The Road to Dissolution* (Cambridge Mass., 1979), and particularly a series of essays by C. Burgess, starting with ' "For the increase of divine service": chantries in the parish in late medieval Bristol', *JEH*, **36** (1985), 46–65 (cf. the bibliography).

[40] L. T. Smith (ed.), *English Gilds* (London, 1870), H. F. Westlake, *The Parish Gilds of Medieval England* (London, 1919), Scarisbrick, *Reformation*, pp. 19–39, G. Rosser, 'Communities of parish and guild in the late middle ages' in Wright (ed.), *Parish, Church and People*, pp. 29–55, and Virginia Bainbridge, 'Gild and parish in late medieval Cambridgeshire' (Ph.D. London, 1994; to be published in 1996).

[41] N. Tanner, *The Church in Late Medieval Norwich* (Toronto, 1984), and S. Brigden, *London and the Reformation* (Oxford, 1989); both Whiting, *Blind Devotion* and A. Brown, *Popular Piety in Late Medieval England* (Oxford, 1995), focus on areas in the South-West; recent doctoral work includes G. G. Gibbs, 'Parish finance and the urban

approach, and argues on the basis of a consistent analysis of ten main sets of churchwardens' accounts from:

- the metropolitan parishes of St Andrew Hubbard and St Botolph Aldersgate, London, and All Saints and St Ewen's, Bristol;
- the market towns of Ashburton (Devon), Halesowen (Worcestershire), Peterborough, and Prescot (Lancashire); and
- the villages of Boxford (Suffolk) and Yatton (Somerset).[42]

This selection of case studies, complemented by evidence from many others, tries to reflect the great variety of surviving records by including vicarages and rectories, metropolitan, urban, and rural parishes, smaller and larger numbers of communicants, coherent and less coherent settlements, southern and northern counties, poorer and wealthier areas. It cannot claim to be a mathematically exact random sample, but the patchy and irregular survival of many sets makes this wellnigh impossible. The intention to quantify the evidence on a long-term basis restricted the choice to the limited amount of continuous and reasonably complete sources.[43] Even so, each case study has its peculiarities and individual starting-date. The All Saints accounts begin in the first decade of the fifteenth century; most others between 1440 and 1490. Two sets survive only from the sixteenth century, but their rare rural (Boxford) and northern (Prescot) origins seemed to justify their inclusion. Another important criterion was the quality of documentation for the first Reformation impact under Edward VI. This was a time of considerable disruption in parish administration,[44] and many a worthwhile case study

---

community in London 1450–1620' (Virginia, 1990), J. S. Craig, 'Reformation, politics, and polemics in sixteenth-century East Anglian market-towns' (Cambridge, 1992), K. L. French, 'Local identity and the late medieval parish: the communities of Bath and Wells' (Minnesota, 1993), and the theses by J. Merritt (London, 1992) on Westminster, C. Litzenberger (Cambridge, 1993) on the diocese of Gloucester, and J. A. Ford (Fordham, 1994) on Kent; among forthcoming dissertations: studies by J. Carnwath (Manchester) on Thame and other market towns (in the meantime see her 'The CWA of Thame c.1443–1524' in D. J. Clayton et al. (eds), *Trade, Devotion and Governance* (Stroud, 1994), pp. 177–97), B. Galloway on the Norfolk marshes, and K. Farnhill on East Anglian communities (both Cambridge).

[42] For detailed references see the List of Abbreviations. I am grateful to Clive Burgess for allowing me to use his transcripts of the early parts of the Andrew Hubbard and All Saints accounts.

[43] The earliest preserved accounts are those of St Michael Bath from 1349 (ed. C. B. Pearson). A limited range of parish activities is illustrated in accounts of Bridgwater for 1318–19: T. B. Dilks (ed.), *Bridgwater Borough Archives 1200–1485* (5 vols, Frome/London, 1933–71), but the fourteenth-century survival is thin; cf. the chronological analysis in Chapter 3.1.

[44] According to Hutton, *Merry England*, p. 69, only 18 sets cover the years 1535–62 fully.

(including Peterborough in this sample) fails on this account.

Each locality would clearly deserve a detailed analysis of its own, but this has not been intended here. With regard to the predominantly local perspective of most ongoing research, it appeared more rewarding to concentrate on what is similar and what is different in the case studies, and to propose some tentative conclusions on late medieval parochial religion in general. Contextualization is limited to a sketch of the basic background and characteristics of each individual set of accounts, and there is no discussion of local architectural, ceremonial, or genealogical features.

Furthermore, to concede other shortcomings of this approach, the style and argument of the chapters necessarily reflect the type of source material used. In other words, churchwardens' accounts rarely yield the sort of local colour, anecdotal asides and literary ornamentation so prominent in other studies of the period. It would be futile to try and wring from them some kind of *histoire totale* of late medieval religion or a feeling of what it was 'like' to be a parishioner, quite apart from the fact that this is no longer a historiographical priority. Drawing on a large number of additional sources such as liturgical texts, confessional literature, architectural evidence, and a great deal of empathy, Eamon Duffy has done just that.[45] The present account has set out to achieve a different and more modest purpose, namely to illuminate the government, resources, and social interactions of a local community. First and foremost, it is an attempt to describe and analyse the available evidence and to test out a more 'objective' approach to contemporary parish life. The aim is not to propose a naïve quantitative empiricism, but to do some preparatory work, to scan the sources for basic trends, and to point to the many remaining puzzles. The tone of the argument has thus been kept rather matter of fact, and the temptation to embellish or personalize has been resisted. This may have affected the quality of the narrative, and so has no doubt the pen of a non-native English speaker. For the latter, however, I can offer little more than a plea for tolerance.

Third, there is now a wideranging interest in parish life on the Continent. Local and regional studies are often compiled with a very strong comparative, national, and international perspective.[46]

---

[45] *Stripping of the Altars.*

[46] See for example the essays of Roland Ganghofer, Jean Gaudemet, Jerzy Kloczowski, Bernard Jacqueline, and Francis Rapp in *Communautés rurales* (Paris, 1984), pp. 39–106, 411–26, and 459–70, and the contributions to *Pievi e parrocchie in Italia nel basso medioevo* (2 vols, Rome, 1984). Recent regional studies include Galpern, *Champagne*, W. A. Christian, *Local Religion in Sixteenth-Century Spain* (Princeton, 1981), and C. Pfaff, 'Pfarrei und Pfarreileben' in *Innerschweiz und frühe Eidgenossenschaft* (2 vols, Olten, 1990), i. 203–82.

Furthermore, a social rather than strictly geographical approach has sparked a series of essays on parochial and subparochial foundations in Central Europe.[47] Their common point of reference is Peter Blickle's concept of 'communalism', which provides an interpretative framework for the increasing emphasis on communal values and institutions among late medieval peasants and townspeople alike. Having achieved a strong political and legal position, many rural and urban communities in Central Europe began to supervise the moral life of their clergy, to administer parish funds, to endow additional masses, chantries, or chapels and ultimately to aspire to create a fully privileged church within their boundaries and under their own control. In the south-western corner of the Holy Roman Empire in particular, political and religious power was anything but a monopoly of traditional feudal elites.[48] Much of this sounds familiar from recent English historiography, even though there is, not untypically, rather less emphasis on the theoretical reflection of such processes here. And yet, England's wealth of serial financial information for the late medieval parish, so sorely missing elsewhere, should be of considerable interest to Continental historians. In order to find some common ground with their findings, it seemed essential to go beyond the local level and to try to determine which general features the English parish shared with local ecclesiastical organization in Europe, and in what respect it may have been a special case. The present study, while attempting to illustrate this international dimension wherever possible, will probably offer more questions than answers. However, it may help to set an agenda.[49]

---

[47] H. Von Rütte, 'Bäuerliche Reformation am Beispiel der Pfarrei Marbach im Sanktgallischen Rheintal' and R. Fuhrmann, 'Die Kirche im Dorf: kommunale Initiativen zur Organisation von Seelsorge vor der Reformation' in P. Blickle (ed.), *Zugänge zur bäuerlichen Reformation* (Zurich, 1987), pp. 55–84, 147–86; see also Von Rütte, 'Von der spätmittelalterlichen Frömmigkeit zum reformierten Glauben', *Itinera*, 8 (1988), 33–44, Fuhrmann, 'Dorfgemeinde und Pfründstiftung vor der Reformation' in P. Blickle and J. Kunisch (eds), *Kommunalisierung und Christianisierung* (Berlin, 1989), pp. 77-112, and Fuhrmann's thesis *Kirche und Dorf* (Stuttgart, 1995) on the canonical aspects of communal foundations.

[48] P. Blickle, 'Kommunalismus: Begriffsbildung in heuristischer Absicht' in his *Landgemeinde und Stadtgemeinde in Mitteleuropa* (Munich, 1989), pp. 5–38, 14ff. Particular emphasis on the ecclesiastical field in his 'Communal Reformation and peasant piety: the peasant Reformation and its late medieval origins', *Central European History*, 20 (1987), 216–28.

[49] I hope to contribute a general survey on 'The English parish in its European context' to the forthcoming collection *The Parish in English Life 1400–1600*, co-edited by K. L. French, G. G. Gibbs, and myself.

The argument opens with a brief account of the origins of the parochial network and the development of its institutions, most notably the office of churchwarden. A social profile and an analysis of the various ecclesiastical and secular responsibilities of the wardens seeks to illustrate their importance for late medieval society as a whole. Chapter 3 contains the empirical core of the thesis. It introduces the selection of case studies, addresses the question of the reliability of churchwardens' accounts as a historical source, and proceeds to a presentation of the details and trends in parish finance. The subparochial level of chapels, chantries, and fraternities forms the subject of the next section, with a special emphasis on the ties which linked them to the main parish institutions. Chapter 5 attempts to place parochial finance in the context of general socio-economic trends and competing demands on parishioners' resources, while an analysis of the effects of the mid-sixteenth-century changes in communal worship, administration, and autonomy will seek to contribute to a closer understanding of what 'Reformation' meant for English towns and villages. At the end and in a rather speculative manner, an epilogue will raise the wider question of the late Middle Ages as a 'communal era' in large parts of Western Europe.

The project has been tackled in full awareness of the considerable practical problems involved, above all in applying computer technology to medieval sources. There are no established formats to fall back on, and it might have been wise to leave such an undertaking to qualified accountants or statisticians. However, to rehearse a well-worn excuse, this study wants to make a start. It will endeavour to show that the overall benefit of a comprehensive look at churchwardens' accounts may eventually outweigh the many legitimate methodological reservations.

CHAPTER TWO

The Community of the Parish

2.1 The canonical perspective: cure of souls and financial dues

2.1.1 Early history

The parish has been defined as 'a township or cluster of townships having its own church, and ministered to by its own priest ..., to whom its tithes and ecclesiastical dues are paid'.[1] In England, local ecclesiastical provision developed in four main stages:

> (i) a system, general in Anglo-Saxon England, of large parishes served by teams of priests operating from important central churches ('the old minsters');
> (ii) the rapid proliferation, between the tenth and twelfth centuries, of 'local' or 'private' churches with resident priests;
> (iii) a major building campaign, during the eleventh and twelfth centuries, of stone church-building at the local level; and
> (iv) the eclipse of the minsters, the division of their parishes between local churches, and the crystallisation of the modern parochial system, a process which was under way in the eleventh century and complete by the thirteenth.[2]

This pattern was not universal. In France, for example, the basic network of local churches took shape in the Carolingian period, while in many areas of northern Italy, minster churches or *pievi* continued to exercise a baptismal monopoly up to the fourteenth century and beyond.[3] England's phase (ii) coincided with the fragmentation of complex royal or ecclesiastical estates into smaller manors which developed religious centres of their own. Church foundations were thus normally seigneurial or episcopal initiatives, but the influence of broad lay demand for easier access to the sacraments should not be discounted.[4] In some areas under Germanic law, collective efforts led to 'communally owned churches' (*genossenschaftliche Gemeindekirchen*). In Norway, for instance, the peasants of one legal district founded a

---

[1] Palliser, 'The parish in perspective', p. 7.

[2] Blair, 'From minster to parish church', p. 1.

[3] M. Aubrun, *La paroisse en France des origines au XVᵉ siècle* (Paris, 1986), pp. 33–4, C. Violante, 'Sistemi organizzativi della cura d'anime in Italia' in *Pievi e parrocchie in Italia nel basso medioevo* (Rome, 1984), i. 23.

[4] Reynolds, *Kingdoms and Communities*, p. 89.

central church which they maintained and whose priest they elected.[5] There are no traces of such a system in rural England, but communal churches may have existed in some towns. Here, two generalizations have been made: 'places with many churches became urban during the Anglo-Saxon period, and the founders of the churches were usually laypeople'.[6] Some certainly did so in a collective capacity, and Domesday Book contains evidence for communal ownership, but normally advowson and profits remained with an individual.[7] Many old English towns distinguished themselves by a large number of parishes: while Braunschweig, Rostock, and Hamburg each contained four, Cologne 12, and Toledo in Castile 28, York possessed 40, Norwich 46, and London 110.[8] A generous supply of clergymen appears to be a general characteristic of the late medieval *Ecclesia Anglicana*. In the pre-Reformation diocese of Geneva, there may have been 50 households per secular priest, in sixteenth-century Castile over 40, but in England just 22.[9]

In contrast to the old minster *parochiae*, the new local units seem to have been imposed upon an earlier landscape in a rather arbitrary fashion.[10] Instead of coinciding with one or more manors, by the time of phase (iv) parishes often cut across secular boundaries.[11] The proliferation of local ecclesiastical provision resulted in a remarkable construction effort, which produced some 2000 stone churches between

---

[5] H. E. Feine, 'Die genossenschaftliche Gemeindekirche im germanischen Recht', *Mitteilungen des Instituts für österreichische Geschichtsforschung*, **68** (1960), 171–96.

[6] Morris, *Churches*, p. 169.

[7] D. Owen, *Church and Society in Medieval Lincolnshire* (Lincoln, 1971), p. 4, and Addleshaw, 'Parochial System', p. 13. Examples of collective town foundations: C. Brooke, 'The churches of medieval Cambridge' in D. Beales and G. Best (eds), *History, Society and the Churches* (Cambridge, 1985), p. 52, and his 'The church in the towns 1000–1250' in G. J. Cuming (ed.), *The Mission of the Church* (Cambridge, 1970), p. 78. The reference to Domesday Book: G. Rosser, 'The Anglo-Saxon gilds' in J. Blair (ed.), *Minsters and Parish Churches* (Oxford, 1988), p. 32.

[8] B.-U. Hergemöller, 'Parrocchia, parroco e cura d'anime nelle città anseatiche del Basso Medioevo' in P. Prodi and P. Johanek (eds), *Strutture ecclesiastiche in Italia e Germania prima della Riforma* (Bologna, 1984), p. 144; Christian, *Local Religion in Spain*, p. 8, 11, 149; Tanner, *Church in Late Medieval Norwich*, pp. 2–3, and Brigden, *London and the Reformation*, pp. 24–5.

[9] Rough estimates calculated from Aubrun, *Paroisse*, p. 159, Christian, *Local Religion in Spain*, p. 14, and Swanson, *Church and Society*, p. 30. These are averages, there were of course great differences between different periods and individual parishes (see below).

[10] T. Williamson, 'Parish boundaries and early fields', *Journal of Historical Geography*, **12** (1986), 247.

[11] O. Reichel, *The Origins and Growth of the English Parish* (London, 1921), p. 7, and Blair, 'From minster to parish church', p. 14; J. Haslam, 'Parishes, wards and gates in eastern London', ibid., p. 41, argues the same case for London, but cf. Brooke and Keir, *London*, chs vi and vii.

*c.*1075 and *c.*1125. By the twelfth century, parochial boundaries could be disputed down to the last yard.[12] A jury of elected townsmen, to take just one example, defined the respective territories of Ely and Wisbech shortly after this date.[13] The priests were estate officials, chosen and invested by local lords, and the rights and endowments of the church were treated as seigneurial property, which could be sold and divided.[14] Tithes in particular, enforceable at law since the tenth century, were often split up and in various lay hands.[15]

The Gregorian reform and the ensuing ecclesiastical legislation from the eleventh to the thirteenth centuries tackled this excessive dependency of the Church by means of measures aimed at a better separation of the spiritual and secular spheres.[16] As a result, benefices were attached to specific clerical offices, and priests subjected to the laws of the Church and the ordinary's supervision. In other words, the ecclesiastical hierarchy reassumed control over parochial religion.[17] Tithes were also effectively reformed. By the thirteenth century, their character as dues on gross proceeds was firmly established, payment enforced on pain of excommunication, and lay encroachment eradicated. Eventually, the Lateran councils and regional synods enforced a 'constitutional and administrative framework, which broadly speaking still functions in England today':[18] patrons' rights were limited to the presentation of suitable clergymen, whom the bishops inducted. Ideally, successful candidates obtained a fully privileged rectory with cure of souls and a benefice for life, but this became rather less common. A side-effect of the church's campaign against lay control was the increase in the ratio of appropriated parish churches from a quarter in 1150 to over a third by

---

[12] Morris, *Churches in the Landscape*, pp. 147 (building effort) and 225–6 (boundaries). The latter no doubt for primarily financial motives.

[13] D. Owen, 'Two medieval parish books from the diocese of Ely' in M. Barber et al. (eds), *East Anglian Studies* (Reading, 1985), p. 127 (early thirteenth century).

[14] Addleshaw, *Parochial System*, pp. 5ff. This is the system Ulrich Stutz refers to as *Eigenkirche*.

[15] O. Reichel, *The Rise of the Parochial System in England* (Exeter, 1905), p. 8.

[16] A convenient summary in R. Rodes, *Ecclesiastical Administration in Medieval England* (Notre Dame/London, 1977), pp. 49ff. There were of course other dimensions to contemporary ecclesiastical reform: A. Vauchez, *Les laïcs au moyen âge* (Paris, 1987), pp. 133–43, speaks of a 'tournant pastoral' in the thirteenth century. Following the lead of Lateran IV, regional synods devised a basic catechetical programme: Duffy, *Stripping of the Altars*, p. 54; a similar emphasis on regular confession and knowledge of fundamental prayers in France: Aubrun, *Paroisse*, p. 172.

[17] 'Contacts grew narrower and narrower between [local priests] and the bishop, and they became, especially from the thirteenth century forward, the latter's representatives': Genicot, *Rural Communities*, p. 119.

[18] Addleshaw, *Rectors, Vicars and Patrons*, p. 3, and for the passages below pp. 6ff, 12ff, and 17ff.

the sixteenth century.[19] In these cases, the rectorship passed to a monastic or collegiate institution, and the cure of souls was delegated to a vicar. The legal and financial terms of tenure for the deputies varied, but they normally received just a third of the tithes to cover all their obligations and ecclesiastical dues. It goes without saying that this diversion of parochial resources must have affected the quality of pastoral provision.[20] Monasteries, friaries, and even cathedral churches could offer some spiritual services to the laity, but basic needs had to be met in the parish.[21]

The fiscalization and meticulous territorial definition of the local church made it increasingly difficult to establish new parishes. Many changes in settlement patterns no longer entailed ecclesiastical adjustments, and historians agree that the 'cold hand of canon law' froze the parochial map around 1200.[22] However, the demand for reform never really abated.[23] The 8838 benefices of the 1534 *Valor Ecclesiasticus* were very unequally divided: they covered on average three or four square miles in the south-east of England, but up to 70 in some areas of the north.[24] The situation in individual counties was similar; a quick glance at, say, a map of Surrey or Lancashire reveals an extreme variation of shapes and sizes.[25] Whalley (Lancs.) contained 30 townships, St Margaret Westminster 3500 souls, while one Vincent Engeham was the sole parishioner of Knowlton in Kent.[26] Size and population were

---

[19] Ibid., pp. 6 and 14. Between 33 and 37 per cent of parishes were incorporated in Bristol, Gloucester and York, but only 6 per cent in Exeter (Skeeters, *Community and Clergy*, p. 101). A total of 3300 benefices were affected at the time of the *Valor Ecclesiasticus*: Swanson, *Church and Society*, p. 44. Elsewhere, the tendency could be much more pronounced: in Scotland, 85 per cent of parishes were eventually appropriated to some other religious body: R. Fawcett, *Scottish Medieval Churches* (Edinburgh, 1985), p. 25. Incorporations are identified as a crucial problem for the pre-Reformation German church: Hergemöller, 'Parrocchia', p. 157.

[20] Reichel, *English Parish*, p. 22. Some monastic rectors did not even establish a proper vicarage: R. Hartridge, *A History of Vicarages in the Middle Ages* (Cambridge, 1930), p. 162.

[21] M. Franklin, 'The cathedral as parish church' in D. Abulafia et al. (eds), *Church and City 1000-1500* (Cambridge, 1992), pp. 173–98. The church itself insisted on the priority of the parish for sacramental provision (*Pfarrzwang*): cf. for example F. M. Powicke and C. R. Cheney (eds), *Councils and Synods* (Oxford, 1964), p. 1085: Statutes of Chichester 1289, c. 19 (no clergyman can administer confession or communion to a layman without his parish priest's licence).

[22] Brooke, 'Churches of medieval Cambridge', p. 54. Similar Blair, 'From minster to parish church', p. 14, and C. Barron, 'The later Middle Ages' in M. Lobel, *City of London* (Oxford, 1989), p. 48. Morris, *Churches in the Landscape*, p. 226, sees the beginning of an age of regulation.

[23] For some of the successful initiatives cf. the cases listed in Chapter 4.3.

[24] A detailed analysis in P. Hughes, *The Reformation in England* (London, 1950), i. 35.

[25] D. Robinson, *Pastors, Parishes and People in Surrey* (Chichester, 1989), p. 5, C. Haigh, *Reformation and Resistance in Tudor Lancashire* (Cambridge, 1975), p. xiii.

[26] Rosser, 'Parish and guild', p. 32 (Westminster), K. Wood-Legh (ed.), *Kentish Visitations 1511-12* (Maidstone, 1984), pp. 96–7 (Knowlton). Engeham's experience was

thus often at odds, particularly in towns. Places like Liverpool or Hull, which had grown after 1200, remained without a parish. And even in Bristol, to take one of the old provincial capitals, the ratio between priests and parishioners varied from 1:28 at St Ewen's to 1:252 at St Michael's.[27] These institutional flaws, and the failure of the Church authorities to tackle them, provided one of the crucial incentives for lay initiative.

2.1.2 Lay duties

Eighteenth-century historiography identified the 1153 constitution of archbishop William of York as the earliest evidence for official lay responsibilities: 'ea primum occasione laici ad fabricas Ecclesiarum vocati sunt'.[28] However, the two parish representatives put in charge of money collected for church repairs look more like an ad-hoc committee than permanent officers. More recent research has provided many further clues and suggestions, but the origins and precise chronology of the institutionalization of collective lay duties remain somewhat evasive.[29] English historians conventionally refer to the various thirteenth-century synodal statutes on the division of responsibility between rector (chancel) and parishioners (nave, churchyard) as the crucial starting-point for their country,[30] but both their uniqueness and practical importance may have been overstated. While they did become nationwide guidelines, local custom could vary, and there was certainly plenty of scope for conflict.[31] Whether or not fixed canonical rules existed, the laity assumed a share in church building and maintenance throughout Western and Central

---

not unique: further examples in R. Swanson, 'Standards of livings' in C. Harper-Bill (ed.), *Religious Beliefs and Ecclesiastical Careers in Late Medieval England* (Woodbridge, 1991), fn. 12, and Thomson, *Early Tudor Church*, p. 287.

[27] Skeeters, *Community and Clergy*, p. 111 (1530s/1540s).

[28] L. Thomassinus, *Vetus et nova ecclesiae disciplina* (Venice, 1766), p. 268.

[29] The main contributions are Drew, *Early Parochial Organisation*, and S. Schröcker, *Die Kirchenpflegschaft* (Paderborn, 1934). See also (for an analysis from the point of view of papal registers) M. Clément, 'Les paroisses et les fabriques au commencement du XIIIᵉ siècle', *Mélanges d'Archéologie et d'Histoire*, 15 (1895), 387–418, and now Fuhrmann, *Kirche und Dorf* (here quoted from her 1991 thesis). Drew, p. 14, concedes that the cause for the development of permanent institutions 'remains at present ... a matter for more or less probable conjecture', while Schröcker, p. 34, asserts that there was no one decisive event.

[30] For example statutes of the synod of Winchester, c. 11 (1224, nave/*corpus* vs. chancel/*cancellum*): Powicke and Cheney (eds), *Councils and Synods*, pt 2, p. 128; statutes of the synod of Salisbury, c. 31 (1238–44, enclosure of yard): ibid., p. 379.

[31] Some London parishes apparently looked after the chancel, too, and the relevant canonical manual recognizes custom as the crucial factor: W. Lyndwood, *Provinciale* (Oxford, 1679), p. 53. There were countless disputes about the respective responsibilities, for example at St Michael Cornhill 1431, when four aldermen had to act as arbitrators between parson and wardens: A. Thomas (ed.), *Calendar of the Plea and Memoranda Rolls 1413-37* (Cambridge, 1943), pp. 253–5. A similar case outside the city at Cressing in 1446: GL, Register Robert Gilbert, f. 211. I owe these references to Irene Zadnik.

Europe at that time. Most German communities introduced special fabric boxes, and patrons or tithe-owners only paid where such funds did not exist. Quite often, there is evidence for the 'English' differentiation between chancel and nave.[32] In France, the emergence of fabric funds was the result of a similar 'nécessité pour les paroisses de supporter certaines charges, de garder des sommes à cet effet et d'accomplir collectivement divers actes'.[33] Here, too, rectors normally maintained the chancel and the parish community the nave, even though this was not formalized until the seventeenth century, and other arrangements co-existed.[34] One exception were the 'communally owned churches' referred to above. Wherever they survived, the entire building was kept up by the parish.[35]

The provision of ornaments and liturgical books became the second main communal responsibility in English canon law from about 1250. The long list of items allegedly compiled by archbishop Winchelsey in 1305 provides the classic example, even though it does not seem to have been observed immediately.[36] In any case, similar duties were specified by synods elsewhere and shouldered by Continental parishioners.[37]

---

[32] W. Schöller, *Die rechtliche Organisation des Kirchenbaues im Mittelalter* (Vienna/Cologne, 1989), p. 358, Schröcker, *Kirchenpflegschaft*, p. 132. F. X. Künstle, *Die deutsche Pfarrei und ihr Recht zu Ausgang des Mittelalters* (Stuttgart, 1905), p. 105, sees at least towers and part of the nave as communal responsibilities, while parsons were required to keep up the chancel (A. P. von Segesser, *Rechtsgeschichte der Stadt Luzern* (Luzern, 1850), pp. 777–8, confirms this for central Switzerland) .

[33] B. Jacqueline, 'Les paroisses rurales en Normandie au Moyen Age' in *Communautés rurales*, p. 423. Similar, for the whole of rural France, Huard, 'Paroisse rurale', 15-6.

[34] The 'bâtiments du choeur' were normally maintained at the cost of the 'gros décimateurs': Goujard, 'Fonds de fabriques', 100. Aubrun, *Paroisse*, p. 153, argues a similar case, but also quotes the example of La Châtre en Berry, where the patron paid one third of the costs and the parish two thirds. For the seventeenth-century legislation: Constant, 'Source négligée', 524.

[35] Feine, 'Genossenschaftliche Gemeindekirche', 178.

[36] There are a series of different versions, for example Powicke and Cheney (eds), *Councils and Synods*, pp. 1122–3 (archbishop John Pecham) and 1385–8 (archbishop Robert Winchelsey, alternatively attributed to archbishop Reynolds). It lists the following: lesson book, antiphonal, gradual, psalter, book of sequences, ordinal, missal, manual, chalice, set of vestments, choir cope, altar frontal, three cloths for the high altar, three surplices, procession cross, censer, lantern/bells to visit the sick, pyx, Lenten veil, set of banners, bells and ropes, bier for corpses, holy water vat and sprinkler, pax, candlestick for the paschal, font with cover and lock, images in nave and chancel, churchyard wall, maintenance of nave, windows, books, and ornaments. J. R. H. Moorman, *Church Life in England in the Thirteenth Century* (Cambridge, 1945), p. 142, however, found little evidence for a uniform system in the early fourteenth century.

[37] For example statutes of the council of Rouen 1335 (Drew, *Early Parochial Organisation*, p. 9). The foundation charter of the parish of Spiringen in Central Switzerland (1299) specifies the duty to provide mass books: Pfaff, 'Pfarrei und Pfarreileben', p. 242.

The Church also suggested ways to distribute communal responsibilities. The statutes of the synod of Exeter in 1287 stipulated that parishioners were liable 'secundum portionem terrae, quam possident in eadem parochia'.[38] Other evidence suggests that 'possessiones et facultates' were also taken into account.[39] Kentish visitation records for Preston in 1511 testify to the continuity of this system, when they state that the repair of a derelict church wall amounted to a serious problem 'for there be but three owners in that parisshe and of little substaunce'.[40]

A survey of canonical requirements should finally allude to those aspects of the 'spiritual economy' of the parish which affected individuals rather than the community as such.[41] Tithes have already been mentioned, but there were many further demands. Priests normally expected fees for specific services, gifts on certain feast days, customary quarterly offerings, and mortuaries upon death.[42] Some parishes also recorded Peter's pence payments to Rome,[43] while others made contributions to their cathedral church.[44]

2.2 The lay response: expansion and local authority

2.2.1 The development of permanent institutions

With reference to the secular field, where the levying of subsidies promoted the development of parliamentary assemblies, it is often argued that financial demands and collective responsibility imposed upon the parishioners 'became the focus of their corporate awareness'[45] and led to a 'bigger say in the running of their parish church'.[46] There is clearly some truth in this, but the development of the churchwardenship

---

[38] Powicke and Cheney (eds), *Councils and Synods*, pp. 1002–4 (c. 9).

[39] Drew, *Early Parochial Organisation*, pp. 12–13. Sutton (1298) and Langar (1310) provide the evidence.

[40] Wood-Legh (ed.), *Kentish Visitations*, p. 234.

[41] See the chapter in Swanson, *Church and Society*, pp. 209–28, which discusses the various charges in more detail.

[42] The level of customary offerings varied greatly and there was only limited general legislation: see Powicke and Cheney (eds), *Councils and Synods*, i. 180, n. 3.

[43] At Morebath, the level was fixed at ½ d. per householder and ¼ d. per cottager: J. E. Binney (ed.), *The Accounts of the Wardens of Morebath* (Exeter, 1904), pp. 34–5. See Boxford in Appendix 3.

[44] For example Halesowen in this sample.

[45] Duffy, *Stripping of the Altars*, p. 133.

[46] E. Mason, 'The role of the English parishioner 1100–1500', *JEH*, 27 (1976), 23.

to its final pre-Reformation stage was a gradual process and arguably rather a lay initiative. In a document of the 1230s, which offers a rare glimpse into early parish administration, there is as yet no trace of communal institutions. Household-based contributions to the 'wax-scot', collected for the lighting of the church, are raised and accounted for by a chaplain on behalf of the rector.[47] By 1261, in contrast, we find the first documentary evidence for the existence of *procuratores parochie* at All Saints, Bristol.[48] This did coincide with a period of increasing canonical legislation, but the charges imposed were of an occasional nature and did not require a permanent and independent communal office.[49]

Similarly, the assessment of the parishioners' landed property, means, and goods to fulfil their canonical duties may have played a part in the political education of the English parish, but it would be hard to prove that this was the Church's intention. While the highest dignitaries actively promoted pious donations to the local church,[50] they did not envisage the creation of corporate lay institutions. Ecclesiastical authorities remained reluctant to see 'parishioners' as more than a series of individuals, and wardens as anything else than representatives acting in proxy of each member of the community. Papal documents could be ambiguous about lay rights over fabric funds,[51] but councils and synods never budged in the question of clerical control over church property. They kept insisting on annual accounting to ecclesiastical authorities and on the involvement of parish priests in the administrative process.[52] The statutes of the synod of Exeter in 1287 are a case in point:

---

[47] Owen, 'Parish books', pp. 121–2, 125–6 (Haddenham). 'Wax-scot' was an ancient 'offering of the altar' and clerical control may not seem surprising. Later churchwardens' accounts, however, often include waxsilver collections and spending on the lighting of the church (see the income/expenditure analysis in Appendix 3). It is tempting to speculate that this duty was gradually taken over by communal organs.

[48] Drew, *Early Parochial Organisation*, p. 6 (in a lay bequest for a light). The first lightwardens are documented in Shrewsbury abbey parish church in 1260: Moorman, *Thirteenth Century*, p. 143.

[49] Schröcker, *Kirchenpflegschaft*, pp. 131–2, quotes examples of communities with church building duties which did not develop independent administrative institutions.

[50] Honorius III asserted in 1225: 'cum saeculares viri assurgunt ad opera spiritualia, tacti timore divini nominis et amore, non est eorum impendienda devotio, sed potius favore benevolo prosequenda' (Clément, 'Paroisses et fabriques', 408).

[51] Innocent IV demanded in 1253 that the fabric of St Giovanni at Florence be returned under clerical control (Schröcker, *Kirchenpflegschaft*, p. 149), while Honorius III seemed to accept the distinct nature of fabric funds under lay administration (Clément, 'Paroisses et fabriques', 404: confirmation of goods belonging to the 'oeuvre' of the church of Béziers in 1216).

[52] Schröcker, *Kirchenpflegschaft*, pp. 147-56.

Precipimus insuper quod de ecclesiarum instauro ipsius custodes coram rectoribus vel vicariis ecclesiarum, seu saltem capellanis parochialibus, et quinque vel sex parochianis fide dignis quos ipsi rectores, vicarii, vel capellani de hoc duxerint eligendos quolibet anno compotum fideliter reddant, et redigatur in scriptis; quam scripturam precipimus loci archidiacono cum visitat presentari. Nec ipsum instaurum in alios usus quam ecclesie ullatenus convertatur; unde si parochiani pro defectibus ecclesie seu pro aliis demeritis amerciari contigerit de proprio satisfaciant, instauro ecclesie integre remanente.[53]

The fabric wardens appear in a subordinate position, clergymen (supported by a few lay *fidedigni*) audit their accounts, and archdeacons are given rights of supervision. Furthermore, disbursements from fabric funds are restricted to strictly defined 'uses of the church'. This does not look like a blueprint for an independent communal office.[54]

More important than canonical impulses may have been the parishioners' desire to keep the newly established communal funds well outside the incumbent's grasp.[55] The distinction between ecclesiastical benefice and fabric funds had emerged after the demise of the *Eigenkirche* system during the twelfth and thirteenth centuries, when the 'parish fabric' started to attract voluntary donations in its own right.[56] Money, land, and tenements were offered as endowments for masses, anniversaries, lights, and chantries, but, as German evidence shows, often on condition of the existence or establishment of independent wardens.[57] Even though the office had many complex legal roots and varied a great deal locally, pious bequests clearly made a substantial contribution to its development.[58] In England, too, priests were not considered to be ideal trustees for communal funds, and after a series of ad-hoc solutions, gifts were increasingly entrusted to special lay representatives. By the mid-fourteenth century, their capacity to hold certain properties was well established, notwithstanding the parish's lack of formal corporate status. It looks as if many of the legal problems had

---

[53] Statutes, c. 12: Powicke and Cheney (eds), *Councils and Synods*, p. 1008. Drew, *Early Parochial Organisation*, p. 7, quotes it as the first authoritative statement on the duties of churchwardens and their accounts.

[54] H. E. Feine, 'Kirche und Gemeindebildung' in T. Mayer (ed.), *Die Anfänge der Landgemeinde und ihr Wesen* (Stuttgart, 1964), p. 55, and Reynolds, *Kingdoms and Communities*, pp. 79–80, both credit the Church with little share in the emergence of lay parochial institutions.

[55] Schröcker, *Kirchenpflegschaft*, p. 92.

[56] Ibid., p. 37, Drew, *Early Parochial Organisation*, pp. 6, 19 (thirteenth century). Aubrun, *Paroisse*, p. 150, and Genicot, *Rural Communities*, p. 102, find the earliest Continental evidence in the twelfth century.

[57] Schröcker, *Kirchenpflegschaft*, pp. 51–59, 93.

[58] Most recently confirmed by Fuhrmann, 'Pfarrei und Kaplanei', p. 79.

simply been 'ignored' or circumvented.[59] Equally informally, parish representatives soon assumed duties other than those connected to the fabric and started to administer a common purse rather than a specific fund. Thus, from the very first preserved accounts of 1349 of St Michael in Bath, we see parishes fulfilling a variety of roles with their own communal resources. Given the Church's reservations about lay custody of church goods, reiterated by some English bishops well into the fourteenth century, not all of this happened smoothly. Widespread conflict about collection boxes had been observed for England around 1300, and many German communities put up similar fights to secure control over fabric funds.[60] Gradually though, most places managed to limit clerical involvement to the presence of the incumbent at the annual audit and to periodical supervision by ecclesiastical visitors.[61]

2.2.2 The office of churchwarden

Once established, the lay officers could be known as *procuratores parochiae, custodes instauri,* or *iconomi,* but increasingly (English starts to dominate from the later fifteenth century) as church-reeves (from 1386), kirkmasters (from 1429), and finally as churchwardens (from at least 1466).[62] Corresponding terms used on the Continent were *mamburni, vitrici, operarii, matricularii, marguilliers, fabriciens, trésoriers, operai, Kirchenpfleger, Kirchenvögte* or *Kirchmeier.*[63] But what exactly did they do?

---

[59] Drew, *Early Parochial Organisation,* p. 23. Canonical literature of the fourteenth and fifteenth centuries, if it deals with the subject at all, starts to recognize the distinct nature of fabric funds and their separate administration: Schröcker, *Kirchenpflegschaft,* pp. 79–89. For the acquisition of quasi-corporate status see the section on the 'office of churchwarden' below.

[60] Drew, *Early Parochial Organisation,* pp. 9, 16–7: first evidence for lay custody at the chapel of Colleton in 1301. When called to adjudicate in matters of lay control and administration, some members of the episcopate supported the idea, others (for example bishop Woodloke of Winchester in 1308) firmly opposed it. Evidence for conflict in Germany in Schröcker, *Kirchenpflegschaft,* p. 48.

[61] C. Drew (ed.), *Lambeth CWA* (London, 1941), p. 1. In this sample, the vicar was present for example at parish assemblies at All Saints, Bristol, St Mary-at-Hill, London (CWA passim), and at a special meeting connected to a building project at Prescot (CWA 1560).

[62] Drew, *Early Parochial Organisation,* p. 6 n. 3, lists the various terms. An early reference to 'churchwardens' in E. Freshfield (ed.), 'Some remarks upon ... St Stephen Coleman Street [London]', *Archaeologia,* 50 (1887), 48 (1466). The first preserved account at St Botolph Aldersgate, London, is headed 'This is thaccompte of Willyam Barolke and Aleyn Johnson Wardeyns of the churche of seynt Botulff' (CWA 1468–70).

[63] Exhaustive references in Schröcker, *Kirchenpflegschaft,* pp. 172–203.

In Peterborough, to start with one of the case studies, the wardens administered, bought, and sold property, organized collections on certain feasts, lent out money and various church goods, received testamentary bequests and contributions by local gilds, staged entertainments, and demanded fees for bell-ringing or burial, while spending money on church maintenance, ornaments, salaries, subsidies, bridge-building, legal matters, priests, and ceremonies.[64] This is a fairly typical list, and yet it has to be modified by countless local varieties. Some wardens looked after lights and wax, collected Peter's pence, brewed ale, traded in cattle and bees, supervised building work, attended manor courts, looked after churchyards, maintained parish gardens, and sued negligent rectors, executors of wills, and independent-minded chapels.[65] On the eve of the Reformation, churchwardens (together with selected 'sidesmen') also attended ecclesiastical visitations, a custom eventually enforced by the canons of 1571.[66] The basic spectrum of activities had developed by the time of the first preserved accounts of St Michael Bath in 1349. 'Thome le Mason et Thome le Tannere procuratorum ecclesie beati Michaelis' received 16 s. 6½ d. in rents, spent £2 6 s. 2 d. (the biggest single item) on a missal, bought a messuage, and apparently had the authority to sell ornaments ('xii d. de veteribus pannis ad dictam ecclesiam legatis venditis') and parish timber. Other activities included the keeping of anniversaries, the purchase of candles, and property maintenance. They incurred a deficit and the account offers a first taste of medieval arithmetic.[67] Most of this could be transferred to their European colleagues, at least as far as the sources allow for comparison. Sixteenth-century French *marguilliers* collected rents, dues, and gifts, and paid for masses, church repair, and ornaments in a very similar way.[68] The administration of fabric funds, ornaments, and minor benefices was the main function of the German *Kirchenpfleger* and Swiss

---

[64] CWA, p. xxxi and passim.

[65] Evidence for these and many more activities can be found in the present sample. See also S. O. Addy, *Church and Manor* (London, 1913), p. 314 (trading), Cook, *Medieval Parish Church*, pp. 248ff (negotiating contracts with masons), W. Ault, 'The village church and the village community', *Speculum*, 45 (1970), 212 (leasing and cultivating of arable parish land), F. A. Bailey (ed.), *Prescot Court Leet* (Preston, 1937), p. 131 (manor court attendance), C. Barron and J. Roscoe, 'The medieval parish church of St Andrew Holborn' in A. L. Saunders (ed.), *London Topographical Record* (London, 1980), p. 44 (garden).

[66] E. Gibson (ed.), *Codex iuris ecclesiastici anglicani* (Oxford, 1761), p. 960; cf. the discussion of medieval visitations in Chapter 6.2.1.

[67] Pearson, 'CWA of St Michael' (1877), 1-4.

[68] Constant, 'Source négligée', passim. However, in addition, they seem to have been charged with the finding of an experienced midwife, whom they had elected by an assembly of the female members of the parish (ibid., 505).

Kirchmeier, who also supervised and reported on the morals of their communities.[69]

As a result of the informal development of the office and the lack of parish incorporation, churchwardens had a delicate status under English law. Their foremost historian has argued that their capacity to hold property was firmly established by 1350,[70] but the situation was rather more complex. A quick survey of Year Book cases reveals that common law courts granted churchwardens the capability to hold goods, but not lands.[71] They 'ne poient prescriber terres al eux & lour successours, car ils ne sont ascun Corporation dauer terres, mes pur biens pur lesglise', was a typical (Law French) legal opinion expressed in the reign of Elizabeth, with similar verdicts dating back to Henry IV.[72] However, it is blatantly obvious that parishes *did* hold landed property as a matter of course. The records of All Saints, Bristol, confidently speak of 'landes and tenementes belongyng to the paresche churche', as in a rental appended to the accounts of 1524–5, or of the house that particular executors 'gave us' (CWA 1515–16). Elsewhere, churchwardens sued and distrained in cases involving landed endowments,[73] and their accounts record payments for the respective legal disputes.[74]

Many benefactors no doubt made informal or cash-based arrangements with the parishioners, and some will have simply ignored legal difficulties,[75]

---

[69] K. S. Bader, *Dorfgenossenschaft und Dorfgemeinde* (Cologne, 1962), p. 208; Pfaff, 'Pfarrei und Pfarreileben', p. 253.

[70] Drew, *Early Parochial Organisation*, p. 23.

[71] Gibson, *Codex*, pp. 215-6 (only London wardens were customarily able to purchase or receive land on behalf of the parish). W. Lambarde, *The Duties of Constables* (London, 1602), pp. 57–8, speaks of wardens as 'persons inabled ... to take moveable goods, or cattels, and to sue, and be sued at Law, concerning such goods for the use and benefit of their parish'. See also Sir E. Coke, *The First Part of the Institutes of the Laws of England* (8th edn, London, 1670), lib. i, cap. i, sect. i, f. 3a, c. A model Year Books case upholding gifts made to a parish was Y.B. Trinity 12 Henry VII, fos 27–9.

[72] H. Rolle, *Un abridgement des plusieurs cases del common ley* (London, 1668), f. 393.

[73] A detailed account of the suits against John Sharp and town bailiff Griffith in St Ewen's CWA, pp. xxxff. In 1457–8, 51 pounds of wax were levied out of Griffith's house as distress for arrears of 10s. per annum, an action upheld in an arbitration by the mayor, sheriff, and town clerk (1463). At St Botolph Aldersgate, the wardens seized a pot of brass for the 11s. owed by Margaret More for a tenement in Blackhorse Alley: CWA, 1493–4. The parish officers of All Saints, Bristol, were accompanied by a sergeant when they distrained for payments due to the Halleway chantry: BRO, P/AS/C/1, 1476–7.

[74] Ashburton CWA, 1526–7 and 1529–30.

[75] The will of William Hall (attached to the CWA of St Botolph Aldersgate, 1504-5) asked the parson and wardens to sell his lands and tenements in the parish for 'as dere a pryce as they may' and to support a variety of causes (torches, poor relief, anniversary) with the profit. A similar (rural) case in F. Mercer (ed.), *CWA at Betrysden* (Ashford, 1928), p. 65: the will of Robert Tepynden, made in 1500, instructs his trustees to sell certain lands and to donate £5 each to a number of churches.

but the most important reason for the gulf between legal theory and parochial practice was the emergence of a loophole, enfeoffment to use, in the fourteenth century. In order to avoid the feudal fees normally payable for the descent of land, tenants could in their lifetime convey it to two or more feoffees, usually friends or acquaintances, who would hold it henceforth 'to the use' of the grantor or any other beneficiary, including collective bodies such as the parish.[76] Feoffees became a permanent institution (the members were easy to replace) and thereafter formal changes of ownership no longer occurred. While common law courts explicitly banned wardens from accepting enfeoffments,[77] it was easy enough to appoint other eminent parishioners, municipal officers, or clergymen instead. This has been observed for chantry and anniversary endowments in fifteenth-century Bristol,[78] but similar evidence can be found outside the big cities. At Bethersden in Kent, for instance, William Glover (d. 1493) ordered his feoffees to 'enfeoff 12 honest persons of the parish' with his land called Wosbriggs for the maintenance of a taper before the sepulchre light and a yearly obit.[79] At Boxford in 1492, Agnes Sergeant left a close called Thorncroft to be enfeoffed to the use of the churchwardens, while 'feoffees of the church' were assessed at £5 in the 1544 lay subsidy for Ashburton.[80] Perhaps the best documented case is Tavistock in Devon, where an elected body of parishioners called the 'feoffees to the uses of the parish church' regularly received and leased landed property. The wardens seem to have been ex officio members.[81]

Circumventing legal restrictions had the drawback that established royal courts could offer no protection against abuses of the system, and

---

[76] J. Baker, *An Introduction to English Legal History* (3rd edn, London, 1990), pp. 283ff, and A. Harding, *The Law Courts of Medieval England* (London/New York, 1973), pp. 101–2.

[77] Y.B. Michaelmas 12 Henry VII, f. 33.

[78] C. Burgess, 'Strategies for eternity' in C. Harper-Bill (ed.), *Religious Belief and Ecclesiastical Careers* (Woodbridge, 1991), p. 17. The rents for the Halleway chantry at All Saints, Bristol, were to be gathered by the wardens, under the general supervision of the vicar, parishioners and town authorities: F. B. Bickley (ed.), *The Little Red Book of Bristol* (2 vols, Bristol, 1900), ii. 199ff. In practice though, churchwardens seem capable of receiving property on their own, as in the case of the obit of ex-vicar Nicholas Pittes at St Mary Redcliffe, Bristol, 1494: C. Burgess, 'A service for the dead', *TBGAS*, 105 (1987), 200.

[79] A. Hussey (ed.), *Kent Obit and Lamp Rents* (Ashford, 1936), p. 12. This must have happened on a regular basis: in 1541, the wardens recorded a total of 24 d. spent 'when the fefement was made': Mercer (ed.), *CWA at Betrysden*, pp. 45–6.

[80] Boxford CWA, p. 90; T. L. Stoate (ed.), *Devon Lay Subsidy Rolls* 1543–5 (Bristol, 1986), p. 192. In CWA 1525–6, the Ashburton wardens recorded fines paid on the feoffees' behalf.

[81] R. N. Worth (ed.), *Calendar of Tavistock Parish Records* (Plymouth, 1887), pp. 11, 77, 85, 92 and *passim*.

much depended on the reliability and honour of the feoffees. From the early fifteenth century, however, Chancery (and later the Court of Requests and Star Chamber) emerged out of the King's council as new tribunals operating on equity principles. In Chancery, issues were decided not according to common law, but in line with the judge's conscience.[82] Furthermore, the new court was free from procedural rigours, it had means to ensure the attendance of defendants (*writs of subpoena*), acted comparatively swiftly, and accepted unwritten evidence. For the parish, this must have come like a gift from heaven.[83] Enfeoffment cases formed the bulk of the court's early activity, and the giving of land to unincorporate bodies 'was not a difficulty that troubled the chancellor'.[84] Parishes faced with legal problems were very much aware of the new opportunities: when suing in the Court of Requests, the wardens of Bapchild in Kent stated 'that thoffice and corporacion of churchewardens whicht your sayed poore supplicantes ... doo now exercise & serve (by the rigor of the common lawes) doth not extend to claime and demaund (such a kynd of inheritans as this is) therefore your sayed suppliauntes ... are without remedy for recouery of the same'.[85] There is indeed an intriguing chronological coincidence between the emergence of equity jurisdiction, enfeoffments, and the 'rise of the parish'. It is questionable whether churchwardens would have ever attained the resources and status they did without these favourable circumstances.

Nevertheless, parishioners continued to appear at common law. Partly this was due to new opportunities presented by actions such as *assumpsit*, particularly from the early sixteenth century.[86] A good illustration of how the courts were used to deal with cases of breach of contract are actions against bell-founders. A written agreement between the parish of Weston (Norfolk) and John Aleyn was submitted as evidence in a case before Common Pleas in 1528. The bell-founder had

---

[82] Baker, *Introduction*, pp. 112ff, and Harding, *Law Courts*, pp. 100ff.

[83] For historians, too. The surviving petitions, answers, rejoinders and so on have left us with much 'viva voce' evidence from wardens and parishioners alike. See the survey of characteristic cases in French, 'Local identity', ch. 6.

[84] J. L. Barton, 'The medieval use', *Law Quarterly Review*, 81 (1965), 576.

[85] I. S. Leadam (ed.), *Select Cases in the Court of Requests* (London, 1898), pp. 196–8 (1553). Similarly, fifteenth-century wardens of Pulloxhill sued in Chancery for money they believed was owed to them from a play because they had 'no remedy' at common law (quoted in Platt, *Parish Churches*, p. 90; profits from a play were also at issue in a Chancery case concerning Bedford: PRO, C 1 146/48).

[86] An action at law in which a plaintiff asserted that the defendant had failed to fulfil a promise to perform a certain act: J. H. Baker (ed.), *The Reports of Sir John Spelman* (vol. ii, London, 1978), pp. 255ff.

promised to cast a new tenor bell which he warranted 'to be of good accorde, perfight Tewne, hole sounde, and swete armony both in Tewne and workemanshypp with the other belles'. Payment by the parish could be withheld if it was found 'defectyff by ij or iij credeble persons of musyk endifferently chosen', and was only due after Aleyn had mended it 'at his proper costes' as many times as necessary.[87] Many other examples could be cited to show that some parishes at least were used to running their affairs on a written, 'business-like' basis.[88] Others, however, continued to prefer more informal oral agreements, particularly when commissioning smaller ornaments or furnishings for the church. Conflicts in such cases could now lead to *assumpsit* proceedings, as in the King's Bench suit Churchwardens of Folsham (Norfolk) *v.* Yarman in 1507, where the parish was clearly dissatisfied with the work done about their new *sedilia*.[89] Much more of course remains to be discovered about churchwardens and the law, suffice it here to say that by the eve of the Reformation, parishioners had come to terms with their peculiar legal status and appeared in virtually all contemporary courts, both secular and ecclesiastical.[90]

Moving to the choosing of wardens, procedures and electorate varied considerably, even though the most common case was probably an election at Easter (or some other traditional feast) by an assembly of all parishioners.[91] German evidence exemplifies the range of local peculiarities. In towns, appointments were normally made by the council, unless parishes had developed a strong identity of their own. Parochial elections were the norm in independent rural communities, while local lords exercised strong influence in the manorial context. In multi-township parishes with mixed secular lordship, procedures could involve different stages and the appointment of special electors.[92] A

---

[87] Ibid., pp. 260–1 (*Shynkwyn v. Larke*).

[88] Cf. the contracts with masons and other craftsmen surviving for example for the tower at Arlingham (1372: J. H. Bettey, *Church and Parish* (London, 1987), p. 146) or the St George image at Wymondham (11 Henry VIII: H. Harrod, 'Some particulars relating to the abbey church of Wymondham', *Archaeologia*, 43 (1880), 271).

[89] Baker (ed.), *Spelman*, p. 261.

[90] See R. E. Rodes, *Lay Authority and Reformation in the English Church* (Notre Dame/London, 1982), pp. 138, 162–3, 222–3.

[91] W. E. Tate, *The Parish Chest* (3rd edn, Cambridge, 1969), p. 86, and D. Meade, *The Medieval Church in England* (Worthing, 1988), p. 47. The same seems to apply to France: R. Mousnier, *Les Institutions de la France* (Paris, 1974), i 433, and Huard, 'Paroisse rurale', 16. Cf. Chapter 6.2 for a definition of the term 'parishioner'.

[92] Schröcker, *Kirchenpflegschaft*, pp. 97, 113, 125, 133-4. D. Kurze, 'Hoch- und spätmittelalterliche Wahlen im Niederkirchenbereich' in R. Schneider and H. Zimmermann (eds), *Wahlen und Wählen im Mittelalter* (Sigmaringen, 1990), pp. 199–200, gives details for the multi-township parish of Leinburg near Nuremberg.

similar variety of systems operated in England: the curate of Holy Trinity, Cambridge, chose two persons, who in turn picked four other parishioners, and these six together elected the wardens.[93] Elsewhere, appointments were made by town authorities (Arundel), manorial lords (Whitington), or patrons (St Marylebone, Middlesex), while some parishes required particular professions (fishermen at Brighton).[94] At Nettlecombe, there is evidence for a periodical rotation system among 15 households, and at Thame, Prescot, and Stanwick a tendency to represent territorial subdivisions of the parish. In the last case, the wardens were elected at the visitation of the prebendary of Ripon, at least in 1464.[95]

More often than not, however, election memoranda are not very explicit and restricted to phrases such as 'custodes tc electes' (Yatton CWA 1451–2), wardens 'now alektyd' (Andrew Hubbard CWA 1541–3), or other ambiguous formulations.[96] Still, some are explicit enough to reveal broad communal participation: 'Memorandum that att the seyd day of accountt the hole parisshe hath elect and Chosen William Dawson William Farsett Gilbert Bull and Cuthbertt Miller Churchwardens for the yere to Cume' (Peterborough, 1546).[97] At Botolph Aldersgate, the wardens recorded in 1525–6 'that the ix[th] day of July … ar chosen by the hole assent of the paryssh for church wardens m. tamworth & Thomas Harlop', and in 1537–8 that John Willoughby and John Wotton were 'chosen churchewardens in the presence of the parisshoners beyng present at the seid accompt'. At All Saints, Bristol, the officers were appointed by the 'most voice' of the whole parish, and at Lambeth they could not continue for another term unless 'they be chosen agayn' by the parisshens'. St Michael Coventry's elections, finally, were made 'yerely by the parisshons of the same chirche at their pleasir' by a simple show of hands.[98] Late medieval parish government, analysed

[93] Cox, CWA, pp. 4–5.

[94] S. and B. Webb, The Parish and the County (London, 1906), pp. 21–2.

[95] French, 'Local identity', p. 60 (the same succession of households recurred every 15 years). Carnwath, 'CWA of Thame', p. 182 (where the wardens from New and Old Thame looked after separate parts of the church!), F. A. Bailey, 'The CWA of Prescot', Transactions of the Historical Society of Lancashire and Cheshire, 92 (1940), 165 (from 1546 the four officers were meant to represent the four quarters of Prescot), J. T. Fowler (ed.), Acts of Chapter of the Collegiate Church of Ripon (Durham, 1875), p. 223.

[96] Elections of some kind, sometimes certainly by a large part of the parishioners, are documented at Ashburton (CWA 1487–8), and presumed at St Ewen's (CWA, p. xx) and Boxford (CWA, p. xii).

[97] CWA, p. 163 (31 October 1546).

[98] C. Burgess, 'The benefactions of mortality' in D. Smith (ed.), Studies in Clergy and Ministry (York, 1991), p. 80 (Bristol), Drew (ed.), Lambeth CWA, p. 1, and C. Phythian-Adams, Desolation of a City (Cambridge, 1979), p. 168 (Coventry).

in more detail in Chapter 6.2, was broadly based and there is no reason to doubt such 'all inclusive' formulations.[99] Once elected, the wardens could be sworn in at visitations,[100] but ecclesiastical officials had no authority to refuse or dismiss them. Their principal loyalty was to the community, not the Church. John Mydell, warden at Croscombe in 1536, made this explicit when he asserted in a conflict with the rector that 'he was but a servant unto the parish'.[101]

Quite frequently, parishes developed systems of phased elections. At St Stephen Coleman Street, London, the community assembled annually on a particular Sunday 'to choose one churchwarden to him that had been last chosen the year before'.[102] The presence of a junior and a more experienced senior warden ensured a certain continuity in parish affairs, and the custom was practised, at least temporarily, at Mary-at-Hill, All Saints, Bristol, Boxford, Ashburton, Thame, Yeovil, and Bethersden.[103] Re-elections of individuals or whole teams occurred for example at Prescot 1530–54, St Edmund, Salisbury, in the fifteenth century, and in the earlier accounts of Peterborough and St Botolph Aldersgate, but whatever the normal practice, particular circumstances, lack of suitable candidates, inner-communal feuds, or pressing parochial needs could disrupt any system. Those appointed were expected to serve and dispensations proved costly: William Sutton refused the office at Prescot in 1534 and was fined 20 d.[104] Such cases were rare though. Someone had to do the job and, on balance, the prestige and power of the office probably outweighed its burdens. Candidates knew that their efforts were appreciated. All Saints, Bristol, kept careful records of the achievements of its wardens in the hope that God would look favourably on their service.[105]

---

[99] 'Wenn man ... von der "universitas parochianorum" ... liest, sollte man nicht an allgemeineren Wahlen oder wenigstens nicht an der Intention dazu zweifeln': Kurze, 'Wahlen im Niederkirchenbereich', p. 205.

[100] 'Juraverunt suam diligenciam exhibere ... et fidelem compotum reddere cum fuerint legitime requisti' (visitation of Stanwick, 1464): Fowler (ed.), Acts of Ripon, p. 223.

[101] Gibson, Codex, p. 215, and R. Gneist, Geschichte und Gestalt der englischen Communalverfassung (Berlin, 1863), pp. 272–3. The Croscombe quote in Marshall, Catholic Priesthood, p. 204.

[102] Freshfield (ed.), 'Stephen Coleman', 48. London, however, knew many different practices: E. G. Ashby, 'Some aspects of parish life in the city of London 1429–1529' (MA London, 1950), p. 164.

[103] CWA, passim, Carnwath, 'CWA of Thame', p. 183 (from 1496), French, 'Local identity', p. 58, Mercer (ed.), CWA at Betrysden, pp. xvi–xvii.

[104] Bailey, 'CWA of Prescot', 138. Alexander Frynd paid £1 for a life-time dispensation from serving as alewarden at Ashburton: CWA, 1555–6. In the same place, T. Cole was fined 10 d. for not helping with the brewing in 1501–2.

[105] For C. Burgess, ' "A fond thing vainly invented" ' in S. Wright (ed.), Parish, Church and People (London, 1988), p. 78, service may have counted as a 'good work'; cf. the opening sections of the All Saints Church Book: BRO P/AS/ChW/1.

Established systems could be overthrown more or less overnight: at Prescot, elections were moved from St Catherine's day to Easter in 1546 and the wardens' number increased from two to four, while at St Edmund, Salisbury, three wardens served up to 1456, four until 1510, and just two afterwards, in the latter case (as often) for no apparent reason.[106] Equally puzzling is the frequent change between cooptation and communal election at Bethersden: in 1519–20, the senior warden nominated his junior officer, in 1527–8 the parish could at least give its advice, while a communal appointment seems to have taken place in 1514–15.[107] The temporary reduction from two wardens to one at Morebath, however, seems to be closely linked to the disruptions of the Reformation period and the decrease in parochial activities.[108]

Audit regulations make it explicit whom the wardens were answerable to. At the end of their term, the church stock had to be returned to its corporate owners, and the audit day was an opportunity for the parish assembly to exercise its sovereignty.[109] Local ordinances laid down carefully what the community expected of its wardens:

> at the yeres ende they shall' geve and make accomptes of their' Receytes paymentes and dettes for the same yere to the person and to the most parte of the most honest' men of the same parisshe for the tyme beyng. And that under the payn' of fourety shillinges to be paied' by the said' church'wardeyns not makyng their' accomptes at the yeres ende as said ys' the which' xls. shall be disposed' and bestowed' to the use and behoff for the most prouffitt of the foresaid church' of Lamehith.[110]

Botolph Aldersgate repeatedly recorded

> that hyt ys ordeynyd aswell by the advyce and assent of Nicholas Lathell, John Peke … and other of the sayd paryssh that the sayd churchewardens now beyng and they that for the tyme shalbe shall bryng in theyr accompte yerely w'in vii wekes next aftyr the fest of candilmas apon peyne thatt eny of theym that byn or shalbe churche wardens shall pay of hys onne goode to the clerke of the same

---

[106] Prescot CWA, p. viii (to allow representation of territorial subdivisions), and Edmund CWA, passim. The general trend seems to have pointed towards fewer wardens: at Ashburton, two instead of four served from 1549, and at All Saints Bristol one name instead of two appears in the headings of the accounts from 1555. However, at Kendal (Westmorland) 12 wardens have served each year from time out of mind (I owe this reference to Patrick Collinson).

[107] Mercer (ed.), CWA Betrysden, pp. 81, 19, 70.

[108] Binney (ed.), Morebath, 1548–53. This is the impression of Eamon Duffy, who is working on a monograph of the parish.

[109] Drew (ed.), Lambeth CWA, pp. xii–xiii.

[110] Lambeth, 19 May 1505. In 1523 the date was fixed on relic Sunday after evensong: ibid., p. 1.

chyrche x^s that ys to sey eny of theym v^s as oftyn as they do contrary to thys ordenannce.[111]

More detailed still are the rules made by the parson, churchwardens, and 22 men of St Stephen, Bristol, on 15 August 1524: the audit day was to begin at 8 a.m. sharp, non-attendance by parishioners incurred a fine of 40 d., and the senior warden had to rehearse the prepared accounts before the whole parish, which scrutinized them carefully. Non-compliance resulted in a penalty of 40 s., half of which went to Worcester cathedral and half to the parish.[112] In certain towns, both in England and elsewhere, accounts had to be rendered to the municipal authorities: this applied to St Martin, Leicester, and Wells, as well as Marburg, Goslar, or Berne. On the whole, however, continental wardens reported to the parish assembly, too.[113]

For the wardens themselves, the sample suggests a quite distinct social profile. Some 700 accounting periods with 1950 officer positions have been scrutinized for the period up to 1560, covering roughly 1050 individuals from about 760 families.[114] This produces an average of two terms per individual and 1.4 wardens per family, but averages are of course misleading. A short run of accounts will normally contain almost as many family names as individuals (20 and 27 at Boxford), while over a longer period the same names are more likely to reappear (43 and 70 at Halesowen; 111 and 192 at Yatton). In many large parishes there may have been a limited supply of families within reasonable distance from the church, but the 43 different surnames in the 62 Halesowen accounts do not suggest a monopoly of a narrowly defined ruling elite. In the big towns, the range of office-holding families appears even bigger: in London, 70 individuals from 63 families served at Andrew Hubbard, and 78 from 73 at Botolph Aldersgate, while the figures in Bristol were

[111] CWA, 1480–82.

[112] F. Fox (ed.), 'Regulations of the vestry of St Stephen', *Proceedings of the Clifton Antiquarian Club*, 1 (1884), 199. The consistency of rendering accounts suggests that there must have been similar ordinances everywhere. Other examples include Peterborough CWA 1477–8 ('ordinatum est per parochianos quod compotus erit redditus annuatim in dicta dominica [=prima post Octabis Epiphanie] Anno Revoluto'. In 1534–6, the fine was fixed at 6 s. 8 d. and Bethersden (1519–20: audit day Sunday after St Nicholas, same fine: Mercer (ed.), *CWA Betrysden*, p. 81).

[113] Thomson, *Early Tudor Church*, p. 275 (Leicester), French, 'Local identity', p. 32 (Wells), and Schröcker, *Kirchenpflegschaft*, pp. 97–8. For communal supervision in France: Constant, 'Source négligée', 527, and Huard, 'Paroisse rurale', 16.

[114] In addition to information from the main sample (for starting-dates of CWA see Table 3.2), officer details from St Edmund, Salisbury (1443–1560) and St Mary-at-Hill (1477-95) have been included here. The figures for individuals and family names are of course approximate; it is often difficult to judge whether wardens of the same name are identical and whether variations in spelling of names reflect different families or different scribes.

112 from 96 at All Saints, and 69 from 64 at St Ewen's. In these cases at least, there must have been a strong feeling that the office should rotate among all parishioners, and the fines for those who refused it point in the same direction. In this sample, only the Geffreys and Wyndeyates at Ashburton had more than four wardens, and not many families could build up a dynasty. Still, there were always more 'open' and more 'closed' parishes. While Yatton belonged to the former category, places like Croscombe and Tintinhull in the same county could be dominated by just a few families. [115]

Long-term office holders and dominant personalities appear almost everywhere: typical examples are Thomas Pernannt of All Saints (seven terms), also a sheriff of Bristol and tenant of a £4 p.a. house in the High Street, and John Dolbeare junior (four terms at Ashburton), a tanner who briefly farmed the local gild market in 1548 and owned £14 in goods in 1524.[116] There were perfectly good reasons to re-elect certain officers: Thomas Dene and William Forbour, for example, were asked by the parson and parishioners of St Ewen in 1457–9 to stay on in order to deal with a complicated legal issue. Elsewhere, some parishioners may have genuinely enjoyed their position, while others were happy not to be called upon themselves. By the mid-sixteenth century, religious motives played a part, as in the case of Prescot's James Watmough who served 1537–43 and returned under Mary. Generally it is rare to find the same wardens elected more than six times, and John Saberton's 25 terms at Peterborough (between 1478 and 1506) must have been a record.[117]

Broad as the social basis may have been, it is equally evident that not everyone was eligible. Residency was a fundamental requirement,[118] and so were basic experience in money and business matters, as well as a certain economic independence. For various reasons, the office could make demands on the wardens' own resources, at least temporarily,[119]

---

[115] French, 'Local identity', p. 63.

[116] All Saints CWA, 1480ff (Pernannt); T. L. Stoate (ed.), *Devon Lay Subsidy Rolls 1524-7* (Bristol, 1979), p. 231, and H. Hanham, 'The suppression of the chantries at Ashburton', *Devonshire Association*, **99** (1967), 120.

[117] Edward Bole served at Croscombe from 1506–31: French, 'Local identity', p. 65. In the same parish, John Bole was another example of a 'traditionalist' reappointed under Mary (ibid.).

[118] The small parish of Mickfield in Suffolk provides an exception: P. Smith, 'The CWs of Mickfield' (Cambridge Certificate in Local History, 1994), p. 35: Thomas Blower served 1546 when he lived in Stonham Aspal.

[119] When an accounting period ended in a deficit, the parish 'owed' the balance to the wardens. This implied that they had advanced the money. Sometimes they were reimbursed the next year (Halesowen CWA 1504–5), but sometimes only over a series of accounts (Ashburton CWA 1487ff).

Table 2.1 Lay subsidy assessments for Ashburton churchwardens
c. 1524

		Wardens (%)			Total (%)	
Wages:		1–4	(1–3)		16	(11)
Goods	£1–4	34–35	(36)		60	(42)
	5–9	18–20	(20)		28	(20)
	10–14	17	(18)		20	(14)
	15–19	10	(11)		3	(2)
	20–24	4	(4)		3	(2)
	25–29	1	(1)		1	(1)
	30+	6	(6)		7	(5)
Lands:		1	(1)		4	(3)
Total:		95	(100)		142	(100)

but sometimes permanently.[120] Martial Dauvergne of Saint-Germain le Vieil, to quote an example from the French capital, reimbursed his parish in 1454 for outstanding rent charges he had been unable to recover in a law suit, while in 1505 his colleagues at Saint-Etienne du Mont found 3000 *livres* between them to cover a deficit the community was incapable of paying itself.[121] Churchwardens thus had to be men of some substance, but not necessarily wealthy. At Ashburton, 95 of the 152 individuals serving between 1479 and 1560 can be identified in the subsidy rolls of 1524, 1525 and 1544. Their assessments were as shown in Table 2.1.[122]

The highest recorded assessment for a warden was Thomas Prediaux's (at £40 goods), while John Ford topped the list overall (£140 goods). The wage earners as well as the lowest goods range (£1–4) are underrepresented among the officeholders, but not absent altogether,

---

[120] 'Hyt ys a greyd by thyes syd awdytors thatt the olde churge wardens Bartylmew Watson & John Smythe schall paye toward the losse of the churge goodes iis.' (Andrew Hubbard CWA 1526–7). One former warden of a Kentish parish, in contrast, thought that he had been unfairly charged with certain sums and started proceedings in Chancery: PRO, C1 226/31.

[121] Constant, 'Source trop négligée', 180.

[122] Stoate (ed.), *Subsidy Rolls 1524–7*, pp. 231–2. Basis: 1524, gaps supplemented by 1525 and 1544 (Stoate (ed.), *Subsidy Rolls 1543–5*, pp. 192–3). If wardens' goods were assessed in several subsidies, the figure closest to their term of office has been chosen. Some names appear twice, assessed once at wages and once at goods, which explains the minimum and maximum figures (1524 assessments only have been included for the 'Total assessed' column).

while the wealthier inhabitants get more than their fair share. On the other hand, neither John Ford nor the most substantial landowner (John Sentclere at £20) ever serve as churchwardens. The only 'landed' warden was John Crocker with property worth £3. The average assessment of the officials is just over £10, but 59 per cent (compared to 73 per cent overall) owned less.

The parish included both the borough and the manor of Ashburton. Was there a territorial bias in the office, too?[123]

	Wardens	Total
Borough	29	83
Manor	41	65

The wardens were clearly more likely to be substantial manorial tenants (the manor's average assessment in goods was £7 5s., the manor wardens' £9), but the parish council, the 'eight men', consisted of an equal number of members from town and country. The burgesses' lower share in the churchwardenship may have had something to do with their additional responsibilities towards the St Lawrence gild.[124]

At Boxford, the sample is smaller and the empirical basis rather more disparate,[125] but the available evidence not dissimilar (Table 2.2). Here, none of the office holders was assessed as a wage-earner, even though over 50 per cent of the subsidy payers belonged to that category. The wardens covered a range from £2 (Thomas Heth) to the £30 of William Coo, junior, with about half assessed at less than £10. Neither the wealthiest landowner (Peter Fen at £10), nor the richest Boxford clothier (Thomas Coo at £200 in goods) recorded in 1524 ever served during the time covered by the accounts.

At Morebath in Devon, to move to a final example, the same analysis results in Table 2.3.[126]

---

[123] This can only be examined for the 1524 subsidy.

[124] Ashburton CWA, pp. 192–3 (eight men); H. Hanham, 'Chantries at Ashburton', 112–13 (gild).

[125] The evidence from 1522 (muster) and 1524 (S. Harvey (ed.), *Suffolk in 1524* (Woodbridge, 1910), pp. 13–15) has been supplemented by 1568: Boxford CWA, pp. 83–93. The comparison with the overall figures (again based on 1524) can thus only provide a very rough idea.

[126] Stoate (ed.), *Subsidy Rolls 1524–7* and *1543–5*; 33 wardens 1520–59. The minimum and maximum figures derive from two identical names with different assessments. The 'total' column is based on 1524 only, when there were no landholders, while the landholding warden Richard Cruce appears in 1545 (£1).

Table 2.2   Lay subsidy assessments for Boxford churchwardens
c. 1524

		Wardens (%)		Total (%)	
Wages:		–	(–)	61	(54)
Goods	£1–4	4	(24)	19	(17)
	5–9	4	(24)	5	(5)
	10–14	4	(24)	10	(10)
	15–19	–	(–)	–	(–)
	20–24	3	(18)	4	(4)
	25–29	–	(–)	1	(1)
	30+	1	(5)	2	(2)
Lands:		1	(5)	7	(7)
Total:		17	(100)	109	(100)

Table 2.3   Lay subsidy assessments for Morebath churchwardens
c. 1524

		Wardens (%)		Total (%)	
Wages:		0–1	(0–3)	13	(24)
Goods	£1–4	21–23	(63–9)	30	(54)
	5–9	4	(12)	5	(9)
	10–14	5–6	(15–8)	7	(13)
	15–19	–	(–)	–	(–)
	20–24	–	(–)	–	(–)
	25–29	–	(–)	–	(–)
	30+	–	(–)	–	(–)
Lands:		1	(3)	–	(–)
Total:		33	(100)	55	(100)

This was a small 33 household community in a rural environment,[127] where the maximum assessment in 1524 was a moderate £14 in goods (for William Morsse) and the majority of parishioners belonged to the lowest goods range. There was a limited supply of potential candidates,

---

[127] Information about the structure of the parish supplied by vicar Christopher Trychay in Binney (ed.), *CWA Morebath*, pp. 34–5.

and even Morsse served repeatedly, but the numerically substantial group of wage earners remained excluded. Levys Trychay and Richard Robyns had been labourers at an earlier stage of their life, but by the time they took office, they possessed goods worth £4 and £3 respectively. Cottager status, in contrast, was no bar to parochial service, as long as the household did not rely on wages alone (cottager churchwarden Harrye Hurlye owned £4 in goods).

Taken together, the evidence from this sample is suggestive. It looks as if the very top and bottom layers of local society were less likely to serve as churchwardens, even though the parish 'heavyweights' were certainly present at the passing of ordinances and the auditing of accounts.[128] At Ashburton, John Ford the elder, a major benefactor and farmer of the lucrative local gild-market, and John Sentclere, active county gentleman in possession of Ashburton manor 1546–51, never held the office.[129] The same is true for the richest Boxford clothier, Thomas Coo, and the various lords of the manors.[130] There is a remarkably small gentry contingent: at Prescot, the warden Henry Holland in 1525 may have been an example,[131] while the Newtons at Yatton were referred to as 'masters', but only once in charge of the office (widow Isabell in 1496/7). This seems to support Colin Richmond's impression of a gentry retreat and his suspicion that the whole tone of parochial life was not very 'gentlemanly'.[132] But the involvement of members of the social elite depended perhaps on how close they felt to the rest of the parish; where differences in wealth and outside contacts were comparatively small and gentlemen/yeomen boundaries blurred, the local 'gentry' could be more actively involved in parochial affairs and offices.[133]

Naturally, many more case studies are needed to substantiate these claims, particularly for the big cities. However, glimpses of practices in

---

[128] For example the exchequer baron and clerk of the pipe Nicholas Lathell at Botolph Aldersgate (P. Basing (ed.), *Parish Fraternity Register* (London, 1982), p. 85) or the gentlemen at Prescot.

[129] On Ford: H. Hanham, 'A tangle untangled', *Devonshire Association*, **94** (1962), 444, 'Chantries at Ashburton', 113 (St Lawrence gild market), and CWA 1521–22 (where he contributes no less than £10 to the rood loft!). However, Ford who may have been an attorney, wrote the accounts from 1509–32 and put them on a 'business-like' basis: CWA, p. vii. The manor belonged to the Bishops of Exeter until 1549, but was always farmed out: H. Hanham, 'A tangle untangled', 444.

[130] Identified in W. A. Copinger, *The Manors of Suffolk* (London, 1905), i. 22ff.

[131] Not described as 'gentleman' in the CWA, but as a juror in the manorial records 1535: Bailey (ed.), *Prescot Court Leet*, p. 84.

[132] 'The English gentry and religion *c*.1500' in C. Harper-Bill (ed.), *Religious Beliefs and Ecclesiastical Careers* (Woodbridge, 1991), p. 137.

[133] B. Galloway, 'Gentry and parish in the Tudor Marshland, 1500–80' (paper to the Cambridge Church History Seminar, 30 Nov. 1994).

other parishes confirm the preliminary impression. The few known wardens of Mickfield were substantial yeomen with goods of between £6 and £22 in the mid-1540s, but neither the highest nor lowest-ranking subsidy payers.[134] At Thame, the two wealthiest inhabitants of New Thame did serve for their half of the parish (but with just £3 goods in 1524–5 they were actually of rather moderate status), while the richest inhabitant overall, Geoffrey Dormer of Old Thame (£3 6s. 8d.), did not.[135] For Bridgwater in Somerset, it seems that the most senior townsmen preferred municipal service to the churchwardenship.[136]

Moving to the capital, Clive Burgess has discovered a fascinating 'social pyramid' among the Mary-at-Hill records, which arranges the contributors to the clerk's wages in a hierarchical manner. The churchwardens appear predominantly in the upper sections, while the top names had either served at a previous stage in their life or not at all. Here again, those from the bottom part of the pyramid are conspicuously absent.[137] Similarly, no aldermen are known to have served at Botolph Aldersgate, and only four styled themselves 'gentlemen'. Straightforward comparisons with the subsidy figures in London and Bristol are hampered by the fact that the assessment bases were wards rather than parishes. Still, those churchwardens who can be identified for St Ewen in 1524, for instance,[138] covered a fairly wide spectrum: from the 20s. earned by Harry Fild to the £80 in goods owned by the warden widow Margery Mathew. An 'average' warden would have paid between 10–20s. in tax, which was more than the average resident of Broad Street (approximately 6s.), but less than the typical inhabitant of Corn Street (38s.), the two main neighbourhoods of the parish.

The professional spectrum confirms the broad middling status of the office holders. In this sample of parishes, the occupations of 129 wardens can be reconstructed (Table 2.4).[139] The list has an unfortunate bias towards urban settings, because of the scarcity of occupational

---

[134] Smith, 'Mickfield', p. 13.

[135] I am grateful to Julia Carnwath for this information.

[136] French, 'Local identity', p. 54.

[137] Paper to the Medieval and Tudor London History Seminar at the Institute of Historical Research (16 May 1991).

[138] PRO, E179 113/192.

[139] Apart from the (rare) direct evidence in the CWA, cf. Basing (ed.), *Fraternity Register*, H. Hanham, 'A tangle untangled' and 'Chantries at Ashburton', Stoate (ed.), *Lay Subsidy Rolls 1524-7* and *1543-5*, Bailey (ed.), *Prescot Court Leet*, Skeeters, *Community and Clergy*, p. 26, PRO, E179 113/192, and the Halleway chantry accounts at All Saints: BRO P/AS/C/1. Many more clues would no doubt result from a systematic search of wills and lay subsidy rolls. Some of the designations may have been 'titles' rather than indications of the actual occupation.

Table 2.4 Occupations of churchwardens

1 Apothecary	2 Coopers	6 Mercers	2 Surgeons
2 Ashburners	1 'Craftsman'	7 Merchants	9 Tailors
2 Attorneys	1 Draper	2 Painters	2 Tanners
1 Baker	3 Exchequer off.	1 Pewterer	1 Tinner
7 Barbers	1 'Forbour'	1 Dr of physics	1 Town clerk
9 Brewers	5 Gentlemen	1 Priest	1 Vintner
1 Butcher	6 Goldsmiths	1 Scrivener	4 Waxmakers
1 Capper	4 Grocers	2 Shoemakers	6 Weavers
1 Chaplain	1 Haberdasher	2 Shopkeepers	2 'Widows'
1 'Clerk'	1 Husbandman	2 Skinners	1 Woolman
4 Clothiers	2 Ironmongers	6 Smiths	1 Wright
4 Clothmakers	2 Masons	1 Stainer	2 Yeomen
2 Cooks			

information elsewhere. However, it goes without saying that at Yatton, for instance, yeomen and husbandmen would have dominated. One noteworthy feature is the fact that tailors, brewers, and barbers were more numerous than merchants or gentlemen. The only members of the clergy to take office were Sir Thomas Blogwyn at Peterborough (1494–6) and Sir Richard Potter at Prescot (1523–4).[140]

A further important element in the construction of a wardens' profile is their broad administrative experience. It is evident that many were active in local fraternities: five looked after stocks at Prescot, at least three were members of St Ewen's Tailor craft gild, and no less than 37 had joined the Holy Trinity fraternity at St Botolph's, with 17 taking office there, too.[141] Chantry and parish accounts were compiled by the same wardens at All Saints until the 1540s, while those of Boxford had normally helped to organize the church ale in a previous year.[142] Their Ashburton counterparts assumed similar responsibilities about parochial social life, be it before, during, or after their term of office. John Strettyng, like most of his colleagues at Yatton, repeatedly served as lightwarden for one of the halves of the parish.[143] Countless overlaps

---

[140] Parson Thomas Hayle (Mickfield, 1546–8) provides another example, possibly linked to a religious 'purge': Smith, 'Mickfield', pp. 8–9, 34.

[141] Bailey (ed.), *Prescot Court Leet*, St Ewen CWA, and Basing (ed.), *Fraternity Register*, passim.

[142] Boxford CWA, p. xii. Yeoman Richard Brond looked after the ale 1537–41, distributed parish money to the poor 1551–3, and serves three times as warden: 1538–9, 1544–5, and 1553–4.

[143] Churchwarden 1526, 1544, 1558; lightwarden 1524, 1531, 1548, 1556.

existed with secular offices in village, manor, town, and even county. At least 13 of the 30 wardens of Prescot between 1523 and 1555 held a manorial position. Taken together, they acted as constables (24 times), members of one of the two juries (122), four men (14), alewardens (16), affeeors (19), overseers of the woods (33), and burleymen (3).[144] In 1549, Robert Worseley, tenant of the manor and churchwarden 1546–50, simultaneously exercised the functions of juror, constable, alewarden, and overseer of the wood. Four former wardens took part in an arbitration of an agricultural dispute in 1536,[145] while others were the object of court presentments. Robert Worseley himself felled a lord's tree during one of his terms as constable (1539).[146]

Elsewhere in this sample, parochial office holders included three common councillors and an alderman deputy (Botolph Aldersgate), four town sheriffs (All Saints), while 15 out of the 115 wardens of St Edmund Salisbury became town mayors at some stage in their life. One office would presumably precede the other in some kind of municipal 'cursus honorum', as it did at Newcastle-under-Lyme.[147] Churchwardens could also appear in hundred and county juries.[148] Evidence for an inner-parochial office sequence has survived, for example, at Morebath and Bridgwater: in the former case, candidates could move from being young men's wardens, via the trusteeship of other church 'stocks' and the main parish store, to the council of the 'five men'. In the latter, William Snothe appeared first as a collector for parish assessments (1444), then as a warden for the St Katherine's gild, and eventually as churchwarden from 1447–50.[149] It is evident that former wardens became something like 'elder statesmen' in many places: at St Bride's, London, they joined the vestry, at Andrew Hubbard the auditors, and at St Edmund, Salisbury, the 'masters'.[150]

---

[144] Bailey (ed.), *Prescot Court Leet*, and CWA, passim. The figures are based on the assumption that persons with the same name were indeed identical. This overlap between manor and parish seems to continue beyond the Reformation: J. S. Craig, 'Ecclesiastical policy and local community' (MA Carleton, 1988), p. 64.

[145] Bailey (ed.), *Prescot Court Leet*, pp. 110–11 (1549) and 87 (1536).

[146] Ibid., p. 92. For other cases of officer offences: S. Olson, 'Jurors of the village court', *Journal of British Studies*, 30 (1991), 251.

[147] Basing (ed.), *Fraternity Register*, index, Edmund CWA, and A. Brown, 'Lay piety in late medieval Wiltshire' (D. Phil. Oxford, 1990), passim. T. Pape, *Newcastle-under-Lyme in Tudor and early Stuart Times* (Manchester, 1938), pp. 7–8.

[148] J. Post, 'Jury lists and juries in the late fourteenth century' in J. Cockburn and T. Green (eds), *Twelve Good Men and True* (Princeton, 1988), p. 68 (a Leicestershire gaol delivery panel in 1380).

[149] Binney (ed.), *Morebath CWA*, passim; French, 'Local identity', p. 55.

[150] I. Archer, *The Pursuit of Stability: Social Relations in Elizabethan London* (Cambridge, 1991), p. 69 (Bride), Andrew Hubbard CWA, passim, and Amy Stratton in the introduction to Edmund CWA, p. xi.

Churchwardens thus represented a relatively wide spectrum of wealth, professions, and secular experience. Quite naturally, they approached their duties with different degrees of energy and commitment. The sources reveal little about their religious orientation, but it is known that even Lollards did not refuse to serve their turn.[151] Yet whatever the variety of individuals, almost all officers were male. Isabell Newton has been mentioned as an exception at Yatton, where her effigy survives in the family chapel of the parish church. A handful of other parishes, predominantly situated in the west country (Trull, Nettlecombe, Tintinhull, Halse, Morebath, St Petrock, Exeter, and St Patrick, Ingestre) appointed female wardens, but almost invariably as widows rather than in their own right. A widow is known to have served at St Ewen (Margery Mathew 1527–8), and the wife of goldsmith Thomas Barry, who deceased during office, accounted for him in 1561 at the same place. Possibly another woman served at Andrew Hubbard,[152] but the number of examples will always be limited. Still, women could look after subparochial institutions or minor parochial offices: Isabelle Tryppe was an alewarden at Yatton in 1525, and maiden's gilds offered opportunities for unmarried women in many parts of the country.[153]

There is as yet no detailed long-term survey of the churchwardenship to allow for comparison, but a few preliminary remarks about post-Reformation developments can be attempted here.[154] While the yeomanry or even the petty gentry may have taken effective control of many early modern parishes,[155] there are some late sixteenth-century case studies to suggest that the participation basis – at least for the wardenship itself – may have stayed broader. Parishes kept appointing men of predominantly middling sort, mostly with some experience from other offices (even though religious fraternities were of course no longer an option) and conscious of their local standing as 'parochiani meliores et antiquores'. The subsidy figures available for some case studies suggest that their economic status had certainly not increased dramatically: in the East Anglian evidence, wardens possessed on average £6 of goods in the 1570s, while 46 per cent of the churchwardens in the London ward

---

[151] R. G. Davies, 'Lollardy and locality', *TRHS*, 6th Series 1 (1991), 206.

[152] Maryan [?] Gerens, CWA 1508 and 1509.

[153] For a detailed discussion of female officeholding and parish roles see French, 'Local identity', ch. 5 ('Gendering the parish'), which concludes: 'Some parishes were more accepting of women's participation in the parish and in its leadership than other parishes. [...] In most communities, however, the parish offered medieval women another building to clean and more laundry to wash' (p. 224).

[154] A long-term study by J. Craig and B. Kümin (*Churchwardens and their Communities 1300-1700*) is in progress.

[155] Summarizing K. Wrightson, *English Society 1580–1680* (London, 1982), p. 36.

of Cornhill were assessed at less than £8 in the following decade. Inclusion among the subsidy payers seems to have been a prerequisite, but economic independence had been just as important in the pre-Reformation context.[156] The office could still form part of a municipal 'cursus honorum',[157] and both long-term office holders as well as reluctant candidates continue to emerge from the records. Not even spiritual motives had disappeared: parish service no longer appealed for penitential reasons, but as an opportunity to participate in the shaping of a godly society.[158]

It is hard to share Sir Thomas Smith's mid-sixteenth-century impression that local offices were now taken up by humble people for the first time.[159] The recruitment basis had always been broad and only towards the end of the century does there seem to be a tendency among the 'better sort' to avoid the churchwardenship and to concentrate on the control of more formalized vestries. By that time, increasing outside interference and growing internal problems had made parish service rather less attractive, but these processes will be examined in more detail below.[160]

Particular tasks, ranging from grave digging to the brewing of parish ale, were sometimes performed by other officials. In addition to the subparochial level of lights and fraternities, bigger churches could offer an impressive amount of positions. The Ashburton accounts refer to sextons, bedesmen, wax- and alewardens, as well as members of the choir.[161] At Botolph Aldersgate, the salary list of 1558–9 includes a clock keeper, a clock maker, an organ keeper, a scavenger, a launderer, and a conduct, paid between 1s. and 45s. each. Yet another function was carried out by the 'sidesmen', usually two to four laypeople chosen by the parish, who assisted the wardens at visitations.[162] The most important minor officer, however, was the parish or holy water clerk, an assistant in lower orders with an intermediary position between laity and clergy. Canon 29 of the Statutes of Exeter (1287) suggests that his election and

---

[156] East Anglian evidence: Craig: 'Elizabethan CWs and parish accounts', 362 ff.; London: Archer, *Pursuit of Stability*, pp. 63–7 and table 3.1. Such comparisons between different places at different times are of course extremely hazardous.

[157] Ibid., p. 65 (London); in 1609, the vestry of St Michael's, Coventry, ordered two newly elected city officers to pay 30s. each to free them of the office of churchwarden (Phythian-Adams, *Desolation of a City*, p. 169).

[158] Craig, 'Reformation, politics, and polemics', pp. 38ff.

[159] *De republica Anglorum*, ed. M. Dewar (Cambridge, 1982), pp. 76–7. P. Collinson, *De Republica Anglorum or, History with the Politics put back* (Cambridge, 1990), p. 34, quotes it as a piece of 'mythical history'.

[160] Chapter 6.2.2.

[161] CWA, pp. xvff.

[162] Meade, *Medieval Church*, p. 41, and E. Hobhouse (ed.), *CWA of Croscombe [etc.]* (London, 1890), p. xvii.

payment were a frequent bone of contention between parsons and parishioners.[163] From a canonical perspective, clerks were appointed by priests and supported by weekly and quarterly collections among the laity, but parochial practice was often more complex.[164] At All Saints, Bristol, a different group of seven parishioners provided him with his board every year, apart from contributing normally to his wages.[165] At Hawkhurst, the parson had to meet a share of the expenses 'without prejudice to the right of the Parishioners to choose the Clerk', while the customs of Torksey stipulated that 'clericus portans aquam benedictam debet eligi per parochianos et non per personam'.[166] Other evidence also suggests that he was an officer of the parish community, who received detailed regulations of his duties.[167] Generally, he was expected to carry the holy water on different occasions and to assist at mass, but he could also be responsible for bell ringing, washing of church clothes, visiting the sick, or cleaning the church.

2.2.3 Collective capacity

Equipped with their own funds and officers, parishioners were able to accumulate a great variety of collective experience. At Peterborough in the early fifteenth century, they decided to move the parish church. Agreement had to be reached with the local abbot, the bishop of Lincoln, and pope Boniface IX, permission was obtained for an alternative place of worship during the period of construction, and the entire costs of the new building were raised from the community.[168] At Rickmansworth, to take another random example, great commotion followed an arson attack in 1522. To repair the damage, the parish secured a licence to collect alms and appointed three collectors for the neighbouring dioceses. However, their accounts were deficient, and the wardens had to

---

[163] Powicke and Cheney (ed.), *Councils and Synods*, pp. 1026–7.

[164] Ibid., and Ashby, 'Parish life in London', p. 179. The parish of Haxey unsuccessfully claimed in 1291 that they (and not the vicar) should appoint the holy water clerk (Reynolds, *Kingdoms and Communities*, p. 95).

[165] Nicholls and Taylor, *Bristol Past and Present*, ii. 93 (t. Edward IV). A similar system operated at Tewkesbury (I owe this information to Caroline Litzenberger).

[166] Drew (ed.), *Lambeth CWA*, p. lii. M. Bateson (ed.), *Borough Customs* (2 vols, London, 1904–6), ii. 212. Similar evidence in Marshall, *Catholic Priesthood*, pp. 202–3.

[167] Owen, *Medieval Lincolnshire*, p. 106 (Louth). The parish book of St Stephen Coleman Street, London, contains a detailed list of duties: Freshfield (ed.), 'Stephen Coleman', 49. So do the records of St Nicholas Bristol (J. R. Bramble (ed.), 'From the records of St Nicholas', *Proceedings of the Clifton Antiquarian Club*, 1 (1884), 143–50). For the complexities of payments to the clerk in parish accounts cf. Chapters 3.2 and 3.4 below.

[168] CWA, pp. xxix ff.

sue for their money in Chancery. In the end, it took 14 years to complete the work, and the parish had learnt a lesson about the advantages of written agreements.[169]

A particularly important source of collective awareness was the relationship between community and clergy. Instead of submitting to clerical control over their resources, parishioners started to monitor the behaviour of their priests. The conscientious performance of spiritual services at an affordable price was one of their top priorities. Boroughs often issued guidelines to limit the financial impact of the 'spiritual economy'. Torksey in Lincolnshire, for example, fixed the tariffs for churchings at 2½ d., for marriages at 4 d., and for the customary quarterly offerings at ½ d.[170] Confronted with a non-resident or negligent incumbent, the parishioners of Thorley had him deprived by the bishop of London in 1443, those of Thundersley in Essex replaced theirs in 1514 without authorization, while at Braughing in 1520, a lay committee was formed to register the comings and goings of the vicar. On a more positive note, the parish of High Wycombe agreed to alleviate the workload of its priest by means of providing for an assistant.[171] Additional financial support for the local clergy became an increasingly common phenomenon, partly, no doubt, because of the diversion of so much of regular parish income.[172] It is not surprising that this nurtured lay expectations. In the mid-fifteenth century, the parishioners of Polruan (diocese of Exeter) claimed that the priest they paid for should be subject only to them, while those of Ludlow solved a dispute about church rebuilding by farming the whole benefice themselves and employing the reluctant rector as a mere salaried official.[173] This may have been an unusual step for an English parish, but French and Swiss communities quite often insisted on elaborate contracts before they admitted their priests.[174]

---

[169] M. Aston, 'Iconoclasm at Rickmansworth', *JEH*, **40** (1989), 524–8.

[170] Bateson (ed.), *Borough Customs*, ii. 210–12 (*c.* 1345). Cf. similar attempts in London: A. R. Myers (ed.), *English Historical Documents* (vol. iv, London, 1969), p. 729 (1382).

[171] GL, Register Robert Gilbert, fos 71v–72 (Thorley; I owe this reference to Irene Zadnik), C. Cross, *Church and People 1450–1660* (Hassocks, 1976), p. 44 (Thundersley), P. Heath, *The English Parish Clergy on the Eve of the Reformation* (London/Toronto, 1969), p. 64 (Braughing), and M. Bowker, *The Secular Clergy in the Diocese of Lincoln 1495–1520* (Cambridge, 1968), pp. 111–12.

[172] Cf. the analysis of the phenomenon in Chapter 3.4.

[173] A. D. Frankforter, 'The Reformation and the register', *Catholic History Review*, **63** (1977), 218 (Polruan), and Swanson, *Church and Society*, p. 218 (Ludlow).

[174] Aubrun, *Paroisse*, document 38, provides an example. Some parishes and towns in central Switzerland equally specified in detail what they expected from their clergy: Pfaff, 'Pfarrei und Pfarreileben', p. 230.

Parish assertiveness about proper status and services for the local church could lead to open conflict with ecclesiastical institutions. In an effort to protect their part of the abbey church of Wymondham from encroachments by the prior, the parishioners and wardens did not shy away from repeated physical intimidation. They walled up doors to deny the monks access and secured an episcopal decree of 1411 granting the parish the right to construct its own belfry.[175] The more conventional channel of a visitation was used by the inhabitants of Waterden (diocese of Hereford) in 1397 to force their rector to re-establish the vicarage he had illegally converted into a mere curacy.[176] At Chester, the parish of St Oswald fought for over a hundred years to obtain a replacement for the church which had been destroyed for the expansion of St Werburgh's abbey. Eventually, the convent was forced to hand over the south transept of the cathedral.[177] But there were yet other ways of parish influence.

A number of parishes acquired communal (municipal or parochial) patronage, in spite of the historiographical convention that this was unknown in medieval England.[178] Starting in London, the mayor, aldermen and commons obtained the manor of Leaden Hall in 1411 and with it the patronage of two churches, St Peter Cornhill and St Margaret Pattens. The city specified minimum standards for both, for St Peter in 1445, where a candidate had to be a graduate in theology, and for St Margaret in 1478, where the degree of Master of Arts was required. In addition, some London parish communities managed to lease or purchase their livings during Henry VIII's reign.[179] Between 1414 and 1459, the city of Norwich acquired the patronage of St Clement of Conisford,[180] and the townspeople of Ipswich appointed in practice to all of their benefices themselves.[181] In Oxfordshire, the villagers of Piddington settled a dispute with the vicar in 1428 by securing a licence

---

[175] Harrod, 'Wymondham', 265ff. For the similar case of Dunster in Somerset c.1500 see French, 'Local identity', pp. 163, 186.

[176] A. T. Bannister, 'Visitation returns of the diocese of Hereford', *EHR*, 45 (1930), 459.

[177] Cook, *Medieval Parish Church*, pp. 127–8.

[178] Reynolds, *Kingdoms and Communities*, p. 95, and D. Kurze, *Pfarrerwahlen im Mittelalter* (Cologne/Graz, 1966), p. 474.

[179] R. Newcourt (ed.), *Repertorium ecclesiasticum parochiale Londinense* (2 vols, London 1708–10), i. 523 and 407ff. The regulations for St Peter and St Margaret are discussed in J. A. F. Thomson, *The Transformation of Medieval England* (London, 1983), p. 311. P. Seaver, *The Puritan Lectureships* (Stanford, 1970), p. 345 (leases and purchases *t*. Henry VIII).

[180] Tanner, *Church in Norwich*, pp. 147 and 176.

[181] D. MacCulloch and J. Blatchly, 'Pastoral provision in the parishes of Tudor Ipswich', *Sixteenth-Century Journal*, 22 (1991), fn. 7 (for example St Clement).

to form their own parish and to elect their own priest,[182] while on 9 March 1538, the parishioners of All Saints, Oxford, leased all the rights of their church from Lincoln College for a period of 30 years, agreeing to keep the chancel in good repair and to pay all customary dues to the ordinary, in return for the right 'that they the saide william [paw] and william [Tylcokes] and their successours chirchewardens shall at all tymes duringe the said terme prouyde procure and gette oon honeste priste of good name and fame to serve and have chardge of the cure of the said parisheners of all seinctes'.[183]

Such formal procedures were not always necessary. Cited before a visitation commission on 11 December 1511 for his failure to provide a secular priest for the Holy Cross parish, the prior of St Gregory's Canterbury conceded 'quod dixit parochianis ibidem quod si velint providere capellanum idoneum, ipse salarium huiusmodi capellani solvere paratus esset'.[184] At Boxgrove priory, where the parishioners shared the church with a religious community, there seems to have been an equally informal arrangement.[185] Less harmoniously, the parishioners of Castle Combe in Wiltshire appointed a chaplain on their own authority in 1408, after the benefice had been vacant for over two years. In a similar case, the bishop of Bath and Wells imposed an interdict on the chapel of Pensford in 1448, because the inhabitants had hired a priest without an episcopal licence.[186] Judging from such evidence, the famous article of the 1549 rebellion ('We pray that priests and vicars that be not able to preach and set forth the word of God to his parishioners may be thereby put from his benefice, and the parishioners there to choose another, or else the patron or lord of the town') may have had a pre-Reformation context after all.[187] Furthermore, patronage by gilds represented another, if somewhat more exclusive means of collective influence. In London, the merchant taylors presented to St Martin Outwich from 1408, the grocers to Allhallows Honeylane from 1471 and to St Stephen Walbrook from 1534, while the drapers acquired the advowson of St Michael Cornhill in 1503.[188]

---

[182] G. Rosser, 'Parochial conformity and voluntary religion in late medieval England, *TRHS*, 6th Series 1 (1991), 182.

[183] A. Clark (ed.), *Lincoln Diocese Documents* (London, 1914), p. 228.

[184] Wood-Legh (ed.), *Kentish Visitations*, p. 71.

[185] Information kindly supplied by the current incumbent, the Reverend Canon Jeremy Haselock.

[186] Brown, 'Medieval Wiltshire', p. 37 (Castle Combe), and Bettey, *Church and Parish*, p. 44 (Pensford).

[187] Quoted in J. Cornwall, *The Revolt of the Peasantry* (London, 1977), p. 149. The passage is often seen as a mere populist borrowing from the German Peasants War (ibid., p. 239).

[188] Newcourt (ed.), *Repertorium*, i. 251–2, 418, 481, and 538.

The phenomenon was yet more prominent on the Continent. The case of 'communally owned churches' has already been mentioned, but parishioners in Italy, France, the Pyrenees, Transylvania, and a fair number of German urban and rural communities enjoyed similar rights of presentation. In Central Switzerland, many a parish hired and fired its priest almost at whim, treating the spiritual pastor literally like the local shepherd. Some 107 cases of communal patronage have been identified for central Europe, and many more advowsons were held by town councils in the same area.[189] These examples may be heterogeneous and scattered, yet they make an important point. Medieval clerical patronage was not necessarily the prerogative of powerful individuals or ecclesiastical institutions, but could also be exercised by gilds, parishes, and towns.

To perform all their tasks and duties, English parishes developed more than just an independent office of churchwarden. Gradually, the community was equipped with the capacity to exercise local authority functions whenever the need arose. Many parishioners were familiar with the ways towns, villages, and manors organized collective decision making and the distribution of responsibilities. It was but logical to transfer such experiences on to the ecclesiastical field, where the opportunities for genuinely communal procedures were even greater. Neither Church nor state took a great interest in the details of parochial government in the Middle Ages, and direct seigneurial control was comparatively weak. Parishes like St Stephen, Bristol, Tavistock in Devon, or Mary Magdalen, Oxford, assertively expressed their distinctive identity by affixing seals to their transactions.[190] In general, three areas deserve closer scrutiny: periodical legislative assemblies, tax authority, and internal peace-keeping arrangements. None of these turned the parish into an officially recognized corporate body, and certain constitutive elements were more pronounced in some places than others, but neither secular activities nor local government capacity should be associated with the post-Reformation parish only.

---

[189] Examples in Feine, 'Genossenschaftliche Gemeindekirche', passim, Genicot, *Rural Communities*, p. 100, Hay, *Church in Italy*, p. 24, Mousnier, *Institutions de la France*, p. 433, R. Ganghofer, 'Les communautés rurales en Europe occidentale et centrale' in *Communautés rurales*, p. 54, Kurze, *Pfarrerwahlen*, pp. 327–42, 435 (number of cases in central Europe), and Hergemöller, 'Parrocchia', p. 157. For Switzerland Pfaff, 'Pfarrei und Pfarreileben', p. 229.

[190] Fox (ed.), 'St Stephen', 202, Worth (ed.), *Tavistock*, p. 77, and Drew, *Early Parochial Organisation*, p. 20. The 'seal' would not have been legally binding, and may have been affixed to a document in order 'to add to its appearance' (Fox, 204), but the symbolism should not be overlooked.

Periodical assemblies and legislation

The sections on the election and supervision of churchwardens have introduced two of the most important responsibilities of the parish assembly, but it acted as the community's sovereign institution in many other respects. At Botolph Aldersgate for example, 'the hole body of the paryssh' ordered the attendance of all householders at the annual audit, consented to important changes in the leasing of parish property or to the waiving of 'desperate' debts,[191] while four men chosen by the officers and 'comonte' assessed the clerk's quarterages at another London parish, St Margaret Lothbury.[192] Elsewhere, the assembly required all parishioners to attend a 'general mind' for the benefactors of their community, or to sit in their proper places within the church.[193] Outside the big cities, there could be agreements between several parishes or townships about the mutual attendance of church ales and minimum contributions on such occasions. At Elvaston (Derbyshire) sometime on the eve of the Reformation, the town of the same name on the one part, and the people of Ockbrook on the other, agreed that the latter were to brew four ales at their own cost and

> y^t eu'y inhabitant of the s'd towne of Okebrooke shall be at the s'd ales, and eu'y husband and his wife shall pay 2 d., and eu'y cottyer 1 d. and all the inhabitants of Eluaston, Thurlaston, and Ambaston, shall come to the said ales.[194]

In return, Elvaston was to brew eight ales within the same one-year period, which the inhabitants of Ockbrook were ordered to attend with corresponding obligations. At Yatton and Morebath, too, the visiting of ales in neighbouring parishes is a regular feature of the

---

[191] Botolph CWA, 1494–5 (attendance) and 1512–13 (new indenture for the tenement without Temple Bar); debts were waived periodically, for example, 1538–9. A new higher rent of 16 s. was fixed for Thomas Went in the presence of the whole parish at All Saints (CWA 1510–11), and at Harmondsworth in Middlesex leases were granted 'with the assent concent of the hole parysheonrs' (Chancery evidence quoted in French, 'Local identity', p. 261).

[192] GL, MS 9,1 71/4, f. cclxxiii (Commissary Court Register of Wills 1438–49). I owe this reference to Irene Zadnik.

[193] General minds are customary for example in Bristol parishes: Burgess, 'Benefactions of mortality', pp. 75–6; seating arrangements are preserved at Littleborough, Lancs.: H. Fishwick, *The History of the Parish of Rochdale* (Rochdale, 1889), pp. 190–1.

[194] F. A. Carrington, 'Ancient ales', *Wiltshire Archaeological and Natural History Magazine*, 2 (1855), 193. An agreement by 'the hole parissners of the Parishe ... by their hole assent & consent' regulates the yearly amount of money due to the alewardens at Woodbury: T. Brushfield, 'Church of All Saints', *Devonshire Association*, 24 (1892), 354 (1536).

accounts.[195] Similar payments graded according to economic status were stipulated in the waxsilver ordinances at places like Ashburton and St Petrock, Exeter. In almost identical wording, they demanded that 'every man & hys wyffe to the wexe schall paye yerely on peny, and every hire servant thatt takyth wayges a halffe peny, and every othe person thatt rescevyth hys Maker at Ester, takyn no wages, a ferthyng'.[196]

Poor relief is another example for the broad authority of pre-Reformation parish assemblies. In March 1518, the audit day presented the legislative of Lambeth with the opportunity to record the following 'acte':[197]

> that the chyrghwardenes off the said chyrgh for the tym' beynge shall have aw[tho]ryte ... to put In to the almus howsse such feble people and thay to remayn ther dewrynge therlyve excepe that they doo offend unreasonably and then yt shall be lawfull to the said wardens apon a reasonable warnyng them to expulsse and put owtt and at the deth off any off the said poore people yt is enacted that such goodes as any off them shall leve in the said almus howsse at the hour off ther deth shall remayn' to the reperac'ons off the said howsse, ther fewneralles reserved, and the reste to be ordrede at the sighet off the sayde wardenes for the tym' beynge.

Most ordinances deal with financial matters, but this reflects the nature of the surviving sources. Other areas of communal involvement are often only alluded to,[198] and need to be reconstructed by means of circumstantial evidence.

Tax authority

Strictly speaking, parishes acquired a rating authority: whenever circumstances demanded the levying of substantial sums, they apportioned the agreed total among their members in accordance with some pre-defined local standard.[199] In the words of Pollock and Maitland, 'money-voting vestries became as indispensable to the rector as money-voting parliaments are to the king'.[200] In contrast to the Elizabethan age, this particular fund-raising device was the result of a

---

[195] For example Yatton CWA, 1512–3: 8 d. was spent at Ken. Other ales were visited at Kingston, Wrington, Banwell, and Congresbury.

[196] Ashburton, CWA, p. 192; F. A. Gasquet, *Parish Life in Medieval England* (London, 1906), p. 129. At Harlestone, a communal decision fixed the 'ceragium' at 3 d. per virgate: Wake, 'Communitas villae', 409.

[197] Drew (ed.), *Lambeth CWA*, pp. 24–5.

[198] Such as the 'instrument of decrees ... for good order in the parish' apparently passed at St Andrew Holborn in 7 Henry VI: E. Griffith, *Cases of Supposed Exemption from Poor Rates* (London, 1831), pp. vif.

[199] E. Cannan, *The History of Local Rates in England* (London, 1912), pp. 4–5.

[200] *The History of English Law* (2nd edition, Cambridge, 1968), i. 613.

genuine parish decision rather than statutory requirements or episcopal orders.[201] Once agreed upon, however, the voluntary element disappeared, and the community applied a variety of enforcement mechanisms. Indeed, custom and a certain peer pressure ensured that many 'collections', too, were more than just discretionary: the paschal money at St Edmund Salisbury was probably as 'compulsory' as the quarterly contributions to the parish clerks' wages elsewhere.[202] The regular amounts collected for particular lights or feast days in parishes like Peterborough or Halesowen strongly suggest a duty which was not easy to avoid.[203] The same applied to the waxsilver duty, as the relevant ordinances have shown above.

Rates were as thoroughly regulated as parish audits or elections. A particularly explicit example are the ordinances passed (with the assent of the parish) at St Stephen, Bristol, on 15 August 1524. The churchwardens and 12 principal men were empowered to set the levies for the clerk's stipend or any other necessity, and 'no manner of manne' was to 'dispyse no proctor or proctors for requyrynge of the churche dewties', on pain of a fine of 6 s. 8 d.[204] A rather more complicated procedure existed at St Christopher-le-Stocks in London: specially chosen assessors put a price tag on all pews and allocated them in accordance with the parishioners' financial resources. Those who refused to accept this decision were reported to the vestry, and, if need be, to the ordinary.[205] Elsewhere, the assembly decided itself: at Wiverton in 1298, inhabitants agreed to contribute 'juxta taxacionem de ipsorum omnium parochianorum communi vel majoris partis ipsorum consilio provide faciendam'.[206] The majority vote was binding, and the respective dues could be enforced by means of presentations to ecclesiastical courts and visitations. The parishes of Westbere, Northbourne, Smeeth, Sheldwich, and St Paul's, Canterbury, did so successfully during the visitations of Kentish deaneries in 1511.[207] At Bridgwater, collectors for the various wards reported defaulters to the churchwardens who sued them in the archdeacon's court, although this was rarely necessary.[208] Parish rates were also upheld by the highest secular courts. In a Year Book case of

---

[201] Drew (ed.), *Lambeth CWA*, p. liii, and Cox, *CWA*, p. 12.

[202] *Edmund CWA*, p. xiv, and Ashby, 'Parish life in London', p. 179.

[203] Cf. similar findings by Drew (ed.), *Lambeth CWA*, p. li, and S. Ware, *The Elizabethan Parish* (Baltimore, 1908), p. 59.

[204] Fox (ed.), 'St Stephen', 200.

[205] W. J. Hardy, 'Remarks on the history of seat-reservation in churches, *Archaeologia*, 53 (1892), 100-1.

[206] Drew, *Early Parochial Organisation*, p. 13.

[207] Wood-Legh (ed.), *Kentish Visitations*, pp. 87, 109, 153, 229, and 62.

[208] Hobhouse (ed.), *CWA of Croscombe [etc.]*, pp. xiif, and K. L. French, 'Lay piety in Bridgwater' (MA Minnesota, 1988), p. 52.

1370, a parishioner of an unnamed parish objected to a distraint for 9 s. imposed for his failure to contribute to a £10 rate for roof repairs. Confronted with the plaintiff's insistence that such a collection could only be enforced by the ordinary and that he had not assented to the rate in the first place, and the parish collectors' plea of immemorial custom, judge Kirton confirmed the validity of a by-law made by neighbours to assess everyone at a certain sum.[209] Vills thus exercised a similar right, and continental parishes, too, resorted to compulsory levies on their members.[210]

The range of activities supported by parochial rates was considerable: voluntary and compulsory contributions went hand in hand when Bodmin Church was rebuilt between 1469 and 1472.[211] At Hartlebury, parishioners were required to maintain specific portions of the churchyard wall at their own cost, while Prescot organized a special 'ley' (rate) for the purchase of new bells.[212] In early sixteenth-century Leicestershire, some parishes rated themselves to supplement the vicar's stipend, and the parish priest at Kingston-upon-Thames was granted an extra 2 d. from each householder in the 1530s.[213] The chaplain of Ayton (Yorkshire) received an annual 8 d. per husbandman, 4 d. per labourer with some landed property, and 2 d. from landless cottagers, while his colleague at Denton could count on 2½ d. per acre without differentiation.[214]

Keeping of the peace
Neighbourly love and peace are crucial elements of the Christian faith, and canon law made a point of promoting them at the local level. Parochial incumbents were ordered to keep peace with all men and admonished that

---

[209] 44 Edward III, fos 18f; discussed in Cannan, *History of Local Rates*, pp. 15–16, and J. T. Smith, *The Parish* (London, 1854), pp. 151 and 532–3.

[210] F. W. Maitland (ed.), *Select Pleas in Manorial Courts* (London, 1889), p. 12 (a 'tallage' at Blakenham, Suffolk, in 1247); Huard, 'Paroisse rurale', 16; Schröcker, *Kirchenpflegschaft*, p. 112 (the wardens of St Kolumban, Cologne, 'legten allein, ohne Mitwirkung des Pfarrers, den Parochianen, sooft es notwendig wurde, eine besondere Steuer auf').

[211] J. Lander, *Government and Community* (London, 1980), p. 149, and J. Harvey, *Gothic England*, (2nd edn, London, 1948), p. 121.

[212] C. Dyer, *Lords and Peasants in a Changing Society* (Cambridge, 1980), p. 364; Prescot CWA, 1523–4.

[213] A. P. Moore (ed.), 'Proceedings of the ecclesiastical courts in the archdeaconry of Leicester 1516–35', *Associated Architectural Society Reports and Papers*, **28** (1905/6), 125 and 208 (Kingston).

[214] E. Cutts, *Parish Priests and their People* (London, 1898), p. 468 (Ayton) and Haigh, *Lancashire*, p. 65 (Denton).

parochianos vestros moneatis, ut in unitate fidei et pacis vinculo unum corpus sint in Christo; inimicitias, si exorte fuerint in parochia vestra, diligenter sedantes, amicitias copulantes, discordantes ad concordiam revocantes; quantum in vobis est non permittentes quod sol occidat super iracundiam parochianorum vestrorum.[215]

Chaplains were similarly required to swear that 'contentiones inter Rectorem & Parochianos nullo modo suscitabunt ... sed quatenus in eis est concordia nutrient & servabunt inter eodem',[216] and the parishioners had to demonstrate their Christian spirit by making special charitable and penitential efforts on their patron saints' feastdays.[217]

Given the inevitability of occasional inner-parochial divisions, it was in the laity's best interest to follow these guidelines. Legal proceedings could be costly and disruptive, and the increasing institutionalization of the parish offered a chance to avoid them. There were no strict divisions between administrative and judicial bodies in pre-modern times, and parochial councils, officers', and assemblies could be used to solve problems locally. There is evidence for arbitration activities for instance at St Dunstan, Canterbury, where the curate and four elderly men dealt with conflicts of various kinds. In case of contempt of this 'court' and a resurgence of arguments, parties were ordered to pay a fine to the parish wardens.[218] Documents survive at St Thomas, Bristol, 'in which persons are bound to the churchwardens in a certain sum of money to keep the peace towards their neighbours', while at St Mary Magdalen Milk Street in London, the vestry held monthly meetings with the vicar to hear matters of 'variance'.[219] A very institutionalized form of parish influence on ecclesiastical jurisdiction can be found in the peculiar of Hartlebury, a manor of the bishops of Worcester, in the fifteenth and sixteenth centuries. 'A panel of parishioners, varying from twelve to seventeen in number, represented villages and hamlets in the parish, and answered the articles of visitation, fulfilling a role similar to the tithingmen and jurors at the view (of frankpledge). There were some coincidences of personnel between those making presentments in both lay and church courts.'[220] The court was presided by an official appointed by the rector, but the

---

[215] Powicke and Cheney (eds), *Councils and Synods*, p. 64: synodal statutes of Salisbury, c. 12 (1217 x 1219).

[216] Ibid., p. 1383 (canon Robert Winchelsey 1295 x 1313).

[217] J. Bossy, *Christianity in the West* (Oxford, 1985), p. 73.

[218] H. M. Smith, *Pre-Reformation England* (London, 1963), p. 124. At Estringham, arbitrators were appointed in a conflict between parish and vicar and approved by the prior of Durham: Thomson, *Early Tudor Church*, p. 284.

[219] Fox (ed.), 'St Stephen', 204; Archer, *Pursuit of Stability*, p. 80 (1564, similar vestry mediation at St Lawrence Jewry and St Margaret Pattens).

[220] Dyer, *Lords and Peasants*, p. 363.

parishioners had a share in its jurisdiction over church attendance, behaviour during services, enforcement of church dues, and questions of morality and public order (strangers, brothels, fornication, and so on). Parish fraternities were another parochial institution with a specific interest in avoiding and solving potential conflicts: founded to facilitate the journey from this world to the other, they laid particular emphasis on neighbourly solidarity and peaceful solution of conflicts. Countless ordinances include passages concerned with arbitration.[221]

If internal mediation attempts failed, parishes could bring their problems before visitors or established ecclesiastical courts. Yet there was a choice even at that stage. The wardens of St Andrew, Canterbury, for example, prepared legal action to recover chantry revenues in secular as well as ecclesiastical courts, before deciding that chances were probably better in the latter.[222] On the whole, it is reasonable to assume that (both secular and ecclesiastical) local communities had a tendency to present only those problems they could not solve themselves.[223]

During the last medieval centuries, the English parish had been shaped by its members into a powerful community with considerable legislative, financial, and jurisdictional powers. It had acquired quasi-corporate status and quasi-state functions which it exercised, not yet on a universal statutory basis, but in the type of locally acceptable mixture which its particular needs demanded. Canonical duties from above and pious initiative from below had both played their important parts in this process, but religious devotion was only one dimension of contemporary parish life. Robert Swanson has argued (with regard to the Reformation) that 'the activities of churchwardens, and lay control over much church wealth ... would foster ideas of lay control in a wider sense',[224] but the same could be said for the parishioners' inclination to diversify outside the ecclesiastical field. This trend shall now be examined in more detail.

---

[221] C. M. Barron, 'Parish fraternities of medieval London' in C. Barron and C. Harper-Bill (eds), *The Church in Pre-Reformation Society* (Woodbridge, 1985), p. 26, and Smith (ed.), *English Gilds*, pp. 74ff (Gild of St George the martyr, Bishop's Lynn).

[222] Swanson, *Church and Society*, p. 189.

[223] Argued for the secular field (for the fourteenth and seventeenth century respectively) by B. W. McLane, 'Juror attitudes towards local disorder' in J. S. Cockburn and T. A. Green (eds), *Twelve Good Men and True* (Princeton, 1988), p. 64, and K. Wrightson, 'Two concepts of order' in J. Brewer and J. Styles (eds), *An Ungovernable People* (London, 1980), p. 30.

[224] Swanson, *Church and Society*, p. 250.

2.3 Secular uses

'Genetically' and legally, the pre-Reformation parish can be seen as a purely ecclesiastical institution,[225] but this was not the perspective of the parishioners themselves. In their eyes, there were no strict divisions between the spiritual and the profane, and communal activities related to both. For a start, the church was their only meeting place and 'a political centre'.[226] St Margaret, Westminster, for example, was rebuilt for a massive £2000 at around 1500 to satisfy the collective desire for a major public building in a town without independent government structures.[227] In many places, church bells were rung to summon inhabitants for the discussion of 'choses touchant la gouernaile de la ville'.[228] At Banwell, the church provided a venue for episcopal jurisdiction, and at Hindolveston for the manorial court.[229] London's St Paul cathedral was notorious for the transaction of respectable and less respectable business, while 'villagers divided between separate lordships or manors may have put on their parishioners' hats to regulate their common affairs'.[230] At Harlestone in Northamptonshire, for example, details concerning the commons and local government were regulated in an agreement between the various lords and representatives 'totius villate' in 1410. Even though it is not made explicit, the inclusion of grants to the rector and the definition of the *ceragium* make it tempting to suspect that the 'vill' referred to here may in fact have acted through the parish.[231] As observed in the churchwardens' profile, there were countless overlaps between secular and ecclesiastical offices, and boroughs or manors often worked hand-in-hand with parochial institutions. At Prescot and Bridgwater, court leet and municipal officers helped to collect parish levies, while numerous

---

[225] F. W. Maitland, 'The survival of archaic communities' in his *Collected Papers* (1911), ii. 339: 'The parish is a purely ecclesiastical institution'. Hobhouse (ed.), *CWA of Croscombe [etc.]*, p. xv: the churchwardens' office is 'wholly free from all civil functions'. W. K. Jordan, *Philanthropy in England* (London, 1959), p. 82: 'the parish in 1480 had few links indeed with secular government'. In H. Jewell, *English Local Administration in the Middle Ages* (Newton Abbot, 1972), 'parishes' are restricted to a few index entries.

[226] Scarisbrick, *Reformation*, p. 45.

[227] G. Rosser, *Medieval Westminster* (Oxford, 1989), p. 264.

[228] W. P. Baildon (ed.), *Select Cases in Chancery 1364–1471* (London, 1896), no. 132 (Grayingham, Lincs.); Cook, *Medieval Parish Church*, p. 35 (Newcastle).

[229] French, 'Local identity', p. 77 (1440s); R. H. Helmholz (ed.), *Select Cases of Defamation* (London, 1985), p. 19.

[230] Smith, *Pre-Reformation England*, p. 108; Reynolds, *Kingdoms and Communities*, p. 143 (quote).

[231] Wake, 'Communitas villae', 409. Terminological changes support this assumption: in 1262, one of the lord's estate book records just a series of individuals, but by 1311 it speaks of a 'commune' (ibid., 408).

places assigned parts of agricultural fines to the repair of the church.[232] On the other hand, parish assemblies – once used to the granting of rates for religious purposes – could soon start 'to interfere with many things'.[233] From an international perspective, the parish has been characterized as 'an important, probably the most important factor in the birth or maturation of the rural community', and it could play an equally prominent part in urban development.[234] Everywhere, Sunday mass and parish affairs served as opportunities for the discussion of current events and an exchange of information, with communal identity strengthened by the interplay of secular and ecclesiastical institutions.[235]

The following cannot be an exhaustive survey of the English evidence, but it attempts to illustrate three main incentives for the secular use of the parochial framework.

2.3.1 National duties

Due to their universal character, parishes provided a convenient platform for the publication of all types of information. Messages from central government, local lords, or bishops were all read out to parochial congregations,[236] with varying success. From the council of Oxford in 1222, the Church had ordered to declare in all parish churches that those who maliciously accused others of serious crimes faced excommunication. And indeed, when one Peter Bencher appeared as a witness in a defamation case in 1415, he told the Canterbury court 'quod sepius audivit pronunciatum sive publicatum in ecclesia sua parochiali ... quod omnes diffamatores sunt excommunicati'.[237] In contrast, the crown's attempt to involve churchwardens in the enforcement of the statute of labourers seems to have left little trace in parochial sources.[238]

---

[232] Bailey, 'CWA of Prescot', 140; French, 'Local identity', p. 103. Examples of relevant agricultural by-laws: W. O. Ault, 'Manor court and parish church in fifteenth-century England', *Speculum*, 42 (1967), 53–67, and Dyer, *Lords and Peasants*, p. 362.

[233] Maitland, 'Archaic communities', p. 364.

[234] Genicot, *Rural Communities*, p. 105 (quote); for the complexities in urban development see the section on 'Town administration' below.

[235] Ganghofer, 'Communautés rurales', pp. 53, 55 (France and Sweden). R. Sablonier, 'Innerschweizer Gesellschaft im 14. Jahrhundert' in *Innerschweiz und frühe Eidgenossenschaft* (Olten, 1990), ii. 104 (Switzerland), Bader, *Dorfgenossenschaft*, ii. 213 (Germany). The mutual strengthening of the various units is stressed in Feine, 'Kirche und Gemeindebildung', p. 54.

[236] For example J. Topham et al. (eds), *Rotuli Parliamentorum*, 21 Richard II, appendix 43 (death of Thomas, duke of Gloucester); Mason, 'English parishioner', 27 (proclamation by Bishop Wolstan of Worcester).

[237] Helmholz (ed.), *Defamation*, p. xv (Chylton vs Garden, 1415).

[238] Hobhouse (ed.), *CWA of Croscombe [etc.]*, p. xv, n. 1.

Royal taxation was another important link to the secular world. The main financial officer was the sheriff, and the township the normal assessment basis, but alternative procedures were not uncommon. Parish juries were involved in the collection of the tithe of Saladin in 1188, royal justices scrutinized parishes for the purposes of the thirteenth from 1207, and the ninths of 1340–2 were 'a wholly secular tax, but used the unit of the ecclesiastical parish for assessment purposes'.[239] A jury of parishioners calculated one ninth of the value of sheaves, wool, and lambs and compared it with the 1291-taxation of pope Nicholas.[240] The most remarkable example, however, was the parish subsidy of 1371.[241] The ecclesiastical framework promised to offer a suitable opportunity to tax clergy and laity alike, even though administrative problems and a lack of reliable information on the number of parishes obstructed the experiment in its early stages. Nevertheless, it proved a great success, and 99 per cent of the target of £50 000 had reached the Exchequer by Easter 1374. The average sum for each unit was 116 s., with due allowances for differences between rich and poor communities. Not surprisingly, the localities applied the most favourable definition to their particular situation, exemplifying the 'precedence of local concerns and local solidarities over and above the interests of the realm'.[242] On the whole, prosperous towns and big rural parishes benefited considerably, and the prerogatives of distant mother churches were for once staunchly defended by many an independent-minded chapel. There is little information about local collection mechanisms, but parish officers and institutions must have played a part. On the evidence of later subsidies, local arrangements varied greatly, yet the 'chief of the parish' were usually involved.[243]

After the temporary switch to a poll tax (which at least in 1377 was also partly collected by parishes rather than vills[244]) the 1371 experiment was repeated in a modified form in 1427. This time, parliament granted a graduated subsidy on condition 'that alle inhabitantz, housholders, withynne every parische of this royaume, so that ther be inhited in the saide parische x persons there holdynge housholde' were to pay a certain sum.[245] Churchwardens also contributed their share to the Tudor lay

---

[239] Jewell, *Local Administration*, pp. 93–4 and 108 (quote).

[240] Ault, 'Village church', 198.

[241] M. Ormrod, 'An experiment in taxation', *Speculum*, 63 (1988), 58–82.

[242] Ibid., 76.

[243] R. S. Schofield, 'Parliamentary lay taxation' (Ph.D. Cambridge, 1963), p. 81; cf. the subsidy payments in many CWA (see the evidence quoted below).

[244] P. Harvey, 'Initiative and authority in settlement change' in M. Aston et al. (eds), *The Rural Settlements of Medieval England* (Oxford, 1989), p. 42 (in Cornwall and Middlesex).

[245] Topham et al. (eds), *Rotuli Parliamentorum*, 6 Henry VI, no. 13.

subsidies: the Bristol parishes of All Saints and St Ewen's were assessed at £36 and £3 in 14–15 Henry VIII respectively,[246] which amounted to about one half to three quarters of their actual annual income at the time. The All Saints accounts duly record the corresponding payments of 36 s. in 1523–4 and 1524–5, and its former (and future) warden John Mansell, a grocer, served as collector for the ward of All Saints. At Ashburton in 1543–4, 4 s. 8 d. were spent for 'our lord the king subsidy', and in an original idea put forward in 1559, the under-treasurer of the Tower mint proposed to meet the costs of a recoinage (c. £400 000) by means of a flat rate contribution of £40 from each of England's parishes.[247]

The first evidence for a military role of the parish dates from 1138. Before the battle of Standard, the archbishop of York promised an assembly of barons that his priests and parishioners would lend aid, and thus the lords of Yorkshire, Nottinghamshire, and Derbyshire were joined by parish levies of 'omnes qui possent ad bella procedere'. In London, to judge from late thirteenth-century evidence, military levies were organized by wards and parishes under the respective aldermen, and on 20 August 1316, the Lincoln parliament decided to include arrays of all the 'fencibles' of the northernmost counties by parishes for the winter campaign against the Scots.[248] While these troops never mustered, parochial funds were certainly used to hire men for the defence of the realm at Hartlebury in 1413.[249] But parishes and military affairs were not only linked in unusual circumstances. The provision of butts for archery was an ancient responsibility reinforced in the 1540s.[250] The legislation of Philip and Mary, which charged parishioners with the maintenance of church armour, could build on a long tradition of ordinary individuals doing military service in times of need.[251] Thus, wars and weapons appear in churchwardens' accounts from an earlier date: in an addition to the regular accounts, the wardens of Ashburton declared in 1543–4 that 'they gave nine men going to war with our lord the king' 20 s., 7½ angelles and 1 riall (gold coins of 7 and 10 s. respectively). The year after, 18 s.10 d. spent 'for the king' included 4 s. 6 d. for helmets and 11 s. for body armour, while another £1 for soldiers appeared as extraordinary expenditure. Substantial military costs also marked the

---

[246] PRO, E 179 113/192
[247] C. E. Challis, *The Tudor Coinage* (Manchester, 1978), p. 119.
[248] M. R. Powicke, *Military Obligation in Medieval England* (Oxford, 1962), pp. 44, 143–4, 254.
[249] Dyer, *Lords and Peasants*, pp. 356–7.
[250] 33 Henry VIII, c. 9.
[251] Drew (ed.), *Lambeth CWA*, pp. xlvi-xlvii.

following account: £3 2 s. were used for ramparts, 4 s. for armour, 12 s. 4 d. for swords and daggers, £1 12 s. 2 d. for soldiers' clothes, and 9 s. 4 d. in cash to their wages. Other parishes made contributions at least through their subsidy payments. At Crondall in Hampshire for example, 4 d. were accounted for as 'money to the chauncelor gathered agenst the Turks' in 1543.[252]

2.3.2 Town administration

The shared recruitment basis for office holders and the use of churches for civic purposes resulted in close links between secular and ecclesiastical communities. Parishes could be subdivisions or constituencies of towns (as in Ipswich), they could precede and support the formation of secular town institutions (as in Cologne), or they could be used casually and unsystematically for particular administrative purposes.[253] Their boundaries were important landmarks, used in deeds, and carefully followed at perambulations.[254] A few examples may illustrate the range of this 'municipal' role of many parishes.

At Bristol, St John's, All Saints, St Nicholas, and St Mary Redcliffe all had conduits and taps, which gave them an important function in the town's water supply, while the clock of St Nicholas provided the standard time. Over the year, the rituals of civic life involved a great range of churches. Mayors and officials visited St Michael at Michaelmas, All Saints on its feastday, and Mary Redcliffe on All Souls, in the latter case to exercise their supervisory function over the Canynges chantry. Eventually, the entire town council attended the boy-bishop ceremony at St Nicholas on 6 December. The parishes also played a part in the outward representation of the town. In 1487 for instance, Henry VII was greeted by a procession representing all 18 parish churches. At Grantham and Folkestone, the mayor and bailiffs were elected in church.[255]

In London, parishes were the units 'viewers' used when they dealt with any form of property or building litigation, and in the lord's court at

---

[252] J. F. Williams (ed.), *The Early CWA of Hampshire* (Winchester, 1913), p. 110. Another example in Peterborough CWA, 1506–7.

[253] Reynolds, *Kingdoms and Communities*, p. 190 (Ipswich). For a survey of the parishes' role in German cities: Hergemöller, 'Parrocchia', pp. 143–51. In places like Cologne they continued to serve as administrative divisions, elsewhere they were gradually replaced by secular wards or neighbourhoods.

[254] D. M. Palliser, 'The sources' in M. W. Barley (ed.), *The Plans and Topography of Medieval Towns* (Leamington, 1976), p. 6.

[255] J. H. Bettey, *Church and Community in Bristol during the Sixteenth Century* (Bristol, 1983), pp. 4ff; Cook, *Medieval Parish Church*, p. 35. For similar urban ceremonies elsewhere see Hutton, *Merry England*, ch. 1.

Torksey in Lincolnshire, presentments were made by 'quelibet parochia'.[256] At York, ecclesiastical boundaries were 'useful as civic units, and both civic rates and national taxes were assessed parochially, while each parish had two or three constables to keep the peace. Justice at its humblest level was enforced there too, for most churchyards contained a pair of stocks'.[257] Here, as well as in Oxford, jurors from 'four parishes' replaced those from 'four vills' normally used in coroners' inquests.[258] At Harwich, the financial competence of churchwardens was apparently so well established that they simultaneously served as chamberlains and treasurers of the borough, while Ipswich parishes served as the assessment basis for town rates from the mid-fifteenth century.[259] On 16 occasions, collectors were named to raise money for purposes as varied as law suits, town charter renewals, common quays, tenths, fifteenths, or the coming of the king.[260]

2.3.3 Parish diversification

Many a parish account book reveals that the community assumed responsibility in local government areas such as highway maintenance. In 1437, the churchwardens of Tintinhull were authorized by their parish to spend 3 s. 5 d. for stones to mend the village road.[261] In 1511, the parishioners of Folkestone presented one William Baker for withholding large parts of the 66 s. 8 d. he had been given for the repair of bad roads, while the conditions attached to a gift make it clear that the parish of Appledore was about to start major works on the highway.[262] A memorandum attached to the Halesowen accounts of 1499–1500 records a contribution to 'the causey at Cachars gate', and £6 18 s. 8 d. were paid for mending the highway from Long Lane to Islington at Botolph Aldersgate in 1550–1. The Highway Act of 1555 has thus been interpreted as a statement of custom rather than a statutory innovation.[263]

---

[256] J. S. Loengard (ed.), *London Viewers and their Certificates* (London, 1989), passim; Bateson (ed.), *Borough Customs*, ii. 54.

[257] D. M. Palliser, *Tudor York* (Oxford, 1979), p. 77.

[258] C. Gross (ed.), *Select Cases from the Coroners' Rolls* (London, 1895), pp. 88–90, 112–13, 119–20.

[259] Newcourt (ed.), *Repertorium*, ii. 218 (at least under Edward VI and Mary); Cannan, *Local Rates*, pp. 18ff.

[260] For example 1545: 'every of the commons shall be rated according to their substance by two honest persons within their parish' (ibid., p. 20).

[261] Ault, 'Manor court and parish church', 64.

[262] Wood-Legh (ed.), *Kentish Visitations*, pp. 124–5 (Folkestone) and 159 (Appledore).

[263] Cannan, *Local Rates*, p. 8. The act stipulated that two surveyors were to be elected by the parish, and that each landholder had to work on the highway on four days designed by the constables and wardens.

A similar picture emerges for the upkeep of bridges and other public works. This was normally a duty incumbent on townships or lords of the manor, but the *coram rege* rolls for 1362 record that 'the men of the parish of Ripon ought with the said archbishop to repair the aforesaid bridge'.[264] Urgent need was a more important motivation than legal obligation for parishes to undertake or sponsor such work. As early as 1250, visitation records of Heybridge reveal that six parishioners looked after the local bridge with the profits from nine sheep bequeathed for this purpose.[265] When the abbot of Peterborough refused responsibility, the churchwardens repeatedly took the initiative themselves. The first payment of the kind was made in 1475–7 and amounted to £1, in 1514, church funds, Corpus Christi money, and the 'increase' of the sepulchre light were all used to finance bridge repairs costing over £7, and further work for £1 was needed less than twenty years later.[266] Staverton bridge at Ashburton was maintained by the local wardens, while the Yatton accounts record contributions to the repair of the sea wall and sluice gate, and the obligation of the wardens to scour the river Yeo for the security of the village.[267] Similarly, some parishes in Lincolnshire charged wardens with the collection of rates for the protection of their coasts or the ringing of bells as a flood warning.[268]

Another important area of secular activity was 'culture' in the widest sense. Recent historiography has provided a wealth of evidence for the importance of parishes in early English drama and the ritual life of the nation. Parish plays were in fact more characteristic for contemporary theatre than the great mystery cycles of York or Coventry, and churchwardens' accounts provide one of the crucial sources for costumes, venues, and performance details.[269] A particularly popular occasion were the Corpus Christi celebrations shortly after Whitsun, which often combined drama with processions and other pageants.[270] Many communities, predominantly outside the big cities, sponsored

---

[264] C. T. Flower, *Public Works in Medieval Law* (London, 1923), ii. 271.

[265] W. S. Simpson (ed.), 'Visitation of churches belonging to St Paul's cathedral, 1249-52', *Camden Miscellany*, 9 (1895), 12: 'isti tenent oves ad emendacionem pontis'.

[266] Peterborough CWA, 1475-7, 1533-4, and p. 94.

[267] Ashburton CWA 1540-1, 42-3, 43-4, 46-7, 48-9 and 1549-50; Yatton CWA 1528-9, and Hobhouse (ed.), *CWA of Croscombe [etc.]*, p. xv.

[268] Owen, *Medieval Lincolnshire*, p. 117. In Suffolk, the Walberswick wardens maintained the quay and managed other town affairs: C. Richmond, *John Hopton* (Cambridge, 1981), p. 178.

[269] I. Lancashire, *Dramatic Texts and Records of Britain: A Chronological Topography to 1558* (Cambridge, 1984), esp. p. 481. The 'Records of Early English Drama' series is an invaluable source in this respect: see for example J. M. Wasson (ed.), *Devon* (Toronto, 1986), pp. 17–30, for an example from this sample (Ashburton; all evidence based on CWA).

[270] Hutton, *Merry England*, pp. 40-4.

companies which travelled to neighbouring towns and villages, raising funds for their parish in the process.[271] The plays were normally religious in character, but also important social events of local and regional reputation. Some accounts in this sample record regular payments for this purpose; pre-Reformation Ashburton spent on average over 3 s. on costumes and actors every year.[272] The ecclesiastical and festive calendar provided plenty of incentives to blend religious ritual, secular entertainment, processions, and formal drama into an appropriate mixture. Parishioners participated in a variety of roles, from waking at the Easter sepulchre to the playful capturing of members of the opposite sex at Hocktide.[273] Music, of course, should also be mentioned in this context. Some urban communities supported a sophisticated polyphonic repertory throughout the liturgical year, and parochial records provide many a clue to the presence of distinguished composers and the purchase of musical literature.[274]

After 1450, an apparent increase in social events led to the emergence of a new kind of community centre, the church house. These were usually rectangular, one- or two-storey buildings with little ornamentation. In Devon alone, 64 appeared in the pre-Reformation decades.[275] Many contained brewing or baking facilities, and the staging of church ales was one of their main functions. For the rest of the year, the house could be let to private tenants or for other social occasions.[276] Communal functions, however, were given priority: the lease of church house tenant John Brode at Whitwell (Isle of Wight) provided that if 'the quarter shall need at any time to make a quarter ale or church ale, for the maintenance of the chapel that it shall be lawful for them to have the use of the said house with all the rooms both above and beneath during their ale'.[277]

---

[271] A. F. Johnston, 'Parish entertainments in Berkshire' in J. A. Raftis (ed.), *Pathways to Medieval Peasants* (Toronto, 1981), pp. 335–8, and ' "What revels are in hand?" Dramatic activities sponsored by the parishes of the Thames valley' (Paper read at the 28th International Congress on Medieval Studies, Kalamazoo, 1993).

[272] CWA, passim.

[273] The ritual calendar is now conveniently summarized in Hutton, *Merry England*, ch. 1.

[274] See, for example, H. Baillie, 'A London church in early Tudor times', *Music & Letters*, 36 (1955), 55–64 (Mary-at-Hill), and F. Harrison, 'The repertory of an English parish in the early sixteenth century', in J. Robijns (ed.), *Renaissance-Muziek, 1400–1600* (Louvain, 1969), pp. 143–7 (All Saints, Bristol).

[275] Lander, *Government and Community*, p. 148, defines them as 'buildings for the communal purposes of the parish'. In Somerset, Croscombe spent £13 2s. 11d. for its construction in 1480 (Smith, *Pre-Reformation England*, p. 119) and Stogursey £29 2s. 7 d. in 1515 (French, 'Local identity', p. 172).

[276] P. Cowley, *The Church Houses* (London, 1970), pp. 53ff.

[277] Carrington, 'Ancient ales', 194 (1574).

Parishes also provided some educational facilities 'with elementary reading and singing schools, and some grammar, all closely linked to training for participation in the church services'.[278] Many of these institutions were attached to chantries, but seldom properly endowed before the sixteenth century. The will of the mercer Richard Collyer of 1532, however, provided for the establishment of a free school for 60 scholars at his parish of origin, Horsham in Sussex. The vicar, churchwardens, and specially chosen schoolwardens were empowered to select the pupils, and the parish was also involved in the choice of the master and usher. The school was operational by 1541.[279]

As for poor relief, parochial institutions played a limited, but important role. Rectors were canonically required to offer a part of their tithes and hospitality, burdens which many tried to shift on to the community.[280] Ancient custom was often ignored or simply abolished. In 1400, the wardens and parishioners from Great Gaddesden in Hertfordshire obtained a court order instructing the priory of King's Langley to resume an annual payment of 10 s.[281] The late medieval parish *qua* parish seems to have entered only occasional commitments, but from the later fifteenth century, it became the unit 'within which most experiments with support of the poor took place'.[282] Anniversaries, chantries, and fraternities usually included provisions for the needy in return for their prayers, while many churchwardens served as executors of wills or administrators of pious bequests. In this capacity, large amounts of money for the poor passed through their hands.[283] Others looked after an almshouse, for instance at Lambeth or Trowbridge in Wiltshire.[284] Given all these alternatives, it is perhaps less surprising that there are so few direct payments to the poor in parish accounts before the sixteenth century, in spite of occasional episcopal appeals for adequate parochial provision.[285] The first evidence in this sample is an

---

[278] Swanson, *Church and Society*, p. 304 (quote); cf. Kreider, *English Chantries*, pp. 38ff.

[279] A. Willson, *A History of Collyer's School* (London, 1965), pp. 195–6. I owe this reference to Annabelle F. Hughes.

[280] M. Rubin, *Charity and Community in Medieval Cambridge* (Cambridge, 1987), pp. 237-45; Rodes, *Ecclesiastical Administration*, p. 131.

[281] Ault, 'Manor court and parish church', 65–6.

[282] M. McIntosh, 'Local responses to the poor in medieval and Tudor England', *Continuity and Change*, 3 (1988), 220.

[283] Scarisbrick, *Reformation*, p. 52. See for example the alms to be distributed by the churchwardens of Horsham in Richard Collyer's will cited above: Willson, *School*, p. 193.

[284] Drew (ed.), *Lambeth CWA*, p. 24 (quoted above), and Brown, 'Medieval Wiltshire', p. 272. McIntosh, 'Local responses to the poor', 221, provides evidence for the marked growth in local almshouse provision from 1460.

[285] Dyer, *Lords and Peasants*, p. 206, quotes John Carpenter, bishop of Worcester (1451).

entry of 11 s. at Ashburton in 1543–4, and a major effort amounting to
£5 8 s. 8 d. at the same place in 1548–9, when contributions for this
purpose were still voluntary. During the first Reformation impact under
Edward VI, poor relief resources were boosted at Boxford by the sale of
church treasures amounting to almost £50. On average, £1 18 s.10 d. or
24 per cent of parish expenses went to the poor in this reign, while
nothing of the kind is recorded for the immediate pre-Reformation
period.[286]

Finally, it should be noted that churchwardens could display a
considerable amount of management expertise. The letting and
administration of parish lands involved both long-term contracts and
occasional court actions.[287] At Peterborough, the parish officers took
over gild property in 1537, because 'the Baylyes therof delt not justly
with the Townsmen'.[288] Quite remarkable is an example of speculative
investment of parish resources. In the presence of all parishioners it was
agreed at the end of the year 1515–16 to lend churchwarden Peter
Edward, a mercer who had coordinated the bridge repair works of 1514,
a sum of £15, which he returned 12 months later with an interest of no
less than £5. It is hardly surprising that the experiment was repeated in
1518:

> Memorandum that Peter Edward hayth receyved of the Cherch
> Mony the xxvj day of July x li. to be payed a yer at the yere end with
> such avauntage as he can brynge yt to by the suerty of William
> Reynes.[289]

The same sum was entrusted to Thomas Bowman, and both returned the
money on 10 July 1519, although this time there is no information about
any 'avauntage'. At the audit day for the 1534–6 accounts, the parish
embarked on yet another experiment, this time in association with a lead
dealer:

> Item payd to Mr Glossopp for ij Fother and iij^c of ledd viij^{li} xij^s iiij^d.
> The seyd William Glossopp promysyd and grauntith that if the
> Churche wardens do nott sell the ledd aboue xx^s geyns before
> Midsomer next that then the seid William Glossopp to gyue to the
> Churche xx^s and thes mony ageyn att the seid fest of seint Jhon
> Baptiste and he to make the best that he can of the ledd.[290]

---

[286] Boxford CWA, 1547ff.

[287] In 1399, the rector and wardens of St Andrew Undershaft let part of the churchyard
for a period of 90 years, with half of the rent going to the church fabric (Newcourt (ed.),
Repertorium, i. 266). The suits *v.* John Sharp at St Ewen's, Bristol, and *v.* John Ford at
Ashburton have been discussed above: St Ewen CWA, pp. xxx–xxxi, and Ashburton CWA,
p. vii.

[288] Peterborough CWA, p. 136.

[289] Ibid., p. 113 (Reynes had been warden in 1513).

[290] CWA 1534–6.

Similar entrepreneurial spirit was revealed by parishes which invested in landed property without waiting for potential benefactors. Peterborough was again among them,[291] and so were many London communities: at St Mary Magdalen Milk Street in 1528-9, capital for the building of a house was raised partly by gifts (£24 7s. 4d.) and partly by sales (£53 12s. 4d.). The first tenant was one John Gresham, and rent payments continued well beyond the Reformation. The 24 chambers built in St Michael Cornhill in 1547-8 proved to be of similar long-term benefit.[292] In 1517, the wardens of St Botolph Aldersgate borrowed £10 from the Holy Trinity fraternity and paid £23 2s. 8d. for the tenement next adjoining the south side of Blackhorse Alley, an area where the parish already held property. Thereafter, an annual rent of 24s. represented roughly a 5 per cent return on the investment.[293] Another effort was made in 1551-2: £20 was paid to Richard Ford 'towardes the Buldyng of one newe tenemente to the churches more advanntage', which sum he could keep 'untill suche tyme as he shall accompte therefore declaring howe every parte and parcell thereof hath ben bestowed to the churches better comodity'. By 1557-8, however, Ford had died, the tenement was 'yet unbuylded', and his widow still owed the parish £4. Clearly, investments could also turn to losses. All Saints, Bristol, used parish plate to increase their holdings: the vicar and community assembled on 31 May 1524 to discuss matters connected to Mr Hawky's lands 'whyche the paryshons of the seid churche hathe bought'.[294] At the same place, the wardens were also in charge of the increasingly ailing Halleway chantry. In order to boost its revenues, repeated initiatives were taken to preserve a brewery on the chantry's Lewensmead property. In 1530-1, John Hewys received an award of 19s. from the parish 'for the grete paynes and labo's that he hath taken abowte owr brewhouse in lewensmed', which the parish repaired at the enormous cost of over £30. In addition, 'berebruar' John Winter obtained a loan of £20, but by 1532-3, the house had passed on to Thomas Haynes. In 1536-7, the tenant was Harry Norbery, equipped with a further £10 loan from the wardens. Whatever their economic fortunes, the parish insisted on repayment, and both Winter and Norbery gradually obliged.[295]

[291] Ibid., pp. xxxii–xxxiii: the wardens and eight other parishioners of Peterborough bought three acres of land near Sexton Barns for 33s. 4d. out of communal funds. The annual rent of 9s. amounted to a considerable return on this investment (1482).

[292] Gibbs, 'Parish finance', pp. 199–200; see GL, MS 2596/1, and W. H. Overall (ed.), The Accounts of the CW of Michael Cornhill (London, 1871), pp. 63–4.

[293] CWA 1516–17.

[294] CWA, 1524–5. Benefactions were still involved: some of the plate sold for this purpose had been the gift of Thomas Snygge 'to furnish money necessary to the churches use' (CWA 1523–4).

[295] Chantry accounts: BRO, P/AS/C/1, 1530–1 ff.

Modern observers have been impressed by the competence and initiative of parish officials.[296] Social historians, in fact, are starting to identify the wardens' increasing involvement in secular affairs as one of the crucial developments in rural England at the close of the Middle Ages. The rise of the parish offered the rather amorphous 'community of the vill' a convenient institutional home and an important impetus for increased local autonomy and self-government.[297] By the early sixteenth century, both rural and urban parishes had certainly come a long way from the first cautious attempts to install collection boxes for church repair purposes.

---

[296] Burgess, 'Benefactions of mortality', p. 79.
[297] Harvey, 'Settlement change', pp. 42–3; C. Dyer, 'The English medieval village community and its decline', *Journal of British Studies*, 33 (1994), 428–9.

CHAPTER THREE

Communal Resources and Responsibilities

3.1 The case studies

Churchwardens' accounts are the primary source material for any description of the financial and communal life of late medieval parishes, but the selection of case studies poses considerable problems. England's copious local archives make it quite impossible to embark on a quantitative analysis of all available sets, and some sort of informed selection procedure is inevitable. In addition to the catalogues of County Record Offices and the publications of local history journals and record societies, a number of reference works supply extensive, if sometimes conflicting, guidance on the survival of parish accounts.[1] By far the most exhaustive survey, however, can now be found in Ronald Hutton's *The Rise and Fall of Merry England*. County by county and in chronological order, it lists all the detailed (and accessible) sets of accounts up to 1690, and provides information about their location, the existence of editions or printed extracts, and the state of the manuscript for the periods covered.[2] This authoritative collection is the result of a monumental research effort by the author, and it would make little sense to duplicate it here. Inevitably though, definitions about starting-dates and inclusion or exclusion of imperfect cases vary, and the *definite* collection must remain evasive, for new sets are being discovered, and existing records lost or damaged all the time.[3] The compilation used for this study,

---

[1] Bettey, *Church and Parish*; L. Blair, *A List of CWA* (Ann Arbor, 1939); Cook, *Medieval Parish Church*; Cox, *CWA*; *CWA of Parishes within the City of London: a Handlist* (London, 1969); Duffy, *Stripping of the Altars*; E. B. Graves (ed.), *Oxford Bibliography of British History: to 1485* (Oxford, 1975); I. Gray and E. Ralph (eds), *Guide to the Parish Records of Bristol* (Bristol, 1963); D. J. Guth, *Late Medieval England 1377-1485* (Cambridge, 1976); Hutton, 'The local impact of the Tudor Reformations'; E. L. C. Mullins (ed.), *Texts and Calendars* (2 vols, London, 1958–83); Boxford CWA; E. Philipps, 'A list of printed CWA', *EHR*, 15 (1900), 335–41; J. West, *Village Records* (Plymouth, 1982); Whiting, *The Blind Devotion of the People*; Williams, *Early CWA of Hampshire*.

[2] In its appendix, pp. 263–93. I am very grateful to the author for providing me with a manuscript copy to collate with my own list.

[3] Ken Farnhill has made me aware of a fragmentary series for Chevington, Suffolk, *c.*1513–43: Cambridge University Library, Hangrave Hall MSS, 17(1). On the other hand, many an item in County Record Offices is now marked as 'lost' (for example East Harling in Norfolk), while others are too fragile for public inspection.

Table 3.1   Geographical distribution of pre-Reformation
churchwardens' accounts *c.* 1300–1547

Beds.	: 1	Dors.	: 2	Leics.	: 4	Som.	:19
Berks.	: 5	Essex	: 7	Lincs.	:10	Staffs.	: 3
Bristol	: 6	Glos.	: 1	London	:26	Suff.	:14
Bucks.	: 2	Hants.	: 6	Midd.	: 2	Surrey	: 8
Cambs.	: 5	Heref.	: 1	Norf.	:10	Sussex	:13
Ches.	: 2	Herts.	: 2	Northants.	: 2	Warw.	: 4
Corn.	: 7	Hunts.	: 2	Notts.	: 1	Westm.	: 1
Cumb.	: 1	Kent	:15	Oxon.	:10	Wilts.	: 7
Derb.	: 1	Lancs.	: 1	Salop.	: 3	Worcs.	: 4
Devon	:18					Yorks.	: 8

printed in Appendix 1, emerged in a pragmatic, rather than systematic way, and benefited from the generous help of many other historians working in the field.[4] It would be tedious to elaborate on each and every discrepancy, but, in essence, this list casts its net a little bit wider, includes examples which are now only known through antiquarian transcripts, and incorporates a small number of modifications suggested by further local research.[5] It thus contains 234 rather than 200 pre-1548 sets, but reveals a very similar geographical (see Table 3.1) and chronological (see Figure 3.1) pattern.[6]

There should be enough material to offer scope for comparison,[7] but the irregularities of source survival complicate the creation of a representative national sample. The evidence is clearly biased towards the immediate pre-Reformation decades and the southern part of the country, with the greatest choice on offer for the cities of London and Bristol, and the counties of Somerset, Devon, Kent, and Suffolk. Furthermore, the emphasis on long-term analysis prohibits the use of random sampling techniques, as over two thirds of the surviving sets do not contain an uninterrupted series of at least twenty years of detailed accounts and/or sufficient evidence from the Reformation period. There

---

[4] I am particularly indebted to Julia Carnwath, John Craig, Judy Ann Ford, Katherine French, and Caroline Litzenberger.

[5] Antiquarian evidence exists for example for Ashstead (*Surrey Archaeological Collections*, 24 (1911), 2–3), Braintree, Essex (*East Anglian*, 3 (1869), 78) or Stanford, Lincs. (F. Peck, *Academia* (1727), lib. xiv, pp. 4–5). Modifications include the pre-dating of the All Saints, Bristol, CWA to 1406 (early accounts in the church book: BRO, P/AS/ChW/1).

[6] *Merry England* lists 2 CWA (1300–49), 6 (1350–99), 26 (1400–49), 43 (1450–99), and 123 (1500–47) compared to 2, 7, 31, 51, and 143 included here.

[7] Hutton, *Merry England*, pp. 49–50, shares this assessment.

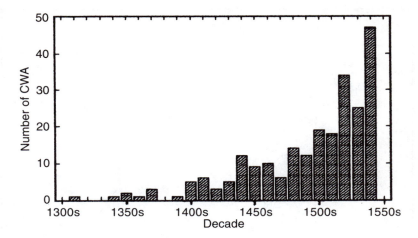

Figure 3.1 Chronological distribution of pre-Reformation CWA *c.* 1300–1547 (by decade containing the first surviving evidence)

is thus little alternative to the active selection of case studies on the basis of a series of criteria intended to reflect the great range of parochial realities:

1. *A broad variety of geographical location and economic prosperity* (see Maps 3.1 and 3.2 for the location of case studies)[8]
In accordance with the overall pattern of survival (which may after all reflect the density of record-keeping in the various areas) the south-east and south-west of England dominate the sample. Prescot and Halesowen, however, allow glimpses into the darker corners. The counties covered represent a broad variety of economic fortunes, ranging from Somerset (ranking second in an assessment of the comparative wealth of English counties made for 1515) to Lancashire (38th), and areas with considerable growth between 1334 and 1515 (Devon improved its position most dramatically in this period), to those with little or no change at all.[9]

---

[8] I am very grateful to J. S. Johnston for agreeing to draw all the maps for this book.

[9] R. Schofield, 'The geographical distribution of wealth in England 1334–1649' in R. Floud (ed.), *Essays in Quantitative Economic History* (Oxford, 1974), pp. 97 (ranking of counties) and 99 (geographical distribution of wealth). A similar assessment of the north-south divide in R. Glasscock (ed.), *The Lay Subsidy of 1334* (Oxford, 1975), p. xxvii.

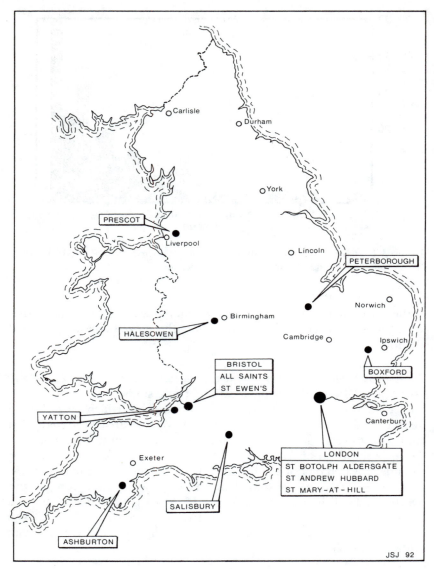

Map 3.1 Location of case studies

2. *Examples from town and country*

Given the predominantly agricultural character of late medieval England, churchwardens' accounts from an unambiguously rural context are comparatively rare. London and Bristol alone, with just 2 to

3 per cent of the total population around 1500, but a more institutionalized character of municipal administration, yield over 13 per cent of
the surviving accounts.[10] Here, they figure even more prominently with
two parishes each, but this may be justified by their disproportionate
economic and political importance.[11] Furthermore, both were constantly
exposed to new influences and ideas, another potentially important
aspect for the assessment of trends in parish life and the changes of the
sixteenth century. Topographically, the surviving Bristol evidence comes
from the town centre, while one central and one extramural parish have
been selected for London.

Most English towns, however, were much smaller, economically less
developed, and not fully differentiated from their countryside.[12] In
addition to including two villages proper (Boxford, Yatton), it has thus
been attempted to integrate further quasi-rural evidence by means of
three smaller, less prosperous market towns with a large agricultural
hinterland (Peterborough, Prescot, Halesowen). Wherever possible,
further light is shed on the experiences of the majority of English people
by juxtaposing the result from the quantitative analysis of these case
studies with evidence from other rural accounts such as those of
Morebath (Devon), Bethersden (Kent), Mickfield (Suffolk), and various
Somerset communities. In a similar way, glimpses at London's St Mary-
at-Hill and St Edmund, Salisbury (for different reasons unsuitable for
detailed scrutiny here[13]) should help to contextualize the urban evidence.

3. *A variety of ecclesiastical and secular status*
Self-governing cities under the control of free burgesses (London and
Bristol), fairly independent (Ashburton) and tightly supervised boroughs
(Peterborough and Halesowen), alongside manorial communities
(Yatton and Boxford) represent the many different forms of lordship.
Parishes often cut across secular boundaries, but at Ashburton the
ecclesiastical unit coincided with the borough and manor of the same
name. As for ecclesiastical status, most had vicars (occasionally pluralists
as in the case of early sixteenth-century All Saints[14]), but some were

---

[10] Calculations based on J. Hatcher, *Plague, Population and the English Economy
1348–1530* (London/Basingstoke, 1977), pp. 33, 71.

[11] See C. Barron, 'The later Middle Ages 1270–1520' in M. Lobel (ed.), *City of London*
(Oxford, 1989), pp. 42-3, and D. Sacks, *The Widening Gate: Bristol and the Atlantic
Economy 1450–1700* (Berkeley, 1991), pp. 22ff.

[12] R. Holt and G. Rosser (eds), *The English Medieval Town* (London/New York, 1990),
p. 1.

[13] Clive Burgess is working on the extraordinarily wealthy community of Mary-at-Hill;
Brown, 'Medieval Wiltshire', has discussed the (fairly patchy) St Edmund material (48
accounts in almost 120 years).

[14] John Flooke, vicar 1517–33 (Skeeters, *Community and Clergy*, p. 93).

Table 3.2   The case studies (with year of first CWA)

London	St Andrew Hubbard (1454)
	St Botolph Aldersgate (1468)
Bristol	All Saints (1406)
	St Ewen's (1454)
Market towns	Ashburton, Devon (1479)
	Halesowen, Worcs. and Shropshire (1487)
	Peterborough (1467)
	Prescot, Lancashire (1523)
Villages	Boxford, Suffolk (1530)
	Yatton, Somerset (1445)

rectories (Andrew Hubbard, St Ewen's, and Boxford) or curacies (Botolph Aldersgate). The 1535 survey reveals a wide spectrum of benefice values: from around £40 at Yatton and Ashburton to the £8 2 s. 8 d. at Halesowen.[15] There are cases of peculiar jurisdiction,[16] others were subject to a commissary court,[17] but most under normal archidiaconal supervision. Patronage, too, was in many different hands. Lord Talbot, earl of Shrewsbury, presented to Andrew Hubbard, and King's College, Cambridge, to Prescot. Generally though, the advowson was in the gift of ecclesiastical bodies.[18]

Avoiding case studies subjected to quantitative work in other local or regional studies,[19] the ten sets shown in Table 3.2 have been included in

[15] J. Caley and J. Hunter (eds), *Valor Ecclesiasticus* (London, 1810–34), i. 187, ii. 364, and iii. 207. No figures survive for Bristol, but other evidence puts the value of St Ewen's at a mere £3 6 s. (Skeeters, *Community and Clergy*, p. 99).

[16] Ashburton (Dean and Chapter of Exeter) and Yatton (Prebendary of Wells Cathedral).

[17] Andrew Hubbard.

[18] Dean and Chapter of St Martin-le-Grand (from 18 Henry VIII Westminster Abbey and its legal successors: Botolph Aldersgate), the Abbot of St Augustine, Bristol (later Bristol Dean and Chapter: All Saints), St James Priory (post-dissolution Henry Brayne: St Ewen's), Dean and Chapter of Exeter (Ashburton), Abbot and Convent of Hales (post-1539 John Dudley and Sir John Lyttleton: Halesowen), Abbot and Convent of Peterborough (from 1539 Dean and Chapter) at the parish of the same name, and the abbot of Bury St Edmund presented to Boxford at least in 1316. See G. Hennessy (ed.), *Novum Repertorium* (London, 1898), pp. 105 and 306-7 (for London), Nicholls and Taylor, *Bristol Past*, ii. 102, and St Ewen CWA, p. xxxii (for Bristol), Peterborough CWA, p. xxiii, Ashburton CWA, p. 113, Copinger, *Manors of Suffolk*, i. 22 (for Boxford), Prescot CWA, p. vii, and T. Nash (ed.), *Collections for the History of Worcestershire* (London, 1781), pp. 531ff (for Halesowen).

[19] Such as those conducted by Judy Ford (Fordham/USA) on Kent or Julia Carnwath (Manchester) on Thame and other market towns. Gibbs, 'Parish finance', has made a comparative analysis of a selection of London accounts at three given points in time rather than over the whole pre-Reformation period.

this sample (starting-dates in brackets; all covered up to 1560). While the selection endeavours to take account of a wide variety of factors thought to influence parish life in the period, it could not hope to reproduce England's complexity in a mere ten case studies. Any sample of this size will struggle to prove its representative nature with statistical accuracy. It cannot recreate the 'average' English parish, which, however, would be a rather meaningless exercise anyway. Rather, it is hoped that the approach will throw more light on ten very individual parochial histories, and, potentially, on a great many similar communities besides. It can illustrate the wide range of contemporary financial strategies and communal experiences in different socio-economic and ecclesiastical contexts. Any general trends emerging from such a heterogeneous sample, or, conversely, any clear discrepancies may reasonably be interpreted as more than mere coincidences. Quite clearly, though, the study can only provide a start and will stand or fall with the analysis of further examples and refined analytical techniques. But first of all, the case studies have to be introduced in some more detail.

3.1.1 London

England's largest city has always enjoyed an unusual degree of autonomy and independence.[20] As the centre of national politics and international trade, the capital grew fastest between 1334 and 1515, pushing its share of assessed lay wealth from 2 to almost 9 per cent of the national total.[21] This accumulation of capital stimulated large-scale investment in both the secular (Guildhall, company halls) and ecclesiastical spheres, with parishes rather than monasteries or the cathedral as the main beneficiaries in the later Middle Ages: St Margaret Westminster, St Andrew Undershaft, and St Giles Cripplegate were extensively rebuilt, many others had aisles, porches, vestries, or spires added. City-centre locations were particularly prosperous, a picture on the whole confirmed by a look at churchwardens' accounts.[22]

Mary-at-Hill, a late twelfth-century foundation which will appear frequently below, is a case in point.[23] Its territory extended from the

---

[20] See the general accounts of late medieval London in Barron, 'Later Middle Ages', and Gibbs, 'Parish finance', pp. 57ff.

[21] Schofield, 'Distribution of wealth', p. 101.

[22] Gibbs, 'Parish finance', p. 124, and R. Finlay, *Population and Metropolis: The Demography of London 1580–1650* (Cambridge, 1981), pp. 74ff.

[23] Cf. Mary-at-Hill CWA, passim; Barron, 'Later Middle Ages', pp. 49 (Abbot of Waltham inn) and 53 (Billingsgate); M. Lobel, *The City of London* (Oxford, 1989), pp. 89–90 (architectural development); C. Kitching (ed.), *London and Middlesex Chantry Certificates 1548* (London, 1980), p. 6 (chantry certificate), Baillie, 'London church' (music); and Clive Burgess' forthcoming essay on parish government in the *Festschrift* for Barbara Harvey.

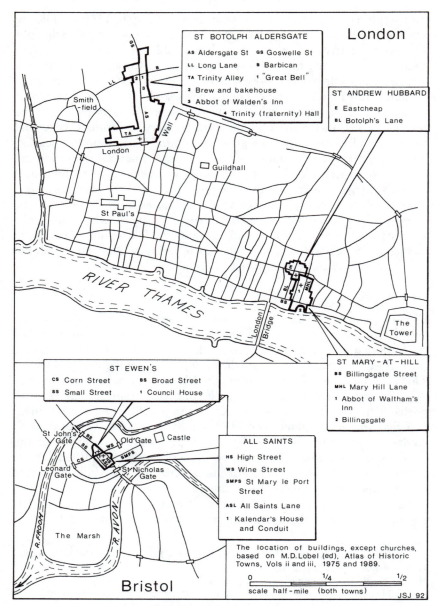

Map 3.2 London and Bristol parishes

Thames northwards and included Billingsgate, an increasingly important area as the Thames waterfront was developed eastwards in the fourteenth and fifteenth centuries (see Map 3.2). Fishmongers were prominent in the parish and sponsored an additional service in the church. The wharf was considerably enlarged in 1449, and shipbuilding flowered between Billingsgate and the Tower. However, parish rentals suggest that no one trade dominated the community,[24] and the churchwardens included representatives from the usual range of professions (grocers, tailors, drapers, ironmongers). The parish also contained the Abbot of Waltham's inn with its chapel, dormitory, yard, hall, and stable to the south of the church. There was a churchyard by 1348, and a further one by the early sixteenth century. A north aisle was added from 1487–1501, and the church included four chapels dedicated to SS Stephen, Katherine, Anne, and Christopher. Most remarkable, perhaps, are the many chantries under direct parish control, which boosted the wardens' incomes to exceptionally high levels.[25]

St Andrew Hubbard

Neighbouring Andrew Hubbard, to move to the first case study proper, was much less fortunate in terms of endowment.[26] It was clearly a poorer area where artisans would settle before they made their fortunes. The church dates from at least 1108, and the yard from 1347. By relying heavily on collections, the parishioners managed to keep up a decent ceremonial life, but there was only a limited amount of gift giving or additional ecclesiastical provision. One moderate endowment derived from the will of Juliana Fairhead made in 1442, whose obit was faithfully kept and provided a steady source of revenue. By 1547, it yielded £4 annually, with little more than £1 devoted to costs. The will also provided for a chantry, but there is no evidence that it was ever established. The accounts contain a few references to a Trinity brotherhood, for instance in 1541–3 (when the parish received 6 s. 8 d. from its wardens) or 1545–7 (when it was decided for some unknown reason to 'delyver unto the wardenns of the brotherhod of the trynnyt

---

[24] Gibbs, 'Parish finance', pp. 132–3.

[25] They regularly account for the Nasing, Causton, Gosselyn, Cambridge, Writtell, Bedham, and West chantries, most combined with an obit. The average annual income 1479–1495 was in the region of £95!

[26] See Lobel, City of London, p. 85 (architectural development); Kitching (ed.), Chantry Certificates, p. 44; Gibbs, 'Parish finance', pp. 183–9 (general profile, relative poverty); W. Jordan, The Charities of London (London, 1960), pp. 34–5 (gift giving); S. Brigden, 'Tithe controversy in Reformation London', JEH, 32 (1981), 289 (tithe dispute in the 1530s), and London and the Reformation, pp. 53, 65, 89, 160, and 201 (nonconformity); R. Sharpe (ed.), Calendar of Wills Proved in the Court of Hustings (London, 1890), ii. 563 (will Juliana Fairhead); Hennessy (ed.), Repertorium parochiale, pp. 306–7 (rectors), and E. Mullins, 'The effects of the Marian and Elizabethan religious settlements upon the clergy of London' (MA London, 1948), pp. 244–5 (parsonage account 1558–60) and 421 (rector William Swift). The CWA are to be edited by Clive Burgess.

iiis. iiiid. every quarter of the yere').[27] There is repeated evidence for disharmony between parishioners and clergy, which may have affected the laity's post-obit generosity. In 1532, Rowland Kendall accused Sir Thomas Kirkham of staying with a married woman, a series of tithe disputes with the rector were heard before the bishop's chancellor and the sheriff's court in the 1530s, while William Swift (1545–68) became a notorious absentee, undeterred even by excommunication. There was also a trickle of nonconformist and radical ideas. Whether religiously motivated or not, communal discontent may well have been behind the parish's most unusual move to take control of the whole benefice under Edward VI and early in Elizabeth's reign.[28]

St Botolph Aldersgate

The extramural church of St Botolph Aldersgate was first mentioned in 1115, and enlarged in 1448.[29] The parish included several prominent landmarks, such as the Abbot of Walden's inn, the Trinity (later wardmote-) hall, and a series of breweries like the Saracen's Head. Here again, lay-clerical relations were not always harmonious: the host was stolen in 1532 (but soon returned in solemn procession), while eight years later, Richard Bostock preached against auricular confession and John Mayler, a grocer and printer, called the Eucharist the 'baken god' of bread.[30] It is impossible to judge how representative such feelings were for the parish as a whole. Outside the walls, the population was generally more mobile and heterogeneous than in the more 'established' city centre, but an equally strong case could be made for the flourishing of the old religion. Significantly, the breaking of windows and shooting of guns recorded in 1549 cannot be safely attributed to one particular denominational faction.[31] There was certainly an intensive traditional life, exemplified by the brotherhood of the Trinity and SS Fabian and Sebastian. Predominantly composed of local people, it supported the community with the services of a morrow-mass priest. There were also a series of obits: the chantry certificates mention those for Thomas Lillingston, Alice Cobwell, (ex-churchwarden) Alan Johnson, Thomas

---

[27] Hubbard CWA, 1541–3 and 1545–7.

[28] Hubbard CWA, 1549–52 and 1558–66. The patron, Lord Talbot (and possibly the rector), sympathized with the old religion.

[29] See Lobel, *City of London*, p. 86 (architectural development); Basing (ed.), *Fraternity Register* (fraternities); Henrey, *St Botolph*, and Staples, *Notes on St Botolph* (parish histories); Kitching (ed.), *Chantry Certificates*, p. 30; Brigden, *London and the Reformation*, pp. 18, 400, 405 (Reformation period); Hennessy (ed.), *Repertorium parochiale*, p. 105 (clergy).

[30] Quoted in Brigden, *London and the Reformation*, p. 405.

[31] H. Walters, *London Churches at the Reformation* (London, 1939), p. 203.

Clarke, the craft of the cutlers, and Philip at Phyn, three of which appear in the parish accounts. In 1390, John Bathe had endowed the rector and churchwardens with the Saracen's Head property for the support of his chantry, and the respective chaplains officiated until 1547. Additional provision was indispensable for the large flock of over 1000 souls, and the Edwardian commissioners agreed that one chantry priest should be retained as a parish assistant. The subsequent accounts duly reveal an annual contribution of £7 from the king's receiver.[32]

3.1.2 Bristol

The second largest town in the kingdom (10–12000 inhabitants around 1500) had become an independent county in 1373 and flourished as an important port and textile industry centre under the government of its merchant elite.[33] The granting of city status and the creation of a separate bishopric, both in 1542, enhanced its position further. From 1499, the ruling oligarchy consisted of a mayor, five aldermen, and a council of 43 very substantial men, but at any time up to 10 per cent of the burgesses held some sort of local office. Competition from London and Southampton had created considerable economic problems in the fifteenth century, but towards 1500 cloth exports and the vine trade recovered. The merchant venturers' contacts with the new world ensured prosperity during the sixteenth century and beyond. Substantial resources were committed to the rebuilding and embellishment of the city's 18 parish churches in the later Middle Ages, with the massive investment of mayor-turned-priest William Canynges at St Mary Redcliffe as the most striking example. Parish accounts only survive from the city centre, and both our case studies were located near the carfax of the ancient borough, the most prosperous area and centre of public life (see Map 3.2).

All Saints
All Saints' parish covered the corner formed by Corn and High Street.[34]

---

[32] Botolph CWA, 1549-50ff.

[33] E. Carus-Wilson, 'Bristol: the fourteenth and fifteenth centuries' in M. Lobel (ed.), *Atlas of Historic Towns* (vol. 2, London, 1975), pp. 10–14 and passim (economic and social survey); E. Williams, *The Chantries of William Canynges* (Bristol, 1950); Skeeters, *Community and Clergy*; Sacks, *Bristol and the Atlantic Economy*, esp. pp. 148 (distribution of wealth) and 160–93 (government).

[34] Clive Burgess is preparing a three-volume edition of the parish records. Many references to All Saints in his 'Chantries in the parish', 'Anniversary in late medieval Bristol', 'Benefactions of mortality' (general mind and parish ordinances), and 'Strategies for eternity' (legal aspects of foundations). See also Nicholls and Taylor, *Bristol Past*, ii.

Its origins lie in the twelfth century, and from the beginning there was a close association with the gild of Kalendars. Composed of lay and clerical members and headed by a prior living next door to the church, the fraternity spent its income (£39 16 s. ½ d. in 1547) on divine service and obits, but it also looked after the town's archives, recorded local events, and ran a public library. There must have been constant informal contacts with the parish, yet the gild kept separate records and hardly ever appears in the churchwardens' accounts. The latter are equally silent about five chantries apparently founded in All Saints before 1450, in stark contrast to the many references to Thomas Halleway's foundation from the later fifteenth century. Managed by the wardens, the Halleway chantry was a very public institution, which required the town mayor and the whole parish to attend the anniversary as well as the annual audit. As often in Bristol, there was a communal 'general mind' for past benefactors, closely regulated by parish ordinances and a prominent item in every financial year. In addition, obits were kept in remembrance of Thomas and Agnes Fyler, William Nawbury, Henry and Alice Chester, Thomas and Maud Spicer, Humphrey Harvey, and Joan Pernannte. Architecturally, the fifteenth century witnessed the addition of a south aisle and belfry, both very typical contemporary features.[35]

St Ewen's

St Ewen's, which covered a tiny area between Corn and Broad Street, may have ceased to exist, but it supplies the oldest documentary evidence of any of the city's parishes.[36] The church was rebuilt in the early fifteenth century, only to be gradually swallowed up by the neighbouring 'Tolzey' or town council house. Having sacrificed their south aisle for an extension of the municipal building in the mid-sixteenth century, the parishioners saw the church disappear completely in the course of further enlargements in 1820. Before the Reformation, the south chapel

90ff (Kalendar gild, church furnishings and benefactors); J. Maclean (ed.), 'Chantry certificates, Glos.', *TBGAS*, 8 (1883/4), 245; Bickley (ed.), *Little Red Book*, ii. 199ff (Halleway chantry arrangements); Williams, *Canynges*, p. 38; BRO P/AS/C/1 (Halleway chantry accounts); Harrison, 'Repertory' (music); E. Atchley (ed.), 'Some documents relating to the parish of All Saints', *Archaeological Journal*, NS 8 (1901), 147–81, and his 'On the Parish Records of All Saints', *TBGAS*, 27 (1904), 221–74.

[35] Cf. Barron, 'The later Middle Ages', p. 48, or Harvey, *Gothic England*, p. 33.

[36] Gray and Ralph (eds), *Parish Records of Bristol*, p. xv (a deed of *c*.1150); further on St Ewen: J. Maclean, 'Notes on the accounts of the CW of St Ewen's', *TBGAS*, 15 (1890/1), 139–82, 254–96; St Ewen's CWA (edition and introduction); Nicholls and Taylor, *Bristol Past*, pp. 249ff; Williams, *Canynges*, p. 39 (fraternity chaplain); Maclean (ed.), 'Chantry certificates', 248; Burgess, 'Strategies for eternity' (chantry), and 'Anniversary in late medieval Bristol'.

had served as the home of the tailors' John Baptist fraternity, whose chaplain received an annual £5 10s. 4d. at the time of the dissolution. A chantry seems to have existed in the same place since 1398, three more altars are known to have stood elsewhere, and there was also a general mind and an obit.[37]

3.1.3 Ashburton

The church of St Andrew accommodated an unusually rich pre-Reformation parish life.[38] Activities took place on the communal as well as a very diversified subparochial level. The worship of images, eight of which can be located within the church, was the devotional focus of some 20 'stores' or 'stocks' which administered offerings and often developed into fully fledged gilds. Some were gender- or age-specific, others open to all with an interest in a particular cult. The parish contained the town as well as the manor, which were never strictly separated, even though tenurial privileges and the gild of St Lawrence gave the borough an identity of its own. The gild maintained a separate chapel with its own priest and looked after municipal affairs such as the school, the market, and the water supply. The bishops of Exeter as faraway landlords and absentee vicars allowed the community a great deal of autonomy. In 1305, Ashburton had been made one of the four official stannary towns, from which point it participated in the ups and downs of the Devon tin trade. Additionally, the borough became a centre of the cloth industry and a considerable local market. The county as a whole greatly enhanced its prosperity in the later Middle Ages,[39] and the large-scale investment in religious life suggests that Ashburton was no exception. Before the accounts open, the church had been extensively rebuilt, ornaments and vestments were purchased in great number, and a spectacular rood loft was added in the 1520s, significantly at a time of a boom in the tin trade.[40] The parish attracted a steady flow of

---

[37] Details for example St Ewen CWA, 1461–2, 1471–2 (mind) and 1514–15 (obit).

[38] Ashburton CWA (edition and introduction); J. Butcher, *The Parish of Ashburton in the Fifteenth and Sixteenth Centuries* (London, 1870); J. Amery, 'Presidential address', *Reports and Transactions of the Devonshire Association*, 56 (1925), 43–102, and W. Hoskins, *Devon* (Newton Abbot, 1972), pp. 132, 320–1 (general Ashburton history); H. Hanham, 'A tangle untangled' (details on manor and borough), and 'Chantries in Ashburton' (dissolution of gilds and confiscation of lands); L. Snell (ed.), *The Chantry Certificates for Devon* (Exeter, 1961), p. 39; Whiting, *Blind Devotion*, passim (Reformation period), and N. Orme, *Unity and Variety: A History of the Church in Devon and Cornwall* (Exeter, 1991), pp. 53–80 and esp. 59 (map of the parish church).

[39] Schofield, 'Distribution of wealth', p. 97.

[40] The Ashburton stannary accounted for 40 per cent of the Devon output in the boom years of the mid-1520s: Hoskins, *Devon*, p. 132.

benefactions and celebrated several obits in return.[41] In 1535, it was valued at a handsome £38 8 s. 9½ d.[42]

3.1.4 Halesowen

Dedicated to St John the Baptist, the parish extended over no less than 10 000 acres, a market town, and 12 townships on the border of the two rather poor counties of Worcester and Shropshire.[43] Places like Romsley, Oldbury, Warley, Ludlow, Lappall, Illey, and Frankley regularly contributed to parish income. Close by was the premonstratensian abbey of Halesowen, which had acquired the manor of the same name in 1251. Relations between monks and tenants were characterized by a fair bit of conflict over services, rents, and other affairs, which may have strengthened the cohesion of the local community. The churchwardens certainly did not hesitate to secure the abbey's rood, organ, and a picture of St Kenelm at the dissolution.[44] Henry III had granted the abbot and convent the right to create a borough, but the burgesses never achieved real independence. After 1538, the manor passed into the hands of Sir John Dudley and later John Lyttelton. The church's earliest structures date from the twelfth century, the south aisle from the fourteenth, while the tower was moved halfway down the nave in the fifteenth. Later still, St Katherine's chapel was added to the north aisle and around 1500 a clerestory built for improved lighting. At least three more chapels existed in the extensive parish: St Kenelm, itself rebuilt in the later Middle Ages and supported by considerable offerings,[45] and those at Cradley (removed at the dissolution) and Oldbury, built in 1529. The parish church contained four altars, a chantry for William Pepwale, a series of lights, and a Jesus service which may have had a gild attached to it.[46] Relics formed a rather unusual part of parochial resources, without ever being a major item in the wardens' reckoning.

---

[41] For example for William Dolbeare at a cost of 3 s. 4 d., William Cosyn 19 d., Thomas Tangkerett 2 s. 4 d., Thomas Stephen 10 d., Walter Pottikyslond 12 d. and 'the benefactors of this churche' (a general mind) 5 d.: Ashburton CWA, 1532–3.

[42] Caley and Hunter (eds), Valor, ii. 364.

[43] Schofield, 'Distribution of wealth', p. 97 (county ranking); Halesowen CWA (edition and introduction by Margaret O'Brien); H. Light, 'Halesowen' in VCH Worcester (vol. iii, reprint London, 1971), pp. 136–53 (borough and manor status); Nash, Worcestershire, i. 508ff (extent) and 531ff (advowson); see also Z. Razi, 'Family, land and the village community', PaP, 93 (1981), 3–36 (village community), and – for a study of the Halesowen court rolls – his Life, Marriage and Death in a Medieval Parish (Cambridge, 1980).

[44] Halesowen CWA, 1537–8.

[45] Caley and Hunter (eds), Valor, iii. 207: £10.

[46] Halesowen CWA 1522-3: 8s. received from the Jesus wardens.

3.1.5 Peterborough

In 1402–7, the parish church of St John Baptist was moved to its present site on the market square opposite the western gate of the cathedral precinct.[47] It served the borough, the four hamlets or 'members' Dogsthorpe, Newark, Eastfield, and Garton (over all of which the abbot exercised comprehensive jurisdiction), as well as the villages of Longthorpe and Oxney. Around 1270, the borough had received a charter with very limited privileges. It freed the burgesses from the heavier services performed by the members and introduced some form of town administration by constables, affeerers, and a grand jury of 12 freeholders. The monastery was dissolved in 1539, but the transition to the dean and chapter of the new diocese proceeded smoothly. The modern municipal organization emerged from the late sixteenth-century feoffees, who repurchased gild and parochial lands for charitable and communal purposes. The ceremonial life of the large parish church focused on four gilds (SS Mary, George, John, and Corpus Christi, each with separate priests and endowments), various lights, and regular obits for individuals and the 'founders' as a whole.[48] Nearby at the cathedral gate stood the chapel of St Thomas the Martyr, with further churches at Oxney and Longthorpe.

3.1.6 Prescot

Prescot was a very large parish in a poor county.[49] Even though the Farnworth half maintained a chapel-of-ease with separate records, the townships of Eccleston, Parr, Rainford, Rainhill, Sutton, Whiston, and Windle (besides Prescot itself) still formed an extensive area on their own. From an early stage, there was conflict about Farnworth's

---

[47] Peterborough CWA (edition and detailed introduction); M. Bateson, 'Borough of Peterborough' in *VCH Northampton* (vol. ii, reprint London, 1970), pp. 421–60 (manor and borough government); A. H. Thompson (ed.), 'Chantry certificates for Northamptonshire', *Associated Architectural Society Reports and Papers*, 31 (1911), 163 (chantry certificate).

[48] For example Peterborough CWA, 1508–9.

[49] Schofield, 'Distribution of wealth', p. 97; Haigh, *Lancashire*, passim (religious conservatism); Bailey, 'CWA of Prescot' (broad discussion of the accounts and officers), *Prescot Court Leet* (secular administration) and Prescot CWA (edition with introduction); D. Bailey, *Prescot Court Leet* (Prescot, no date); W. Farrer and J. Brownbill, 'Prescot' in *VCH Lancaster* (vol. iii, reprint London, 1966), pp. 341–413 (manorial descent); *Prescot Parish Church* (Publication of Prescot Museum, no date; early rate); F. Raines (ed.), *A History of the Chantries within the County of Lancaster* (Manchester, 1862), p. 78 (chantry certificate); Craig, 'Prescot' (later sixteenth century; gentry role; poverty). Walter King is engaged on a detailed study of Prescot material.

responsibilities towards the mother church of St Mary the Virgin, which ranged from the upkeep of the fabric, churchyard, and bells to contributions to the costs of ornaments and books. Both the archdeacon and the bishop of Chester were repeatedly called upon to resolve these delicate matters. In 1500 – in a most unusual pre-Reformation interference in parochial financial autonomy – the ecclesiastical mediator demanded the introduction of compulsory rates or 'leys', while in 1555 communal government was reorganized with the establishment of the 'eight men'. Elected by a parish assembly, they were to choose the wardens, to audit their accounts, and to set the necessary rates. In 1448, ecclesiastical (rectory) and secular lordship (of the manor of Prescot) had passed to King's College, Cambridge, which exercised a rather indirect supervision. The vicars were often prominent university men and not often seen in the parish, despite their handsome income of £24 9 s. 5 d.[50]

The rectory's farmers, the Earls of Derby, their stewards, the Ogle family, and further local gentry like the Bolds of Whiston were of more immediate local importance. While fairly inconspicuous in day-to-day parochial life, they supervised all essential business such as the rebuilding effort of 1610. There can be little doubt about the conservative religious mood of the parish; reformed practices were slow to take root and innovations caused considerable disruption (the wardens reported 'notter receyued ner payd nothyng' for two years during the Edwardian reign[51]). The accounts reveal the existence of 'stocks' dedicated to the rood, Our Lady, and St Katherine, each with separate priests and endowments, which were reallocated to the support of a school in Edward VI's reign. The Bolds had founded a chantry in the parish church, and further clergymen served here as well as in the chapels at Farnworth, Windle, and Rainford. Their number was drastically reduced during the Reformation years, with obvious consequences for the religious provision of an ever-increasing population.

3.1.7 Boxford

St Mary's parish covered the manors of Boxford, Peyton Hall, Coddenham Hall, and Boweshouse in a wealthy woollen cloth making area.[52] The manorial lords, who included Sir Robert Peyton, High Sheriff

---

[50] Caley and Hunter (eds), *Valor*, v. 220.

[51] Prescot CWA, 1552 and 1553.

[52] Boxford CWA (edition and introduction); Copinger, *Manors of Suffolk*, i. 22ff (manorial descent); Schofield, 'Distribution of wealth', p. 97 (county ranking); V. Redstone (ed.), 'Chapels, chantries and gilds in Suffolk', *PSIA*, **12** (1906), 42 and 73 (gild and altars), Caley and Hunter (eds), *Valor*, iii. 453–4 (1535 valuation), and Harvey (ed.), *Suffolk in 1524*.

of Cambridge and Huntingdon, left hardly a trace in parochial sources and officeholding was in the hands of clothiers, clothmakers, weavers, yeomen, and husbandmen. In spite of Boxford's trading functions, the area retained its predominantly rural character. The setting, however, was very different from Prescot: the parish formed part of one of the most prosperous counties with one of the densest ecclesiastical networks. The neighbouring parishes of Edwardstone, Groton, Hadleigh Hamlet, and Polstead were very close and boundaries intermingled. Boxford church (rebuilt in the fifteenth century and valued at £20 10 s. 7½ d. in 1535) contained an altar and image of St Thomas the Martyr as well as a Trinity fraternity supported by lands in Southfield. The gild contributed to the purchase of parish ornaments (CWA 1532–3) and to fabric maintenance costs (for example to the steeple works in 1537–8). It was assessed at £2 in the 1524 lay subsidy, a source which reveals the existence of two other 'stocks': those of St John's and St Peter's, valued at £2 and £3 respectively. The Reformation shifted parish emphasis quickly on to local government matters: superfluous church plate was sold at an early stage to finance an extensive poor relief and money-lending system.[53]

3.1.8 Yatton

Situated within a prospering county and on the Bristol Channel, the parish of St Mary produced one of the best preserved sets of rural churchwardens' accounts for the late Middle Ages.[54] The rebuilding and embellishment undertaken in the fifteenth century, most notably the famous rood loft,[55] earned it the title of 'cathedral of the moors'. Yatton and Cleeve, in the western part of the parish, belonged to the see of Wells, while the manor of Claverham on the eastern side was held by the de la Sores and Rodneys. Dependent churches were located at Claverham and Court de Wyke, seat of the important Newton gentry family, while a chapel dedicated to St James, and also associated with the Newtons, occupied the north-eastern part of the mother church. Close links existed

[53] Boxford CWA, 1547ff.

[54] Hobhouse (ed.), *CWA of Croscombe [etc.]* (CWA extracts, introduction, manorial descent); A. Edwards, 'The medieval CWA of St Mary, Yatton', *Notes and Queries for Somerset and Dorset*, 32 (1986), 536–47 (description of parish life and finances); E. Green (ed.), *The Survey of Chantries in Somerset* (London/Frome, 1888), pp. 88 and 269–70 (chantry certificates); Caley and Hunter (eds), *Valor*, i. 187, and Schofield, 'Distribution of wealth', p. 97 (county wealth).

[55] Yatton CWA, 1446ff. Overall payments to the craftsman John Crosse exceeded £70; cf. Smith, *Pre-Reformation England*, pp. 121ff, and Cook, *Medieval Parish Church*, p. 160.

to the neighbouring parishes of Congresbury, Ken, Kingston, and Wrington, especially with regard to the mutual attendance of church ales. Yatton's own ales reflected its territorial subdivisions, being held and organized separately by 'lightmen' for the eastern and western parts of the parish. The vicarage was valued at £36 in 1535.

3.2 The sources

Very little has yet been written about the potential and pitfalls of churchwardens' accounts. The editors of most sets provide a more or less detailed introduction to their specific material, but only Charles Drew has embarked on a general discussion of the sources.[56] There are of course specialized studies on medieval accounting in manors, monasteries, or lay and clerical households,[57] but the peculiar non-seigneurial and non-commercial character of churchwardens' records calls for separate analysis. Any sort of quantitative approach, in particular, must be preceded by an assessment of contemporary administrative practice to ascertain that there was sufficient consistency to allow long-term comparative analysis. This chapter will attempt to scrutinize the evidence for clues about the compilation and comprehensiveness of parochial records.

England trailed leading financial nations like Italy by a considerable margin. The first printed vernacular manual appeared as late as 1543, and single-entry bookkeeping remained the norm far into the sixteenth century and certainly for all parochial accounts.[58] Yet, from the point of view of monetary historians, it seems that by 1400 (the time of the

---

[56] Drew (ed.), *Lambeth CWA*, esp. pp. xii–xvi. For a study on the post-Reformation period, with particular emphasis on Mildenhall, see Craig, 'Elizabethan churchwardens and parish accounts'.

[57] Those used here include Woolf, *Short History of Accountants*, and A. Littleton and B. Yamey (eds), *Studies in the History of Accounting* (London, 1956; general surveys); N. Denholm-Young, *Seignorial Administration in England* (Oxford, 1937), ch. 4, and P. Harvey (ed.), *Manorial Records of Cuxham* (London, 1976), pp. 12–71 (manors); E. Myatt-Price, 'Cromwell household accounts 1417–76' in Littleton and Yamey (eds), *History of Accounting*, pp. 99–113, and C. Dyer, *Standards of Living in the Later Middle Ages* (Cambridge, 1989), pp. 49–84 (household); S. Hockey (ed.), *The Account Book of Beaulieu Abbey* (London, 1975), and J. Greatrex (ed.), *The Account Rolls of the Obedientiaries of Peterborough* (Wellingborough, 1984; monastic); P. Heath (ed.), *Medieval Clerical Accounts* (York, 1964), and Swanson, 'Standards of livings' (clerical).

[58] Manual: A. Woolf, *A Short History of Accountants and Accountancy* (London, 1912), p. 131 (a translation of the pioneering work of Luca Pacioli by Hugh Oldcastle); single entry: R. de Roover, 'The development of accounting prior to Luca Pacioli' in Littleton and Yamey (eds), *History of Accounting*, p. 160.

earliest accounts in this sample) 'all groups in society were regularly involved in transactions using money and credit'.[59] There were a number of seasonal peaks, such as Michaelmas in the countryside, and significant differences in terms of contact with higher (gold) denominations, but London and the ports in particular were well stocked with money in the fifteenth century.[60] Even so, everyday financial transactions were hampered by a shortage of small change. Metal was a precious commodity, and mints did not derive much profit from striking halfpence and farthings. The increased silver influx from the Continent gradually improved the situation, but small coins remained scarce throughout the Tudor period. Payments in kind were therefore a matter of course; at Yatton, for instance, rings and bushels of wheat or barley are a regular feature of parish income, even though the wardens expressed their value in monetary terms.[61]

Accounts of some description must have been kept by churchwardens from the very beginning, but perhaps on loose sheets and therefore liable to loss and oblivion. At St Edmund, Salisbury, parchment rolls are known to have existed for at least 52 years before 1443, the date of the first surviving records.[62] Quite frequently, all we have are miscellaneous memoranda, fragmentary, or selective entries, pointing to a peculiar mixture of oral and written culture.[63] At this stage of administrative development, quantitative approaches would clearly be futile and misleading. Very often, however, a special effort or building project seems to have prompted more formal proceedings. Fundraising purposes and the sheer scale of many initiatives must have made better record keeping or at least better storage highly desirable. At Louth, the early surviving accounts coincide with the construction of the spire, at Bodmin with the rebuilding of the whole church, at Prescot with high expenditure for bells, and at Yatton with works on the new church house and rood loft.[64] At St Ewen's in 1455, the purpose of the new church

---

[59] P. Spufford, *Money and its Use in Medieval Europe* (Cambridge, 1988), p. 338.

[60] Ibid., pp. 385ff.

[61] Yatton CWA, e.g. 1495–6 and passim.

[62] St Edmund CWA, pp. ix ff (introduction by Amy M. Straton). The same point has been made for other parishes: Carnwath, 'CWA of Thame', p. 181; Barron and Roscoe, 'St Andrew Holborn', p. 31.

[63] The Chevington accounts are in essence lists of names and 'churchpott' dues: Cambridge University Library, Hangrave Hall MSS, 17 (1). Many court cases about parish administration reveal idiosyncratic blends of oral and written practices: French, 'Local identity', p. 237.

[64] R. Dudding (ed.), *The First CWs' Book of Louth 1500–24* (Oxford, 1941), pp. xiiiff; J. Wilkinson (ed.), *Receipts and Expenses in the Building of Bodmin Church 1469–72* (London, 1874); Prescot CWA, 1523 ff, and Yatton CWA, 1446 ff. Croscombe started to record expenditure in detail when the parish embarked on the construction of a church house: French, 'Local identity', p. 172 n. 133.

book, financed by a spicer and a brewer, may have been to take stock (it opens with an inventory) and to record the expensive purchase of a great processional cross weighing 116 ounces of gold and silver.[65] Elsewhere, conscientious officers clearly felt that they needed to improve their archives: John Halhed, grocer and churchwarden at Mary-at-Hill in 1486–7, decided to compile a church book because of the parish's lack of evidence in a recent lawsuit, while at All Saints, Bristol, the same action may have been taken as a consequence of a legal dispute with Thomas Fylour in 1467.[66] Both books include accounts as well as wills or deeds, quite intentionally preserving them for subsequent generations (and historical research). A similar need could be felt much later, as at Halesowen where the book dates from the later sixteenth century (1571–3[67]), or as late as the nineteenth, when the Andrew Hubbard or Boxford accounts were bound. Places like Botolph Aldersgate, however, produced loose rolls of such an elaborate character that they were meant to last without formal rearrangement. Whatever the parish's strategy, there is no such thing as guaranteed survival: the early Prescot reckonings, transcribed from the originals only a few decades ago, have now been lost.[68]

The basic structure of parish accounts was very similar throughout England (and probably beyond[69]):

1. Heading (including names of wardens, parish, accounting period)
2. Balance from previous account/arrears
3. Individual items of income (the 'charge')
4. Total income (sum of '2' and '3')
5. Individual items of expenditure (the 'discharge')
6. Total expenses[70]
7. Balance[71]/acquittal of officers

---

[65] St Ewen CWA, p. xix.

[66] Clive Burgess (paper to the Cambridge Church History seminar 6 May 1992) and 'Anniversary in late medieval Bristol', 203. At All Saints, both the original loose accounts and bound copies survive : BRO, P/AS/ChW/1 (church book) and P/AS/ChW/3 (loose accounts). They are substantially the same, but the church book provides less detail. The parish looked after it carefully and rebound it if needed (for example 1524–5).

[67] Halesowen CWA, transcriber's note.

[68] Information kindly supplied by the present vicar of Prescot, the Reverend Thomas M. Steel.

[69] Cf. the similar sequence of items of income, sum total, expenditure, and balance at Meudon in France: Constant, 'Source négligée', 511.

[70] Very rarely expenses were entered before or balances struck after the income, as in Yatton CWA, 1548–9.

[71] Either 'et sic remanet in manibus gardianorum' (in the case of a positive balance, for example Halesowen CWA, 1502–3) or 'the parishe doyth the church wardenes' (in a year with a deficit, for example Prescot CWA, 1546–7).

8. Memoranda about sums unpaid, money in other hands, parish decisions, and so on.

Even though the wardens were fully responsible for their reckoning, they did not necessarily write it themselves. Most, after all, were 'amateurs' with little experience of formal record keeping.[72] Literacy was only starting to spread down the social scale, and early modern office holders tended to employ scribes throughout Europe.[73] At St John's in Bristol, an ordinance of 1472 acknowledged this explicitly by stating that:

> thay beyng no clerkis nothir hauyng the connyng of wrytyng shalle now take thayme a wryter to write such thynges as is necessary and behovable as towchyng to theyr accompte ... and to geve the sayd writer for his labor xijd.[74]

Many accounts were written by clerical scribes: at Yatton, the vicar obliged in 1446–7 (for a fee of 14 d.), the parish clerk in 1543–4, or other priests like Sir John Smith in 1555–6 (24 d.). Much of the writing for All Saints in the 1470s and 1480s was done by the clerk and later vicar John Thomas, who may have been responsible for the whole church book.[75] The incumbent was used in sixteenth-century Morebath, the priest and organist John Cawood at Louth, the deacon Roger Wellow at St Edmund, Salisbury, and unspecified 'clerks' at All Saints (Roger Rise in 1554–5) or for the Trinity fraternity at Botolph Aldersgate (1453–4, when the same person also gathered rents and quarterages).[76] From the later fifteenth century, however, the situation seems to be changing: Ashburton's records (1479–1580) were compiled by ten different people, nine of them lay, and some of them attorneys, for fees of originally 12 d. and later 6 s. 8 d.[77] John Thurbane, at one stage a parochial 'lightman', was paid for the job at Yatton in the 1460s, while Thomas Alcherton wrote at Botolph Aldersgate from the 1480s for 3 s. 4 d. and

---

[72] Drew (ed.), *Lambeth CWA*, p. xv. Few of the Somerset wardens wrote themselves: French, 'Local identity', p. 24.

[73] In the French example of Meudon, the scribe received 40 *sous* as late as 1572: Constant, 'Source négligée', 511.

[74] St John's Book, f. 10ʳ (quoted in St Ewen CWA, p. xvi).

[75] I owe this information to Clive Burgess.

[76] Binney (ed.), *Morebath*, introduction (unpaginated); Dudding (ed.), *CWs Book of Louth*, p. xvii; St Edmund CWA, pp. 74–5, and Basing (ed.), *Fraternity Register*, p. 35 (Trinity gild). A clerical scribe was also used at St Mary, Grimsby: Morris, *Churches in the Landscape*, p. 358.

[77] For example John Ford (1509–32), Thomas Predyaux (1537–42), and George Dabernon (1542–73). Only John Saunder (1532–6) seems to have been a parish clerk: Ashburton CWA, p. vii. In manorial administration, the reeves seem to have written their own records from the fourteenth century. Local professional scribes were available from the late thirteenth: Harvey (ed.), *Cuxham*, p. 41.

subsequently 6 s. 8 d. Eleven hands have been distinguished at Halesowen (known by name are John Jeks 1498–1514 and Roger Paston 1548–70), and there is no indication that they were in holy orders.[78] The possibility of wardens writing themselves should not be discounted either. There is evidence at St Ewen's (where 'I' is often used in the sixteenth century) or All Saints, Bristol (in the case of Arthur Richard in the 1550s).[79] This may have had something to do with the city's advanced economic position, but the wealthy yeoman Robert Sheppard wrote his own accounts in rural Suffolk, too, and so did the wardens of Banwell in Somerset (both in the 1530s).[80]

The idiosyncrasies of each scribe left their marks on the sources. Within the same set, the character and comprehensiveness of entries can vary considerably, and sometimes hands and style change within the same year (Yatton CWA, 1529–30). The costs of obits, general minds, repairs, or purchases are sometimes reported extensively in one account, and very summarily in the next. Equally, collections may appear in the form of quarterly instalments or as a lump sum for the whole period: at Botolph Aldersgate, the accounts for 1512–13 are very detailed, but comparatively brisk in 1511–12 or 1525–6. As long as the sums for the various items are given, quantitative analysis remains possible. However, where only overall totals or balances survive, it must fail.[81]

Even more variety in form and presentation results from a juxtaposition of several sets: as starting-date, Boxford chose Plough Monday (Monday after 6 January), Botolph Aldersgate Candlemas (2 February), All Saints the Annunciation of Mary (25 March; from 1503), Ashburton St John the apostle (6 May), Halesowen Michaelmas (29 September), Prescot St Catherine's day (25 November) or Easter, while many different days were used at Andrew Hubbard. Accounts normally covered a one year period, but the minimum found in this sample is a quarter and the maximum five years.[82] Sometimes, items were entered in the chronological order in which they occurred, as at Andrew Hubbard,

---

[78] Botolph CWA, e.g. 1480–2 and Halesowen CWA, transcriber's notes. They received between 8 d. and 2 s.

[79] St Ewen CWA, p. xvi, and All Saints CWA, 1554–5 (3 s. 4 d.).

[80] The first evidence for double-entry bookkeeping survives from Bristol (but not in parish accounts): Morris, *Churches in the Landscape*, p. 360; Smith, 'Mickfield', p. 6; French, 'Local identity', p. 24 (Banwell). According to Carnwath, 'CWA of Thame', p. 183, several late fifteenth-century wardens were literate in that parish, too.

[81] For example St Ewen CWA, 1525–47 (no information at all survives 1518–24).

[82] Botolph CWA, 25 Dec. 1518 to 25 March 1519 (¼-year), and Andrew Hubbard CWA, 1460–5. In order to facilitate comparison, all averages given in this study have been calculated on a yearly basis, and longer periods split up accordingly. Shorter terms, which are extremely rare, have been discarded for this purpose.

where the costs of decorating the church at Easter, Corpus Christi, Midsummer, or Christmas provide a regular rhythm. At All Saints in 1538–9 and 1542–3, expenditure was carefully arranged in quarterly units, but this was not common.[83] Occasionally, there are discrepancies between regnal and calendar years and question marks about the date of entire accounts. In several places, identical headings appear for different accounting periods,[84] at Yatton, volume 3 of the parish accounts opens with the date '1530' instead of '1540', and elsewhere important passages are simply lost (Botolph CWA, rolls 43 and 46) or confusing.[85] Some mistakes can be corrected on the basis of circumstantial evidence, arithmetic, or individual items,[86] but often there are no proofs either way, only probabilities, and with fragmentary passages such as Andrew Hubbard 1517–20, the correct chronology is anyone's guess.

Quantitative analysis should thus focus on longer-term general trends rather than short-term fluctuations of individual items. Here, the graphs and tables compare – wherever possible – an equal number of years from four particularly significant periods: the first surviving accounts of each set, the immediate pre-Reformation evidence, the Edwardian years, and the reign of Mary. Individual accounts have not been divided, but placed into the period which covers the bulk of the wardens' term. Due to the uneven pattern of source survival, the period headings may cover slightly different dates in different parishes. However, this should still allow a broad comparison of the characteristics of each set at these distinctive points in time.

Some parish accounts were in Latin, interspersed with vernacular terms (Ashburton, Edmund Salisbury), others used English throughout (Botolph Aldersgate, Bethersden). The arrangement of items could be in the form of narrative prose under different headings with figures within the text, or a neatly structured list with separate columns for the units of pounds, shillings, and pence on the right margin.[87] The latter was rare in

---

[83] Exceptions include the ledger written at Yatton on 13 October 1482 or the dating at Andrew Hubbard (for example CWA 1528–9).

[84] Michaelmas 9–10 Henry VIII (Andrew Hubbard) and 1500–1 (Yatton).

[85] Cf. the editor's comments for Boxford CWA, 1557ff.

[86] In a few cases this has led to the chronological rearrangement of the evidence: Boxford CWA, 1557–9; Peterborough CWA, 1540–3, Prescot CWA, 1530s and 1550–2; All Saints CWA, 1555–9 (where churchwarden Roger Myllward's dating of 1554–5 should probably read 1555–6).

[87] Continuous text for example at Botolph Aldersgate, lists of items at Andrew Hubbard, partly at Yatton (and in the French example of Meudon: Constant, 'Source négligée', 511). All Saints Bristol occasionally uses separate columns for the different monetary units (e.g. CWA 1515–16 or 1549–50). In terms of presentation, the fifteenth century was a period of transition: Woolf, *History of Accountants*, p. 96.

this country, and 'the addition of the items must have been a matter of some difficulty'.[88] Mechanical helps like the abacus were used at least in towns, but arithmetic remained a hazard, as generations of scholars will testify.[89] One example may illustrate the problem. In 19 Edward IV, the wardens entered the following list into the All Saints accounts:

The costs of the General Mind

In primis for loaf bread, cakes and spices and to the baker for his labour	iv^s v^d
Item for a dozen of ale	xviii^d
Item for wine	iv^s v^d
Item to vii priests	xxii^d
Item to the clerk for ringing	xii^d
Sum	xiii^s iii^d
	[recte: 13 s. 2 d.]

Some inconsistencies can be explained by careful scrutiny of the manuscripts, for instance where corrections were made to the original list without adjusting the totals. Others resulted from the cumbersome nature of roman numerals, enhanced by ambiguous symbols, and abbreviations which (in certain hands) must have been as difficult to decipher for contemporary parishioners as for present-day historians.[90] Arabic figures hardly ever appear in pre-Reformation sources and were not in universal use until the mid-seventeenth century.[91] Similarly, textbooks on arithmetic, and calculations on paper (rather than by means of an abacus) were only slowly gaining ground between 1500 and 1700.[92] Reckoning was not easy, and the accountants of parishes, vicarages, gilds, lights, manors, and monasteries all struggled to make

---

[88] Ibid., p. 82.

[89] Abacus: the typical marks appear, for example in the margins of Botolph CWA, 1512–13, 1518–19, and 1535–6. For a general discussion of medieval reckoning: F. Yeldham, *The Story of Reckoning in the Middle Ages* (London, 1926). Arithmetic: 'The totals are often incorrect' (Boxford CWA, p. viii); 'the churchwardens' accountancy went mainly by rule of thumb' (Drew (ed.), *Lambeth CWA*, p. x); 'it will occasionally be found that the printed figures and totals do not tally, and sometimes this is clearly the churchwardens' own error' (J. Farmiloe and R. Nixseaman (eds), *Elizabethan CWA* (Streatley, 1953), p. vii); 'CWA seldom add up or balance' (French, 'Local identity', p. 36).

[90] In the Yatton CWA 'xl' and 'xv' or the symbols used for shillings and pence are often very similar.

[91] The odd Arabic figure, for example in the heading of All Saints CWA, 1528–9, or in Andrew Hubbard CWA, 1548–50. Woolf, *History of Accountants*, p. 97, and Constant, 'Source trop négligée', 173 (for France), confirm the tenacity of Roman symbols.

[92] K. Thomas, 'Numeracy in early modern England', *TRHS*, 5th Series 37 (1987), 103.

their figures tally.[93] Given these problems, all assessments and interpretations in this study are based on fresh additions of all individual items. In Appendix 3, these new 'totals' appear alongside the 'wardens' total' and discrepancies between the two derive not only from errors by the scribes (or this author), but also from the fragmentary nature of some accounts, the impossibility to reconstruct elements of the wardens' totals, or the illegibility of particular passages. Still, the two figures are often similar or even identical,[94] and it is not unreasonable to claim that what is being argued on the basis of these fresh figures does not misrepresent the original material.

Moving to the compilation and auditing process, one crucial problem is the 'arrears' or 'balances' which normally open the accounts. In principle, they included both outstanding payments and the cash surplus from previous years.[95] These items do not necessarily reflect the overall size of communal resources, even where they were carried forward more or less unchanged from the preceding account.[96] It is more likely that churchwardens kept what could be called 'current accounts' for daily use, while the church normally possessed a separate treasury chest or 'deposit account' for special needs. Occasionally, there are glimpses of the latter. Having incurred a deficit in 1554-5, Boxford miraculously provided the next wardens with £5 each when they took office. At Peterborough in 1477-8, the accountants struck an overall balance of almost £7 after a reckoning which – in itself – only produced a profit of 7 s. Explicit evidence survives at Ashburton for 1524-5, when there were £14 17s. 10½ d. in the treasury box besides the churchwardens' balance of £17 16s. 10d. Even more detailed is the information for All Saints, where wardens were entrusted with only a fraction of the church's resources:

> delyvered to John Mawncell senior proctor of the seid sum [= the balance of £9 3s. 1½ d.] v^{li} iij^s he to bring it in agayn at hys accomte

---

[93] Ibid., 118. On the arithmetical problems of vicars: Heath (ed.), *Clerical Accounts*, p. 25; lightwardens: Barron and Roscoe, 'St Andrew Holborn', pp. 55-6; gilds: Basing (ed.), *Fraternity Register*, e.g. p. 27; monks: Hockey (ed.), *Beaulieu Abbey*, pp. 41-2, and manors: Woolf, *Story of Accountants*, p. 82.

[94] For example Yatton CWA, 1518-19; Peterborough CWA, 1488-9; Boxford CWA, 1536-7; Ashburton CWA, 1527-8. Generally and not surprisingly, the figures seem to correspond more frequently in London and Bristol.

[95] Denholm-Young, *Seignorial Administration*, p. 127, or Botolph Aldersgate CWA, where it was usually a mixture of the two. In the eyes of the wardens, the 'balance' included everything that was due to them, regardless of whether it had already been paid.

[96] As at Boxford or Ashburton; at St Ewen's, however, it was only from 1540 that the full balance went to the next set of wardens rather than to the 'bursa' of the church (St Ewen CWA, p. xxii).

and the rest that is to sey iiii[li] is put in the Tresor cofer in the presens of the seyd parisshons.[97]

The system was refined from 1537–8:

Also the paryshe ys a greyde that the seneor proctor shall delyver unto hys mate yongyr proctor at the Fest of candylmas iiii[li] yn money For the use of the paryshe and soo to be contynewyd For a custom always.

The purpose of this gradual shift in responsibility from the senior to the junior warden was to enable the latter to pay the necessary expenses during the period between the formal closing of his predecessor's account at the end of March and the audit sometime during May, when the balance was physically handed over. The reserves stored in the treasury box would remain untouched, unless for special purposes such as the purchase of a new expensive ornament.[98] It is perhaps less important to know exactly how much money parishes had at any one point, than to realize that they could produce large sums in very short time, as the £47 raised at Boxford from the sale of church goods in the 1540s or the £65 invested in lands at All Saints Bristol in 1525.[99]

The money the wardens received to carry out their duties had to be stored carefully. An unfortunate incident at Botolph Aldersgate reveals the exact location, when the accountants asked allowance for £11 14 s. 6¼ d. 'which was stollen owte of the Roodeloft which at all tymes hath bene a place convenyent to leve ther money and other Juelle'.[100] Nevertheless, the locks and keys bought in later years suggest that it continued to serve this function (for example CWA 1522–3). The treasury box itself was hidden carefully and opened only with the consent of a variety of important people who all held their own keys.[101] In addition, wardens had some money in their own pockets or at home, which usually comes to light when it was returned to the church by the

---

[97] All Saints CWA, 1517–8 and similar 1520–1, 1526–7. At St Thomas, Bristol, £4 10 s. 'goeth from proctors to proctors': C. Taylor (ed.), 'Regulations of the vestry of St Thomas', *Proceedings of the Clifton Antiquarian Club*, **1** (1884–8), 194.

[98] For example a cross in All Saints CWA, 1523–4.

[99] Boxford CWA, 1547–8, and All Saints CWA, 1524–5. The peasants' ability to raise astonishing sums for secular purposes has been noted by Dyer, *Standards of Living*, p. 179.

[100] Botolph CWA, roll 32 (an emergency intermediate account from Christmas 1511). Churches often served as places of safe storage (see for example the evidence of a fifteenth-century Chancery case concerning Devon: PRO, C 1 28/289), but thefts were not unusual: C. Oman, 'Security in English churches 1000–1548', *Archaeological Journal*, **136** (1979), 90–8.

[101] See the cover illustration of this study or the court leet chest still on display at Prescot Museum. In a typical arrangement, the parson, one 'auncyant man' of the parish, and the senior CW each held a key to the 'cofin' at St Stephen, Bristol: Fox (ed.), 'St Stephen', 202.

widows of those who died in office.[102]

Turning to the question of arrears, 'desperate debts were a perpetual plague on early modern financial administration'.[103] Manorial officers, for instance, were haunted by them for years after their term and faced prosecution if any irregularities occurred.[104] The increasing assertiveness of late medieval villagers made rent collection more and more difficult for them, and arrears could reach astronomical proportions.[105] It is thus essential to investigate whether parish accounts represent an idealistic picture with imaginary figures no churchwarden could ever expect to collect. At first sight this might be suspected, when in some reckonings half of the theoretical balance remained in other hands or unpaid.[106] The problem, however, was tackled energetically. For a start, debts were carefully recorded, as any quick glance at the growing appendix to the Botolph Aldersgate rolls will show.[107] When paid, they were ticked off and this happened frequently: £2 9s. 2d. or half of the arrears recorded in 1497–8 are marked in this way. Most of the case studies regularly list payments of debts (2s. 8d. on average at Botolph Aldersgate, 5s. 9d. at All Saints, and 18s. 1d. at Boxford, where the parish served as a credit institution). If further measures were needed, churchwardens could exercise pressure by means of reminders (as the expenses of 19d. 'made and done apon suche persons as wuld nat pay the clerke wage' at Botolph Aldersgate in 1501–2), law suits (as at St Ewen's *v.* John Sharp and Ashburton *v.* John Ford), or even distraints (as at St Botolph in 1493–4, when Margaret More owed 11s. 'For the whyche the aforsayd accomptantes have distressyd and takyn a pot of bras'). Nevertheless, some debts remained impossible to collect and reappeared year after year: the abbot of Kirkstead was a constant offender at St Botolph, and

---

[102] Andrew Hubbard CWA, 1554–7 (widow of Harry Batman), St Ewen CWA, 1560–1 (Thomas Barry, goldsmith), and All Saints CWA, 1511–2 (John Baten).

[103] P. Carter, 'The records of the court of first fruits and tenths 1540-54', *Archives*, **21** (1994), 63.

[104] It was never too late to pay: the arrears of the sheriff of Holderness dragged on from 1264–66 to 1277, when his executors were faced with a bill of £50 (Denholm-Young, *Seignorial Administration*, p. 151).

[105] Dyer, *Lords and Peasants*, p. 276.

[106] At Botolph Aldersgate, for instance, the information is complex and calculations can only be approximate: where both balances and explicit arrears survive, the theoretical balance was on average £20 and the actual money transferred around £10.

[107] Cf., for example, Botolph CWA, 1497–8 with 1512–3. The same can be observed in manorial accounts: Harvey (ed.), *Cuxham*, pp. 70–1. It looks as if new wardens took responsibility of the whole theoretical balance and in turn discharged themselves of anything not yet recovered at the end of their term. To investigate each and every case would be a massive and frustrating task. In 1486–7 the wardens of St Botolph asked allowance for a bad debt of 9½ d. dating back to 2 Edward IV.

the case was described as 'hopeless' in 1493–4.[108] The parish periodically acknowledged this by waving such entries 'for as moche as all the parysshons beyng at the yeuyng up of thys accompt callyd hyt Desperat dette',[109] but it was not a decision they took lightly.

There is a good deal of information on administrative practice in late medieval parishes. Documentation is better for the big cities, but much must have been similar elsewhere. It is clear for instance that wardens made notes of their financial transactions: at Mary-at-Hill there was a 'boke of parcellis', at St Ewen's a small paper book, at All Saints a 'book of rekenyng', and the Botolph accounts include regular expenses for 'papyr to wryte in parcelles'.[110] Sometimes there were separate records for certain communal responsibilities, such as the book for the gathering of the clerk's wages at Lambeth and Andrew Hubbard, or the special rolls at All Saints. The 'prykyng byll' at Andrew Hubbard was a list of parishioners' names and their contributions to various types of collections.[111] Botolph Aldersgate seems to have gathered its dues on the basis of streets or neighbourhoods, and individual payments ranged from 4 d. to 2 s.[112] In most bigger places, the main parish officers were assisted by auxiliary personnel with closely defined responsibilities and sometimes separate records: alewardens operated at Ashburton with a cash advance from the parish (1558–9: £2), and occasionally they attached summary statements to the churchwardens' accounts (as in 1556–7). At All Saints, pew fees were collected separately (1497–8), and there was a waxmaker's book (1539–40[113]), while brewery accounts exist for Yatton (amounting to £3 8 s. 8 d. in 1545–6), or poor relief reckonings for Boxford in the Reformation period.[114]

---

[108] Four shillings were due yearly from a tenement in 'Ratton Rowe', a gift of London citizen Ralph Rattespray from 1307 (Botolph CWA, 1498–9).

[109] Botolph CWA, 1502–3. Similarly 1538–9, where over £19 were 'dyschargyd by the assent of the hole parysshe' or 1559–60, when the confiscation of rents and tenements by the crown made recovery of any outstanding payments from them unlikely.

[110] Mary-at-Hill CWA, pp. xiv and 95, 99, 100, St Ewen CWA, p. xvii, All Saints CWA, 1480–1, and Botolph CWA, 1505–6. Household (and probably most other) accountants equally relied on memoranda or day-books: Myatt-Price (ed.), 'Cromwell household', p. 111. Their existence and importance is confirmed by a case at St Ewen's on 17 March 1501, when an official who had lost his 'rekenyng' was cited to appear before the parson and 11 parishioners: Maclean, 'St Ewen's', 285–6.

[111] Drew (ed.), *Lambeth CWA*, p. xv, All Saints CWA, 1528–9, and Andrew Hubbard CWA, 1531–2 (for the clerk) and 1521–2 (other collections).

[112] 'For the clerkes wages in dyvers aleys' (Botolph CWA, 1538–9). Individual payments can be reconstructed from outstanding debts, listed, for example in 1525–6 and 1539–40.

[113] The old wax was delivered to the waxmaker, the new wax received, and the difference debited to the parish. The waxmaker also received a few pence for 'making it' (cf. the details recorded for the Halleway chantry 1532–3: BRO, P/AS/C/1).

[114] Only those listed in detail alongside (and not summarized within) the CWA have been entered in the database.

The gathering of rents was also often delegated to other parishioners or specialized 'estate agents'. Gilbert Allen did the job for Botolph Aldersgate with an annual allowance of 13 s. 4 d. to cover defaults and general costs. In return, he was responsible for the delivery of the full £4 11 s. 4 d. due from the tenements in Blackhorse Alley. The parish, however, continued to bear the costs of repair and maintenance.[115] At All Saints in 1489–90, the accounts record £1 5 s. 10½ d. for rent collectors, but both here and at St Botolph the wardens later shouldered the burden themselves with a similar allowance of 6 s. 8 d. at the former and 13 s. 4 d. at the latter.[116] Methods of recording rents varied: sometimes an attempt was made to write down the actual payments received (this seems to be the case at Boxford or Ashburton), while elsewhere the full theoretical rent roll was charged to the wardens, with vacations deducted in another part of the accounts.[117] The accuracy of these entries can sometimes be checked by collation with separate rent rolls, another set of records kept alongside the wardens' accounts and compiled (at All Saints) at a yearly cost of around 3 d.[118] The comparison reveals that every item of the 'reddit' assise' and the 'tenementes in highstrete' was carefully transferred from one to the other. Furthermore, the receipt of quarterly payments was acknowledged by clipping holes alongside the respective names on the rent roll, and all those without a full set of four marks subsequently appear as 'vacacyons' in the accounts.[119] If so desired, the wardens supplied 'acquitannces' or receipts to the tenants (at Botolph Aldersgate in 1520–1 a total of seven at a cost of 12 d.). For some of their tenements, parishes owed quit rents in return, and the wardens were expected to prove that they had actually made the respective payments: in 1515–16, the 2 s. 6 d. customarily due to the prior and convent of St Bartholomew were disallowed by the auditors of St Botolph because there was no written evidence for the transaction. Having learnt a lesson, the wardens of 1517–18 attached a slip to their reckoning which carried prior William's sealed acknowledgement of 'duobus solid' & sex denar'.

The intricacies of parish management are not adequately reflected by the state of the surviving evidence. Originally, accounts were not just single pieces of paper or parchment, but comprehensive files with scores

---

[115] Botolph CWA, Xmas 1511–12.

[116] For example All Saints CWA, 1525–6, and Botolph CWA, 1525–6.

[117] At All Saints vacations appear on the expenses side, for example, in CWA 1473ff (similarly Botolph CWA, 1494–5), and at the end of the income in CWA 1499ff.

[118] BRO, P/AS/ChW/2. For the cost of writing cf. All Saints CWA, 1487–8.

[119] Cf. for example the rent roll from Xmas 1489 to Xmas 1490 (MS is dated 1488–9, but Pernannt/James were CWs a year later) and CWA Xmas 1489 to Xmas 1490. Only those marked with an 'f' did not pay at all.

of notes and bills attached. At Botolph Aldersgate, the phrase 'as apereth by a byll shewyd apon thys accompt and among the memorandes of thys accompt remaynyng' is ubiquitous and refers to indentures, wills, waxmakers' bills, costs of vestments, and repairs to tenements. The prior's receipt is a rare survival, and so are the two slips of parchment drawn up in 1518–19 by a plumber for casting a new gutter and the carpenter Thomas Hall for timber and workmanship. They contain detailed lists of their costs, while only the totals found their way into the wardens' accounts.[120] Evidence for this is widespread; at Ashburton in 1517–18, £13 14s. 8d. spent for building the house and appurtenances in North Street were 'itemised in a bill shown and approved with this account'.[121]

The wardens must have felt a need to discuss and coordinate their activities. One 'business meeting' is recorded at Peterborough in 1467–8, and occasionally they employed assistants (a warden's clerk is mentioned at Ashburton in 1530–1). On the other hand, each may have had his own duties, and some formulations suggest that they worked fairly independently: 'I have paide' is not uncommon at Yatton in the 1470s, and the 1507–8 account ends with four lines carefully recording what each officer had received and spent. Similarly, in a deficit year at Boxford (CWA 1554–5), the wardens 'have payed more ... than they have Receyved xxvˢ xjᵈ whereof Rychards [Brond= warden 1] part ys [blank] & Wylliam coes part ys vijˢ vjᵈ ob ...'. At Andrew Hubbard in 1521–2, the wardens actually accounted separately.[122] Where large sums were involved, the parish and especially its elite insisted on being consulted, even in the middle of an officer's term. Wardens who failed to do so took a considerable risk: at Yatton in 1470–1, Thomas Kewe and John Hurt, who had served in 1468–9, still owed £1 'that they delyvered to the peynter withowte leve of the parasche'. A formal spending ceiling was imposed on the officers at Botolph Aldersgate in 1551–2:

> it is aggreed by thassent of the parochians ... that the said Robert Lee & Thomas Ryoll nor eny other the churche wardens hereafter to be chosen shall bestowe in Reparaciones of any one house or

---

[120] Botolph CWA, 1486–7 (phrase referring to a new suit of gold vestments), 1491–2 (indenture concerning the lease of a parish tenement), 1504–5 (copy of the will of William Hall, made for 8d. and attached with a piece of string and still surviving), 1482–3 (waxmaker's bill) and 1525–6 (repairs done on tenements in Blackhorse Alley totalling £7 9s. 9d.).

[121] This 'meta-level' of accounting is noted in Carnwath, 'CWA of Thame', p. 182, French, 'Local identity', pp. 31–2, and Constant, 'Source négligée', 509. In manors, too, the reeve or bailiff would keep track of his payments and sales by means of tallies (pieces of wood notched with the appropriate sums) or slips of parchment containing bills: Dyer, *Standards of Living*, p. 28. The attachment of detailed accounts was also standard procedure: Harvey (ed.), *Cuxham*, p. 67.

[122] In some French cases, the keeping of accounts was assigned to a specialized warden, the *trésorier*: Constant, 'Source négligée', 506.

tenement or in the making or Repayring of any other thing neccisarie touching the use of the said churche above the some of xx^s at ane tyme & in one yere withowt the speciall aggreamentt & assent of vj honest & elderlie neighbours of the parishe or by the speciall assentt of foure of them at the leaste [and added in another hand] to be made prevy unto the said charge at the fyrst beginnyng of the same.

Offending wardens were punished, as in 1567–8 when an unapproved expense of £11 5s. 8d. resulted in a fine of 3s. 4d. payable to the poor men's box.[123] However, wardens could not be blamed for everything that diminished communal wealth. Edward VI's government dealt a double blow to parish finance by large-scale confiscation of church treasures and by its monetary policy. Debasement hit the country in 1551, when the existing bad silver money was decried by 25 per cent.[124] Parish records reveal the immediate impact of this measure. The allowance for the fall of money at All Saints in 1551–2 (£6 of a balance of £26 13s. 10 d.) represented a 22.5 per cent cut, and the Andrew Hubbard wardens lost £1 in their 1550–2 account. An atmosphere of speculation and shaken confidence sparked further government action, and both stages were neatly reflected at Botolph Aldersgate with two devaluations of 25 per cent each and an overall loss of £2 14s. 9d.[125] The result could be dire straits, as in the parish of St Nicholas, Guildford, which blamed its poverty partly on 'the severall proclamacons for the abaten … of the kynges majestes coyne, whereby the money … was dymynyshed and abated to the half'.[126]

The many references to allowances and precautions raise the question of audit procedures. Quite often, there is evidence for the compulsory attendance of all parishioners at the rehearsing of their accounts: it was a community receiving its common stock 'coram parochianibus'[127] and using the opportunity of an 'annual general meeting' to discuss current concerns. Judging from suggestive formulations in the records of Morebath, Yeovil, or Banwell, the reckonings were probably read out

---

[123] At Lambeth, too, 'the prudent warden, before embarking on unusual expenditure, would seek the consent, if not of an ad hoc parish meeting, at least of a Sunday congregation': Drew (ed.), *Lambeth CWA*, p. xiv. All Saints attempted to curb expenditure for the general mind in 1503–4, when the upper limit was fixed at 13s. 4d. The 1519–20 CWA, however, record 18s. 8d. for the purpose.

[124] Challis, *Tudor Coinage*, pp. 301 (debasement effects in general) and 105–6 (1551).

[125] Botolph CWA, 1551–2 asks allowance 'for the losse of certayne money remaynyng in their handes at ether of the proclamacions touching the debasement of money'.

[126] In a petition to the Edwardian commissioners: R. Roberts (ed.), 'Further Surrey inventories', *Surrey Archaeological Collections*, 24 (1911), 35.

[127] Drew (ed.), *Lambeth CWA*, p. xii, and the phrase from Yatton CWA, 1448–9 (the audit took place on 24 February 1449). At All Saints, the balance was delivered 'in the presencs of the parysshe' (for example CWA 1550–1).

aloud.[128] In some (particularly rural) places this may have never changed, but others started to leave the cumbersome work of auditing to a committee which prepared the books for a more or less ritual approval by the whole parish. A good example dates from 17 January 1547 at Andrew Hubbard, when the (normally six to eight) 'auditores chosen be the parishioners for the same purpose' supervised the transfer of the cash balance to the new wardens, passed a burial fee ordinance, defined the clerk's duties, and decided on a yearly contribution to the Trinity guild. They alone signed the respective ordinances, but not without adding that they acted 'yn the nayme of the holl paryshe'.[129] Similar bodies elsewhere all consisted of a broadly defined parish elite: at Prescot on 13 October 1526 the committee included Mr Halsall and 'other the gentilmen of the paroch' (but from 1555 the institutionalized non-gentry 'eight men'), at St Ewen's a group of eight local householders together with the parson, at St Botolph in 1503–4 Thomas Hobson, gent., and 'dyverse of the parysshons', while the 1513 accounts of Thame were shown to 'magistro Johanni Parker ibidem vicario Galfrido Dormer generoso et aliis venerabilibus parochianis'. Explicit evidence for the existence of auditors at All Saints only dates from 1559–60, but the marks and corrections in some of the earlier accounts suggest that they were not a recent innovation.[130] The custom recorded for the Trinity fraternity at Botolph Aldersgate may reflect a more common practice:

> it is ordeyned that the wardeynes of the olde yere schal ben suffareyne auditoures of the maystres [=wardens] that ben ychosen by hem for the new yere in the day of her acountes. And thus euery yere sewyng the olde maystres schullen be auditoures vppon the newe but yif the bretheren thenken othere mor profytable.[131]

At Salisbury, at least, the balance was handed over to the new set of officers in the presence of the mayor and the 'masters', a body consisting of past churchwardens.[132]

The date of the audit could be the day of the formal closing of the accounts (as in fifteenth-century St Ewen's), but normally there was some delay, probably to allow time for the preparation of all the necessary

---

[128] Binney (ed.), *Morebath*, passim; French, 'Local identity', p. 25.

[129] Andrew Hubbard CWA, 1545–6. The reference to election by the whole parish in CWA 1554–7, similar in CWA 1526–7.

[130] Bailey, 'CWA of Prescot', 138 and 177–8; Craig, 'Prescot', p. 55; St Ewen CWA, p. xxi; Botolph CWA, 1503–4, Carnwath, 'CWA of Thame', p. 188, and All Saints CWA, 1539–40 (corrections). At Meudon in France, the accounts were yielded to the vicar and those parishioners 'représentant la plus grande et saine partie des habitants': Constant, 'Source négligée', 527.

[131] Basing (ed.), *Fraternity Register*, register number 13.

[132] St Edmund CWA, p. xi (introduction by Amy Mary Straton).

paperwork.[133] Parishioners were anxious to keep this down to a reasonable period. When Roger Miller of All Saints gave his reckoning as late as 2 September 1540 (for a term which had ended on 25 March), they complained that it 'should ben gevyn ... in the begyning of the month of maij last past according to the olde lawdable custom'. Three years later the date was fixed on Hock Tuesday in the second week after Easter.[134] The parish expected the wardens to produce the whole balance physically at their audit,[135] which was not always possible: at Boxford in 1555–6, William Coe could only put 2 s. 3 d. in the church box and still owed £3, while his colleague Thomas Osborn paid 12 s. 4 d., £3 15 s. short of the overall sum (which both acknowledged with their signature). At All Saints in 1505–6, warden John Dee delivered plate as surety for the 32 s. missing from his balance, and in 1522–3, the parish accepted a gilt cup in lieu of £8 from the wardens' reckoning. Some of the income took the form of plate anyway, which was passed on to the next officer 'to the entent that he shall make salys thereof to the most avawntage of the church'.[136]

As for the actual auditing procedure, manorial and household administrations held a 'view' roughly half way through an officer's term for an intermediary assessment of the situation,[137] but no trace of this survives in parochial records. The purpose of the audit proper was to make sure that all receipts were entered, all expenses justified, and all additions correct.[138] There is no detailed evidence about how this was done, but it must have involved an examination of all the paperwork, a comparison with last year's account, and a common-sense assessment of the accuracy of individual entries. The mere existence of an audit may have helped to prevent dishonesty,[139] but there is evidence to suggest that mistakes and oversights were actually detected. At All Saints in 1539–40, another hand added 'here lackith shere thursday and good friday abowt iii s' to the receipts, crossed out two items mentioned twice, disallowed 6 s. 2 d. entered for a conduit (since the expense was borne by someone

---

[133] St Ewen CWA, p. xxi; a delay for example in the case of the audit held on 19 January 1541 at Andrew Hubbard for the term 7 January 1539 to Xmas 1540.

[134] All Saints CWA, 1539–40 (quote) and 1542–3 (Hock Tuesday). The corresponding ordinance at Botolph Aldersgate demanded the production of the accounts within seven weeks after Candlemas, when they normally closed (CWA 1480–2).

[135] 'The whyche som of xii^li xvj^s xj^d q^a was brought in to the churche' (Botolph CWA, 1547–8).

[136] All Saints CWA, 1526–7.

[137] Myatt-Price, 'Cromwell household', p. 111.

[138] Harvey (ed.), *Cuxham*, p. 52. The last point often remained wishful thinking (cf. the discussion of arithmetic above).

[139] Dyer, *Standards of Living*, pp. 28 and 94.

else), reduced the allowance for carrying banners in rogation week from 3 d. to 1 d., and reminded the accountant that 3 s. 11 d. earmarked for an obit had not yet been paid. At Botolph Aldersgate in 1520–1, the auditors noted in the margin that the wardens should be charged with the whole parish rental without deductions, and in 1522–3 deleted an item worth 18 s. 2 d. for repair work, while accepting 34 s. for lime spent in Blackhorse Alley and 'nott allowed in the laste accompte precedent'. At Mary-at-Hill, the waxmakers had 'misRekonyd' in 1524–5, while warden Robert Howtyng was in the position of having accounted for 5 s. 10 d. 'mor than he sholde haue done'.[140]

Offenders could be called upon quite some time after they had left office: in 1551–2, Botolph Aldersgate got hold of a bill recording an unauthorized sale of certain church goods by a gentleman in 1550, 'wherunto the same John Longe is to be called & to be chardged & annswerable'. More serious still was the offence of ex-warden William Kenyngthorpe, who had embezzled some jewels and was sued and arrested as a common thief in 1468–70. On the other hand, if they had acted with due care, wardens were not held responsible even for major losses. In the same parish, £11 14s. 6¼ d. were pardoned 'ffor asmoche as the seid money wasse takyn owte off the Rode loft the chyste beyng lokked'. The high level of expenditure for locks and keys had a very practical background.[141] Nevertheless, parish auditors could not detect everything: at Ashburton, for instance, £3 14s. 4½d. miraculously appeared in 1538–9 'received in the past years and not accounted for'.

Auditors were not normally paid for their services, but Peterborough allowed them 3 s. 4 d. in 1493–4 when a good deal of cash had to be counted in the vestry. It was probably as much of a social as a financial occasion: some places record dinners or drinks on their audit day. At All Saints in 1551–2, a large number of parishioners must have gone to the 'new inne', where two women treated them to chicken, mutton shoulder, veal, bread, butter, sugar, ale, three gallons of white, and two gallons of claret wine. The hat was passed round on such occasions, but the wardens still contributed an astonishing £2 9 s. 6 d. from communal funds.[142] At Andrew Hubbard, there was originally a 'breakfast' for a modest 4 s. 2 d., but at a later stage dinners were held there, too, with expenses of up to £1 1 s. 8 d.[143]

---

[140] Mary-at-Hill CWA, 1492–3.

[141] Botolph CWA, 1516–17. Keys or locks for the jewel box bought for example, in All Saints CWA, 1505–6 or 1512–13.

[142] All Saints CWA, 1551–2 (the women were paid 16 d.). Collections of 5 s. are mentioned in 1538–9 and 1557–8, where only the 'maysters' contributed.

[143] Andrew Hubbard CWA, 1541–2 and 1550–2.

It must now be attempted to turn this information into an overall assessment of the suitability of churchwardens' accounts for historical and quantitative analysis. Contemporaries certainly valued them highly: carefully compiled and stored, they became the 'memory' of the parish and – like other legal documents – a source of pride and power.[144] As any other type of evidence, however, historians have to establish their scope and limitations.[145] In essence, churchwardens' accounts reflect the financial responsibilities of the main parochial officers in a particular local context. Given the common nature and origin of the position, they offer some scope for comparison. Wardens tackled a basic set of duties with a limited range of strategies all over the country. Every account reflects a parish's idiosyncratic mixture of a number of standard ingredients: collections or rates (particularly prominent at Halesowen, Prescot), ales (Ashburton, Boxford, Yatton), rents (all parishes with landed endowments), burial fees, and sales on the income side, wages of parish employees (the greatest range at Botolph Aldersgate), quit rents or property maintenance (as at All Saints), church decorations (Andrew Hubbard), and the inevitable spending on ornaments, wax, and building work on the expenditure side. The careful compilation and auditing techniques applied in fully developed parochial regimes ensured that all the financially relevant transactions entrusted to the wardens featured in their accounts.[146] In fact, most complete sets follow a very regular pattern, and some appear like pre-printed forms ready to be filled in with the relevant figures for a particular year.[147]

A closer look at some potentially 'delicate' areas reinforces this impression. One apparent difficulty relates to the fact that substantial numbers of bequests known from sources like wills never appear in parish accounts.[148] This is puzzling, but not necessarily the wardens'

---

[144] Cf. the fierce struggle for possession of the Penkevell accounts between the patron and the parish wardens: French, 'Local identity', pp. 22–3, 240.

[145] Cf. the note of caution sounded in C. Burgess, 'Late medieval wills and pious convention' in M. A. Hicks (ed.), *Profit, Piety and the Professions in Later Medieval England* (Gloucester, 1990), pp. 14–33 (and for the Reformation period Duffy, *Stripping of the Altars*, pp. 504–23) with regard to the use of wills in measuring popular piety. Much remained unrecorded due to custom, outside pressures, or arrangements made during the lifetime of testators.

[146] Even in the Reformation period: Hutton, 'Local impact'.

[147] For example Botolph CWA, 1500–1, where the space next to the beam collection has been left blank and filled in by another hand; similarly, the names and rents of current tenants were added to the standard list of parish property. Various items appear with the usual detailed explanation, even though no money was actually raised for them in that particular year.

[148] At Norwich for example, over 90 per cent of parishioners left money to their church: Tanner, *Church in Norwich*, pp. 222–3. Here, the corresponding CWA have not survived,

fault: for a start, identification is often complicated by vague formulations such as 'from a bequest' or 'by a stranger'. Some gifts, moreover, were intended for the parson rather than the community (the ubiquitous 'for tithes forgotten') and many were thwarted by the manoeuvrings of irresponsible executors or feoffees.[149] Other benefactors simply overestimated their resources, while a number of gifts bypassed the wardens altogether, either because they went straight to a parochial creditor or the custody of other eminent parishioners. Documentary proof for such informal arrangements is naturally hard to come by,[150] but given all these options, the levels of gift giving (recorded in Appendix 3) are quite respectable and omissions perhaps less surprising.

Another problematic area are the responsibilities delegated to subparochial officers and ad-hoc collections earmarked for a particular purpose;[151] both raise the question of how much of communal activity the churchwardens failed to record. Years with an independent, but not sufficient, collection for the clerk's wages may illustrate the point: at Boxford in 1554–5, for instance, 11 s. 8½ d. were paid to Richard Smith 'besyd that we gathered of the pares' (a collection not recorded on the income side). Yet again, such discrepancies reflect administrative complexity rather than inaccurate accounting. In many places, the clerk received a fixed salary from an independent collection and contributions from general parish funds only as top-up payments or rewards for additional services.[152] The reasons for this were straightforward: the levying of quarterly contributions from all parishioners was a cumbersome exercise, and the wardens may have been simply too busy to do it themselves. There were detailed lists of individual dues (Mary-at-Hill is a particularly elaborate example[153]) and the routine work could easily be left to assistants. A great variety of systems was in operation at Botolph Aldersgate: in 1482–3 the wardens were in charge, the year after there were special collectors, in 1487–8 no money was received by the accountants 'for asmoche as the clerke gadereth hyt hymsylf', while from 1507 the wardens resumed responsibility.[154] As seen above, other

---

but in a case study from Gloucestershire (Tewkesbury), over 50 per cent of gifts fail to materialize. Some of course do: the £3 6s. 8d. specified in the will of Richard Hatter appear in All Saints CWA 1457–8 (I owe these examples to Caroline Litzenberger and Clive Burgess).

[149] Examples in French, 'Local identity', pp. 255–6.

[150] At Thame, a bequest of 5s. made to the churchwardens appears to have been enfeoffed to two other parishioners: Carnwath, 'CWA of Thame', p. 191.

[151] Drew (ed.), Lambeth CWA, p. xv.

[152] For example St Ewen's CWA, p. xxiii, or at Hawkurst: Drew (ed.), Lambeth CWA, p. xvi. At All Saints, 2s. 2d. were 'lackyng off hys wages' in 1500–1, while in 1517–18, the amount was above what 'cowde be gedred in the pareshe the hole yere'.

[153] Mary-at-Hill CWA, pp. 126–7.

[154] A similar variety in the first Andrew Hubbard CWA.

narrowly defined duties were dealt with in the same way. There were rent collectors at All Saints, Bristol, playwardens at Bethersden in Kent, light- or alemen at Yatton, and waxwardens at North Curry in Somerset.[155] Clearly, churchwardens' accounts may not always reflect 100 per cent of a parish's financial commitments. But how much exactly do they hide?

Any answer to this is an argument from silence and necessarily speculative. It is unlikely, however, that the surviving records present us with a completely deficient picture of communal activities. Churchwardens, after all, were the main officers who represented the parish to the authorities and the outside world. Very often, they included at least a summary statement of the financial transactions of their assistant officers in their accounts, for instance the totals raised by the rent collectors in the big cities, the lightmen at Yatton, or the wax- and alewardens at Ashburton. For quantitative purpose, this is all we need. Furthermore, extraordinary projects with separate funds and officers were likely to come under particularly searching public scrutiny. In fact, they are frequently documented in separate accounts alongside the normal records. This applies to the church house constructions at St Ewen's (from 1493) and Andrew Hubbard (1476–86), as well as to the purchase of new bells at Peterborough (1540–3) and Halesowen (1517).[156] These, too, can be included in the quantitative analysis under the respective years. Still, a grey area remains. The Bethersden playwardens may have been active in years without a surviving account,[157] some parishes may have had separate Peter's pence collectors (in this sample only the Boxford wardens refer to it), and there may have been other ad-hoc fundraising efforts, but – to remain unrecorded – they would have had to be undisputed and to produce exactly the right amount at the right time. If there was a surplus or some uncertainty about the allocation, they normally left some traces.[158]

Two basic conclusions seem to emerge. First, churchwardens' accounts can be subjected to quantitative analysis and, second, they provide an insight into a very large proportion of everyday *communal* activities.[159] To use them, is to look at parishes through the eyes of their 'chief executives' and this, in essence, is the perspective of this study. Its

---

[155] Mercer (ed.), *CWA at Betrysden*, pp. 3–5; Yatton CWA, passim; French, 'Local identity', p. 147.

[156] All to be found at the relevant chronological place besides the CWA, except St Ewen CWA, pp. 11–24.

[157] Mercer (ed.), *CWA at Betrysden*, p. x.

[158] A case in point is the sale of plate at All Saints supervised by the vicar and David Lawrens in 1524, which appears in the form of an assembly discussing the matter.

[159] Cf. the similar verdicts in Gibbs, 'Parish finance', p. 43, or St Ewen CWA, p. xxiii: 'the surviving pre-Reformation accounts may fairly be described as full and detailed'.

findings stand and fall with the conscientiousness of the accountants,[160] but it is difficult to see how this could be avoided.

A *histoire totale* of parochial life, however, would have to rely on a great number of additional evidence. Accounts offer occasional glimpses of individual generosity or leadership, for instance through references to bequests, building initiatives, or the resulting communal response,[161] and they allow an insight into the many related and affiliated institutions of which, not unlike a present-day holding company, the parish formed the centre.[162] But we would look in vain for evidence of informal arrangements, private devotion, or anything without an immediate financial dimension. Neither will there be references to tithes, certainly an important aspect of the social and economic life of the community, but not a collective responsibility.[163] Individual parishioners and subparochial institutions such as lights, gilds, or chantries recorded most of their devotions, customs, and celebrations elsewhere. To construct too precise a chronology of local life and ritual on the basis of churchwardens' accounts is to tread on thin ice indeed.[164] For the same reason, quantitative methods cannot be pushed too far. They should attempt to produce basic trends rather than definitive figures or sophisticated financial analysis. Churchwardens' accounts were compiled by officers who wanted to be 'dyscharged and acquyted'; details about the profitability and cashflow of their institution (or the more colourful aspects of local parochial life) took a markedly lower place on their list of priorities, however much we may regret it.[165]

---

[160] See Chapter 6.2 for (the very limited) evidence of fraud and negligence among parochial office holders.

[161] The south porch at Yatton was sponsored by the Newton family (G. Keily, *A Guide to the Parish Church of St Mary* (no date), pp. 6–7); at Louth, the merchants and vicar Thomas Sudbury provided leadership, but the whole community was involved in the building of the spire (Dudding (ed.), *CWs Book of Louth*, pp. xivff); an impressive list of ornaments bequeathed to All Saints in Nicholls and Taylor, *Bristol Past*, pp. 99–100.

[162] The relationship is examined in Chapter 4.

[163] For tithes in general: A. Little, 'Personal tithes', *EHR*, 60 (1945), 67–88; J. Thomson, 'Tithe disputes in later medieval London', *EHR*, 78 (1963), 1–17; Brigden, 'Tithe controversy'.

[164] See the recent attempt in Hutton, *Merry England*, ch. 2, to date local rituals on the basis of their first entry in CWA and certain other local records. The possibility that, previously, they had taken place without financial implications or under the auspices of different institutional sponsors cannot easily be discounted. The author, of course, acknowledges the problem, but sees it as an argument from silence. For him, the burden of proof rests with his critics.

[165] The phrase from Edmund CWA, 1552–3. For the emphasis on the officer and the character of contemporary accountancy: D. Oschinsky, 'Medieval treatises on estate accounting' in Littleton and Yamey (eds), *History of Accounting*, p. 91; Denholm-Young, *Seignorial Administration*, p. 127; Dyer, *Standards of Living*, p. 92; Morris, *Churches in the Landscape*, pp. 358-9.

3.3 Parish income

The remainder of this chapter discusses the churchwardens' financial activities in some more detail. To facilitate comparison, the evidence has been rearranged into a number of categories reflecting the different types of income and expenditure:[166] 'collections', 'ales', or 'pews' are terms borrowed from the sources themselves, and headings such as 'ceremonial life' or 'landlord' summarize several items of a related kind. There are of course many different ways to structure the material, each with its particular advantages and disadvantages.[167] Here, transactions have normally been classified on a functional rather than personal basis; £1 paid for a carpenter's work on a statue, for instance, has been entered under 'ornaments', not 'labourers'.[168] The perspective is that of the warden, and priority is given to the identification of general trends rather than architectural or liturgical details. No attempt has been made to document individual projects or to distinguish between different types of ceremonies and ornaments. More ambitious approaches are hampered by the wardens' reluctance to elaborate on their activities, and even a limited type of analysis depends on circumstantial evidence to supply essential clues.[169] Consultation of previous accounts is often needed to recover missing figures or to clarify ambiguous phrases. Some transactions can only be classified with reference to the general political or chronological context: the whitewashing of a parish church in the reign of Edward VI, for instance, was more likely to be a Reformation-related measure than a routine maintenance expense. Even so, ambiguities remain: does window repair involve stained glass, and therefore an ornament rather than a part of the fabric? Is the phrase 'from a stranger' used in connection with a gift or a burial? Was a particular payee in holy orders and the transaction therefore made to a 'priest'?[170] In view of these difficulties, it has been attempted to achieve consistency by classifying only explicit bequests as 'gifts', by considering only 'Sirs' and 'clerks' as priests, and by interpreting all expenditure on windows or glass as spending on 'ornaments'. Unspecified labour costs, meanwhile, have been entered under 'building'. In other cases, informed

---

[166] The categories are defined in Appendix 2.

[167] Another (but not fundamentally different) arrangement in Gibbs, 'Parish finance'. The choice of categories naturally reflects the evidence and the particular emphasis of a study.

[168] With one exception: all payments to persons in holy orders have been entered under 'priests'.

[169] For example other local records like Basing (ed.), *Fraternity Register* (for St Botolph), or Bailey (ed.), *Prescot Court Leet* (for the parish of the same name). As seen above, the amount of detail supplied in CWA could vary from year to year.

[170] The latter can be a problem in the later All Saints CWA (for example 1526–7).

guesses were used to determine whether, for instance, a 'book' had been purchased at the instigation of the king's commissioners ('crown') or the parishioners themselves ('ornaments').[171] Detailed local research (architectural development, manor court rolls, wills) was resorted to only if the question seemed to have a major impact on the general trends. The analysis in this section concentrates on the pre-Reformation developments, the Edwardian and Marian changes will be dealt with below.

Two separate (but structurally similar) database files were created for each case study, one for the income and one for the expenditure. Both consist, to use the software's terminology, of an identical number of 'records' (one for each year) and an appropriate number of 'fields' (one for each category). For technical and practical reasons, the common monetary unit is old pence.[172] A spreadsheet programme helped to split up bi- (or multi-)annual accounts and to draw the various figures. Due to the delicate nature of the evidence, it has not been attempted to undertake sophisticated statistical analysis. The material is basically presented as it appears in the manuscripts, apart from the arrangement in categories and the use of yearly or moving averages.

Turning to the development of total income, Figure 3.2 shows the inflation-adjusted 11-years averages of all case studies.[173] In spite of their shortcomings, absolute figures have been preferred to index figures in order to give an impression of the actual size of the financial transactions.[174] To avoid distortions by outstanding debts, the graphs include only the fresh income raised in any given year.[175]

The first striking feature is the great variety of turnovers. The spectrum ranges from nearly £30 for All Saints in the 1530s to the

---

[171] For example the two 'new' service books in Botolph CWA, 1548–9.

[172] To express amounts in pounds, the figures have to be divided by 240 (by 12 to arrive at shillings).

[173] Averages give a fairer impression of the actual burden carried by the parishioners in this period than medians, which would yield 'typical' or 'model' figures. The 11-years average figure for the total income (explained in Appendix 2) has been divided by the 11-years average of the index calculated by E. Phelps-Brown and S. Hopkins ('Seven centuries of consumables', *Economica*, **23** (1956), 296–315) for the same year and then multiplied by 100 to express it in the monetary value of the stable 1451–75 period, which the authors chose as the basis of their presentation. The method is basically that adopted by W. Bittle and R. Lane, 'Inflation and philanthropy in England', *EcHR*, 2nd Series 29 (1976), 203–10. Like any other index, it has its methodological drawbacks, but it remains the most authoritative one and a 'useful aid' (Dyer, *Standards of Living*, p. 229).

[174] Furthermore, the heterogeneous nature of the evidence and the diversity of parochial experiences prevents the choice of a meaningful common index basis.

[175] An idea of the size of arrears in each case study can be gained from the tables in Appendix 3. As argued above, parishes made great efforts to recover any outstanding dues.

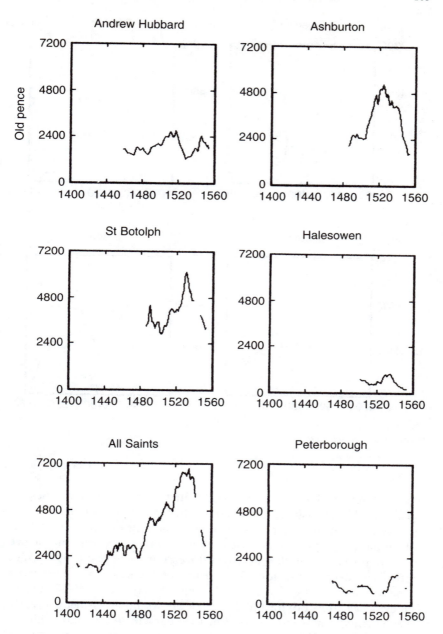

Figure 3.2   Inflation-adjusted 11-years averages of parish income in 10 case studies 1400–1560; unit: old pence (2400 d. = £10). See Table 3.2 for full parish details

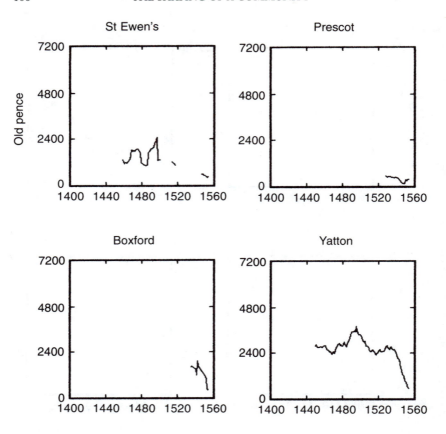

Figure 3.2 *concluded*

modest level of Halesowen, whose deflated average never reaches £5 (=1200 d.). Unsurprisingly, each case study tells its own story, but there are common features: the picture is certainly not one of universal decline, but (in most cases) of an increase in several waves to a peak on the eve of the Reformation, with a downward trend at some point after 1520. Particularly steep and steady pre-Reformation increases can be observed in the urban context of All Saints, Botolph Aldersgate, and Ashburton. The evidence from Boxford and Prescot allows no assessment of early developments, but seems to confirm the character of the latter phase, even though the Suffolk parish achieved a temporary reversal of the trend through the sale of plate in 1547. The only other example of a recovery around 1550 at Andrew Hubbard was due to extraordinary

Table 3.3   Average growth in parish income

Andrew Hubb.	1.013	Ashburton	1.015	Prescot	0.955
Bot. Aldersgate	1.014	Halesowen	1.007	Boxford	1.029
All Saints	1.014	Peterborough	1.011	Yatton	1.001
St Ewen's	1.011				

circumstances.[176] On the whole, parish turnovers peaked at some point between 1520 and 1540, with the exception of St Ewen's (no evidence in this period), Yatton (shortly before 1500), and Peterborough (shortly after 1540). The prevailing pattern is one of real growth up to a remarkably late date,[177] and of decline at some point late in Henry VIII's reign. This is not merely a reflection of trends in inflation, currency circulation, or population increases,[178] but apparently of genuine parochial developments.[179] The average growth figures shown in Table 3.3 confirm the basically rising trend for all pre-1548 accounts.[180] The only exception is Prescot, where the surviving evidence is of a rather late date. All this seems to be more easily compatible with recent revisionist assessments of parochial life than with the traditional picture of late medieval decline.[181]

---

[176] The parish administered the benefice under Edward VI and early in Elizabeth's reign: Hubbard CWA, 1549ff (these separate 'parsonage accounts' have been integrated into the respective years).

[177] Later even than in the case of testamentary bequests for religious purposes which peaked in the 1510s (according to the deflation of W. K. Jordan's data in Bittle and Lane, 'Inflation and philanthropy', 209).

[178] The Phelps-Brown/Hopkins index starts rising from the 1510s and continues to do so up to the 1550s and beyond. The greatest size of the circulating medium in the early Tudor period was reached in 1551 (with an estimated £2.66m: Challis, *Tudor Coinage*, p. 242), that is much later than the peak in parish finances (even for the undeflated figures). Rising parish income was not likely to be a reflection of increasing population either: the losses caused by the Black Death were not recovered until well into the sixteenth century (Hatcher, *Population and the English Economy*, pp. 63ff), and many places record growing revenues well before this date.

[179] See for example the growing reluctance to invest in areas (such as the cult of images) targeted by the crown's reforming policies: R. Whiting, 'Abominable idols', *JEH*, 33 (1982), 44. For possible socio-economic influences cf. Chapter 5.

[180] Growth has been calculated by dividing the fresh income (in unadjusted 11-year averages) from year $x + 1$ by the figure for year x. If the result is >1, the revenue increased, if it is <1, it fell. The average pre-Reformation growth is the average of all these results from the earliest evidence to 1547.

[181] Fundraising is admittedly only one, but an important aspect of the general religious climate. The critical view of the state of late medieval parishes held by historians like G. G. Coulton still influences Dickens, *English Reformation*, pp. 68–74. In contrast, Duffy, *Stripping of the Altars*, p. 479, contends 'that into the 1530s the vigour, richness, and creativity of late medieval religion was undiminished'; similar Haigh, *English Reformations*, p. 38.

It would take up too much room to elaborate on the specific composition of the churchwardens' resources in each of the case studies. The emphasis here has to be on a general and comparative discussion.[182] The stacks shown in Appendix 4 (i), representing an addition of the percentage figures scored by each of the major categories in the ten parishes, allow an assessment of the aggregate distribution of income.[183] Concentrating on the overall and pre-Reformation graphs, rent appears as the leading category of fresh income with 200 points or a fifth of the total, followed by collections and ales, which contribute over a tenth each, and everything else trailing at some distance. Gilds and money lending made noteworthy contributions, the latter especially at Boxford from the last pre-Reformation account.[184] The prominence of regular quarterly items such as rents and collections gave parochial finance a certain predictability and ensured a steady cash flow throughout the year. The wardens did not depend on the more variable elements such as burials or gifts, and extraordinary efforts could serve as an option to boost revenues for particular needs.[185] Sales were very common, but of modest financial importance; they may have served stock-clearing rather than fundraising purposes.[186] Most parishes shared the same basic range of income categories, even though local custom and socio-economic circumstances could offer other, more 'exotic' fundraising opportunities, ranging from indulgences, market profits, or contributions of shipowners, to a share in the profits of the tin mining industry.[187] Rents, collections, ales, and casuals, however, seem to have been the core items, even across the Channel.[188]

---

[182] Summary tables for each parish can be found in Appendix 3 (based on the definitions of categories made in Appendix 2).

[183] The maximum score for a category would be 1000, that is if it formed 100 per cent of the income in each case study.

[184] Shepton Mallet in Somerset lent no less than £52 to three individuals in 1507–8 and 'loaning money to parishioners was not an uncommon practice': French, 'Local identity', pp. 241–2.

[185] Boxford CWA, 1535–6 includes a special play account with income of over £20.

[186] Occasionally, they helped to subsidize a major special effort, as in the case of the land purchased at All Saints (CWA 1524–5). Everywhere, surplus building material (wood, tiles, lime, lead and so on) was sold on a regular basis.

[187] Halesowen raised some money from its relics; Thomson, *Early Tudor Church*, pp. 267–71, provides examples for indulgences and income influenced by the local economy; I. Leadam (ed.), *Select Cases before the Star Chamber* (vol. ii, London, 1911), p. cxxi (market surplus to three Bristol parishes); French, 'Local identity', p. 237 (tin mining profits).

[188] Constant, 'Source négligée', 511–19.

Given the 'merry old England' image associated with much of late medieval parish life,[189] the dominance of rents is somewhat surprising. Property revenues in fact supplied the communities with a constant source of income despite the inevitable administrative and maintenance costs: by the end of Henry VIII's reign, rent surpluses at Peterborough and Ashburton had soared from rather modest levels to £6 and over £8 respectively. Andrew Hubbard possessed but one major tenement yielding some £2 annually, but wealthy All Saints enjoyed a steady profit of over £20 by the late 1540s.[190] We have observed that wardens gradually acquired landholding capacity, but it is worth investigating how so *much* property found its way into the parish portfolio.

The overwhelming part was a consequence of penitential bequests.[191] Recent historiography has provided ample evidence for the importance of intercession and reciprocity in late medieval religion: the 'dead' supported the 'living' through their benefactions, and the latter in turn offered their prayers for the health of the donors' souls.[192] In addition to chantries and lights placed under parochial supervision, anniversaries provided another reason for large-scale gifts of rents and property. This was by no means just an English phenomenon. In late medieval Germany, the increasing number of foundations left an ever more prominent mark on the liturgical life of the parish,[193] and the same must have been true elsewhere in Europe. At Frizet in present-day Belgium, commemorative masses had been commissioned by no less than half of the resident families with endowments to the value of 200 days of a labourer's pay, while at Floreffe near Namur, the parish had accumulated 353 rents from 180 donations.[194] The financial benefit for the community derived from the fact that the costs of its obligations (typically the celebration of a 'placebo' on the eve of the anniversary and a 'dirige' and requiem mass on the day itself) were normally much lower than its income from the property.[195]

---

[189] For example Jessopp, 'Parish life', 431–47; Hutton, *Merry England*, ch. 1. The broadest, if impressionistic, surveys of parish income to date in Swanson, *Church and Society*, pp. 217–28, and Thomson, *Early Tudor Church*, pp. 264–300.

[190] Calculations based on 11-year-averages of rent income minus expenses for maintenance, quit rents, and vacations.

[191] As seen in Chapter 2.3.3, parishes did also actively invest in landed property themselves, but gifts from benefactors could still be involved (for example the parish plate used for the land purchase in All Saints CWA 1524–5).

[192] The concept is most poignantly expressed in Burgess, 'Benefactions of mortality', and Duffy, *Stripping of the Altars*, p. 134. Brown, 'Medieval Wiltshire', argues a similar case.

[193] P. Schuler, 'Das Anniversar' in his *Die Familie als sozialer und historischer Verband* (Sigmaringen, 1987), pp. 87, 108 (I am grateful to Prof. K.-H. Spiess for making me aware of this essay).

[194] Genicot, *Rural Communities*, pp. 95, 106–7; Aubrun, *Paroisse*, p. 169.

[195] Details about foundation and celebration in Burgess, 'Anniversary in late medieval Bristol'.

Numerous examples of pious benefaction can be cited from this sample: at Botolph Aldersgate, Ralph Rattespray had left an annual 4 s. from a tenement in Ratton Rowe for a lamp, Andrew Newport £1 from the 'Helm' in Cornhill for an obit, while 12 d. from the Barbican tenement belonging to the St Stephen gild in St Sepulchre 'were geven … to the mantennance of Lampes Lightes & soch like'. The obit of the former churchwarden Alan Johnson cost the parish some 10 s. every year, but the property received to pay for it yielded between £1 and £2.[196] All Saints, Bristol, derived an annual profit of roughly 6 s. from the quit rent given by William Newbury of a house in Baldwin Street, while at St Ewen's across the road, John Mathew's gift of a house worth 33 s. 4 d. *per annum* was dependent only on the payment of 6 s. 8 d. each for an obit, the poor, and weekly prayers.[197] At Ashburton, 5 s. from a messuage and garden held by George Wyndeyate, three closes in the tenure of John Medytt, and two closes held by Lawrence Elys supported one obit and one light, while 3 s. 4 d. out of 'Sumpter Parkes' and 'Leynhill Close' were linked to another anniversary.[198] In the accounts of more rural places like Yatton or Halesowen, endowment often took the form of livestock rather than land. And yet, the influence of the 'dead' and of contemporary ideas about salvation extended beyond the devising of property. Countless parishioners invested money on an ad-hoc basis to ensure an appropriate ceremonial and ornamental framework for their funerals and obits, and others readily paid the more or less standard charge of 6 s. 8 d. (a reduced rate of 3 s. 4 d. applied to children) for the privilege to be buried within the nave rather than the churchyard. There was a strong preference for parish burial even in a place like London with many potential alternatives (cathedrals, friaries and so on), and the same can be observed in other English or Continental cities.[199] Fees for interment in the church made up 10 per cent of All Saints' income as early as the first decade of the fifteenth century, and financial contributions by local gilds were yet another consequence of this ubiquitous interest in regular and corporate intercession.

---

[196] Botolph CWA, 1559–60 and 1516–17 (Johnson). At Andrew Hubbard, the obit of Juliana Fairhead (£1) was more than provided for by the £4 from the property devised in her will of 1442 (Sharpe (ed.), *Calendar of Wills*, ii. 563, and Kitching (ed.), *Chantry Certificates*, p. 44).

[197] Burgess, 'Anniversary in late medieval Bristol', 200.

[198] To name but two: H. Hanham, 'Chantries at Ashburton', 118.

[199] V. Harding, 'Burial choice and burial location in later medieval London' in S. Bassett (ed.), *Death in Towns* (Leicester, 1992), p. 122; see also R. Dinn, ' "Monuments answerable to men's work" ', *JEH*, **46** (1995), 242, Bury. 'L'étude des lieux de sépulture a confirmé que la structure paroissiale occupe une place centrale dans la vie religieuse des laïcs lausannois': V. Pasche, *'Pour le salut de mon âme'* (Lausanne, 1989), p. 117. Burial within the church was, of course, a sign of social status.

The overall impact of the phenomenon on parish finance can be illustrated in two stages: first, by means of a closer look at the chronological development in this sample, and second, by attempting to place the emerging pattern in a more general context.

The pie charts in Figures 3.3 (a), (b), and (c) shall help us to tackle the first task. Each individual pie represents total parish income in a given period with the exception of balances or arrears. In all of them, the chequered slice indicates the share of the various elements connected to the cult of the 'dead', the lighter section active fundraising activities by the 'living', and the darkest slice those items not clearly belonging to either category, for instance debts or gifts which could come from both present or past parishioners.[200]

Starting with the summarizing pie charts of Figure 3.3(a), the importance of the 'dead' is immediately apparent: they account for 35 per cent of total income in the sample, both in the pre- and post-Reformation periods (to 1560). The pies on the right-hand side, however, show that a refined chronological analysis reveals change rather than stability. The accumulation of bequests from generations of benefactors led to a marked increase from 27 per cent in the first ever accounts to 44 per cent on the eve of the Reformation, with a reversal of the trend in the wake of the Edwardian attack on prayers for the dead (dissolution of gilds, confiscation of rents for 'superstitious' purposes[201]) and little change under Mary.

The development emerges even more sharply if each case study is analysed separately (Figures 3.3(b) and (c)). Focusing on the earliest accounts first, comparison of the two columns of pie charts is striking: the 'dead' slice is much more prominent on the left, while the 'living' slice dominates on the right. Looking at their headings, it would appear that financial regimes varied according to the social milieu: in market towns or rural areas, the lion's share of parish income derived from active fundraising by the living, in central

---

[200] The items included in each category are listed in Appendix 2. In Figures 3.3(b) and (c), the number of yearly units scrutinized appears in brackets alongside the name of the parish. To enable comparisons with the Reformation period, the number reflects the amount of evidence available for the reign of Edward VI. The exception is Botolph Aldersgate in Figure 3.3(b), where a longer period has been preferred to reduce the distorting effect of extraordinarily high rent revenues in CWA 1471–2. Absolute figures (in old pence) are the unit in Figures 3.3(b) and (c), but percentage points (scored in the whole sample) in Figure 3.3(a).

[201] The percentage points for this reign only add up to around 900, because of the lack of Edwardian evidence for Peterborough. For the practical consequences of the chantries act of 1547 on obits see Hutton, 'Local impact', pp. 121ff.

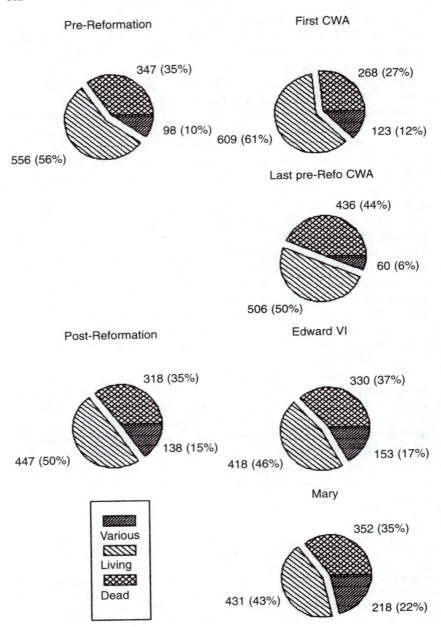

Figure 3.3 (a) Aggregate income from the 'living' and the 'dead' in a sample of 10 parishes (9 parishes *t*. Edward VI): summary of pre-and post-Reformation development; unit: percentage points

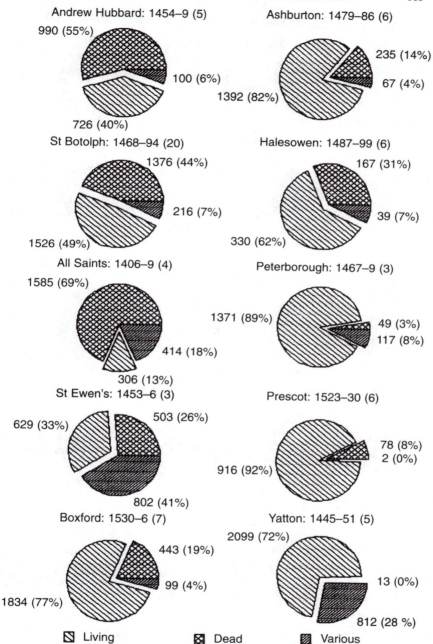

Figure 3.3(b)   Income from the 'living' and the 'dead' in 10 case studies: earliest accounts, with dates and number of years analysed; unit: averages in old pence

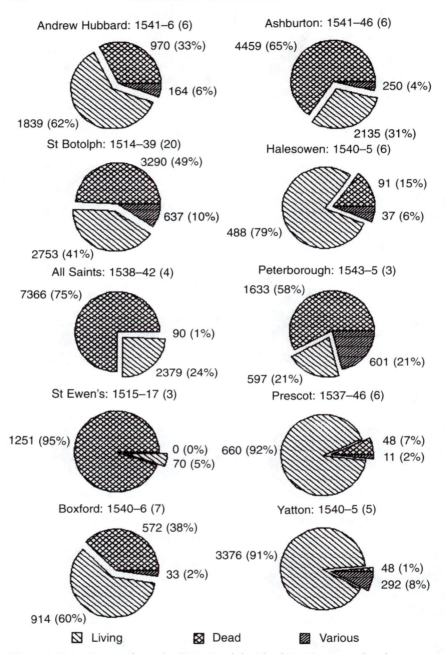

Figure 3.3(c) Income from the 'living' and the 'dead' in 10 case studies: last pre-Reformation CWA, with dates and number of years analysed; unit: old pence a/v

London and provincial capitals like Bristol, it tended to come from the dead.[202]

The term 'tendency' should be stressed: at Halesowen, for instance, turnover was so low that the modest sums of around 10 s. from rents and 4 s. from lifestock amounted to 31 per cent of overall income,[203] a figure higher than at St Ewen's with over £2 of rent revenue. The Bristol parish, however, steadily accumulated more and more property: extending the analysis to the first 20 accounts, the 'dead's' share rises to over 49 per cent, clearly in line with a more general trend. By the last pre-Reformation years (Figure 3.3(c)), contributions by the living were down in five out of ten cases,[204] unchanged at Prescot (a parish which never acquired landed endowment), and up only at Halesowen, Andrew Hubbard, All Saints, and Yatton.[205]

Evidence from other sets of accounts seems to confirm the pattern in this sample. In late fifteenth-century London, rents contributed 68 per cent of Stephen Coleman Street's income and a staggering 90 per cent at St Mary-at-Hill.[206] Outside the capital, landed revenue increased for instance at Bath and Bridgwater in Somerset, or Tavistock in Devon.[207] The same could happen even in wealthy rural communities: the share of the 'dead' at Boxford grew from 19 to 38 per cent over a relatively short period, and a similar analysis for Tilney in Norfolk would show a yet more pronounced development.[208] On the other hand, some London

---

[202] Ales/entertainments dominate in the 'living' regimes of Ashburton, Boxford, and Yatton (for a general discussion see J. Bennett, 'Conviviality and charity in medieval and early modern England', *PaP*, **134** (1992), 19–41), collections at Peterborough and Halesowen, rates at Prescot. The Bristol-based assessment of Burgess, 'Benefactions of mortality', p. 78, that such items were little more than 'pin money' compared to pious benefaction should clearly not be transferred to England as a whole.

[203] A similar picture in Mercer (ed.), *CWA at Betrysden*, for example pp. 68–9 (1514–15), where modest revenues from livestock, rents, and burial fees dominate the village's small budget almost totally (income in that year: £3 15 s. 9 d.).

[204] Not necessarily in absolute terms, but their relative importance decreased due to the faster rise of overall parish income.

[205] Ales had been introduced at Halesowen, an environment more likely to be dependent on the living anyway, and there had been no further landed benefactions at Andrew Hubbard, a relatively poor parish with some internal problems. The increases at Yatton and All Saints are probably optical illusions caused by a large amount of unspecified items inflating the 'various' category in the first CWA.

[206] Gibbs, 'Parish finance', p. 190 (1480s); Mary-at-Hill CWA, 1477–94.

[207] French, 'Local identity', pp. 89, 102. At Bridgwater, property-related income rose from virtually nil to 50 per cent by the 1470s: T. Dilks (ed.), *Bridgwater Borough Archives*, passim. At Tavistock, a mere 9 s. 9 d. (= 8 per cent) derived from rents in 1385–6, but £6 10 s. 10 d. (= 46 per cent) in 1470–1: Worth (ed.), *Tavistock*, pp. 1, 11.

[208] In the latter, the CWA of 1485 record a mere 9 d. from a gild and 8 s. 8½ d. from rents as part of a total income of over £4, while in 1545, the rent revenue of £3 11 s. 4 d. made

parishes moved into the opposite direction: examples include the 'living' orientated Andrew Hubbard, but also All Hallows London Wall, and All Hallows Staining, both from the less prosperous periphery of the metropolis.[209] An interesting case is St Michael Cornhill, where a gap in the sources (1476–1547) divides a 'living' from a 'dead' orientated phase of parochial history.[210] Prosperity was clearly another important factor in the development of a parish's financial regime, and a simple urban/rural differentiation would not do justice to the complexity of the phenomenon.[211]

Nevertheless, wealthy city-centre communities tended to depend more strongly on the 'dead' than those in humbler market towns and the countryside. Norwich or York, unfortunately, cannot be studied in detail, but glimpses into other provincial capitals are suggestive. In the case of St Petrock, Exeter, rents dominated from an early stage and increased during the pre-Reformation period.[212] In rural Somerset, on the other hand, ales all but monopolized revenues at Tintinhull, Trull, Nettlecombe, and Stogursey (where they extinguished the early flickers of a rent regime), while Banwell's finances relied predominantly on collections.[213] At Morebath and Chagford in Devon, ales supported the parish as well as various 'stores': in 1540, for instance, they provided over three quarters of both the high warden's and young men's income in the former,[214] and similar proportions of the revenues of the St Michael and St Katherine stores in the latter.[215] Moving outside the south west, the market town parish of Thame possessed some landed endowments, but collections and ales remained the more important items, and at

up most of the total revenue of £5 5s. 2d.: A. Stallard (ed.), *CWA of Tilney All Saints* (London, 1922), pp. 62 and 166. I am grateful to Berendina Galloway for drawing my attention to these accounts.

[209] Gibbs, 'Parish finance', p. 190.

[210] Overall (ed.), *Michael Cornhill*, passim.

[211] See the note of caution sounded in M. Rubin, 'Religious culture in town and country' in D. Abulafia et al. (eds), *Church and City 1000–1500* (Cambridge, 1992), pp. 3–22.

[212] Seventy-four per cent in CWA 1452–3 and 90 per cent in 1512–13: R. Dymond, 'The history of St Petrock', *Devonshire Association*, 14 (1882), 419ff and 441. For Norwich, the quota of over 90 per cent of Norwich parishioners who made testamentary bequests to their church points in the same direction: Tanner, *Church in Norwich*, pp. 222–3.

[213] French, 'Local identity', pp. 91, 94, 104, 137–8.

[214] 55s. 6½d. out of £3 10s. 10½d.: Binney (ed.), *Morebath*, p. 114–15. In the same year, the young men's wardens raised 24s. 4½d. from their ale (total income: 27s. ½ d.).

[215] Ales raised £3 13s. 8d. out of a total of £5 10s. 11d. for the wardens of St Michael in 1501, and over £7 out of £11 for the officers of St Katherine's store in 1536–7: F. Osborne (ed.), *The CWA of St Michael's Church, Chagford 1480–1600* (Chagford, 1979), pp. 29, 130–1.

Mickfield and Mildenhall in Suffolk, the accounts point to an equally important role of active fundraising activities by the living.[216]

As for the reasons for the apparent dichotomy, little more than speculation can be offered at this stage.[217] Originally, the 'living' must have been the basis of all parochial regimes, and most wardens continued to expect some sort of financial contribution from them throughout our period. Collections, perhaps the most elementary fundraising device, may have emerged as a natural equivalent to the rhythm of the seasons and seigneurial demands, but they were soon supplemented by the financial benefits of communal rituals and entertainments associated with certain dates (such as Whitsun or Corpus Christi) in the liturgical calendar.[218] By the eve of the Reformation, English parishioners participated in an extensive ceremonial life which combined universal observations on major feasts with local specialities such as Hocktide games and Corpus Christi processions (documented predominantly in urban communities) or the Plough Monday collections of many rural parishes.[219]

But how can we account for the gradual socio-economic differentiation of parochial finance? Two factors may have promoted the 'living'-orientation in agricultural environments: the stronger and more persistent collection impetus provided by seasonal and seigneurial forces on the one hand, and the more 'central' role of the parish on the other. Only the latter, of course, can be put on a firmer empirical footing. Towns normally contained a number of rivalling ecclesiastical and secular institutions: monasteries and cathedrals for alternative religious provision, crafts or gilds for conviviality, and company or town halls for the conduct of any type of secular business.[220] In these circumstances, parish celebrations had to be particularly elaborate and spectacular to catch the eye, and the organization of processions and ritual gatherings normally drained rather than augmented the churchwardens'

---

[216] Carnwath, 'CWA of Thame', pp. 190–2; the Mickfield CWA are in the Suffolk Record Office, Ipswich (FB 19/E4/2) and feature plays, collections and ales, for example in 1538–9. I am grateful to Pauline M. Smith for this information. For Mildenhall see the forthcoming edition of the parish accounts by John Craig.

[217] This and many related points have been elaborated in C. Burgess and B. Kümin, 'Penitential bequests and parish regimes in late medieval England', *JEH*, **44** (1993), 610–30.

[218] The liturgical and ritual year is now exhaustively discussed in the opening chapters of D. Cressy, *Bonfires and Bells*, Duffy, *Stripping of the Altars*, and Hutton, *Merry England*.

[219] Hutton, *Merry England*, pp. 17–18, 23–6.

[220] A particularly well-documented example is Coventry: C. Phythian-Adams, 'Ceremony and the citizen' in P. Clark and P. Slack (eds), *Crisis and Order in English Towns 1500–1700* (London, 1972), pp. 57–85.

resources.[221] Outside the big cities, however, the 'living' were offered few of these distractions, and regular parish entertainment became an important fundraising device. The key element in the financial success of rural festivities was their association with church ales (hugely profitable at Yatton in this sample) and – often – plays or music as additional attractions.[222] At places like Ashburton, dramatic activities occurred on a regular basis, while Boxford and Bethersden staged them as parts of particular fundraising campaigns.[223] In the Thames valley, to take another suggestive example, parish-sponsored acting increased in direct correlation to the distance from the capital. There was of course urban drama, too, but the famous mystery cycles were organized by gilds and municipal authorities rather than churchwardens.[224]

On the other hand, there are several potential explanations for the prevalence of pious benefaction in major towns. From the beginning, many urban parishes depended on communal rather than seigneurial gifts,[225] and parishioners may have felt a more immediate responsibility to make generous voluntary donations. Towards the end of the Middle Ages, the doctrine of purgatory provided further incentives, and the friars as the principal promoters were most active in the bigger towns.[226] The two most important factors, however, must have been the boroughs' superior wealth and greater tenurial freedom. The mercantile elites of London and Bristol could dispose of much more extensive spare resources than their counterparts in smaller towns or manors.[227] From a legal point of view, burgage tenure allowed the devising of property by

---

[221] For the 'centrality' of the rural parish and town/country fundraising differences in Somerset: French, 'Local identity', pp. 81, 123, 187.

[222] 'The major fund raising effort during the year [in Berkshire villages] was the church ale held annually at Whitsun': Johnston, 'Parish entertainments', p. 335; 'especially in the countryside, [ales] were the largest single source of parochial revenue': Hutton, *Merry England*, p. 28.

[223] Wasson (ed.), *Devon*, pp. 17–30 (Ashburton); Boxford CWA, 1535–6; Mercer (ed.), *CWA at Betrysden*, pp. 3–5. Some churchwardens went to court to claim their share of parish plays profits (see the evidence quoted in Chapter 2.2.2, p.26, n. 85). London parishes seem to have used plays only in very exceptional circumstances: Thomson, *Early Tudor Church*, pp. 266–7.

[224] Johnston, 'What revels are in hand' (Paper at Kalamazoo 1993) and 'The plays of the religious gilds of York', *Speculum*, 50 (1975), 80, 87.

[225] See the collective foundations of urban churches discussed in Chapter 2.1.1.

[226] W. Southern, *Western Society and the Church in the Middle Ages* (London, 1970), pp. 279–99.

[227] It is estimated that London and other provincial capitals experienced a 15-fold increase in their prosperity between 1334 and 1515, while growth was much slower elsewhere: Schofield, 'Distribution of wealth', p. 101. As mentioned above, prosperity could differ significantly within the same town: Gibbs, 'Parish finance', pp. 124 and 191, points to the discrepancy between central and extramural London parishes.

will, a privilege otherwise unknown before the Statute of Wills (1540). This must have made pious benefaction easier, even though the contrast should not be overstated. The seigneurial classes, after all, were able to alienate property everywhere,[228] and legal loopholes could be exploited all over the country: the importance of enfeoffment to use has been emphasized above, and the socio-economic climate after the Black Death eased conditions even for customary tenants.[229] One particularly significant development was the acceptance, at least in some manors, of arrangements made by peasants on their deathbed, which allowed them to 'fashion true strategies of inheritance' and to benefit charitable and pious purposes if they wished.[230] This may help to explain why rent regimes could make headway in all social contexts, even though rural levels of endowment normally remained well below those in metropolitan communities.

The evidence from both regimes suggests that the laity must have had a greater understanding of the Church's teachings than is often assumed. Benefactors seem to have responded to contemporary penitential doctrine not only out of some dumb fear of the torments of purgatory, but with confident and informed strategies to secure their souls' salvation.[231] The 'living', meanwhile, realized that adequate parochial provision depended on their regular contributions, and the rising parochial budgets show that many offered more than was required. There were of course penalties for those who did not pay their share,[232] but also potential spiritual rewards for those who did.[233] Recent scholarship increasingly questions the conventional scepticism about the level of 'Christianization' among the late medieval population. It has been legitimately said that the emphasis on paganism, magic, and superstition in many accounts of the period does 'insufficient justice ... to the ability and readiness of lay audiences to assimilate the complexities of doctrine'.[234] Such views tend to ignore the laity's

---

[228] Their religious priorities, however, often lay outside the parish: C. Richmond, 'Religion and the fifteenth-century English gentleman' in R. B. Dobson (ed.), The Church, Politics, and Patronage in the Fifteenth Century (Gloucester, 1984), 193–208.

[229] Pollock and Maitland, History of English Law, pp. 260–313, 325–30, and Bateson (ed.), Borough Customs, ii. 90–102, 201–4 (burgage tenure); R. Hilton, The Decline of Serfdom in Medieval England (London, 1969), pp. 44–51; Dyer, Lords and Peasants, pp. 210ff, 373 (tenurial changes).

[230] L. Bonfield and L. Poos, 'The development of the deathbed transfer in medieval English manor courts', Cambridge Law Journal, 47 (1988), 417, 426 (quote).

[231] Burgess, 'Fond thing', p. 69; Schuler, 'Anniversar', p. 104.

[232] Examples of presentments for example in Wood-Legh (ed.), Kentish Visitations, pp. 87, 153 (outstanding contributions to the wages of parish employees).

[233] Swanson, Church and Society, p. 250.

[234] Rosser, 'Parish and guild', p. 42. Thomas, Decline of Magic, and Delumeau, Catholicism, are perhaps the prime exponents of the sceptical 'school'.

orthodox attitude towards the most important sacraments, and the countless examples of deliberate and informed investment in religious services, both in England and the Continent.[235] 'There is absolutely no evidence' that the people who kept the many customs and rituals of the late medieval calendar year 'were anything but Christian', and 'the question of pagan origins' of their pastimes need not enter into the discussion.[236] Not everything was as pure and sophisticated as leading contemporary theologians (and modern observers) might have wished, but at this local level at least there was 'no substantial gulf ... between the religion of the clergy and the educated elite on the one hand and that of the people at large on the other'.[237]

On a more prosaic note, the two regimes made a great difference to parish administration. Churchwardens in collection- and entertainment-based regimes had to organize and supervise a continuous series of events to make ends meet. Their main preoccupations must have been of a financial nature, and ordinary parishioners were almost constantly involved in the day-to-day running of their own affairs. In a generously endowed parish, on the other hand, the emphasis on property-management and intercession resulted in a different pattern of communal participation. Revenues from lands and rents could be administered more effectively by a smaller executive body,[238] but the presence of all inhabitants was required to meet the benefactors' stipulation for prayers of the whole community. If parishioners neglected these duties, property passed on to other beneficiaries.[239] Small wonder, then, that obits and anniversaries were kept so meticulously.

The comparison of per-capita revenues within the sample provides further indications that the financial profile of a parish was influenced by its social context. Methodological problems, however, make it difficult to arrive at more than approximate figures. Parish income can be calculated relatively easily, but reliable population information is

---

[235] Brigden, *London and the Reformation*, pp. 12–23 (parochial attitudes to the Eucharist); Blickle, 'Communal Reformation', 223–6 (the 'Christianization' of the late medieval German peasantry).

[236] Hutton, *Merry England*, p. 72, with reference to Cressy, *Bonfires and Bells*, p. 3.

[237] Duffy, *Stripping of the Altars*, p. 2.

[238] As observed in the chapter on 'sources', rural communities tended to govern by a full parish assembly, while wealthy urban parishes left a great deal to a few 'masters' or 'auditors' (cf. Chapter 6.2).

[239] Burgess, 'Anniversary in late medieval Bristol', 200–1. John Causton's chantry endowment had originally been given to St Helen's Bishopsgate, but was in the possession of St Mary-at-Hill by the late fifteenth century: Mary-at-Hill CWA, pp. 4–9.

notoriously difficult to find. For our purposes, clues have to be extracted from heterogeneous sources such as poll taxes, lay subsidies, muster rolls, ecclesiastical censuses, and (predominantly) chantry certificates. Quite apart from the pitfalls presented by each of these records individually, there are major hazards in trying to compare data deriving from all these different types of evidence. The population figures included in Table 3.4 are thus at best rough guidelines, and the per-capita estimates in the last column have to be treated with great caution.[240] The three most doubtful areas are, first, whether chantry certificates, compiled in the late 1540s on a parish-per-parish basis and therefore the most appropriate sources, provide rounded or accurate figures of the number of communicants (especially if they clash with information gained from early baptismal registers[241]), second, to what extent population levels were higher, if at all, in the 1540s compared to the late 1370s,[242] and, third, what sort of multiplier should be used to extrapolate from lay subsidies[243] or household-based assessments.[244] None of these

---

[240] Most of the methodological information (multipliers for chantry certificate or taxation figures to arrive at total population; conversion formulas to compare different types of evidence) has been taken from E. A. Wrigley and R. S. Schofield, *The Population History of England 1541–1871* (Cambridge, 1989 edn), pp. 565–8. R. M. Smith, *The Population History of England 1000–1540* (2 vols, Manchester, forthcoming) will soon provide a new authoritative survey for the medieval period. The per-capita figure in the last column results from a division of annual income (average of last ten available pre-Reformation accounting years) by the estimated total population.

[241] The chantry survey figures are taken from the editions quoted in Chapter 3.1. Certificates and registers very rarely survive for the same parish, but at Andrew Hubbard the registers reveal an annual average of 17.77 baptisms between March 1540 and March 1550 (GL, MS 1278/1) which – assuming a ratio of 30 births per 1000 inhabitants – suggests a population of some 592. The adjusted chantry certificate figure (that is multiplied by 100/75.1 to account for all inhabitants), in contrast, amounts to 375. The former yields a per-capita average of 6.23 d., the latter 9.83 d.

[242] The conversion formula used for Peterborough assumes that the 1377 figure has to be multiplied by 1.645 to arrive at the number of communicants on the eve of the Reformation. It should be noted, however, that in some regions mid-sixteenth-century population levels were still lower than in the 1360s: L. Poos, *A Rural Society after the Black Death: Essex 1350–1525* (Cambridge, 1991), for example, p. 98. The per-capita figure for Peterborough could thus be an underestimate.

[243] In the case of Boxford, Harvey (ed.), *Suffolk in 1524*, pp. 13–15, provides 111 taxpayers in 1524, and Boxford CWA, p. xii, 101 names for the muster roll of 1522; Wrigley and Schofield suggest a multiplier of 10/3 for both which results in a total population of 370 (subsidy) and 336 (muster). The higher figure features in the table, and it has to be kept in mind that this is probably still an underestimate of the population in the 1540s. No such restriction applies to Ashburton, where the estimate is based on the 1544 subsidy with 231 names (total population 770): Stoate (ed.), *Devon Lay Subsidy Rolls 1543–5*, pp. 192–3.

[244] In a paper to the Cambridge Group for the History of Population and Social Structure (21 October 1991), David Palliser suggested a multiplier of 5.1 for the bishops' census of

Table 3.4 Pre-Reformation per-capita income in 12 parishes (last 10 available years; currency unit = old pence)

Parish	Size/Type	A/V total income	Population info. (Source)	Total pop.[1]	Per-capita figure
All Saints, Bristol	S/Ca/Ce	12197 (1530–42)	180 (Chantry)	240	50.82
Mary-at-Hill, London	Me/Ca/Ce	22636 (1479–94)	400 (Chantry)	532	42.55
St Ewen's, Bristol	S/Ca/Ce	2054 (1492–1517)	56 (Chantry)	75	27.39
Yatton, Somerset	Me/R	9086 (1535–45)	500 (Chantry)	666	13.64
Ashburton, Devon	Me/T+Ma	9976 (1537–46)	231 (1544 subsidy)	770	12.95
Botolph Aldersg., London	L/Ca/E	14910 (1524–39)	1100 (Chantry)	1465	10.18
Andrew Hubbard, London	Me/Ca/Ce	3687 (1535–46)	282 (Chantry)	375	9.83
Boxford, Suffolk	Me/R	3017 (1537–46)	111 (1524 subsidy)	370	8.15
Peterborough	L/T+Ts	5036 (1536–45)	790 (Poll Tax 1377)	1730[2]	2.91
Edmund, Salisbury	L/T/Ce	5328 (1523–43)	1700 (Chantry)	2263	2.35
Halesowen, Worcs.	L/T+Ts	999 (1536–45)	280 families (1563)	1428	0.69
Prescot, Lancs.	L/T+Ts	700 (1531–46)	1000 (Chantry)	1332	0.53

Key: S = small (population under 250); Me = medium (under 1000); L = large (over 1000)
Ca = (provincial) capital; Ma = manor; R = rural; T = market town; Ts = townships
Ce = central; E = extramural; [ ] = rough estimate (data from different periods)

1. For multipliers and methodology see the notes in the text and Wrigley and Schofield, *Population History*, pp. 565–8.
2. Poll tax figure multiplied by 1.645 to arrive at an estimate of communicants in the late 1540s and the latter multiplied by 100/75.1 to represent total population.

questions can be answered with any certainty, and inaccuracies in the absolute figures are almost inevitable. Nevertheless, the table reveals very distinct differences between different types of parishes and even major modifications in population estimates would not alter the overall trends. General prosperity and religious enthusiasm mattered of course, but on the whole smaller parishes raised more than larger ones and central metropolitan communities more than those situated outside the walls, in market towns, or rural environments. In this sample, city-centre churches in (provincial) capitals levied most, prosperous rural places considerably less, and moderate market towns with a large territory least from each inhabitant. All Saints' 50.82 d. (= 4 s. 3 d.) are an impressive testimony to the size of parochial turnovers in its category.[245] Much of this derived from landed bequests by past parishioners, but the rents still had to be paid by the 'living' tenants at the time.

How big or small were these sums in contemporary terms? The inhabitants of larger towns may have had easier access to money and more spare resources, but standards of living varied greatly, and many must have found it difficult to divert cash to the parish. In about 1500, a wholesaler could earn up to £100, but labourers had to cope with just £2, and there was of course an increasing problem of poverty.[246] For the majority of Englishmen and -women, ecclesiastical dues were a formidable expense, and it has to be emphasized that Table 3.4 covers only a fraction of their overall commitments. Tithes, customary dues, contributions to gilds, voluntary offerings, and especially payments for the upkeep of outlying chapels are all not included here. This is particularly relevant for Halesowen and Prescot at the bottom of the list, where the churchwardens raised less than a penny from each member of their congregation. Due to the large territorial size, many parishioners must have lived too far away to participate fully in the life of the mother church, and local chapels probably provided a more convenient centre for their social and religious needs (see Chapter 4.3). Still, this was little comfort for the parish wardens, and the contrast to other communities

families in 1563. Given that this survey was compiled some 15 years after the chantry survey (and thus at a time of higher population) the per-capita figure for Halesowen is probably an underestimate.

[245] Mary-at-Hill in London, another metropolitan city-centre community, would probably score an even higher average in the mid-sixteenth century, but the relevant CWA have not been available. The division of the late fifteenth-century average by the 1547-population figure – as a rough but inadequate guide – produces the per-capita income of 42½d. (3 s. 6½d).

[246] Dyer, *Standards of Living*, p. 196. Parish accounts contain a lot of incidental information on wages: a craftsman could expect roughly 6 d. a day (for example Edmund CWA, 1500-1: John Plummer), but payments varied according to qualification and location.

is probably too pronounced to be explained by unfortunate structural circumstances only. Yatton, for instance, levied over 1 s. per inhabitant in an equally 'living'-based regime. Admittedly a smaller and more focused parish, it is difficult to see how such a discrepancy could be explained without some (unquantifiable) differences in resources or attitudes as well. Compared to the few shillings surplus income of many a peasant, 13.64 d. (c. 1 s. 1½ d.) was a very remarkable sum indeed.[247] This was by no means a unique case of rural extravaganza. As early as 1430, Tintinhull levied the 'considerable' figure of 2 d. from each inhabitant'.[248] At Morebath, socio-economic conditions may have been rather modest, but the community's 'hyperactive' support of traditional religious and social life meant that the main wardens could expect some 5 d. per inhabitant in an average year on the eve of the Reformation. If all other gilds and stores are taken into account, the figure rises to over 14 d.[249] Just as in modern peasant societies, 'ceremonial' purposes absorbed a considerable part of agricultural resources in late medieval England.[250]

Whatever the general trend, there were always 'special cases'. Andrew Hubbard confirms its peculiar position, raising much less than its London or Bristol city-centre counterparts, but still significantly more than for instance St Edmund Salisbury. Botolph Aldersgate, situated in a less prosperous extramural location, appears behind Yatton, while Ashburton comes a surprising fifth. The parish consisted of a closely connected borough and manor, and the coincidence of secular and ecclesiastical boundaries may have provided an additional impetus. In such circumstances, the church could become the unrivalled centre of religious as well as social life and attract additional investment as the outward symbol of the secular community. Ashburton, however, yields just a particularly pronounced illustration of the general trends observed

---

[247] Dyer, *Standards of Living*, p. 149: having met all his basic needs, Robert Smith, a half-yardlander at Cleeve, could expect a surplus of just 7s. after the Black Death (but conditions had probably worsened by the mid-sixteenth century).

[248] Ibid., pp. 182–3.

[249] In 1540, the high wardens recorded an income of £3 10 s. 10½ d. in this 33-household parish (with perhaps 165 inhabitants). In the same year, the total revenue of all parish stores exceeded £10: Binney (ed.), *Morebath*, pp. 35, 114–18. At Bethersden, calculations are hampered by the disparate population information: some 105 householders contributed to a Marian rate (thus representing a population in excess of 500: Mercer (ed.), *CWA at Betrysden*, pp. 110–14), but there were only 20 subsidy payers in 1524 (which suggests a mere 67 inhabitants: J. Sheail, 'The distribution of regional wealth in England, 1524/5' (Ph.D. London, 1968), subsidy listings in vol. 2). The 30-year gap between the two counts can hardly explain the difference. In the year of the subsidy, the wardens' income was £4 3 s. 10½ d. and the per-capita figure, based on the contemporary low estimate, over 15 d.

[250] E. Wolf, *Peasants* (14th edn, Englewood Cliffs, 1966), pp. 7–9; Dyer, *Standards of Living*, p. 182.

in this chapter: churchwardens could count on considerable and, on the whole, increasing contributions from their parishioners until the very eve of the Reformation, and the specific composition of their resources depended less on ad-hoc decisions and coincidence than on established fundraising strategies which tended to reflect a community's particular socio-economic context.

3.4 Parish expenses

Churchwardens, like all accountants, were expected to balance their books, and it seems that they tried hard to do so. The moving averages for total income and expenditure follow a very similar course, with the latter running at a slightly lower level. Average growth figures, too, varied only marginally: for the pre-Reformation period, differences are restricted to the second decimal, with expenditure increasing slightly more.[251] In a long-term perspective, there was considerable expansion, even if inflation is taken into account. Figures 3.4(a) and (b) highlight three particularly prominent examples: looking at the (deflated) lower graph (b), expenses peaked at Yatton in the 1490s, but at Ashburton and All Saints well after 1520, and – in marked contrast to the Phelps–Brown/Hopkins index – there was a sharp downward trend in all three from the 1530s.[252] In some parishes, peaks are linked to major construction campaigns such as the addition of a chapel at Yatton, the building of the church house at St Ewen's (both in the 1490s), the setting up of the rood loft at Ashburton (1521–2), the purchase of new bells at Prescot (early 1520s), or the repairs to the church roof at St Botolph (around 1530). Adding to this the investment on Boxford's steeple in 1537, there is plenty of evidence that the 'great age of parish church (re-) building' reverberated in this sample, too, even if none of the communities commissioned a completely new house of worship.[253] To mark their extraordinary efforts, St Ewen's parishioners kept a separate building account, staged one of their few ales, and received over £10 in

---

[251] The only exception is Boxford, where income (average growth: 1.029) was boosted to a figure over 1 by the extraordinary sale of plate, while the expenses (the more reliable guide to the immediate pre-Reformation situation; 0.967) decreased.

[252] Later peaks were 'special cases', caused by the transfer of gild responsibilities to the parish at Peterborough (from the late 1530s), the administration of the benefice at Andrew Hubbard (under Edward VI and Elizabeth), and the need for massive reinvestment at Prescot (in Mary's reign). Only in the first case, however, did this amount to more than a temporary reversal of a falling trend.

[253] Some of them (for example St Ewen's, Ashburton) had of course done so before the accounts open; see Chapter 3.1.

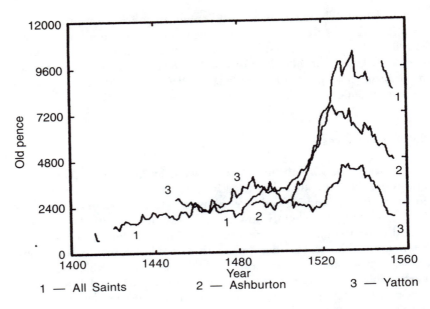

Figure 3.4(a) Parish expenses in three case studies 1400–1560 (11-years averages of absolute figures); unit: old pence

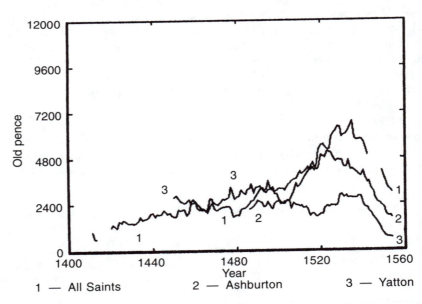

Figure 3.4(b) Adjusted for inflation in accordance with the Phelps-Brown and Hopkins index; unit: old pence

various gifts and contributions, while Prescot rated its townships and Ashburton recorded soaring revenues from gilds and gifts.[254]

An analysis of churchwardens' balances underlines the sound state of parish finance. Deficit years did occur (only Yatton never made the experience), but no accountant could regularly live beyond his means. Comparing expenditure with fresh income, eight out of ten parishes produced a positive average balance, ranging from the £3 6s. at All Saints to the 8 d. at Halesowen.[255] Only the two London examples were less fortunate, with a (moderate) average deficit of 5 d. at Andrew Hubbard and a considerable 13 s. 2 d. at Botolph Aldersgate. Both clearly needed regular injections from the 'reserves' in the parish chest to make ends meet. In the case of St Botolph, the church roof repairs in the early 1530s were the most dramatic cause of overspending with costs of over £109. Generally though, the wardens' funds proved adequate for their current needs.

The first surviving accounts were dominated by the three categories of 'building/fabric', 'ornaments', and 'wax/candles', which absorbed roughly a fifth of total expenditure each.[256] No other item took up more than a twentieth, and the wardens clearly concentrated on their basic duties. It should be noted, however, that the spending on wax and candles went far beyond the bare necessity of lighting the church, and that ornamentation was almost as costly as church building and maintenance, in spite of the fact that all unspecified labour costs have been assigned to the latter. Moving to the last pre-Reformation accounts, the picture changes significantly. 'Wax/lights' is now the single most important category, no doubt largely as a result of the countless candles maintained before altars and images. It scores less percentage points than at the beginning, but in seven out of ten cases increases its importance in absolute figures, most prominently at Yatton from an average £1 3s. 8d. in the 1440s to £4 5s. 10d.[257] 100 years later. This underlines both the continuing importance of the cult of saints as well as its communal

---

[254] St Ewen's CWA, 1492–3 (the special building accounts which open the church book have been included in the database at their chronological place); Prescot CWA, 1523–4, and Ashburton CWA, 1520ff (John Ford alone contributed £10 in 1521–2).

[255] To avoid distortions by subsidies from the parish chest, previous balances or arrears have been excluded from this analysis: the figures result from the subtraction of average pre-Reformation expenditure from the average fresh income in the same period. The result is approximate, since for some years only the income or only the expenses survive (cf. the notes to the graphs and tables in Appendix 2).

[256] That is a score of between 175 and 275 percentage points in the sample. For details see the 'Expenditure in Ten Parishes' stacks and the notes to the graphs and tables (in Appendices 4 (ii) and 2).

[257] Or £2 9s. 3d. expressed in the monetary value of the 1440s.

quality.[258] The biggest relative drop affected 'building/fabric' and 'ornaments' (a loss of some 125 percentage points each), as a clear indication of the diversification of parish activities away from the basic duties. In turn, there was a considerable increase in spending on priests and landed property, reflecting the ever more prominent influence of the 'dead' in late medieval parishes. Confirming the socio-economic differentiation of parish finance, city parishes spent considerable resources on an elaborate ritual and ceremonial life, while expenditure for drama, entertainment, and 'social life' was more common in the communities which relied predominantly on the 'living'. However, given the latter's fundraising priorities, the sums were kept as small as possible, and only in Yatton's immediate pre-Reformation years did they amount to a figure of more than five per cent.[259]

The expenditure for priests and clerks deserves a digression, not least because of the important part played by 'anticlericalism' in the debate on the English Reformation.[260] Once considered an essential prerequisite for the religious changes of the sixteenth century,[261] and exemplified with reference to heresy, tithe disputes, non-residence, clerical education, and ecclesiastical jurisdiction, there is now a tendency to see hostility towards priests as exceptional and motivated by particular circumstances rather than as an endemic feature of the later Middle Ages.[262] Many historians have pointed to the political, financial, and legal motives behind contemporary attacks on the Church, and some associate deteriorating lay-clerical relations with the Reformation period itself rather than the

---

[258] Duffy, *Stripping of the Altars*, pp. 155–63. The spending levels of the 1540s are particularly striking when seen on the background of the 1538 injunctions against images attracting pilgrimages and offerings, which marked a crucial turning point in the veneration of saints (ibid., p. 407).

[259] Constant, 'Source négligée', 519–24, allows a glimpse into (late) sixteenth-century French parish accounts. In the case study of Meudon, expenditure covered a similar range of wax, ornaments, fabric maintenance, and visitation costs, supplemented by the occasional extraordinary communal effort.

[260] This section is based on B. Kümin, 'Parish finance and the early Tudor clergy' in A. Pettegree (ed.), *The Reformation of the Parishes* (Manchester, 1993), pp. 43–62.

[261] For example G. G. Coulton, *Ten Medieval Studies* (Cambridge, 1930), pp. 124, 137–8, and Dickens, *English Reformation*, pp. 90–102.

[262] Swanson, *Church and Society*, p. 259, and Frankforter, 'The Reformation and the register', 215. 'The majority of men paid their tithes, in accord with local custom, without recorded complaints' and most arguments centred on specific questions such as to whom they were owed or on what products they had to be paid rather than on the principle of paying itself: G. Constable, 'Resistance to tithes in the Middle Ages', *JEH*, 13 (1962), 184.

preceding decades.[263] A series of recent studies on the pastoral, educational, and moral standards of rectors, vicars, and chaplains have modified conventional ideas about late medieval decline, and visitation presentments fail to suggest intolerably high levels of local dissatisfaction.[264] Compared to the rampant anticlericalism found in south-western Germany in particular, it would certainly seem that England was confronted with far less serious problems.[265] One of the principal reasons, perhaps, was the comparatively late emergence and strict secular monitoring of ecclesiastical courts, which appear to have operated more freely (and oppressively) in Central Europe.[266]

The discussion of these issues, however, has tended to focus on a limited range of evidence. Court cases and complaints literature form the mainstay of the debate, and their frequency or intensity is taken as indicative of the esteem or contempt in which the clergy were held by parishioners. The study of the laity's financial investment, in contrast, is an aspect which the debate has only touched upon. Christopher Haigh suggested that individual bequests were at least an indirect index for the popularity of priests and concluded on the basis of a few isolated examples and the revised data on philanthropy in England, that they 'peaked in the 1510s and fell rapidly only in the 1530s and after'.[267] The communal dimension of financial support for the clergy, however, escaped quantitative analysis, in spite of the long-term evidence contained in churchwardens' accounts. Given the parishioners' room for

---

[263] Political motives are stressed in all recent revisionist accounts; the interest of common lawyers for example in M. Bowker, 'The commons supplication against the ordinaries', *TRHS*, 5th Series **21** (1971), 61–77. Marshall, *Catholic Priesthood*, ch. 8, acknowledges the existence of pre-Reformation tensions, but stresses that they appear 'with greater frequency and urgency from the 1540s' (p. 228). Christopher Haigh, of course, has turned the tables completely by suggesting that anticlericalism was a result rather than a cause of the Reformation ('Anticlericalism and the English Reformation' in his *The English Reformation Revised*, p. 74).

[264] Bowker, *Secular Clergy*, Heath, *English Parish Clergy*, Marshall, *Catholic Priesthood* (general discussion); Harper-Bill, *Pre-Reformation Church*, pp. 48–51, 77 (visitation evidence).

[265] See for example H. Cohn, 'Reformatorische Bewegung und Antiklerikalismus in Deutschland und England' in W. Mommsen (ed.), *Stadtbürgertum und Adel in der Reformation* (London, 1979), pp. 303–30, and R. Scribner, 'Anticlericalism and the German Reformation' in his *Popular Culture and Popular Movements in Reformation Germany* (London, 1987), pp. 243–56. A broad comparative approach (with select bibliography) to the phenomenon now in P. Dykema and H. Oberman (eds), *Anticlericalism in Late Medieval and Early Modern Europe* (Leiden, 1993).

[266] P. Kirn, 'Der mittelalterliche Staat und das Geistliche Gericht', *Zeitschrift für Rechtsgeschichte*, kanon. Abt. **15** (1926), 197.

[267] Haigh, 'Anticlericalism', p. 72, based on Bittle and Lane, 'Inflation and philanthropy', 209.

manoeuvre in the allocation of spare resources, communal investment
into pastoral provision clearly offers another important indicator of the
popularity of clerical services, and most importantly, it seems to have
involved much larger sums than wills and life-time bequests. In W. K.
Jordan's sample of ten counties and 2685 parishes, a total of £12 918 5 s.
given for clergy maintenance can be traced between 1480 and 1560.[268]
Expressed as an annual quota of 1 s. 2½ d. per parish, this was much less
than the average annual contribution made by the wardens of the ten
parishes examined here, which amounted to almost £2 in the same
period. This is not to claim that individual gift giving and support was
indeed that much smaller in real life, but it is certainly worthwhile not to
neglect any additional evidence. Particularly, when it reaches as far down
the social ladder as churchwardens' accounts.

It is now generally accepted that many of the church's shortcomings
such as absenteeism or pluralism had less to do with negligent clerics
than with an institution which failed to provide its members with an
adequate living. It is thought that around 1500 a parochial incumbent
needed an annual income of at least £10 to make ends meet. In practice,
however, very many English benefices were worth less than £7, and over
a third had been appropriated to monasteries and other ecclesiastical
institutions, which retained the greater part of parochial income for their
own uses. For the (far more numerous) clergymen without a parochial
living, the economic situation was even worse.[269] No surprise then that
many gladly accepted the additional job opportunities created by the
laity in this period. It is well known that religious gilds and chantries
employed a great many priests,[270] but so did the parish as a whole, thus
adding voluntary contributions to the established payments of tithes and
customary dues which, in theory, should have been sufficient to meet its
spiritual needs. The size of investment could vary considerably:
expressed in percentages of total parish expenditure, the spectrum ranges
from practically nil in the cases of Salisbury, Prescot, and Halesowen to
the 53 per cent (or over £30 *per annum*) at St Mary-at-Hill in the late
fifteenth century. On the whole though, the figure lay somewhere
between 10 and 35 per cent, or about £1 to £5.[271]

---

[268] Jordan, *Philanthropy*, pp. 24, 28, 375. The considerable methodological problems
need not concern us for a very rough comparison of the overall size of financial investment
in surviving wills and CWA.

[269] Harper-Bill, *Pre-Reformation Church*, pp. 45–6.

[270] Scarisbrick, Reformation, ch. 2, and Barron, 'Parish fraternities' (gilds); Wood-Legh,
Perpetual Chantries, and Burgess, 'Chantries in the parish'.

[271] Mary-at-Hill CWA, 1477–95 (annual average). Most places had at least one period of
high spending on priests: for example St Ewen's 47.6 per cent under Mary (6.6 per cent
overall) or Yatton 22 per cent in the last pre-Reformation years (2.6 per cent overall).

Who was this money spent on? The most common recipient was the parish or holy water clerk, who appears in all but one of the parishes in this sample.[272] The canonically required quarterly collections are documented in London and Bristol parishes, but payments could vary from year to year (between 2 s. 5 d. and a full annual salary of £4 at Andrew Hubbard) and were often only meant 'to make up his wages'.[273] Individual contributions, revealed in the form of lists or outstanding debts, varied (according to social status) from a few pence to something like 2 s. and were normally raised from householders only.[274] At Boxford, the clerk was apparently paid out of the receipts of the waxsilver gatherings in the pre-Reformation period, but additional parish collections and full yearly payments seem to have become necessary when old and possibly 'superstitious' ways of fundraising were disrupted under the new religious regime.[275]

Apart from men in lower orders, parishioners also supported the rectors and vicars themselves.[276] Churchwardens sometimes appealed to the bishop to convince impropriators of livings to increase the incumbent's salary, or as in some parishes in the archdeaconry of Leicester on the eve of the Reformation, 'there was a custom, or probably a byelaw passed by the majority of the parishioners assembled in vestry, to supplement the stipend of the vicar by parochial contributions'.[277] The evidence from the sample shows that such contributions were not unusual. At Yatton, the wardens paid their incumbent 6 s. 8 d. in 1462–3, at Ashburton, a neighbouring vicar received the same sum in 1496–7, while payments to the parson boosted the clergy's share of St Ewen's expenditure to over a third in the reigns of Edward and Mary. In both 1551 and 1552, the rector was supported with payments of £2 13 s. 4 d., probably in an attempt to make up for

---

[272] The exception is Halesowen.

[273] Churchwardens' accounts often fail to supply full financial details about the office; see the discussion of the various arrangements in chapter 3.2.

[274] At St Ewen's, John Mathew left 6 s. 8 d. yearly in his will on condition that the poorest householders would be relieved of their contributions to the clerk's wages: CWA, p. xxiii. 'The Booke of the clarkes wages' in Mary-at-Hill (CWA, pp. 126–7) lists only a certain number of people and not every communicant (cf. Chapter 6.2.1).

[275] Boxford CWA, for example 1551–2 (19 s. 3 d.) and 1553–4 (£1 4 s. 8 d.) on the income side; 1551–2 and 1552–3: £2 13 s. 4 d. among the expenses. Similarly, fixed contributions of £3 were recorded at Ashburton from CWA 1558ff.

[276] For an analysis of parochial contributions from the incumbents' point of view see Swanson, 'Standards of livings', which – in an interesting contrast to the trends in CWA – stresses the scarcity of sources and the overall decline of clerical incomes.

[277] Hartridge, *Vicarages*, pp. 112–14; Moore (ed.), 'Archdeaconry of Leicester', 125 (quote).

the inadequacies of the tithe system.[278] Under Edward VI and again in the early Elizabethan period, St Andrew Hubbard found itself in the very unusual position of administering the whole benefice itself. As a notorious absentee, undeterred even by excommunication, rector William Swift capped a whole series of troublesome clergymen,[279] and probably convinced either ecclesiastical authorities or the parish to transfer his responsibilities into communal hands.[280] After a few preliminary payments in the regular accounts of 1546–8, the wardens went on to yield a separate reckoning for the parsonage from 1549–52. Over these four years, the parson's duty (or tithe) amounted to over £71, the rent revenues from the parsonage to £4 3s. 4d., the regular offering days brought almost £7, and contributions to the holy loaf £2 14s. Even a marriage fee of 8d. was paid to the wardens. On the expenses side, the parson received £30, the curate almost £34, and £1 10s. was spent on bread and wine for the communion. The parish also commissioned two sermons, met the clergy's expenses at episcopal visitations, and even paid £10 16s. 8d. to the king for subsidies and tenths.[281] This extraordinary effort raised the priests' share of parish expenses to 53 per cent and suggests that Andrew Hubbard's apparently lacklustre performance in terms of gift giving and parochial fundraising may have had something to do with disruptions in lay-clerical relations as well as with poverty or weak communal structures.[282] During these years, at least, parishioners must have come very close to complete local control over their religious affairs.

Between the two extremes of providing for a clerk and administering a whole benefice, there was of course a great range of opportunities for parochial investment in better religious services. A very popular object were the various auxiliary clergymen who helped or substituted for incumbents in providing for the cure of souls. In 1541–2, 21 of the 315 assistant priests in 11 deaneries of the diocese of Chester were financed

---

[278] See CWA, p. xxxiii. 'The parishioners of St Ewen apparently were aware of the economic hardship faced by their incumbent and were supplementing the tithe income of parson John Rawlins from parish receipts ... . Inadequate livings were already blurring the line between incumbents and stipendiary curates.': Skeeters, *Community and Clergy*, p. 109.

[279] Mullins, 'Clergy of London', pp. 69, 421 (described as excommunicated in 1561). Swift was presented to the benefice in 1545 and died in 1568: Hennessy (ed.), *Repertorium parochiale*, pp. 306–7.

[280] Occasionally, bishops entrusted parish representatives with the administration of benefice revenues in case of a vacancy or sequestration (Thomson, *Early Tudor Church*, pp. 19, 284; Skeeters, *Community and Clergy*, p. 119), but this could also be an example of deliberate farming by the whole community.

[281] Andrew Hubbard CWA, 1546ff.

[282] See the section on Andrew Hubbard in the presentation of the case studies.

'ex stipendio parochianorum'.[283] The pattern of support in the denser parochial network of the South was not fundamentally different. At St Leonard Foster Lane, London, parishioners subscribed for an additional priest to help their rector out 'of devotion and good will at their own charge'.[284] In the diocese of Winchester at Christmas 1541, one in eight of a total of 300 auxiliary clerics derived his livelihood not from any regular ecclesiastical fund, but from additional resources raised by the flock in his local community.[285] At about the same time, parishioners at Bassingbourn, Holy Trinity, Ely, and St Andrew and St Peter, Cambridge, are known to have employed chaplains or curates.[286] In this sample, the Andrew Hubbard accounts include payments to a Sir Richard in 1468-9, a Sir Roger 1485-6, a Sir William in 1486-7, and a Sir John in 1506-7. The biggest single cash sum of £5 (both in 1454-6 and 1458-60) went to an anonymous priest to sing for a benefactor's soul. At Ashburton, the curates William Austyn and Nicholas Laneman received regular payments of between 3 s. 4 d. and £1 4 s. for specific supplementary services,[287] while the first ever record of a similar expense at Prescot dates from Mary's reign, when a Sir James Jackson was hired for 11 d. This is not necessarily an indication of a complete lack of previous initiatives, but probably a reflection of the fact that communal investment in such vast parishes was more likely to be diverted to the many chapels of ease.

Characteristic for most places, however, is the provision of additional and especially morrow masses. The importance of the sacrament of the Eucharist for late medieval religion cannot be overstated and there is plenty of evidence to suggest that the elevation in particular lay at the heart of lay devotion:[288] in a fifteenth-century petition to the court of Chancery, the parishioners of Grayingham in Lincolnshire complained that due to an image placed in the church by their parson Robert Conyng they could no longer see 'la leuacion ne diuine seruice',[289] while the

---

[283] W. Irvine (ed.), *A List of Clergy in Eleven Deaneries of the Diocese of Chester* (Manchester, 1896), passim. In Lancashire, notorious for its large parishes and the constant need of additional clergy, only 33 of these priests in 1541 were paid by the local parson, 70 however by individual gentlemen, and a considerable 26 by the local population at large: Haigh, *Lancashire*, p. 65.

[284] Barron, 'Parish fraternities', p. 36.

[285] H. Chitty (ed.), *Registra Stephani Gardiner et Johannis Poynet* (Oxford, 1930), pp. 174-85.

[286] Cambridge University Library: Bishop Goodrich's Register, EDR G/I/7, fos 162ff. I am grateful to Patrick Carter for these references.

[287] Ashburton CWA, for example 1497-8, 1512-3 and so on.

[288] Smith, *Pre-Reformation England*, p. 95; J. Bossy, 'Essai de sociographie de la messe 1200-1700', *Annales*, 36 (1981), 44-70; Brigden, *London and the Reformation*, p. 16.

[289] Baildon (ed.), *Select Cases in Chancery*, case 132.

inhabitants of Minster Lovell in the archdeaconry of Oxford felt justified to present their vicar for his refusal to grant them access to the chancel 'ut videant levacionem'.[290] The more opportunities, the better, and parish, gild, and chantry priests celebrating in the same church obliged by coordinating their services to allow the laity to see several sacrings within a short time.[291] Adding to the existing range of services, mass endowments multiplied all over the country, and many were aimed specifically at travellers or other people unable to participate in regular parochial worship. At Wakefield, the parishioners introduced a morrow mass for all servants and labourers, at Rotherham, resources were found for a weekly Saturday morning mass at the Lady altar and a service of St Katherine, while communally funded mass priests officiated in the Norwich churches of St Peter Mancroft, St Stephen's, and St Gregory's.[292] In the present sample, morrow mass priests were paid, at least partially, by the wardens of Peterborough, All Saints, Bristol, and Andrew Hubbard, London,[293] and services devoted to Jesus, the Blessed Virgin Mary, or St Katherine appear in the accounts of Ashburton, again All Saints, and Halesowen.[294]

But parochial support could take yet further forms: the generally close relationship between parishes and their religious fraternities is expressed in the contributions made to gild chaplains, as in the case of Ashburton, where John Vyne was paid £3 for half a year each in 1519–20 and 1520–21. The need for additional clerical provision was explicitly endorsed by the chantry commissioners for the large extramural parish of Botolph Aldersgate with its 1100 communicants. The crown henceforth paid the salary of an assistant, while on top of this the parishioners (at least temporarily) employed former fraternity priests.[295] In the rural context of Yatton, chaplains like Sir Richard York in 1510–11 could count on regular contributions from the parish wardens, and occasionally, the vicar or clerk got a few pence from reciting the

---

[290] 'Churchwardens' presentments, 1520', *Reports of the Oxfordshire Archaeological Society*, 70 (1925), 103.

[291] Duffy, *Stripping of the Altars*, p. 98.

[292] Cutts, *Parish Priests and their People*, p. 481 (Wakefield), and *VCH Yorkshire*, iii. 41–2 (Rotherham, c.1500); Tanner, *Church in Norwich*, p. 94 (1520s).

[293] Peterborough CWA, 1470–1; Andrew Hubbard CWA (for example £5 in 1465–6 and smaller sums in 1539–40 and 1541–2). At All Saints, various priests received up to £1 10 s. a quarter (for example CWA 1527–8).

[294] For example Sir Roger Channce and Sir John for singing a St Katherine's mass (Halesowen CWA, 1502–3, 1505-6 ff).

[295] Kitching (ed.), *Chantry Certificates*, pp. xxvii, 30. The assistant received £7 from CWA 1551–2 and Sir Olyver, former chaplain of the Holy Trinity Fraternity, £1 in the CWA of 1548–9.

bede-roll.[296] Payments to friars or monks, however, are very rare, and only Andrew Hubbard spent a few pence in 1485–6, 1494–5, and 1535–7. Just as scarce and late is the evidence for the provision of sermons, with a mere 1 s. 10 d. recorded at Botolph Aldersgate in 1557–8 and 3 s. 4 d. at Boxford in 1560–1. This does not necessarily point to a lack of interest in religious instruction: late medieval incumbents were, after all, required to preach four times a year themselves, and certain tendencies in fifteenth-century church building and furniture could be taken as indications for growing preaching audiences.[297] In addition, a number of lectureships were endowed in the later Middle Ages, but normally as a result of municipal or individual rather than parochial initiative.[298] Much more common, however, are payments of a few pence or shillings to vicars, priests, clerks, and sextons on the occasion of obits or anniversaries for past parishioners, particularly in the metropolitan parishes of London or Bristol, but also in humbler urban communities such as Peterborough. The important role of chantries (and their priests) in parish finances should also be mentioned, but this will be discussed in more detail below.

In a comparative perspective, it is once more apparent that the social milieu and relative wealth of a particular parish affected its financial profile: almost no additional clerical services are recorded at St Edmund, Salisbury, Halesowen, and Prescot, all market-town based communities with (in the case of the latter two) a heterogeneous territory of seven and 15 townships respectively. Here, one would expect local religious provision to take preference over investment in the distant parish church. As for St Edmund, 30 per cent of its budget was spent on a rich ornamental and ceremonial life, we know about the existence of gilds and of at least ten altars, but it seems that the churchwardens did not have to make direct payments to the clergy themselves. The daily mass sponsored by the Jesus Fraternity at a cost of £5 6s. 8d. may have met the most pressing communal needs.[299] If such evidence were taken into account, St Edmund would hardly differ from a structurally similar place

---

[296] For example All Saints CWA, 1450–1 (8 d. for the vicar), or St Edmund CWA, 1478–9 (6 s. for the parish priest).

[297] Heath, *English Parish Clergy*, pp. 4ff (preaching requirement); Owen, *Medieval Lincolnshire*, pp. 109–10 (larger naves at Croft and Ingoldmells, Lincs.; introduction of benches and pulpits).

[298] For example the engagement of friars by the city authorities of York (Palliser, *Tudor York*, p. 227), the preaching almshouse priest sponsored by the Coventry merchant Thomas Bond in 1507 (Scarisbrick, *Reformation*, p. 169), or the sermons requested of the cantarist at Havering (M. McIntosh, *Autonomy and Community* (Cambridge, 1986), p. 236).

[299] Brown, 'Late medieval Wiltshire', p. 86 (altars) and pp. 141ff (the Jesus gild).

like Peterborough. Meanwhile, prosperous rural communities like Boxford and Yatton could – at least temporarily – devote up to a quarter of their budget to the support of the local clergy. In Edwardian Boxford, this may have amounted to an astonishing 5d. from each of the perhaps 100 households.[300] In big city parishes, the evidence becomes yet more plentiful and the sums involved even more impressive. In the late 1540s and 1550s, communal contributions could reach the level of 10–16d. per inhabitant (in the Bristol case studies, at Mary-at-Hill, and Andrew Hubbard), which was more or less the equivalent of the per capita revenue of the respective rectors![301] Large peripheral parishes, on the other hand, were less likely to involve their members to the same extent: the extramural St Botolph Aldersgate with its over 1000 souls spent a maximum figure of just 2½d. per parishioner.[302]

Whatever the local circumstances, it is clear that testamentary bequests and tithes reveal only parts of the laity's financial engagement. Any attempt to discuss contemporary attitudes towards the clergy without due reference to churchwardens' accounts presents only a very partial picture, and one which may seriously understate the degree of involvement of many parishioners in providing for the local ministry. Whether in the form of occasional support, regular payments, or the initiation of new services, the cumulative effect of the amounts spent by churchwardens all over the country must have been considerable. The organization of this sustained fundraising effort was no mean feat, and its success testifies to the strength of late medieval parochial institutions.

What can be said about the development over time? It seems that it would be difficult to argue for a fundamental dissatisfaction with the old religion on the eve of the Reformation: in all the case studies, the clergy's share of parish resources is higher in the last years of the old regime than over the whole pre-Reformation period. The absence of references to preachers or sermons does not suggest that the parishioners opted for

---

[300] The population in the 1520s has been estimated at 370 and may have exceeded 500 around 1550 (see Table 3.4). These 5d. have to be added to the payment of tithes, offerings, mortuaries, and other customary dues. As suggested above, the disposable surplus income of a half-yardlander at that time may have been as little as 7s.: Dyer, *Standards of Living*, p. 149.

[301] The rectors per-capita (that is communicants multiplied by 1.33: Wrigley and Schofield, *Population History*, pp. 565–7) revenue was roughly 1s. at Hubbard (Kitching (ed.), *Chantry Certificates*, p. 44) and 1s. 6d. at Mary-at-Hill (ibid., p. 6; here it has to be remembered that the figures for priest-support date from the late fifteenth century). According to the reconstruction of rectorial incomes for Bristol in Skeeters, *Community and Clergy*, p. 98, the incumbent received 10½d. per head at St Ewen's, but a mere 4.17d. at All Saints.

[302] Kitching (ed.), *Chantry Certificates*, p. 30. The rector's income was just £12, that is even less than 2d. per inhabitant.

'advanced' religious opinions. However, churchwardens' accounts only record one aspect of the wide spectrum of lay support for the clergy. Without an overall assessment of all types of financial investment (given the uneven survival of sources an unrealistic prospect), conclusions have to be tentative. Looking at the absolute figures first, two parishes peaked in the immediate pre-Reformation years,[303] but no less than five, including all metropolitan examples, did so later. In the reign of Edward VI between 1547 and 1553, Boxford spent a record yearly average of £2 3 s. 4 d., St Ewen's £2 15 s. 9 d., and Andrew Hubbard £15 19 s. 4 d. All Saints invested an average of £8 14 s. 3 d. during this period – about a third more compared to the years 1538–42, but went even further under Mary by reaching £10 17 s. 8 d., while Botolph Aldersgate raised its Edwardian average of £11 12 s. 8 d., a three-fold increase of the immediate pre-Reformation figure, to £14 2 s. 6 d. in Mary's reign. Thus, in contrast to the overall expenditure and W. K. Jordan's revised data from wills, there is neither an all-time high in the early sixteenth century nor a collapse in the first Reformation years.

The graphs in Figure 3.5 reveal a different pattern. Two curves are shown for each parish: the absolute annual expenditure expressed in 11-years moving averages in old pence and the inflation adjusted figures below. The largest graph at the top depicts the development of the annual average of all eight parishes with significant expenses on priests and clerks (always excluding tithes and customary dues): steadily increasing support from the earliest evidence, more rapid growth after 1500, and a peak (in real terms) in 1546–7. It is questionable, however, whether contemporaries would have judged the level of their expenditure in accordance with this particular index, and subjectively, their heaviest burden would have come under Edward or with the absolute peak of 1554–5.[304] There were no doubt many different local reasons for this, but on the whole two factors may have played an important role: certainly the Marian return to the old religion, but also (throughout these early Reformation years) the loss of clerical services provided by subparochial and 'superstitious' institutions. The existing network of gilds, chantries, and monasteries had been dismantled, and the parish community seems to have picked up the bill.[305] Forty per cent of Bristol's ex-religious and at

---

[303] Ashburton: £5 10 s. (1541–6; 22 per cent of total expenditure); Yatton £3 14 s. 5 d. (1541–5; 22 per cent).

[304] Under Edward, 'priests' reached the highest score in percentages (cf. Appendix 4 (ii). In 1554–5, the 11-year average of the expenditure in all eight parishes was £5 16 s. 4 d.

[305] Cf. for example the payments to gild chaplains at Botolph Aldersgate or the sudden increase in payments to clerks at Boxford (formerly paid out of 'superstitious' waxsilver collections).

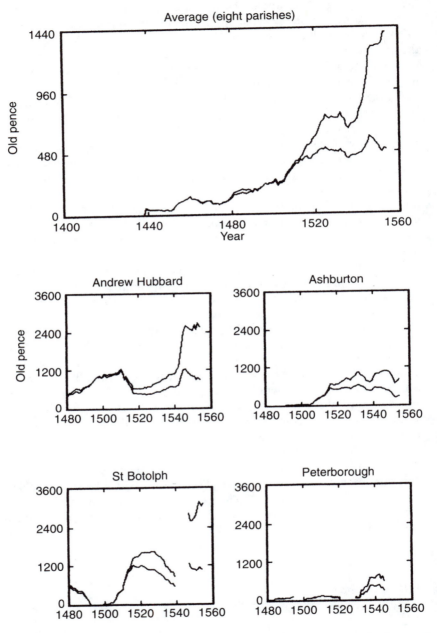

Figure 3.5 Payments to priests and clerks in eight parishes, in absolute and inflation-adjusted 11-years averages; unit: old pence

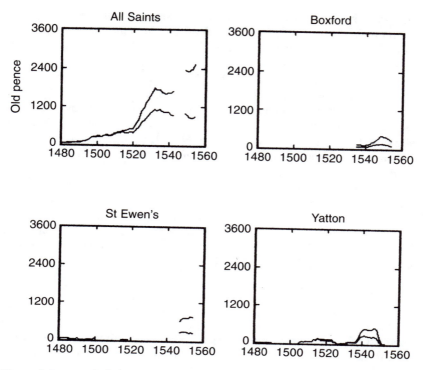

Figure 3.5 *concluded*

least three former chantry priests became involved in the local cure of souls, and, by the early 1540s, they made up one third of the stipendiaries employed by the city parishes; one, Humfrey Hyman, became vicar of All Saints in 1541. Inflationary pressures and the disappearance of many a traditional source of extra revenue made the city's notoriously poor livings even poorer, and, as seen at St Ewen's, the parishioners started to supplement or replace tithe payments with rates organized by the churchwardens.[306] One wonders, too, whether Andrew Hubbard's takeover of the whole benefice under Edward VI was motivated by the fact that the disappearance of clergymen connected to 'superstitious' institutions had rendered the non-residence of its rector even more offensive.

Clearly, if part of the English reformers' motivation for changing the country's religious system derived from the impression that the church had too high a share of the nation's resources,[307] then their initiatives

---

[306] Skeeters, *Community and Clergy*, pp. 85–6, 105, 114.
[307] W. Sheils, *The English Reformation 1530–70* (London, 1989), pp. 6 and 26.

backfired, not for crown or gentry of course, but at least for parish communities and their wardens. Rather than freeing energy and resources for other purposes, most places ended up spending most on priests after the religious changes. Increasing royal taxation in the wake of the Act of First Fruits and Tenths (1534) may have accentuated the problem: the official valuation of many benefices greatly overestimated parochial resources, and incumbents turned to their congregation for help in meeting the heavy fiscal burdens. During an inquiry into the decay of the living of St Gregory at Northampton, for instance, the parishioners argued 'that they could not secure the services of a priest "without the further charges of the said parissheners to be contributories to the salarie and here of the saide priste"'.[308] All this, it should be recalled, at a time when parochial income was on a steady downward trend. It certainly looks as if parishioners concentrated increasingly limited pastoral resources on their communal institution; something which would have been quite unnecessary, had they severely disapproved of the clerical services that were on offer.

However, it would be inadequate to interpret this process and many others exclusively in religious or even denominational terms. First and foremost, all the figures point to a general strengthening of the parishes' communal institutions and the increasing importance of secular dimensions. Financial support for the clergy was partly a pious initiative, but certainly also an important aspect of lay control over the late medieval Church.[309] It was always an attractive prospect for lay people to be able to hire and fire their own priests,[310] even if it involved considerable resources and the odd legal headache.[311] After all, most of the generosity had some strings attached: strict residence and performance requirements created a new type of parish employee who had every interest not to scandalize his communal patrons and paymasters by negligence or immorality.[312] Collective parochial investment thus served the multiple purpose of augmenting divine service, enhancing lay control, and improving clerical discipline. The

---

[308] Carter, 'First fruits', 61 (1546); see also his 'Royal taxation of the English parish clergy 1535–58' (Ph.D. Cambridge, 1994) .

[309] Swanson, *Church and Society*, pp. 256–7; Pfaff, 'Pfarrei und Pfarreileben', p. 229.

[310] Barron, 'Parish fraternities', p. 33.

[311] A priest of St Lawrence, London, who had been employed on a seven-year contract, sued the churchwardens in Chancery for his dismissal after just nine months: French, 'Local identity', p. 248.

[312] Payments to clergymen contributed to an increasing 'value for money' attitude among the parishioners: Marshall, *Catholic Priesthood*, p. 199.

religious changes did little to alter this attitude: Bristol parishioners, for instance, were willing to support impoverished curates in the later sixteenth century, but not in a manner which would have made them truly independent.[313] Landed endowments are another case in point. Most were certainly given to the church out of a religious impulse and – as evident from the stacks for the last pre-Reformation years in Appendix 4 (ii) – added to the ceremonial life with a growing number of obits. For the wardens, however, the consequences (maintenance costs, legal issues, and a great many financial decisions) were of a predominantly secular nature.[314] Property management gradually became their second largest expenditure item (even without the costs of anniversaries), and long before any official highway legislation, public works were recorded in parish accounts.

One way of assessing this trend away from traditional ecclesiastical duties is to group expenditure into the three main areas of 'fabric' (everything connected to the upkeep of the lay part of the church), 'worship' (ceremonial and religious life), and 'administration' (accounting, parish employees, property management, local government functions).[315] From the pie charts in Figure 3.6, again based on an addition of percentage points scored in all ten parishes, it is clear that the most prominent growth area was not worship,[316] but administration: from a modest 11 per cent at the beginning, to 27 per cent in the 1540s, and over a third under Edward.[317] The most explicit illustration of how religious initiatives turned the churchwardenship from an ecclesiastical into a managerial position is All Saints. In this increasingly better endowed parish, basic parochial duties were losing ground quickly: in absolute terms, spending on worship may have grown from an annual £4 14s. 7d. (1406–9) to £12 18s. 9d. (1538–42), but administration rose from virtually nil to over £18.

In the benefaction-orientated regimes, the wardens' secular competence was well developed by the early sixteenth century, and (an

---

[313] Skeeters, *Community and Clergy*, pp. 117–21.

[314] Anniversaries were not kept if the resources dried up, as for example the Newbery obit at All Saints, because 'we be unpaid of ye Tailors' (CWA 1519–20).

[315] Full details for these categories can be found in the notes to the figures and tables (Appendix 2).

[316] Religious and ceremonial life maintained a share of roughly half of parish expenditure throughout the pre-Reformation period, which amounted to a significant increase in absolute figures. This is of course what the revisionist mean when they claim that the English people did not want the Reformation (Scarisbrick, *Reformation*, p. 1), but it is only part of the picture.

[317] Under Mary, the re-equipment of parishes with ornaments reversed the trend temporarily.

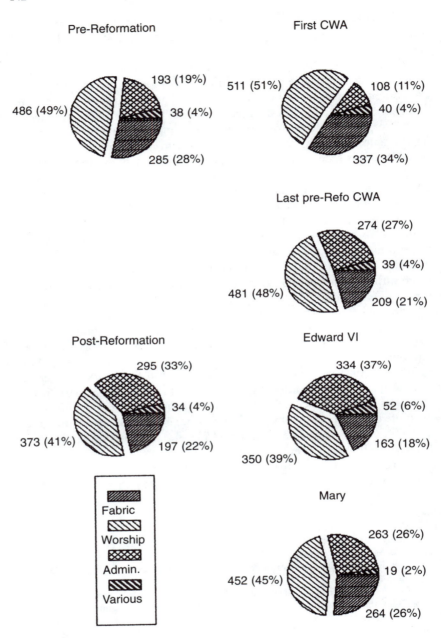

Figure 3.6 Aggregate expenditure on fabric, worship and administration in a sample of 10 parishes (9 parishes *t*. Edward VI); unit: percentage points

important difference to the Elizabethan period) the pace and scope of their activities were set by the parishes themselves rather than by parliament or justices of the peace. In the 'living' regimes, however, the same move away from ecclesiastical duties owed more to outside stimulation: at Ashburton and Boxford, around one tenth of expenditure in the early 1540s concerned military purposes, or the payment (and organization?) of subsidies. Elsewhere, the decisive impulse came with the implementation of the crown's Reformation injunctions:[318] Halesowen spent just 4 per cent on administration in the years before 1547, but 38 per cent between 1547 and 1552. Whatever the exact date and impulse, it would be wrong to associate the 'secularization of the parish' only with the post-Reformation period.[319]

A reassessment of another of Christopher Hill's notions, the claim that the post-Reformation parish was 'breaking down', is now under way.[320] For a long time, historians saw little room for voluntary initiatives within the mainstream of the old religion, and many associated the 'triumph of the laity' with the changes of the sixteenth century.[321] This implied almost supreme powers of incumbents over all aspects of medieval parish life and an essentially compulsory character of all communal activities, leaving only Lollardy to cater for those who wanted 'to be free of hierarchical control and canon law'.[322] In many respects, such a view has now proved untenable: far from breaking down, the parochial framework survived for many centuries, and there was little left in post-Reformation churches to distract from the towering role of pulpit and incumbent. As for late medieval worship, chantries and fraternities provided ample scope for voluntary and independent activities, and pageants, plays, and local shrines augmented the

---

[318] The timing and efficiency of removing altars, purchasing bibles, and whitewashing walls (Hutton, 'Local impact'; an impression confirmed by this sample) is on the whole better explained as an execution of government orders (hence 'administration') than by genuine religious feelings ('worship'). The latter would have led to many more parishes pre-empting the crown's policy, and many more to resist it (see Chapter 6.1).

[319] C. Hill, *Society and Puritanism in Pre-Revolutionary England* (London, 1964), pp. 420–42. Much of his evidence (use of the church for business and entertainment; secular aspects of the office of parish clerk) date back much further than the sixteenth century. P. Slack, *Poverty and Policy in Tudor and Stuart* England (London, 1988), p. 131, sees the roots of the parish's civil functions only in its traditional welfare role and the government impulses of the Tudor age.

[320] Hill, *Society and Puritanism*, p. 484.

[321] Subtitle of Cross, *Church and People*. For a more detailed discussion of this topic (particularly for the urban context) see B. Kümin, 'Voluntary religion' in P. Collinson and J. Craig (eds), *The Reformation in English Towns* (Basingstoke, forthcoming).

[322] Cross, *Church and People*, esp. pp. 31–52 (the limited room for lay initiatives); Dickens, *English Reformation*, p. 32 (quote).

parishioners' options further.[323] But an analysis of churchwardens' expenses suggests that the adjective 'voluntary' can also be applied to many *communal* parochial activities. In this sample, churchwardens' funds helped to cover a chantry's deficit, to make up a fraternity chaplain's stipend, or to purchase wax for the veneration of a particular saint.[324] This did not make the respective institutions or cults 'compulsory', but points to the coordinating role of communal officers and to the availability of choice in the late medieval parish.[325]

The classification of expenditure is admittedly not always straightforward and circumstantial information often too scarce to judge whether, for instance, a particular ornament was purchased out of the parishioners' initiative or as a result of an order by their ecclesiastical superiors. Still, an attempt can be made to group expenditure into items with an established basis in canon law or secular legislation and those made without such outside encouragement. Hence, any vestment, book, or roof repair can be assigned to the former category, and lights, additional clergy, parish employees, or local ceremonial life to the latter.[326] Strictly speaking, the classification applies to the activities of 'churchwardens' rather than the 'parish', but this should not undermine the argument put forward here: given the 'official' nature of the evidence, we can expect fuller coverage for the narrower field of 'compulsory' activities than the wider range of 'voluntary' initiatives.[327] With this in mind, the results appear unambiguous: while 'membership' of the parish was enforced throughout our period (and indeed much beyond), the scope for voluntary activities supported by the parish wardens always existed and increased over time. Looking at Figure 3.7,

---

[323] Palliser, 'Parish in perspective', p. 17. For a detailed discussion of the 'Parochial substructure' see Chapter 4 below.

[324] Support for chantries for example All Saints CWA, 1521–2, for gilds: Ashburton CWA, 1519–20.

[325] Parishes and 'voluntary' fraternities shared many similar features and the contrast should not be overstated: Swanson, *Church and Society*, p. 280: see Chapter 4.1. below.

[326] Upkeep of nave, churchyard, and bells as well as provision of ornaments and payment of the clerk were undisputed duties under canon law, while subsidy and military expenses resulted from demands made by the crown. On the other hand, no legal responsibility existed for the support of additional altars, images, or clergymen, and no parliamentary legislation (yet) for the performance of public works, poor relief, and the maintenance of landed property. For a full list of the categories in the two groups see the notes to the graphs and tables in Appendix 2.

[327] The compulsory element may be underestimated in those parishes which delegated payments to the clerk to officers other than the wardens, but this is more than compensated by the fact that *all* spending on ornaments has been classed as compulsory. As for the 'grey area' of unrecorded activities, ad-hoc communal initiatives were certainly more easily omitted from CWA than canonical or official secular duties.

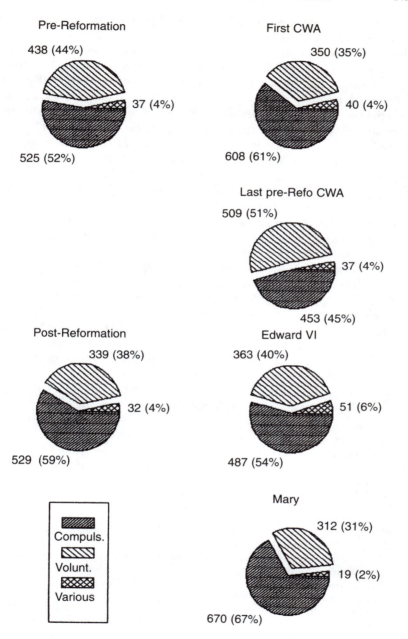

Figure 3.7 'Compulsory' and 'voluntary' spending in a sample of 10 parishes (9 parishes *t*. Edward VI); unit: percentage points

35 per cent of expenses could be described in this way in the first ever accounts, but over 50 per cent in the last pre-Reformation years. The first Reformation impact under Edward VI and Mary reversed the trend, and compulsion reassumed its dominant role in parochial life: lights before images had been outlawed by the reformers, additional priests were no longer necessary, and a series of royal injunctions defined acceptable parochial worship ever more closely.[328] For further comparisons with the Elizabethan period, the categories would have to be redefined to take account of the increasing legislation on parochial duties,[329] but it is unlikely that this would change the picture fundamentally. Voluntary religious activities were bound to be given a lower priority by officers who had more than enough to do with all their new local government responsibilities.[330]

Overall, it seems that sixteenth-century change can be observed less in the appearance of voluntary and secular activities, than in their form and motivation. Parishes, fraternities, and chantries do not fit the traditional image of compulsion for the later Middle Ages, and all could be engaged in considerable secular activities: a chantry priest might hold a school, a gildwarden support the smooth running of a port, and parishioners pay for military expenses, subsidies, or property management.[331] The Tudors simply continued the parish's trend towards a local government unit, and enhanced the element of compulsion in its administration.[332] At the same time, the Reformation outlawed many religious activities only to provoke their reappearance in a more detached if not sectarian form.[333] In line with the increasing particularization of the religious landscape, the laity's emphasis was no longer on providing more variety of

---

[328] W. Frere and W. Kennedy (eds), *Visitation Articles and Injunctions of the Reformation Period* (3 vols, London, 1910), passim; for a brief summary see Chapter 6.1.

[329] The shadows of compulsion in terms of poor relief, for instance, intensified between 1552–63: McIntosh, 'Local responses to the poor', 235.

[330] The classic study of the parishes' early modern administrative role remains the Webbs' *English Local Government*.

[331] Examples in Kreider, *English Chantries*, pp. 38ff, and Scarisbrick, *Reformation*, p. 26 (Holy Trinity Guild, Hull).

[332] Rates for example replaced ales as a fundraising method in many seventeenth-century parishes (Bennett, 'Conviviality', 36), a change which provoked both intensified external supervision (Drew (ed.), *Lambeth CWA*, p. liii) and greater innerparochial compulsion (Hill, *Society and Puritanism*, p. 432).

[333] The doctrine of the priesthood of all believers challenged the role of the clergy, turning every house into a 'little church': ibid., p. 458. The scope for individual worship, beyond clerical or parochial control, was further enhanced by the emphasis on sermons (often commissioned by towns rather than parishes) and the gradual emergence of many doctrinal varieties: P. Collinson, 'Shepherds, sheepdogs, and hirelings' in W. Sheils and D. Wood (eds), *The Ministry: Clerical and Lay* (Oxford, 1989), p. 203.

(doctrinally) more or less the same thing, but on supplementing a reduced parochial service with tailor-made forms of worship catering for a now much more differentiated spectrum of religious creeds.

CHAPTER FOUR

Parochial Substructure

Parishioners did not always appear *in corpore*. They were individuals with particular religious needs, and a discussion of late medieval parish life cannot ignore the existence of chapels, chantries, and fraternities. This chapter will look in turn at the main subparochial institutions, highlight their principal characteristics, and then examine their relationship with the community as a whole. The main aim will be to assess whether these services simply complemented existing religious options, or whether they posed a serious threat to the parochial system.[1]

4.1 Lights and fraternities

Lights placed before altars and images were an important part of the veneration of saints. Their maintenance required some collective organization, and regulations were drawn up on various levels within the parochial system. Ashburton's communal waxsilver ordinance, which graded financial contributions in accordance with social status, is just one of a great many similar examples.[2] The amounts it specified may have been small, but the church contained some 20 other lights (three alone in honour of the virgin Mary), many of which were supported by specific 'stores' or gender groups such as the young men or maidens.[3] Generous endowments could accrue to these institutions, and part of the income was often allotted to church repair or poor relief purposes.[4] At Prescot, where candles survived well beyond the reforming injunctions of 1538, the churchwardens supervised the purchase and 'making' of wax themselves.[5] It is often difficult to differentiate between parochial and subparochial responsibilities. An ever-increasing proportion of communal funds was absorbed by the cult of saints, and in turn many bequests to lights were explicitly intended to relieve the parishioners of some of this burden. The maintenance of candles formed an integral part

---

[1] Gilds in particular have been described as somehow opposed to the official Church: see for example Bossy, 'Counter-Reformation', 58–9, and *Christianity*, p. 63.

[2] CWA, p. 192.

[3] A plan of Ashburton church and its images in Orme, *Unity and Variety*, p. 59.

[4] J. Oxley, *The Reformation in Essex to the Death of Mary* (Manchester, 1965), p. 68.

[5] Bailey, 'CWA of Prescot', 153–4.

of the corporate worship of the parish, and – complicating distinctions further – it could become the focal point of a fully fledged gild. The boundaries were blurred.[6] Administrative links and similarities reinforce this impression: lightwardens' accounts were often submitted to parish representatives and revealed the same sort of bookkeeping techniques, resources, and spending priorities as those kept by the churchwardens themselves. The reckoning made by Thomas More and Richard Batts for a light at Andrew Holborn in London (1477–8) is one of the few surviving examples: with an income of £7 raised from rents and collections, the wardens spent just over £6 for materials, ornaments, and certain ceremonies.[7]

A fraternity or gild can be defined as 'an association of layfolk, who under the patronage of a particular saint ... undertook to provide the individual member of the brotherhood with a good funeral ... together with regular prayer and mass saying thereafter for the repose of the dead person's soul'.[8] In addition, it normally staged an annual feast and engaged in some charitable or ceremonial activities.[9] The earliest documentary evidence surviving from the Anglo–Saxon period reveals a mixture of Christian and pagan elements. In an often violent social environment, gilds fulfilled important peace-keeping or administrative duties and 'helped to prepare the laity for the responsibilities which would come to them from c.1100 onwards as members of the new parish'.[10] Even at that stage, however, their *raison d'être* was the provision of intercession and funeral rites, and this pious impulse should remain at the heart of their activities throughout the Middle Ages, both in England and on the Continent.[11] In towns, of course, many gilds were linked to particular crafts, but economic motivations were secondary to

---

[6] Duffy, *Stripping of the Altars*, pp. 146–9.

[7] Barron and Roscoe, 'St Andrew Holborn', pp. 55ff (the arithmetic is poor). Records for the SS Clement and George lights at St Michael, Oxford, are preserved at the Bodleian Library (MSS D.D.Par Oxford, St Michael), and there is a single folio of accounts of the keepers of St Christopher's light at March in the Cambridgeshire County Record Office (P116/5/1).

[8] Scarisbrick, *Reformation*, pp. 19–20. The terms 'g(u)ilds' and 'fraternities' are interchangeable regional varieties for parish-based associations, while 'confraternity' referred to a layman's association with a monastery, which – in return for his financial support – included him in its prayers.

[9] G. Rosser, 'Going to the fraternity feast: commensality and social relations in late medieval England', *Journal of British Studies*, 33 (1994), 430–45.

[10] Rosser, 'Anglo-Saxon gilds', p. 33 (quote) and passim.

[11] Vauchez, *Laïcs*, p. 116, speaks of the dominance of the 'confrérie funéraire', Genicot, *Rural Communities*, p. 103, of 'piety' as the basic motive for the popularity of fraternities.

those connected with religion, mutual charity, and conviviality: 'spiritual brotherhood had been the first reason for the existence of the trade gilds, and in the sixteenth century the first reason still mattered'.[12]

By the eleventh century, pagan remnants had disappeared, and the doctrine of purgatory provided a further incentive for the spread of the fraternity movement. Members were required to attend the funerals of all their brothers and sisters as well as the annual feast, which consisted of a mass in honour of the dead, the audit of accounts, and a common meal. Wealthier institutions like the Corpus Christi gild at Grantham in Lincolnshire proceeded with great ceremonial pomp and provided their own silver cutlery, table cloths, and livery for the purpose:

> Before the time of procession on Corpus Christi Day they assemble at the church, the two priests in the sacred vestments carry the Body of the Lord attended by two boys in albs carrying the gild candles, followed by the brethren and sisters with candles. At the mass each offers as he pleases. After the mass the two candles are carried to the high altar by the boys and remain there. Of the other candles, two burn daily at the high altar and one at Corpus Christi altar during mass. After the mass they eat together and each couple – i.e. husband and wife, gives food to a poor man. To the friars minor ... in front of the procession they give fourteen loaves, a sheep, half a calf etc.[13]

Parish gilds appealed to both sexes and a wide variety of social groups, with the exception perhaps of the poorest and wealthiest members of local society. The former were deterred or excluded by the existence of entry fees. In country parishes, this was a rather symbolic amount, but the prestigious Holy Cross fraternity at Stratford, for instance, levied a considerable 3 s. 4 d.[14] Nevertheless, some organizations were deliberately aimed at the humbler sort of parishioners. The regulations of the Corpus Christi gild at St Michael on the Hill in Lincoln stipulated that 'whereas this gild was founded by folks of common and middling rank, it is ordained that no-one of the rank of mayor or bailiff shall become a brother of the gild, unless he is found of humble and good conversation, and is admitted by the choice and common consent of the brethren and sisters of the gild'.[15] As for the wealthiest and most influential groups, London's elites, for instance, had many alternative

---

[12] Brigden, *London and the Reformation*, p. 35 (quote); Reynolds, *Kingdoms and Communities*, pp. 67ff.

[13] Westlake, *Parish Gilds*, p. 162.

[14] Scarisbrick, *Reformation*, p. 25.

[15] Quoted in an unpublished paper by Robert Goheen ('Deference and Authority' (1987), p. 5): see Smith (ed.), *English Gilds*, p. 178. There was also a fraternity for the poor of the parish at St Augustine, Norwich: Rubin, 'Town and country', p. 6.

options to meet their religious or social needs, and parish fraternities were 'predominantly a "middle class" artisan movement'.[16] And yet there were prestigious top-flight institutions such as the Holy Trinity gild at Coventry or the St George fraternity at Norwich with a very distinguished, interparochial, and even national membership.[17] The social basis of a gild clearly depended on its location, particular purpose, and social context, but on the whole it seems to have appealed most strongly to the middling sort.[18]

Numerically speaking, fraternities were one of the most impressive features of late medieval social and religious life: London contained nearly 200 gilds between 1350 and 1547, early sixteenth-century Northamptonshire 100, and Lincolnshire 120. York's biggest institution was joined by 70 000 members in the course of the late Middle Ages and Ludlow's Palmer gild admitted 1176 new brothers and sisters between 1505 and 1509. Even a town of a mere 1500 inhabitants like Whittlesey (Cambs.) could accommodate ten fraternities and a single church like Holy Trinity, Hull, 12.[19] A typical gild would be headed by elected wardens, aldermen or masters, supported perhaps by chamberlains (for financial matters), stewards (collection of membership fees), and almoners (administration of charitable work).[20] Most parish-based institutions were not very complex, but additional officers and clerks could be added if activities expanded beyond the basic religious and ceremonial duties.

The performance of some charitable acts, ranging from funeral doles to the running of fully equipped almshouses, was very common, while services such as schools, unemployment benefits, insurances, or legal aid remained the preserve of a few more sophisticated organizations. The fraternity of the Holy Cross at Abingdon was incorporated in 1442 and used its landed endowments to build roads and bridges for the town.[21]

---

[16] Barron, 'Parish fraternities', p. 30.

[17] Phythian-Adams, 'Ceremony and the citizen', pp. 59ff; Scarisbrick, *Reformation*, p. 22.

[18] The majority of members were 'artisans indépendants et ... commerçants', with only the 'noblesse la plus huppée' und 'ouvriers' normally excluded: Vauchez, *Laïcs*, p. 115.

[19] All figures from Scarisbrick, *Reformation*, pp. 28ff, except London (Barron, 'Parish fraternities', p. 13) and Hull (P. Heath, 'Urban piety in the later Middle Ages' in R. Dobson, *The Church, Politics and Patronage* (Gloucester, 1984), p. 222). As early as the thirteenth century, 40 per cent of French parishes contained one or more gilds: Genicot, *Rural Communities*, p. 102.

[20] Scarisbrick, *Reformation*, p. 23.

[21] G. Cook, *Medieval Chantries and Chantry Chapels* (London, 1963), pp. 25ff. The churchwardens of Trowbridge told the chantry commissioners in 1545 that the Corpus Christi brotherhood had spent all its revenues of the last five years on highways: quoted in Brown, 'Late medieval Wiltshire', p. 33.

From this point, it was only a short way to quasi-municipal status. Late medieval Stratford was effectively governed by the Holy Cross gild: founded for the support of priests, it built a chapel and hospital in the fourteenth century, and its members gradually proceeded to the discussion of all sorts of local issues. They even passed ordinances 'per totam communitatem villate Stratford'.[22] The inhabitants of Wisbech, too, must have regarded the Holy Trinity gild, which repaired dykes and maintained a grammar school, as some kind of town authority. Here, as in Saffron Walden or Bury St Edmunds, there were direct links between pre-Reformation fraternities and later town governments.[23] In various forms and ways, gilds with important secular functions and personal connections to urban authorities existed at Newark in Nottinghamshire, Chester (gild of St George), Lichfield (St Mary), Norwich (St George), and countless other places.[24] In towns without independent government institutions, they gave 'some corporate identity to the leading citizenry and prepared the way for full legal identity – by providing a centre of gravity over and against surviving manorial authority'.[25] Parishes, of course, could serve the same purpose, and this is a first indication of the structural and functional similarities of the two institutions.[26]

The relationship between parishes and gilds was complex and potentially delicate. Both flourished in the fourteenth and fifteenth centuries: parish life became increasingly institutionalized and diversified, while fraternities multiplied to an unprecedented extent, particularly in areas of insufficient or geographically inadequate parochial provision.[27] In other words, they could cater for particular local needs which had earlier been met by the creation of a new parish. All but one of the 16 large extramural London parishes contained one or

[22] R. Hilton, *The English Peasantry in the Later Middle Ages* (Oxford, 1975), p. 93.

[23] M. McIntosh, 'Local change and community control in England 1465–1500', *Huntington Library Quarterly*, **49** (1986), 238. Other examples include Newark, Notts. (Cook, *Medieval Parish Church*, p. 30), while at Boston the property of the local gilds was used to endow the newly created town institutions: C. Cross, 'Communal piety in sixteenth-century Boston', *Lincolnshire History and Archaeology*, **25** (1990), 36.

[24] D. Jones, *The Church in Chester 1300–1540* (Manchester, 1957), pp. 116ff; A. Kettle, 'City and close' in C. Barron and C. Harper-Bill (eds), *The Church in Pre-Reformation Society* (Woodbridge, 1985), p. 160 (Lichfield); Tanner, *Church in Norwich*, p. 81. Further examples in: C. Phythian-Adams, 'Urban decay in late medieval England' in P. Abrams and E. A. Wrigley (eds), *Towns in Societies* (Cambridge, 1978), pp. 175–6.

[25] Scarisbrick, *Reformation*, p. 22.

[26] Rosser, *Medieval Westminster*, p. 248, and cf. the Chapter 2.3 on 'Secular uses' above.

[27] Scarisbrick, *Reformation*, ch. 2 (proliferation). In many cases, their origin may be connected less to the Black Death than to the 'virtual cessation of new parochial creations after 1300': Rosser, 'Parish and guild', p. 33.

more fraternities,[28] and at places like Baslow in Derbyshire or Weymouth in Dorset, brotherhoods of neighbours erected chapels because of the inconvenient distance from the mother church.[29] As a means to relieve inflexible social or religious structures, new gilds were often founded in areas of great social mobility or by groups of newcomers and strangers to help them settle in a new surrounding.[30] Occasionally, gilds could shoulder communal administrative duties or develop into fully fledged parochial institutions themselves: at Bassingbourn, the Holy Trinity chaplain John Hubbard acted as parish secretary, while officers of the lay fraternities of Shrewsbury or Bridgwater gradually evolved into churchwardens.[31] An important incentive for lay participation was provided by the possibility of direct supervision over clerical services. Dozens of London gilds could employ chaplains whose 'livelihood depended upon the whim of the lay people'.[32] Elections and dismissals were normally made by the wardens and eminent members of the gild in consultation with the parochial incumbent, but sometimes lay people decided on their own: 'when the masters of the guild of the assumption in St Margaret's, Westminster, took boat for London to find a priest for their brotherhood, they neither consulted their vicar, nor went in search of a spiritual director – they wanted a minister who would do as he was told, and probably found him in the nave of St Paul's'.[33] Standards of clerical discipline were regulated in great detail: the chaplain of St Peter's gild in St Peter Cornhill needed his employers' permission for any period of absence from the benefice, and he was required to keep respectable company throughout his term of office.[34]

Ecclesiastical authorities naturally monitored the phenomenon with a certain suspicion: on the one hand they could only encourage pious activity, but on the other there was always a danger that independent sworn associations drifted out of clerical control.[35] The emergence of institutions with considerable assets, voluntary membership, and a certain secrecy within the existing parochial framework was an ominous development. Rectors and vicars had some grounds to fear that the new priests would absorb parts of their income or challenge their authority. It would be naive to claim that this never happened, but on the whole recent scholarship agrees that 'a hypothesis of fundamental opposition

---

[28] Barron, 'Parish fraternities', p. 28.
[29] Rosser, 'Anglo-Saxon gilds', p. 32 (Baslow in 1349), and 'Parish and guild', p. 35.
[30] Ibid., pp. 33ff (for example the German colony in London).
[31] Duffy, *Stripping of the Altars*, p. 149; Drew, *Early Parochial Organisation*, p. 22.
[32] Barron, 'Parish fraternities', p. 33.
[33] Smith, *Pre-Reformation England*, p. 115.
[34] Westlake, *Parish Gilds*, p. 79.
[35] Reynolds, *Kingdoms and Communities*, p. 73.

between the fraternities and the parochial clergy cannot be substantiated', that the large majority of gilds were firmly based within and working for the parish.[36] For a start, they shared the same orthodox belief in sacraments and intercession, as exemplified by the two Cambridge gilds which joined forces in 1352 to endow Corpus Christi College for the education of priests.[37] Rather than undermining parochial worship, gilds strove to provide further and more specialized opportunities for religious worship. They were not necessarily 'exclusive' outlets for growing lay individualism. Fraternities such as the 'laudesi' of northern Italy may have promoted more contemplative forms of lay devotion, but in western Europe they were on the whole of a more ritualistic character and sometimes comprised a very large part, if not the whole population of a village, town, or parish.[38] Such 'confréries territoriales' can be found in southern France ('Saint-Esprit' fraternities) or Lombardy ('consortia plebis'), but also at Keele in Staffordshire, Bardwell in Suffolk, and the market town of Ashburton.[39] Even a gild with more restricted membership included at least the poor and ancestors in its wider community. Most importantly though, there were countless ways in which fraternities supported their parishes.

Very often, they provided important financial backing: at Stamford, 'certain poor men noting the poverty of the Rector to be such that the Church in its feeble state scarcely provided for his maintenance, decided at their own charges to found a fraternity in augmentation of divine worship. Each one gives as he pleases to the Rector's maintenance, and the gild provides 16 candles before Trinity and has a feast at the rectory on Corpus Christi day'.[40] The St Mary gild at West Tarring (Sussex) was founded in 1528 to provide an auxiliary priest for the whole community, and even a very select association like the Jesus fraternity at St Lawrence,

---

[36] Rosser, 'Parish and guild', p. 40 (the vicar of Pillerton for instance actively supported the recruitment of new members), Duffy, *Stripping of the Altars*, p. 145, and Thomson, *Early Tudor Church*, p. 294 (England); 'it seems unlikely that [brotherhoods] were created or used against the institutional church': Genicot, *Rural Communities*, p. 103 (90 per cent of gilds in central Italy were set up with priestly approval).

[37] Cook, *Medieval Chantries*, p. 26.

[38] Vauchez, *Laïcs*, p. 120.

[39] Keele was in the gift of the order of St John and of extra-parochial status. A gild comprising all households provided the framework for local ecclesiastical life: Swanson, *Church and Society*, p. 280. The St Peter fraternity at Bardwell 'seems to have included nearly all the adult population of the village': D. MacCulloch, *Suffolk and the Tudors* (Oxford, 1986), p. 141. All burgesses were entitled to membership of the St Lawrence gild at Ashburton; it was 'synonymous' with the town and served as a convenient sub-unit in a parish which also comprised the manor: H. Hanham, 'Chantries at Ashburton', 112.

[40] Westlake, *Parish Gilds*, p. 177. Another example at Baldock in Hertfordshire (Rosser, 'Parish and guild', p. 29).

Reading, could offer to pay the parish sexton's wages.[41] Particularly frequent were contributions to general parish funds or specific building projects: Ashburton, Pilton, and Croscombe derived over 10 per cent of their pre-Reformation income from 'stores', the rebuilding of Bodmin church attracted money from no less than 40 fraternities, and gilds were the most substantial backers of the same undertaking at Westminster.[42] At All Hallows London Wall or Bottisham in Cambridgeshire, brotherhoods were specifically formed for church repair purposes.[43] But if needs be, it could work the other way: the Bridgwater churchwardens, for instance, repaired the Holy Trinity gild chapel at their own cost.[44]

The Ashburton accounts offer a few glimpses into the financial life of subparochial institutions: in 9 Henry VIII, the profits of the roughly 20 stocks amounted to £42 13s. 2½d. or over three times the figure generated by the churchwardens themselves; this as another reminder that parish accounts reveal only a fraction of total lay investment.[45] In the West Country in general, parish substructure seems to have been more differentiated (or merely better documented?) than elsewhere. The churches at Morebath and Chagford accommodated a similar variety of 'stocks', each with separate officers and accounts, and sometimes higher turnovers than the churchwardens themselves.[46] At Chagford, for instance, the patron saint store of St Michael was rather less wealthy than that of St Katherine, but from 1513 at the latest, the four communal wardens ('general receivers of the Church') emerged as the most important officers with responsibilities about the church fabric and general supervisory powers.[47]

The financial dimension of subparochial activities can be illustrated in some more detail for another parish in this sample. At Botolph Aldersgate, a few reckonings survive for the Trinity fraternity both before and after the merger with the gild of SS Fabian and Sebastian. Figure 4.1 illustrates their similarities with parish accounts:[48] revenues dominated by rents from landed bequests and expenditure focusing on

---

[41] Scarisbrick, *Reformation*, p. 22 (West Tarring), and Duffy, *Stripping of the Altars*, p. 152 (Reading).

[42] Ashburton CWA, 1479–1546, French, 'Local identity', p. 71, Harvey, *Gothic England*, p. 121 (Bodmin), and Rosser, *Medieval Westminster*, p. 270. Further examples from Louth and Walberswick in Thomson, *Early Tudor Church*, p. 294.

[43] Cook, *Medieval Chantries*, p. 25 (London); Duffy, *Stripping of the Altars*, p. 146.

[44] French, 'Local identity', p. 71.

[45] CWA, p. 58–9.

[46] Wasson (ed.), *Devon*, p. xxii, sees this as the typical parochial structure for Devon and 'a way of keeping the community involved in church and temporal affairs'.

[47] Osborne (ed.), *CWA of Chagford*, pp. 40ff, 130.

[48] Basing (ed.), *Fraternity Register*, pp. 18ff; unit: absolute figures in old pence.

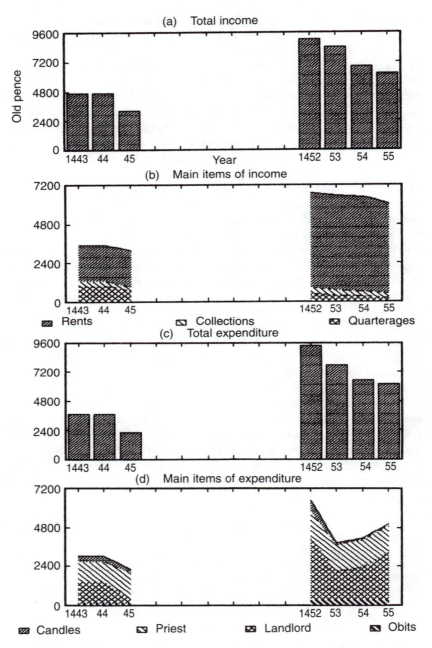

Figure 4.1 Accounts of the Holy Trinity and SS Fabian and Sebastian fraternity at St Botolph Aldersgate, London, 1443–55; unit: absolute figures in old pence

candles, priests, and property maintenance. The average post-merger income of £31 15 s. 9 d. (1452–5) is considerably higher than that of the first surviving parish accounts (£10 14 s. in 1468–81), but tables had turned at the dissolution: the fraternity was valued at just £17 16 s., while the churchwardens accounted for over £30 (excluding balances) in the last pre-Reformation years.[49] This reversal provides a suggestive example for the 'rise' of communal institutions, even though the laity's priorities had always been clear: the Trinity chaplain assisted the parish, his morrow mass service benefited all inhabitants, and office holders had to be drawn from among the parishioners.[50]

The participation of gild chaplains in the parochial cure of souls, divine service, or the church choir was not unusual, and many testators stipulated that their gifts were to pass on to the parish should the fraternity as the original beneficiary cease to exist.[51] This attitude was shared by the officials themselves: the St Mary gildwardens at Hatherleigh in Devon managed to forestall the Chantries Act of 1545 by transferring their assets to a group of trustees which were to hold 'the property for the service and use of the parish'.[52] Elsewhere, parishioners benefited from the fraternities' support of music and plays, the promotion of new feasts (Corpus Christi), efforts to beautify the church, or the endowment of additional masses to meet the needs of particular groups or professions.[53]

But relationships could be more formal than that. The parish as a whole or its representatives often exercised some sort of supervisory functions over gild property, finances, or discipline. At Rickmansworth in 1532, George Belch, a former warden of the Virgin and St Katherine gild, was sued by the parish for insufficient accounting, the masters of the fraternity of St Mary at Brinkhill in Lincolnshire were reprimanded for not rendering their accounts 'coram parochianis', Cambridgeshire churchwardens presented gild members for outstanding debts and disobedience to their officers, and the Botolph Aldersgate parish wardens

---

[49] Kitching (ed.), *Chantry Certificates*, p. 30, and Botolph CWA, 1533–9. The fact that the fraternity was one of the wealthiest parish gilds in London (see C. M. Barron's review of Basing (ed.), *Fraternity Register*, in *London Journal*, 10 (1984), 94–5) makes the change even more significant.

[50] Basing (ed.), *Fraternity Register*, pp. xii, xvii and 3. When needed, the gild also made loans to the parish, for example Botolph CWA, 1497–98.

[51] Westlake, *Parish Gilds*, pp. 63ff, Thomson, *Early Tudor Church*, p. 297, and W. Sheils, 'Religion in provincial towns' in F. Heal and R. O'Day (eds), *Church and Society in England* (London, 1977), p. 175 (various forms of assistance in the cure of souls; see the rewards paid to John Vyne, 'capellanus fraternitatis' for special services in Ashburton CWA, 1519–20 and 1520–1); Duffy, *Stripping of the Altars*, p. 149 (testators).

[52] J. Manaton, *Hatherleigh History in Brief* (Exeter, 1951), p. 12.

[53] Rosser, 'Parish and guild', pp. 42ff.

helped with the auditing of reckonings of the Trinity fraternity.[54] The communal body of the 'four men' at Chagford was in charge of 'all the goods of every store of the church', which meant that it issued the new set of subparochial officers with some start-up capital and then collected their profits at the end of their term.[55] At Peterborough, to take a final example, the parish assumed responsibility for gild lands in 1537, 'becawse the Baylyes thereof delt not justly with the Townsmen'. At the same place, it also stored money for the gilds and even made appointments on their behalf.[56]

Summing up, in large and heavily differentiated communities, gilds had a potential to be 'exclusive' or 'divisive', but in a more coherent parish the similarities in membership, office holding, religious orientation, and social life must have outweighed the differences. As in the relationship between crafts and towns, each had a life and character of its own, but the existence of separate units was the result of different functions rather than fundamental opposition. Parishioners who joined a fraternity made an additional effort, some financial contributions, and accepted particular regulations, but so did those who chose to opt for other 'voluntary' activities in- or outside the parish such as the veneration of specialized saints, pilgrimages, parochial offices, the minor orders, bequests, or endowments of additional masses. Mutual respect and internal arbitration were not a prerogative of gilds, either.[57] Membership in a fraternity with strict moral and ethical rules could convey a 'certificate of moral qualification' not unlike that associated with later protestant sects,[58] but – quite in contrast to the latter – differences had not yet become so marked to prevent the same people from taking an active part in both institutions.[59] In many ways, the parish was itself

---

[54] Aston, 'Iconoclasm', 530; Thomson, *Early Tudor Church*, p. 295; W. Palmer (ed.), 'Fifteenth-century visitation records of the deanery of Wisbech', *Proceedings of the Cambridge Antiquarian Society*, 39 (1938–9), 69–75; Basing (ed.), *Fraternity Register*, p. 29 (Botolph).

[55] Osborne (ed.), *CWA of Chagford*, pp. 130–1. A similar system operated at Morebath, and the fraternities of St Edmund, Salisbury, too, returned their 'increases' to the parish wardens: Binney (ed.), *Morebath*, 'introduction', and Morebath and St Edmund CWA, passim.

[56] CWA, pp. 136, 91–2, 158: Robert Merchauntt was chosen 'by ther hole assent ... [to sing] within the seyd Churche for the brethren and systers of all the Gyldes' (memorandum of 6 Nov. 1544).

[57] Cf. the peace-keeping role of the parish discussed in the Chapter 2.2.3.

[58] Rosser, 'Parish and guild', p. 37.

[59] See the evidence quoted in Chapter 2.2.2 and C. Louis (ed.), *The Commonplace Book of Robert Reynes of Acle* (New York, 1980), pp. 29ff (overlap of parochial and fraternity

some kind of fraternity, 'a point perhaps not usually given the emphasis it deserves'.[60] The distribution of the Holy Loaf manifested the brotherly nature of parochial worship, and the annual fraternity feast had its parallel in parochial 'general minds' which all members of the community were expected to attend.[61]

Both gilds and parishes combined orthodox religious devotion with increasing lay control, a mixture of compulsory and voluntary activities, collective rather than individual worship, and an involvement in secular affairs.[62] Gilds, however, were much the more flexible instrument, be it for the establishment of tailor-made devotional services or for the provision of means to ease the constraints of an inflexible parochial network.

4.2 Chantries

Gilds and chantries were different incarnations of the same intercessory impulse.[63] A chantry was a temporary or perpetual endowment of daily masses celebrated by one or more priests for the souls of certain named beneficiaries. Normally attached to a side altar of a parish church, it could also be founded in chapels, specially erected churches, monasteries, or cathedrals. Temporary chantries were relatively easy to set up and required only limited monetary resources and contractual arrangements, but the creation of a perpetual ecclesiastical benefice was a protracted process which depended on the consent of all the relevant parties and the securing of a mortmain licence for the alienation of landed property. The establishment of the Halleway chantry in All Saints, Bristol, for instance, was preceded by an inquiry conducted by the bishop of Worcester in 1452. In its course, the foundress was questioned about her motives, the abbot of St Augustine as rector of the church approached for his permission, and the vicar, Sir William Robert, churchwardens, and two other parishioners consulted about any

---

interests), or Brown, 'Late medieval Wiltshire', p. 153 (the stewards of the Jesus mass fraternity at St Edmund, Salisbury, went on to become churchwardens two to three years later). 'The same men generally appear at the head of the different bodies': Genicot, *Rural Communities*, p. 104.

[60] Swanson, *Church and Society*, p. 280.

[61] Burgess, 'Benefactions of mortality', pp. 75ff.

[62] Both had a share in preparing parishioners for the local government functions of the Tudor Age, perhaps in the form of a gradual replacement of gilds by parish institutions: see V. Bainbridge's forthcoming monograph on *Gilds in the Medieval Countryside*.

[63] Many gilds could be described as 'poor men's chantries': Cook, *Medieval Chantries*, p. 25.

potential objections. Satisfied that there were none, the episcopal licence was granted on 6 May 1452.[64]

The total number of foundations, from the first evidence at Chichester in 1180 to the badly timed initiative of the royal servant Robert Burgoyne in 1545, must have exceeded 2000.[65] On the eve of the religious changes, London still contained 200 chantries, 13 of which had been established in the sixteenth century. In the country as a whole, 2374 priests may have been attached to perpetual institutions in 1529.[66] In most areas, foundations peaked in the fourteenth century, but in counties like Lancashire only in the late fifteenth. Norwich recorded the highest percentage of bequests for temporal chantries halfway through Henry VIII's reign, which may have reflected the government's ever more hostile attitude towards alienations into the dead hand. At the dissolution, all 'superstitious' foundations were earmarked for confiscation by the crown, and in March 1549 alone, the Court of Augmentations raised £18 000 out of the sale of chantry and gild property.[67]

Chantries are often seen as an expression of increasing individualism and shortcuts to the Reformation have been made by interpreting foundations as 'at once a symptom of the low esteem into which monasteries had fallen, and of the growing individualism in religion which finally expressed itself in Protestantism'.[68] From a late medieval perspective, however, they much rather reveal the sort of mixture between individual and communal motives which was so typical for the period. On top of prayers for the founder's souls, chantries often provided 'an increase of divine service' in their host communities.[69] Cantarists were expected to assist the parish clergy, and to keep the canonical hours. The ordinance of the Vavasour chantry at Badsworth in Yorkshire, for instance, stated that the chaplain was to sing in the choir each Sunday and festival day, wearing his surplice. Churchwardens' accounts sometimes record small payments for such services, which could become more time-consuming than the 'core' responsibilities

[64] Ibid., p. 46.

[65] Moorman, *Thirteenth Century*, p. 17 (Chichester), Scarisbrick, *Reformation*, p. 9 (Burgoyne). The (conservative) estimate in Cutts, *Parish Priests and their People*, p. 442; Kreider, *English Chantries*, pp. 16–17, found 2189 institutions supporting at least one priest in a survey of just 4620 parishes, but these include hospitals and gild priests.

[66] Cook, *Medieval Chantries*, p. 49; Lander, *Government and Community*, p. 109.

[67] Kreider, *English Chantries*, pp. 88–9 (early peak), Haigh, *Lancashire*, pp. 71–2, Tanner, *Church in Norwich*, p. 101 (44 per cent of wills made in the 1520s), and Scarisbrick, *Reformation*, p. 122 (crown profit).

[68] Oxley, *Essex*, pp. 63–4; similarly Cross, *Church and People*, p. 44.

[69] Burgess, 'Chantries in the parish'. See the evidence quoted there and, for the following examples, Cook, *Medieval Chantries*, pp. 15–16.

towards the founders. At St Ewen's, Gloucester, the cantarist was required to step in whenever the vicar was sick or absent, while the foundation of the chantry of our Lady in St Nicholas, Bristol, provided for a priest 'to be at all Divine Service and assistance to the curate and others in administration of the sacraments to the great multitude of people in the parish'. The fact that some chaplains bequeathed musical literature to their churches testifies both to their close ties with the parish and to their share in its ceremonial life.[70] Cantarists were also required to swear an oath of allegiance to the parochial incumbent which included an assurance not to take oblations or to stir up strife. Not all of them were conscientious, of course, but negligent chaplains faced presentments at visitations. At Reculver in Kent in 1511, parishioners complained that two priests would not 'come yn to syng divine service as it hath been used aforetime',[71] while at Christopher-le-Stocks in 1521, proceedings were initiated to deprive Sir William in the wake of allegations of incontinence made 'by the greater part of the said parish, and by all the churchwardens'.[72]

Many cantarists fulfilled preaching or educational duties. Schools were attached to 10 out of 91 Lancashire chantries, and there must have been well over 200 in England as a whole.[73] But chantries, like gilds, were also used to amend the inadequacies of the parochial network: at Leverington (Cambs.) in 1459, an insufficiently endowed institution was moved to the chapel of Parson Drove with the intention that the local population should make up the priest's wages in return for pastoral services.[74] By the time of the dissolution, up to a quarter of the chaplains may have participated in the cure of souls, many in outlying villages or hamlets.[75] Parishioners also benefited from occasional loans from chantry funds and the assets of expired temporary institutions.[76] And poor relief payments must have been welcome in most places, even before the worsening socio-economic conditions of the sixteenth century.[77]

---

[70] William Warens, incumbent of a chantry in All Saints, Bristol, bequeathed a book of pricksong to the parish in 1480 (Burgess, 'Chantries in the parish', 58).

[71] Cook, *Medieval Chantries*, pp. 15–16.

[72] Greater London Record Office, DL/C/207, f. 50ᵛ.

[73] Haigh, *Lancashire*, p. 33; Wood-Legh, *Perpetual Chantries*, pp. 268ff.

[74] Swanson, *Church and Society*, p. 302.

[75] This was explicitly recognized by the chantry commissioners for 21 Lancashire institutions: Haigh, *Lancashire*, p. 33; 214 out of 913 chantries in Essex, Warwicks., Wilts., and Yorks. were essential for the local cure of souls: Kreider, *English Chantries*, p. 48.

[76] At Croscombe, the parish borrowed 40s. for repair works in 1526–7 (Hobhouse (ed.), *CWA of Croscombe [etc.]*, p. 38); founders often stipulated that all the possessions of temporary chantries were to go to the parish: Burgess, 'Chantries in the parish', 63.

[77] Six shillings and eight pence were a standard figure, for example for the Cornborough chantry at Romford (McIntosh, *Autonomy and Community*, p. 236) or at St Mary, Scarborough (D. Smith (ed.), *A Calendar of the Register of Robert Waldby* (York, 1974), pp. 19–20).

Another reason not to overestimate the individual character of chantry institutions is the evidence for collective initiatives and communal control. Almost a third of all lay foundations at Norwich were the result of collective efforts.[78] The first chantry founded by a local community in Lancashire dates back to 1235 and 11 out of a total of 139 originated in this way. Five alone were based in the huge parish of Whalley, no doubt as another indication of their pastoral functions.[79] Whatever the precise circumstances, the advowson of many urban and some rural foundations 'was assigned to the parson and churchwardens or a specific number of the better sort of parishioners, usually four or six, but sometimes as many as twelve'.[80] Countless examples could be quoted: from the late thirteenth century, the rector, churchwardens, and 'chief of the parishioners' of St Mary Woolnoth in London became patrons of a chantry in their church, while the wardens and rector of St Peter Cheap possessed the advowson of a perpetual institution at the altar of the Blessed Virgin Mary. On 15 December 1436, John Martyn, rector of St Ethelburga within Bishopsgate, and Richard Person, John Burvayn, John Piers, Philip Jakes, William Brammyng, and John Sperhawke, 'comparochiani', presented to the St Mary chantry in their church.[81] Due to their failure to do so in 1416, we know that the parishioners of Sudbourne with Orford normally appointed a chantry priest, while the chapelwardens of Romford exercised the same right in conjunction with the manorial bailiff.[82] Eight and 12 'principal men' respectively acted as electors for cantarists at Croydon and St Lawrence, Ipswich.[83]

The involvement of the local community could extend into the daily affairs of many chantries. Bristol parish ordinances often legislated on relevant matters,[84] and rather than being entrusted to monasteries or the priest himself, late fifteenth-century foundations were normally

---

[78] Tanner, *Church in Norwich*, pp. 212ff.

[79] Raines (ed.), *History of Chantries*, i. xxxiiiff. The greatest density of institutions supporting at least one priest can be found in the West Riding of Yorks with an equally inadequate parochial network: Kreider, *English Chantries*, pp. 16–17.

[80] Wood-Legh, *Perpetual Chantries*, p. 66; similar Cook, *Medieval Chantries*, pp. 59, 74.

[81] Newcourt (ed.), *Repertorium*, i. 461–2 and 520; GL, MS 9531/6, f. 25. Between 1426 and 1447, the registers of the bishops of London record the (sometimes repeated) involvement of the 'custodum bonorum et ornamentorum' or 'parochianorum principalium' in presentations at All Hallows the Great, Nicholas Shambles, Stephen Coleman, St Bride, Edmund Lombard Street (Register of William Gray: GL, MS 9531/5, fos 19ᵛ, 21, 28, 33, 50ᵛ), Mary Abchurch, Mary Woolnoth, and Mildred Poultry (Reg. Robert Gilbert: GL, MS 9531/6, fos 34, 53ᵛ, 95ᵛ). I am grateful to Irene Zadnik for these references.

[82] Wood-Legh, *Perpetual Chantries*, p. 71; McIntosh, *Autonomy and Community*, p. 236.

[83] Cook, *Medieval Chantries*, pp. 17, 59.

[84] For example Fox (ed.), 'St Stephen', 201 (1524).

established as 'service' chantries under parochial control.[85] By 1500, the wardens were commonly the trustees of such institutions, and their powers could extend to the payment of the priest.[86] Mary-at-Hill in London was a particularly striking example: the parishioners presented for instance to the Wrytell chantry,[87] and the churchwardens accounted for the income and expenses from a total of seven institutions. A detailed profit-and-loss statement made for the Causton foundation reveals revenues of over £18 and costs of just £12, with the difference benefiting the parish.[88] The seven cantarists, one specifically responsible for the morrow mass, received £6 13s. 4d. a year each from the wardens, who also managed the landed endowments, collected the rents, and – occasionally – started legal proceedings against reluctant tenants. Elsewhere, chantries were dealt with in separate records, allowing further glimpses into the financial dimensions of the subparochial level. At All Saints, Bristol, the churchwardens were in charge of the Halleway chantry in much the same way as their London colleagues.[89] The founder had stipulated that

> the seid procuratours and thair successours yerli at such time as thei yelde thair commune accomptes of the profites of the liflood and other thinges of the saide chirch shall dueli, truli and effectualli ... yelde accomptis of all thinges and summes of money bi tham paide and resceiued of the liflood and profites belonging to the saide Chaunterie.[90]

Their reckonings survive from the 1460s to the dissolution, and both the first and last decade are summarized in Figure 4.2.[91] The overall trend is unambiguous: comparatively high rents and modest expenses at the beginning, but reduced revenue and soaring costs at the end. The priest's wages remained relatively stable at between £6–7,[92] but the landed endowments were apparently in great need of repair, and the accounts

---

[85] Burgess, 'Strategies for eternity', p. 23. A service chantry used trustees or feoffees drawn from parish and town to circumvent mortmain restrictions.

[86] Swanson, *Church and Society*, p. 218. Parish control could of course date from a much earlier period: in 1390, John Bathe entrusted the property of his chantry to the rector and churchwardens of St Botolph Aldersgate, with any surplus going to repairs or the ornaments of the church: Basing (ed.), *Fraternity Register*, p. xix.

[87] Cook, *Medieval Chantries*, p. 59.

[88] Mary-at-Hill CWA, 1494–5.

[89] Halleway chantry accounts: BRO, P/AS/C/1. This was not restricted to the big cities: the churchwardens of Bridgwater in Somerset, for example, were also in charge of the Holy Cross chantry: French, 'Bridgwater', p. 37.

[90] Bickley (ed.), *Little Red Book*, ii. 205.

[91] Unit: absolute figures in old pence.

[92] The median income of chantry priests at Bristol has been estimated at £6: Skeeters, *Community and Clergy*, p. 88.

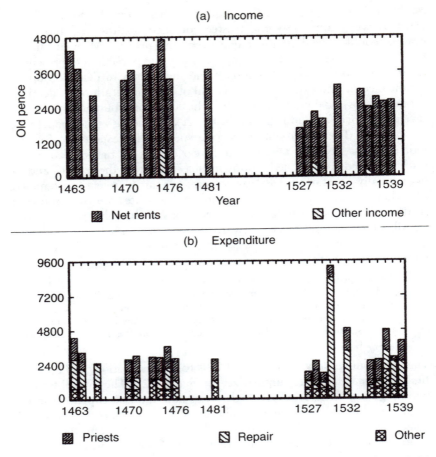

Figure 4.2   Accounts of the Halleway Chantry at All Saints, Bristol, 1463–81
and 1527–39; unit: absolute figures in old pence

repeatedly record statements like: the warden 'askith to be allowid v^s x^d
which he hath payd more then he hath recevid of the emolimentes of the
chantree as it apperith more playne in the booke of the chantre this
yere'.[93] The parishioners put up a fight, tried to boost revenues by
attracting new business,[94] but to little effect: in these last ten years they
were forced to contribute no less than £55 to cover the chantry's deficits.

[93] All Saints CWA, 1521–2. The worst year was 1530–1 when the chantry account made
a loss of over £30.
[94] See the example discussed in Chapter 2.3.3; similarly, the St James churchwardens in
the same town adopted a long-term strategy to save the Spicer chantry from extinction:
Burgess, 'Strategies for eternity', p. 22.

There would have been little need for this had the community not felt responsible for the subparochial institutions and appreciated their services. Comparing the Halleway chantry's financial fortunes (and those of Botolph's Trinity gild examined above) with the steadily rising revenues of churchwardens' accounts, it is clear which way the trend was going. Lagging marginally behind in the mid-fifteenth century, the parish raised over four times more than the chantry on the eve of the Reformation.[95]

Chantry founders often integrated other institutions, most notably municipal bodies, into the complex web of supervision mechanisms.[96] The involvement of parochial incumbents in the election process helped to prevent clerical rivalries, and reliance on municipal corporations provided a means to secure 'perpetual' adherence to the founders' wishes. The city authorities took their duties seriously:

> Sir William Yattes, the chantry priest of the chapel of St Thomas the Martyr, upon the High Bridge, being deceased, and the place must be filled up within eight days by the mayor and commons, it is agreed that a kalender shall be made of such honest priests as will labour for it, and they that have the most voices to be presented to the dean and chapter to have the chantry.[97]

Many towns exercised at least rights of nomination or presentation, but some had far greater powers: candidates for the Halleway chantry at All Saints, for instance, were subjected to a full-scale examination by the mayor of Bristol.[98] In 1499, the mayor and corporation of York issued detailed regulations governing the conduct of four priests in the bridge chapel of St William. Punishment for offenders started at 6 s. 8 d., rose to 13 s. 4 d. in case of a relapse, and culminated in the loss of the benefice. These were not empty threats: in 1544, the town authorities withheld a

---

[95] Income of the first chantry account 1463–4: £18 1 s. 1 d./ CWA: £16 15 s. 3½ d.; last chantry account 1539–40: £10 15 s. 6 d./ CWA: £47 3 s. 4 d. In humbler, less well-endowed rural parishes, chantry incomes would of course remain higher: at the time of the *Valor Ecclesiasticus*, the chantry of St Mary, Bethersden, was valued at £7 7 s. 8 d. (A. Hussey (ed.), *Kent Chantries* (Ashford, 1936), p. 18), while the churchwardens' income amounted to £5 17 s. 7 d. (Mercer (ed.), *CWA at Betrysden*, p. 32).

[96] Burgess, 'Strategies for eternity', p. 19. The supervision of chantry priests may well have served as a precedent for the establishment of town lectureships in the Elizabethan period.

[97] Lincoln city register of 16 May 1520, quoted in Wood-Legh, *Perpetual Chantries*, p. 158.

[98] 'Ad cantariam ... in villa Castribernardi vacantem et ad meam presentacionem ex nominacione communitatis ville Castribernardi spectantem ...': extract from a presentation by vicar Roger de Kyrkeby in 1412: R. Storey (ed.), *Register of Thomas Langley* (Durham, 1957), ii. 6-7; Bickley (ed.), *Little Red Book*, ii. 199ff (Halleway chantry).

chantry priest's income until he resumed his neglected duties.[99] At Sandwich, to take another example, chaplains faced imprisonment if they refused to take a full part in the community's ceremonial life.[100] It goes without saying that towns also appreciated the prestige and material benefits associated with their responsibilities. The Thurscrosse chantry at Hull was endowed with £200, of which a mere £5 13s. 4d. went to the priest, and many foundations specified financial rewards for the attendance of town authorities at anniversaries. This was motivated partly by the fact 'that their presence might add to the splendour of the occasion, but also to recompense them for their trouble in supervising the affairs of the chantry'.[101] As for the clergy, they seem to have accepted this extensive lay control and some made similar arrangements themselves.[102]

A good example for the range of communal benefits and powers is the chantry set up at the Virgin Mary altar of Scarborough church in 1397.[103] Founded for the souls of Emery Edwyn, Reginald Milner, their ancestors, 'all the faithful departed, and for the commonalty of Scarborough, both living and dead', it was endowed with various lands and possessions in the town. The right of presentation was vested in the commonalty in perpetuity, and provision was made to remove negligent or scandalous priests. The incumbent's duties included the saying of daily masses, obits, and anniversaries for the beneficiaries, the maintenance of all ornaments and religious utensils, the presence in choir for all matins, masses, vespers, and processions, the upkeep of an almshouse and the distribution of money to its inmates.

On the whole, chantries, too, could hardly be described as a constant thorn in the parishioners' side, and the abolition of subparochial institutions must have caused problems in many places. At the dissolution in 1547, the crown's military and financial needs were given priority over the promised reinvestment of chantry possessions for educational and social purposes.[104] Some towns were able to repurchase at least parts of the endowments, but for many parishioners the losses in

---

[99] Wood-Legh, *Perpetual Chantries*, pp. 169ff.

[100] P. Clark, *English Provincial Society* (Hassocks, 1977), p. 37.

[101] Wood-Legh, *Perpetual Chantries*, p. 178. The CWs of All Saints paid the mayor 6s. 8d., the sheriff 3s. 4d., the bailiffs 20d., the town clerk 12d., and themselves 6s. 8d. each for their attendance at Joan Halleway's obit: Chantry Accounts, 1463–4.

[102] Wood-Legh, *Perpetual Chantries*, p. 179.

[103] Smith (ed.), *Register of Robert Waldby*, pp. 19–20.

[104] Cook, *Medieval Chantries*, pp. 76–7; cf. Chapter 6.1 below.

terms of pastoral provision and other benefits must have been very considerable.[105]

4.3 Chapels

Social mobility, demographic change, and the emergence of new settlements posed constant challenges to the established parochial network. The *raison d'être* for a chapel at Garsdale in the parish of Dent (Yorks.), for instance, was a distance of over three miles from the mother church, and 'the necessetie therof ... to have one prist to celebrate ther, beinge in the mounteynez, so that in wynter many tymez ther can nothinge passe betwixt the same and the paroch churche'.[106] In places like these, separated from the main centre of worship by rivers, moors, or other topographical hazards, petitions by local inhabitants for better religious provision normally pointed to the very grave consequences 'both in body and soul ... if it should chance any child to be born into this world or any other person to be sore vexed with sickness (the said water then being overflowed) they should perish before they should have the sacraments and sacramentals of the holy Church be ministered to them'. Elsewhere, raids on deserted hamlets and even invasions of foreign troops were among the fears expressed by distant parishioners.[107] At Newchurch in Rossendale (see Map 4.1 depicting the location of some Lancashire churches), the chapel owed its existence to recent colonialization:

> whereas before that time there was nothing else but deer and other savage and wild beasts, there is since, by industry of the inhabitants, grown to be very fertile ground, well replenished with people. And forasmuch as their parish church is distant twelve miles from the said forest, and the ways very foul, painful and perilous, and the country in the winter season is so extremely and vehemently cold, that infants borne to church are in great peril of their lives ... and the dead corpses there like to remain unburied at such times for want of carriage, till such time as great annoyance doth grow thereby: the premises considered, the inhabitants of the said forest, about thirty-eight years past, or thereabouts, at their proper costs made a chapel of ease in the said forest; since the disforesting of which from eighty persons in the forest they are grown to 1000, young and old.[108]

---

[105] Sheils, *Reformation*, pp. 38–9.

[106] W. Page (ed.), *The Certificates of the Commissioners Appointed to Survey the Chantries ... in the County of York* (Durham, 1893), ii. 269.

[107] Examples from Henley-in-Arden (quote *t.* Henry VIII), Aldenham (Herts.), and Weymouth (Dorset) in Kreider, *English Chantries*, pp. 55ff.

[108] T. Whitaker, *An History of the Original Parish of Whalley* (Manchester, 1872), p. 318 (extract from a petition for the preservation of the chapel at the time of the Reformation).

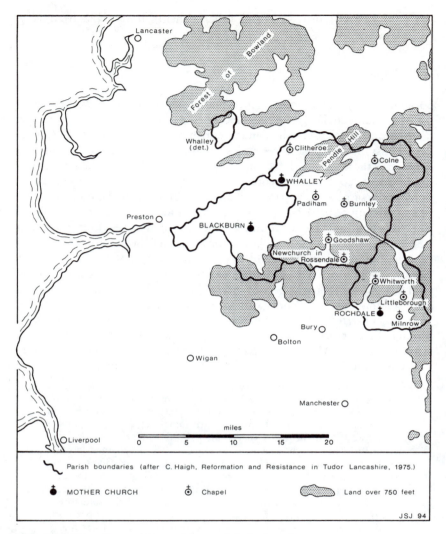

Map 4.1   Some Lancashire parishes and their chapels

Whatever the circumstances, a safe and easy access to the sacraments was the common denominator of all these initiatives. Progress, however, was piecemeal and always had some strings attached: at Ripponden and Luddenden, the inhabitants obtained the right to celebrate daily masses (with the exception of certain feast days, when – typically – wax had to be offered to the high altar of the mother church), but they were not dispensed from paying tithes and fabric maintenance duties to the parish of Halifax.[109] Similarly, the population of Boterworth and Honorsfeld was allowed to celebrate mass at the newly erected chapel of Littleborough (Map 4.1), but again under the strict condition that the parish would suffer no financial damage.[110] This was common canonical practice, both in England and on the Continent; the fiscalization of church administration demanded careful consideration of all existing rights and dues.[111]

Lancashire, to take a particularly striking case study, was a county with an inadequate parochial network. Benefices were well endowed, but areas too large for efficient pastoral provision. Fifty-six per cent of parishes had been appropriated and the high income attracted absentee pluralists. With the exception of Lytham, mother churches were responsible for at least three separate settlements, and an average of 1700 parishioners.[112] The demand for additional places of worship was obvious, but poverty and economic underdevelopment prevented large-scale investment into better religious provision until the late fifteenth and early sixteenth centuries, when most of the (datable) chapels were built.[113] Over half are located in the south east of the county, where the incipient textile industry created some spare resources. Taken together with the contemporary increase in chantry foundations and the popularity of the cult of saints, this amounted to the clearing of a considerable backlog in terms of contemporary religious fashions.[114] Most initiatives were taken locally and collectively:

> whereas hitherto the initiative in providing places of worship had been taken by monastic or other religious communities and by individual clerics and landowners, now groups of local parishioners are seen to be raising money to build modest churches for themselves and sometimes also to support their ministers. Ten of the new chapels are said to have been built 'by the inhabitants'.[115]

---

[109] A. Thompson, *The English Clergy and their Organization in the Later Middle Ages* (Oxford, 1947), pp. 127–8 (both examples; 1466 and 1496).

[110] One fifth of the dues received by the chaplain had to be passed on to the incumbent at Rochdale: Fishwick, *Rochdale*, pp. 189ff (1471).

[111] Ottobuono Fieschi legation, 1268: Powicke and Cheney (eds), *Councils and Synods*, ii. 766; Schöller, *Kirchenbau im Mittelalter*, pp. 353ff (for example Langen-Trechow: a third of all bequests to go to the fabric of the mother church at Bützow; 1329).

[112] Figure based on 1563 survey (compared to 167 parishioners in the diocese of Salisbury): Haigh, *Lancashire*, pp. 22ff.

[113] Ibid., pp. 31 and 66; G. Tupling, 'The pre-Reformation parishes and chapelries of Lancashire', *Transactions of the Lancashire and Cheshire Antiquarian Society*, 67 (1957), 9 and 12ff: chapel foundation sequence: 1100–1200: 24 (with some of even earlier origin), 1200–1300: 16, 1300–1400: 13; 1470–1548: 46.

[114] Haigh, *Lancashire*, pp. 21 and 67ff, for a more detailed discussion.

[115] Tupling, 'Chapelries of Lancashire', 9 (of a total of 46 between 1470–1548).

By 1550, a quarter of all Lancashire households were looked after by chapels and quite immune to central control or outside interference.

Social reality meant that broad local initiatives stood a better chance if they were headed by lords, influential gentlemen, or the more substantial members of the community. When pope Boniface IX approved burial rights for the chapel of Carleton in the East Riding of Yorkshire, he granted them to the temporal lord Brian de Stapulton 'et habitatoribus ville'.[116] Across the Pennines, it was Robert Holt Esq. who 'at the earnest motions and request of the inhabitants' coordinated the endeavours to secure sufficient endowment for a chapel at Whitworth. The actual building work, however, was supervised by a larger group of 14 local householders and the day-to-day business entrusted to a 'chapel vestry' of four men, which 'shall ever have the placeing and setting of ye priest', as well as the power to allocate pews.[117] At Goodshaw in the neighbouring parish of Whalley (see Map 4.1), the foundation details emerge from a contract between eight prominent yeomen – four each from the two interested parties. Written in 1540–1, it confirmed that

> 'they shall found, Edifie, and Build one Chapel in the Honour of God, our Blessed Lady, and all saints, in a certain place within the forest of Rossendale named Morrell Height, for the Easement of the said parties and of their neighbours'. As for the financial arrangements, it was stated 'that they, the said George Ormerod ... and the said Co-fellows, with and towards the help and supportation as they shall happen to get of their neighbours the Inhabitants of Crawshawbooth, Gambleside, Nutshaw, and Dunnockshaw ... shall make, stand to, and bear the Moiety of all manner of costs and charges concerning the foundation and Building of the said Chapel; and in like manner the said Thurstan Birtwistle ... covenanteth ... that [he] and his Co-fellows, with the help and supportation of other their neighbours, Inhabitants of the Goodshaw and Loveclough beforesaid, shall make, stand to, and bear the other Moiety of all manner of costs and charges concerning the foundation and Building of the said chapel'.[118]

Further details concerned the structure, size, and ornamentation of the new building. The involvement of 'co-fellows' and 'neighbours' clearly points to a broad communal effort, and given the financial dimensions of the undertaking it could have hardly been different. The building of even a small church could easily cost several dozen pounds and local or

---

[116] P. Zutshi (ed.), *Original Papal Letters in England 1305–1415* (Vatican City, 1990), pp. 209–10 (1391).

[117] Details for Whitworth appear in a series of articles set up in 1532: Fishwick, *Rochdale*, pp. 164ff. The vestry at the time consisted of Edward Leach, Randal Howarth, Lawrence Smith, and Adam Holt.

[118] T. Newbigging, *A History of the Forest of Rossendale* (Rawtenstall, 1893), pp. 177–8.

regional collections must have been standard procedure.[119] Once set up, the priest's wages were the most substantial part of a chapel's budget. Endowments were often too small to cover the full stipend, and ad-hoc contributions of the inhabitants were again needed to make up the difference. This was true in the five Lancashire cases of Goodshaw, Milnrow, Whitworth, Denton, and Billinge, and some communities even rated their members.[120]

In spite of all this financial engagement, the right of presentation proved elusive: in order to win support for the project, advowsons were often ceded to influential gentlemen, abbots, or parochial incumbents. Still, some places did choose their own priests: the inhabitants of the chapelry of Wellow (in the parish of Edwinstowe, Notts.) acquired the right of presentation as early as 1250,[121] and Whitworth and Edesforth could be named as two Lancashire examples.[122] But formal grants were not always necessary: many appointments were the result of local agreements with the parochial incumbent,[123] while places like Pendle (Lancs.) or Hindon (Wilts.) seem to have hired and fired clergymen 'atther pleasure'. These cases may stand for many others.[124]

The relationship between chapels and mother churches was often strained. Bishops were well aware of the problem and insisted that all new foundations required their approval.[125] 'There was always a tendency for the chapelry to build up a church life of its own, especially if access to the parish church was difficult, or the chaplain was conscientious and energetic, or the rector was non-resident.'[126] The

---

[119] Smith, *Pre-Reformation England*, p. 119 (the costs of St George's chapel at Croscombe were £29 11 s. 8 d. *c.* 1500), and Haigh, *Lancashire*, p. 66 (collections for Billinge chapel near Wigan).

[120] Tupling, 'Chapelries of Lancashire', 9 (collections in 5 chapels); rates were levied for example at Denton (Haigh, *Lancashire*, p. 65) or Ayton in Yorks. (Cutts, *Parish Priests and their People*, p. 468).

[121] Reynolds, *Kingdoms and Communities*, p. 95 (agreement with the Lincoln dean and chapter). The chapel goers of Coombe in the parish of Enford were granted episcopal licence to appoint two priests in 1365, and the lord of the manor duly consulted the chief inhabitants when he presented in 1387 (Brown, 'Late medieval Wiltshire', p. 29).

[122] Fishwick, *Rochdale*, pp. 164ff; Raines (ed.), *History of Chantries*, ii. 237.

[123] Thompson, *English Clergy*, p. 128.

[124] Haigh, *Lancashire*, p. 28 (Pendle in 1535), and Brown, 'Late medieval Wiltshire', p. 44 (the quote from the chantry certificate for Hindon; the papal licence of 1405 had granted the advowson to the local rector). Cf. the independent appointment of chaplains at Romford (McIntosh, *Autonomy and Community*, pp. 236ff). Sometimes other communal bodies presented, as in the case of the mayor and burgesses of Thetford (Norfolk) from 1480: Rosser, 'Voluntary religion', 178.

[125] The relationship was a frequent issue at medieval synods: see for example Powicke and Cheney (eds), *Councils and Synods*, p. 766 (Ottobuono legation), or Cutts, *Parish Priests and their People*, p. 113 (Westminster, 1102).

[126] Tupling, 'Chapelries of Lancashire', 10.

records of ecclesiastical courts provide ample evidence for the frequency of struggles about financial and sacramental rights. Many chapels found it difficult to accept that they were only allowed to celebrate masses, when burials and baptisms presented them with even more serious problems. The great plague lent additional weight to their arguments: Grasmere and Windermere were granted a cemetery in 1348, Didsbury near Manchester in 1352,[127] and by the sixteenth century, most Lancashire chapels had achieved quasi-parochial status.[128] Even so, the remaining stigmas of subordination (contributions to the repair of the mother church, periodical attendance) were still resented. The case of Prescot *v.* Farnworth is an illustration from this sample. The first mediation attempt by the archdeacon of Chester dates from 1291, but lawsuits about the collection of rates continued well into the sixteenth century. Eventually, the problems had to be settled by an episcopal decree in 1555.[129] At Colne in 1544, the local inhabitants challenged the vicar of Whalley's authority by refusing him entry to their chapel and by boycotting his masses; in the end there were serious doubts about Colne's actual status. Over at Burnley in the same parish (see Map 4.1), the existence of an ancient chapel with auxiliary clergy and a grammar school induced the wardens to the confident (but unsubstantiated) claim that theirs was neither a 'chantry nor free chapel, but has time out of mind been called a Parish Church'.[130] This was clearly not an attack on the parochial system as such, but an expression of the desire to have a fully privileged church in one's own village. Excessive distance was a frequent and legitimate argument, but communal feeling arguably even more important. A petition made by the vicar of Barton Stacey in the diocese of Winchester is a case in point: the inhabitants of the township of Newton, he complained to pope Eugene IV, expected him to perform all parochial services not only in his own church, but also at their local chapel, even though it was no more than one mile away and not separated by any topographical obstacles whatsoever.[131] But how widespread were such

---

[127] Thompson, *English Clergy*, p. 124 (Grasmere/Windermere), C. Kitching, 'Church and chapelry in sixteenth-century England' in D. Baker (ed.), *The Church in Town and Countryside* (Oxford, 1979), p. 283 (Didsbury).

[128] Tupling, 'Chapelries of Lancashire', 10, that is the combined rights of mass, baptism, and burial.

[129] Prescot Museum: *Prescot Parish Church* (no date), p. 1; Haigh, *Lancashire*, p. 32; CWA of Prescot, p. vii.

[130] Haigh, *Lancashire*, p. 32 (Colne), and H. Fishwick (ed.), *Pleadings and Depositions in the Duchy Court of Lancaster* (vol. iii, Manchester, 1896), p. 159 (Burnley).

[131] J. Twemlow (ed.), *Papal Letters* (vol. ix, London, 1912), p. 335 (1443).

feelings and is it not true that the parochial map was frozen at some point around 1200?[132]

To achieve a formal separation was no mean feat and often required several attempts: the bishop or pope had to be presented with a convincing case for the inadequacy of existing pastoral arrangements, and he wanted to see evidence that there were sufficient resources for the endowment of the new as well as for the compensation of the old benefice.[133] The variety of experiences in Continental countries is instructive. Faced with a similar fossilization of parochial boundaries from the thirteenth century,[134] initiatives were taken more or less everywhere with very similar arguments and identical aims: the inhabitants of the Schächental (in the Swiss canton of Uri), for instance, petitioned the bishop of Constance in 1290 'quod ipsi tempori hyemali interdum etiam proper innundationem aquarum, interdum propter glaties et nives ad parochialem ecclesiam pervenire minime valerent, et ob hoc etiam, quoniam homines in morte constituti sine viatico et extrema unctione decederent'.[135] This was to be a successful attempt, but the outcome varied from case to case and region to region: most of the late medieval initiatives in Central Switzerland achieved at best chapel-of-ease status for their churches,[136] and the same seems to be true for northern Germany. In the south of the Empire, however, the situation was more flexible, particularly on the eve of the Reformation. It has been calculated that in the Palatinate left of the Rhine, no less than 15 per cent of dependent communities separated from their mother churches between 1400 and 1525, very often as a result of a concerted corporate

---

[132] 'Occasionally a chapel separated from the mother church and became an independent parish, but this was not common': Moorman, *Thirteenth Century*, p. 13. In Scotland, the network of parishes was 'virtually complete' by the late thirteenth century: Fawcett, *Scottish Medieval Churches*, p. 24.

[133] A convenient summary of the relevant canonical proceedings in Fuhrmann, 'Kirche im Dorf', pp. 169ff.

[134] 'Le réseau paroissial ... est fixé au XIIIᵉ siècle, parfois même plus tôt': J. Gaudemet, 'La vie paroissiale en occident au moyen âge et dans les temps modernes' in *Communautés rurales* (vol. iv, Paris, 1984), p. 73 (quote); similar J. Kloczowski, 'Communautés rurales et paroissiales en Europe médiévale et moderne', ibid., p. 96, and Künstle, *Die deutsche Pfarrei*, p. 7.

[135] The aim of securing full parochial rights for the local church (Bader, *Dorfgenossenschaft*, pp. 187, 194) was pursued with almost stereotypical references to bad roads, raging torrents, and foul weather: Fuhrmann, 'Kirche im Dorf', pp. 177–8; this example from T. Schiess (ed.), *Quellenwerk zur Entstehung der Schweizerischen Eidgenossenschaft* (Abt. 1, vol. 1, Aarau, 1933), p. 739.

[136] Pfaff, 'Pfarrei und Pfarreileben', p. 220.

effort.[137] A similar regional differentiation can be observed in Italy, where the break-up of the minster style *pievi* system with its great number of dependent chapels without baptismal rights was apparently more successful in the countryside north of Rome than in the cities. However, the process was slow and gradual, starting in eleventh-century Lazio and accelerating as a consequence of new forms of settlement and the growth of popular complaints in the later Middle Ages.[138] In exposed coastal areas such as North Brabant, on the other hand, where land was continually lost or reclaimed, the network had to be rather more flexible.[139]

Returning to the British Isles, there seems to have been some room for manoeuvre in England, too. Several factors worked against easy adjustments: the main settlement period was completed at an earlier stage than on the Continent, and cases of advowson were judged by royal courts, where possessionary aspects may have been given priority over pastoral necessity.[140] Compared with the south-western part of the Holy Roman Empire in particular, England lacked the kind of institutionalized local political communities to provide efficient backing for separation initiatives.[141] English urban and rural self-government was less developed, and local loyalty to the parish as an important focus of secular activities possibly more pronounced. Many a hamlet was faced with the problem that the necessary administrative experience for the creation of a new ecclesiastical unit could only be found in the institutions of the old, which was understandably reluctant to support its own division. But in spite of all these factors, there is a wealth of

---

[137] Hergemöller, 'Parrocchia', pp. 137–8; Fuhrmann, 'Kirche im Dorf', pp. 151–2, 169 (Palatinate). On the whole, the network seems to have been immobile in the twelfth and thirteenth centuries, but somewhat more flexible in the fourteenth and fifteenth: W. Müller, 'Der Beitrag der Pfarreigeschichte zur Stadtgeschichte', *Historisches Jahrbuch*, 94 (1974), 79–80. According to Immacolata Saulle, 'Die Kommunalisierung der Kirche in den drei Bünden' (Diss. phil., Berne, forthcoming), there were over 20 separations in Graubünden on the eve of the Reformation.

[138] D. Hay, 'Il contributo Italiano alla riforma istituzionale della Chiesa' in P. Prodi and P. Johanek (eds), *Strutture ecclesiastiche in Italia e in Germania prima della Riforma* (Bologna, 1984), p. 49; Violante, 'Sistemi organizzativi', pp. 17, 36–8.

[139] A. Bijsterveld, *Laverend tussen Kerk en Wereld* (Amsterdam, 1993), p. 390.

[140] Reynolds, *Kingdoms and Communities*, pp. 86 (settlement) and 95 (crown control over advowson). I am grateful to Susan Reynolds for her comments on the different circumstances governing the developments in England and on the Continent.

[141] Blickle, 'Kommunalismus', pp. 8ff. The motivation for initiatives was both secular and spiritual: a local parish church would provide a welcome chance for expansion onto the ecclesiastical field, but 'communal endowments always have the parallel purpose of elevating the sacral attributes of the political community': Blickle, 'Communal Reformation', 224.

evidence to suggest that inconvenient ecclesiastical structures were tackled throughout the later Middle Ages. Apart from the 'soft' options of founding gilds or chantries,[142] 'there may have been a considerable readjustment in the internal patterns of parish life'.[143] Some attempts were clearly abortive, like those of the inhabitants of Carlton or the chapel of Hollym (both in Yorkshire),[144] but often it is a matter of definition whether an initiative is classified as a success or a failure. The term 'chapel' is hardly appropriate for places like Stanford in Bromyard, which administered its own tithes and dues, or Farnworth, with its separate registers and churchwardens' accounts.[145] There can be little doubt that the local residents – in all but name – led a full and quite normal parish life. The more or less arbitrary list of examples below may illustrate the nationwide scale of the phenomenon:

In Cumbria, the people of Eskdale complained that they were separated by three rivers and ten miles from the parish church of St Bees, which made it impossible to obtain adequate sacramental provision. In 1445, they were given episcopal licence to elevate their chapel to parochial status.[146] The inhabitants of Hesket High owed the building of a new and independent church to the plague in the 1530s and the reluctance of the city of Carlisle to bury their dead.[147] In Lancashire, Brindle, formerly an outlying part of Penwortham, was given parochial status between 1341 and 1369. The ancient chapels of Bispham and Goosnargh were increasingly treated as parish churches in the early Tudor period, while Dean was elevated by Henry VIII in 1541 on the grounds of its distance of eight miles, an increasing population, and a sufficient financial and ornamental basis. Altcar, formerly subject to Walton, was a separate parish at least by 1552.[148] A flexible system can also be found in the West Riding of Yorkshire, 'where a small population increased considerably between the Conquest and the Reformation, new parishes were created out of old dependent chapelries, while some of the churches serving villages deserted in the fourteenth and fifteenth

---

[142] Cf. Rosser, 'Voluntary religion', and the evidence in the two preceding chapters.

[143] Frankforter, 'The Reformation and the register', 223 (increasingly by means of direct recourse to papal licences).

[144] Carlton had purchased papal bulls to obtain a chapelry, but the parish of Snaith reasserted its sovereignty in a lengthy conflict which involved the abbot of Selby and the future Henry IV; Hollym secured an archiepiscopal mandate granting it independent status when the old parish church was abandoned, but here, again, the mother church of Withernsea managed to reverse the decision: Swanson, *Church and Society*, pp. 219, 259.

[145] Kitching, 'Church and chapelry', p. 283 (Stanford); Prescot CWA, p. vi (Farnworth).

[146] Bettey, *Church and Parish*, p. 45.

[147] Cook, *Medieval Parish Church*, pp. 21–2.

[148] VCH *Lancs.*, ii. 25 (Brindle) and 37 (Bispham, Goosnargh and Dean; cf. Haigh, *Lancashire*, p. 31); Tupling, 'Chapelries of Lancashire', 6 (Altcar).

centuries were demolished'.[149] St Mary, Beverley, previously a chapel of ease of St Martin, was given the rights of tithe, offerings, and mortuaries by an ordinance of archbishop Melton in 1325.[150] In Lincolnshire, the chapel of Barkston had become a parochial church by the fourteenth century, although the precise date and circumstances are obscure.[151] Staffordshire as a whole was a county of late ecclesiastical development, and the structure was far from frozen in the thirteenth century. 'The 84 parishes [of 1291] increased to between 125 and 150 at the Reformation, the difference depending on the borderline status of some churches between parishes and chapelries.'[152] This implies at least 41 secessions, although there is some uncertainty about the comprehensiveness of the 1291 figures.[153] St Mary, Lichfield, for instance, was converted from a chapelry of the extramural parish of St Michael into an independent vicarage in the 1530s.[154] In Warwickshire, the acquisition of parochial functions at Ditchford Frary involved a quarter of a century of struggles and compromises with the reluctant rector, Merton College, Oxford.[155]

Change was also possible in the denser network of the South. At Piddington (Oxon) in 1428, the villagers acquired a licence which granted them both parochial status and the election of their priest. Nevertheless, they continued to make voluntary visits to Ambrosden church after the separation.[156] In Essex, St Michael, West Donyland, which had temporarily been annexed to Holy Trinity, Colchester, was re-edified and created a parish in 1539 on the authority of the abbot of St John's.[157] Even in London adjustment was possible in the fifteenth century. St Stephen Coleman Street, a chapel of St Olave Jewry and

---

[149] Palliser, 'Parish in perspective', p. 10.

[150] Cook, *Medieval Parish Church*, p. 22.

[151] D. Owen, 'Chapelries and rural settlement' in P. Sawyer (ed.), *Medieval Settlement* (London, 1976), p. 67.

[152] D. Palliser, *The Staffordshire Landscape* (London, 1976), p. 74.

[153] *VCH Staffs.*, iii. 28–9. The same caveat applies to Wiltshire, where a comparison of the parishes listed in 1291 and 1535 suggests that 15 chapels were elevated in the period: Brown, 'Late medieval Wiltshire', appendix I.

[154] Swanson, *Church and Society*, p. 5 (the new parish did not have burial rights).

[155] Swanson, 'Standards of livings', p. 174: a papal licence was secured in 1400, but Merton challenged it in various Roman and English courts. Compromise attempts included a separation of the tithes of the chapel from those of the mother church at Great Wolford. For details see R. Swanson, 'Parochialism and particularism: the dispute over the status of Ditchford Frary' in the forthcoming *Festschrift* for D. Owen (*Medieval Ecclesiastical Studies*, pp. 241–57).

[156] Rosser, 'Voluntary religion', 182, and *VCH Oxon.*, v. 256. In the same county, Yarton is described as a former part of Cassington at a visitation in 1520: 'Churchwardens' presentments', 95.

[157] Gibson (ed.), *Codex*, p. 1536.

appropriated to the priory of Butley in Suffolk, was situated in a rather poor and densely populated area between Lothbury and London wall,[158]

> but in ... 1456 on the 6th of November this Church or Chapel was made Parochial, and a Vicarage ordain'd and endowed by Thomas [Kemp] then Bishop of London, who convening before him the Prior and Convent of Butley aforesaid ... and the Parishioners of this Parish (between whom, and the said Prior and Convent there had been great Contests about the same) and the Vicar of S. Olaves ... did with the Consent of them all create and ordain this Chapel from thenceforth to be a Parish-Church, and a Vicarage, and out of the Profits thereof the Vicar and his Successors to have eleven Pounds per Ann. which was to be paid by the said Prior and Convent, or their Deputy, yearly at the four usual Feasts by even and equal Portions. Provided, that if the Vicar did not reside in the said Parish, but lived out of it anywhere else without the Bishop's Licence, he was then to have but 10l. per Ann.
> From this time it continued a Parish Church, and a Vicarage distinct of itself, and in the Gift of the Prior and Convent of Butley, till the Suppression of that House.[159]

In spite of the strained relationship between rector and community, it had been possible to find a solution which maintained the links to the priory. Outside the city walls, Henry VIII created a parish at St Martin-in-the-Fields, apparently because of the nuisance caused to the palace by the transport of corpses to St Margaret, Westminster.[160] In Surrey, the chapel of Ewkenes, south of Dorking, became independent in the fourteenth century, while Thorpe was granted independence from Egham by bishop Beaufort in 1428.[161]

Moving to the South-West, the moorland Somerset parish of Weston Zoyland was divided into three separate parts by the institution of vicarages at Middlezoy and Othery in 1515. Promoted by a sympathetic incumbent, matters progressed extraordinarily smoothly: master Roger Churche started proceedings by informing the abbot of Glastonbury as his patron that Othery (with over £10) and Middlezoy had adequate resources and well-equipped chapels. At an inquiry summoned by the local archdeacon, the initiative was supported by all parties, and the ordinance for the division of the parish could be issued on 23 September. In the same county, Trull had obtained independence from Taunton by a

---

[158] Freshfield (ed.), 'Stephen Coleman', 17 (4000 souls in the sixteenth century).

[159] Newcourt (ed.), *Repertorium*, i. 535–6. Stephen Coleman Street's status seems to have been somewhat flexible: at the time of an episcopal inquiry in 1436 (Register Robert Gilbert, GL, MS 9531/6, fos 24–24ᵛ) it was referred to as a parish, but in a presentation document of 1427 (Register William Gray, GL, MS 9531/5, f. 28) as a chapel.

[160] Cook, *Medieval Parish Church*, p. 22.

[161] Robinson, *Surrey*, p. 3.

papal grant in 1476.[162] Finally, no less than 11 new creations have
been identified for Devon between 1291 and 1535: three in the early
fourteenth century, one in the later fourteenth, three in the early
sixteenth, and four more at some unknown point during this period.[163]

Unions of parishes are of course only the other side of the coin, and
predate the formal act passed by parliament in 37 Henry VIII, c. 21. As
early as 1229, St Peter Chichester was merged with the hospital of St
Mary by royal letters patent.[164] Settlements could appear as well as
disappear, and insufficient endowments were just as detrimental to an
efficient cure of souls as an excessively large territory. In marginal areas
of Yorkshire, at least 24 churches were lost between 1400 and 1600,
while 30 disappeared in fifteenth-century Norfolk and as much as 90 in
the sixteenth. A 'model' urban case is Winchester, where ecclesiastical
provision decreased from originally 57 churches to 15 by 1550.[165] The
reasons were normally the proximity of neighbouring parishes and the
inadequacy of endowments for the support of a priest. As in the case of
divisions, claims were carefully investigated by the ordinaries, who only
acted with the broad assent of all parties concerned.[166] Further examples
would include Ringstead in Dorset, where the various subunits were
deemed too small, or Christchurch Newgate, which was created out of
two impoverished London parishes in 1546.[167]

This lengthy, but far from exhaustive collection of examples underlines
the point that the rigidity of the system should not be overestimated,
neither in England nor on the Continent. Creating or changing the
parochial network in the late Middle Ages was certainly more difficult

---

[162] H. Maxwell-Lyte (ed.), *The Registers of Oliver King and Hadrian de Castello*
(London, 1939), pp. xviii, 176–7 (Weston Zoyland); Twemlow (ed.), *Papal Letters*, xiii.
561–2; French, 'Local identity', pp. 56, 103.

[163] N. Orme, 'The medieval parishes of Devon', *Devon Historian*, 33 (1986), 8: Broad
Nymet, Jacobstow, Nymet Rowland (early fourteenth), Calverleigh (late fourteenth),
Templeton, Welcombe, and Woolfardisworth (early sixteenth). The Templeton efforts date
back to 1439, when the local population, supported by the lord of the manor, brought in
a friar bishop to consecrate their chapel and cemetery against the vigorous but ultimately
futile resistance of the parish of Witheridge: Orme, *Unity and Variety*, p. 69.

[164] D. Yale (ed.), *Sir Matthew Hale's 'The Prerogatives of the King'* (London, 1976), p.
155.

[165] Morris, *Churches in the Landscape*, pp. 334–5 (Winchester figures based on D.
Keene, *Survey of Medieval Winchester* (vol. i, Oxford, 1985), p. 2).

[166] Detailed records of proceedings survive for example for the diocese of London in the
early fifteenth century: union of St Augustine Pappay and All Hallows on the Wall (Register
William Gray, GL, MS 9531/5, fos 66ᵛ–67), Ashingdon and Hawkwell (ibid., fos 74ʳ+ᵛ) and
West Lee and Langdon (Register Robert Fitzhugh, GL, MS 9531/4, fos 234ᵛ–6). I owe these
references to Irene Zadnik.

[167] Ringstead 1488: Swanson, *Church and Society*, p. 45; London: Newcourt (ed.),
Repertorium, i. 318–19.

than in the heyday of the tenth to twelfth centuries, but even the 'cold hand of canon law' could not stop determined pressure groups from tackling the structural problems which prevented an adequate cure of souls.[168] Religious needs and local prestige combined to ensure that independent ecclesiastical status remained a desirable asset for rural and urban communities throughout the later Middle Ages. The conflicts that followed put severe strains on the parties involved, but, generally speaking, they testify to the vitality rather than decline of the parochial system.

4.4 The common motives

Subparochial institutions undoubtedly added new dimensions to the religious and social life of the parish, but an overall assessment of their impact is a matter of perspective. The presence of additional clergymen could reduce the incumbents' importance, the emergence of gilds and chantries expand the range of individual religious choice, and the formation of subgroups such as territorial fraternities and chapelries undermine the coherence of particular communities. From the point of view of institutions, established rights, and Church authorities this must have looked threatening, but for the laity, stability for its own sake was less of a priority. What mattered to them was the definition and, if necessary, redefinition of appropriate religious boundaries, activities, and devotions. The parish itself, of course, was shaped and reshaped to meet changing local circumstances, and its constituent parts, too, endeavoured to keep pace with, say, increasing mobility, literacy, and professional fragmentation. Different tastes and needs were catered for, but these developments are best viewed as 'supplementing or overlapping with the parish rather than competing with it'.[169] The increasing turnovers of churchwardens' accounts would certainly point in this direction. Inner-communal relations were not always harmonious, but the parish *system* as such, conceived as a network of (reasonably defined) units of religious life, was never fundamentally challenged.

It would be futile to try and disentangle the idiosyncratic mixture of spiritual and worldly motives in each and every case, but the large majority of initiatives shared four important common characteristics.

---

[168] The phrase in Brooke, 'Churches of medieval Cambridge', p. 54; see the discussion in Chapter 2.1.1. Many more examples of change would result from a systematic search of bishops' registers and papal archives.

[169] Palliser, 'Parish in perspective', p. 12 (quote); Swanson, *Church and Society*, p. 280. The appeal to different religious tastes: Harper-Bill, *Pre-Reformation Church*, p. 96.

First, they reflected an orthodox religious desire to improve sacramental provision in the interest of salvation.[170] The conclusions reached for many recent English and Continental case studies are virtually interchangeable: 'the most distinctive feature of popular religion was its preoccupation with death and the ensuring of salvation'; 'an extraordinary effort was made to cultivate reciprocal aid among Christians. No man stood alone before the Divine'; 'popular parish life was marked by penitential piety and caring for the dead'.[171] The combined effect of the Church's pastoral offensive and lay-sponsored catechetical efforts cannot be overlooked. Parish drama, for instance, quite apart from its fundraising dimension, brought the laity into regular contact with 'a good summary of cosmic history from the Creation to Doomsday',[172] and there is plenty of evidence that complex theological issues reverberated at the grass-roots level.[173] From a modern point of view, of course, many practices look mechanical and tainted by superstition. Contemporary Christians looked at their church as a 'repository of supernatural power', prayers were used as magic formulae, and the consecrated host subjected to all sorts of questionable uses.[174] All this, however, occurred at a time when the 'official' Church promoted something as inexplicable as the doctrine of transubstantiation, readily accepted the miraculous, and deliberately used it to reinforce orthodoxy.[175] Ambiguous clerical attitudes towards applications of the sacred for everyday purposes blurred the distinctions further.[176] 'Popular'

---

[170] Cf. the prominence of 'orthodoxy' on the main parochial level observed in Chapter 3.3; for the pre-eminent role of masses see Harper-Bill, *Pre-Reformation Church*, p. 64, for the acceptance of traditional doctrine as a whole Swanson, *Church and Society*, p. 279.

[171] Quotes taken from Haigh, *Lancashire*, p. 68; Galpern, *Champagne*, p. 28; Pfaff, 'Pfarrei und Pfarreileben', p. 269 ('das volkstümliche Leben im Rahmen der Pfarrei war ... geprägt von Bussfrömmigkeit und Totensorge': Central Switzerland; even in one of the future reformed cantons, Berne, religious life on the eve of the Reformation could only be described as (enthusiastically) orthodox: F. Häusler, 'Von der Stadtgründung bis zur Reformation' in P. Meyer (ed.), *Berner – Deine Geschichte* (Wabern, 1981), p. 96).

[172] Tanner, *Church in Norwich*, p. 72 (cycle of Norwich mystery plays), and Palliser, *Tudor York*, p. 232 (quote). In sixteenth-century Essex alone, 46 places staged mystery plays: Oxley, *Essex*, p. 28.

[173] The bede-roll at All Saints, Bristol, explained that 'by the purgative mercy of Almighty God, by the intercession of our blessed Lady and of all blessed Saints of heaven ... you may come to everlasting bliss' (quoted in Burgess, 'Benefactions of mortality', p. 76).

[174] Thomas, *Decline of Magic*, pp. 32 (quote), 34ff (host) and 41 (prayers).

[175] Swanson, *Church and Society*, p. 290 (for example miracles connected with the Eucharist against Lollard teachings). Officially recognized saints were attributed with spectacular powers, but also served the didactic purpose of propagating crucial Christian values: Duffy, *Stripping of the Altars*, pp. 157–61.

[176] See for example the 'grey area' between officially sanctioned uses of sacramentals and their popular applications: R. Scribner, 'Ritual and popular religion in Catholic Germany at the time of the Reformation' in his *Popular Culture and Popular Movements in Reformation Germany* (London, 1987), pp. 17–47.

and 'official' religion still differed in emphasis and doctrinal purity, but given an age of poor communications and heretical alternatives, the degree of 'Christianization' of late medieval society was remarkable indeed.

Second, popular initiatives were of a strikingly visual and ceremonial character. 'Lay people seem to have had an insatiable appetite for the spectacular and magnificent'.[177] The elevation of the host at mass, the maintenance of lights in front of colourful images, the annual feast days of gilds, the Rogation Week processions, the beautification of churches, the lavish endowment of chantries – they all had their firm place somewhere in the wide spectrum between spiritual needs and secular aspirations.

Third, the coexistence of individual and communal dimensions emerges as a *Leitmotiv* of all parochial religion: personal efforts were indispensable elements in the quest for salvation, but many of their features contributed to the strengthening of communal ties. At the same time, individual needs were accommodated by collective institutions. To draw too sharp a distinction is to break up a whole, and recalls the futile attempt to distinguish pious and charitable bequests in the same period.[178] Churchwardens supported additional masses and services to suit minority demands, chantry priests participated in parochial service, gilds enriched the ceremonial life of the church, the same individuals took office in allegedly 'rival' institutions, and every corporate initiative was made up of countless individual efforts. While social relations were fragile and conflicts always a possibility, there is no need to 'deconstruct' the concept of community for an age where it had such obvious real meaning.[179] Gilds, chantries, and chapels coexisted with parish institutions for several centuries; to see them as openly 'hostile' and fundamentally incompatible is to take the 'longue durée' approach to historical evidence rather too far.[180] In fact, they could all be seen as contributing to what has been called the 'communalization' of local ecclesiastical life in the period.[181]

---

[177] Cross, *Church and People*, p. 48.

[178] J. Thomson, 'Piety and charity in late medieval London', *JEH*, 16 (1965), 180 (a critical assessment of W. K. Jordan's division).

[179] As attempted in Rubin, 'Small groups', p. 135. For this period at least, the communal dimension deserves to be restored to the picture painted in A. Macfarlane, *The Origins of English Individualism* (Oxford, 1978).

[180] Gilds date from the Anglo-Saxon period (Rosser, 'Anglo-Saxon guilds') and chantries from the twelfth century (Moorman, *Thirteenth Century*, p. 17).

[181] K. Frölich, 'Die Rechtsformen der mittelalterlichen Altarpfründen', *Zeitschrift für Rechtsgeschichte*, kanon. Abt. 20 (1931), 539 ('Kommunalisierung des Kirchenwesens'); Schröcker, *Kirchenpflegschaft*, p. 107, speaks of a 'Kommunalisierung des städtischen Kirchenvermögens'.

Fourth and last, parochial and subparochial initiatives were part of an increasingly 'natural' lay control over late medieval church affairs on all levels of society.[182] At the top, papal sovereignty became subject to royal restrictions, and convocations of the clergy a forum for fiscal demands.[183] Among the gentry, religious initiatives were marked by ever more detailed stipulations, local peculiarities, and family interests.[184] On the local level, the control over services, finances, and discipline of the clergy appealed to gild members, chantry founders, and parishioners alike. Communities of common people supervised church property, appointed priests, and regulated their own religious affairs. Every self-endowed benefice made the local church less susceptible to clerical or seigneurial influence and reinforced parochial ties and power.[185] Towns in particular were continuously eroding rivalling ecclesiastical rights and privileges: Norwich succeeded in limiting the extent of the priory's jurisdiction and economic influence long before the Reformation, and similar advances were made by other towns such as Chester and Exeter.[186] At Newcastle-under-Lyme, borough authorities appointed the churchwardens, audited their accounts, and used the church as a meeting place for municipal business. From the late fourteenth century, 'the church affairs, financial and other, were all ordered by the corporation', and the same could be said for many Continental cities.[187] Lay assertiveness and participation seem the more likely 'ancestors' of the religious changes of the sixteenth century than doctrinal discontent or increasing individualism, not necessarily determining future denominational preference, but certainly preparing the laity to decide spiritual matters themselves.[188]

---

[182] Swanson, *Church and Society*, p. 250. For a general account of lay influence over church goods in the Middle Ages: J. Hashagen, 'Laieneinfluss auf das Kirchengut vor der Reformation', *Historische Zeitschrift*, **126** (1922), 377–409.

[183] Harper-Bill, *Pre-Reformation Church*, pp. 9ff.

[184] B. Thompson, 'Habendum et tenendum' in C. Harper-Bill (ed.), *Religious Belief and Ecclesiastical Careers in Late Medieval England* (Woodbridge, 1991), pp. 232ff.

[185] Fuhrmann, 'Dorfgemeinde und Pfründstiftung', pp. 109ff; von Rütte, 'Religionspraxis der Bauern', p. 40.

[186] Tanner, *Church in Norwich*, pp. 141ff; Jones, *Church in Chester*, p. 41; A. Green, *Town Life in the Fifteenth Century* (2 vols, London, 1894), i. 333ff.

[187] Pape, *Newcastle-under-Lyme*, pp. 18–23; 'Das herrschende Bürgertum ... beansprucht ... mehr und mehr ein sachliches Mitspracherecht in kirchlichen Angelegenheiten': U. Weiss, *Die frommen Bürger von Erfurt* (Weimar, 1988), p. 283.

[188] Places with an extreme extent of lay control could stay firmly catholic (H. Guggisberg, 'The problem of "failure" in the Swiss Reformation' reprinted in his *Zusammenhänge in historischer Vielfalt* (Basel, 1994), pp. 115–33), but the ultimate decision about the 'right' doctrine was made by lay authorities, be it the councils of German town communities (R. Scribner, 'Paradigms of urban reform' in L. Grane and K. Hørby (eds), *The Danish Reformation against its International Background* (Göttingen, 1990), p. 127) or Henry VIII's parliament.

CHAPTER FIVE

The Social Context

Increasing lay investment in parishes and fraternities certainly had something to do with religious motives. The Black Death must have been an awe-inspiring experience, and the daunting prospect of purgatory may have been reason enough for contemporary parishioners to try and improve their chances of salvation. Some must have followed the Church's guidelines in a rather unreflected fashion, but many acted out of genuine devotion and a deep belief in the efficacy of intercession. Such activities, however, did not take place in a social vacuum. They could be expensive and depended on a variety of circumstantial factors. Parish life should not only be discussed on the basis of (Reformation-inspired) questions concerning the popularity of religious practices and/or potential roots of sixteenth-century change, but also with reference to contemporary socio-economic conditions. The absolute figures spent on priests or the embellishment of churches mean little, unless they are interpreted in light of the size of available resources and other spending purposes. This chapter will tackle some of these issues, even though the evidence does not always permit more than a very tentative assessment.

5.1 Setting the scene

The last decades of the Middle Ages were a period of transition. At the top of local society, seigneurial institutions struggled to maintain their powers. Due to the protracted slump in population, there was little demand for land, lords suffered from a deep economic recession, and some accumulated debts of 'phenomenal' proportions. The income of rectors and other parish incumbents was also in decline.[1] Many manorial courts saw their authority undermined, and villagers acted with increasing self-assertiveness. The remaining traces of serfdom were now deeply resented and the peasants' successful fight for better tenurial conditions changed medieval social organization beyond recognition.[2]

---

[1] Hatcher, *Population and the English Economy*, pp. 36ff; Swanson, 'Standards of livings', p. 195 (for example the revenues of the rectors of Great Yarmouth).

[2] Hilton, *Decline of Serfdom*, pp. 44ff, 57, and A. Bridbury, 'The farming out of manors', *EcHR*, 2nd Series, **31** (1978), 520. For an example of the problems of seigneurial jurisdiction: Dyer, *Lords and Peasants*, pp. 264ff (Bishops of Worcester).

For the population at large, standards of living improved:[3] more spare cash was available in town and countryside, and due to the relative stability in the value of money, purchasing powers increased. Compared to the 1310s, a carpenter had to work four times less for a basket of basic consumables in the 1490s, while at the same time the peasantry was 'better fed, housed, clothed, and equipped than their ancestors had been'.[4] As for the two cities in this sample, Bristol's trade recovered after a difficult phase at the end of the fifteenth century, and London reinforced its economic position throughout the period. The long-standing debate on other urban experiences has remained somewhat inconclusive: advocates of wide-spread decline in the later Middle Ages have focused on architectural and fiscal evidence, while others differentiated between the fate of towns as a whole and the varied economic fortunes of their inhabitants.[5] On the whole, however, the development of rents, prices, and wages suggests that conditions improved for a very large part of the population.

Yet another contributing factor was the decreasing level of direct lay taxation. By the late fifteenth century, crown revenues were on a much lower level than they had been around 1400, in absolute as well as relative terms.[6] The fifteenths and tenths levied on moveable goods from 1334 could not keep pace with economic developments: whenever parliament made a grant, local communities simply apportioned a fixed quota among their members. Assessments probably excluded goods for basic daily needs, and the (limited) distribution evidence for boroughs and townships suggests 'that only a relatively small number of people in

---

[3] Experiences varied of course from region to region and progress was not linear; the late fifteenth century, which still awaits detailed research, could contain periods of considerable strain: McIntosh, 'Local change'.

[4] D. Farmer, 'Prices and wages 1350–1500' in E. Miller (ed.), *The Agricultural History of England and Wales* (Cambridge, 1991), pp. 491–2 (quote and carpenter's wages); Dyer, *Standards of Living*, pp. 149 (cash in the countryside) and 196 (towns). Monetary inflation only picked up from the 1510s: R. Outhwaite, *Inflation in Tudor and Early Stuart England* (London, 1969), pp. 9-15.

[5] Carus-Wilson, 'Bristol', p. 12; Barron, 'Later Middle Ages', pp. 53–4 (London); R. Dobson, 'Urban decline in late medieval England' reprinted in R. Holt and G. Rosser (eds), *The English Medieval Town* (London, 1990), pp. 265–86, and Phythian-Adams, 'Urban decay' (arguments for worsening economic fortunes); D. Palliser, 'Urban decay revisited' in J. Thomson (ed.), *Towns and Townspeople in the Fifteenth Century* (Gloucester, 1988), 1–21, stresses regional variations; Holt and Rosser (eds), *English Medieval Town*, p. 17, point to the varying experiences of individuals.

[6] I am grateful to Mark Ormrod for allowing me access to his unpublished data on crown revenues and taxation, compiled for the European State Finance Database (\orm\engg010 and \orm\engg024). The index is based on the period 1451–75.

each community paid tax'.[7] Indirect taxation, too, was a comparatively light burden, which in practice affected wool and cloth exports only. But even the latter were not adequately reflected: the cloth trade generated more and more money, but yielded just a fraction of export tax revenues.[8] It was only in the 1520s that lay subsidies were restructured on the basis of fresh assessments of income from lands, goods, and wages. The crown's net was now cast much wider, and very few persons managed to gain an exemption.[9] Before these reforms, however, most people found themselves in the pleasant situation of a relatively favourable economic climate unspoilt by inflation or oppressive fiscal demands.

It is tempting to relate these macroeconomic processes to other noticeable trends in the period. There was, for instance, a significant shift in the public profile of the various social groups: while twelfth and thirteenth-century observers must have been dazzled by the construction of monasteries and secular cathedrals, it was building at a lower level which caught the eye at the close of the Middle Ages. In London, to take but one example, ecclesiastical dignitaries sponsored the most prominent projects in the thirteenth century, merchants those of the fourteenth, but corporate groups of citizens the halls and churches built on the eve of the Reformation.[10] In line with this (relative) trend away from old established elites, the aristocracy played 'their most philanthropic tune earlier than other classes of lay benefactors, for by the second half of the fifteenth century the evidence is that their activity was becoming quite minimal'.[11] Further down the social scale, however, gift giving in wills stood at an all-time high: over 29 per cent of the wealth of Londoners was disposed for philanthropic purposes between 1480 and 1540, more than in any other period between 1400 and 1660.[12] At the same time, churchwardens disposed of ever larger resources, not just as part of indiscriminate investment into any available religious service, but as the result of a clear shift of priorities away from monasteries and friaries to the parish, which had now emerged as the undisputed centre of local

---

[7] R. Glasscock (ed.), *The Lay Subsidy of 1334* (Oxford, 1975), pp. xiiiff. and xxiv (quote).

[8] Mark Ormrod, 'Financing the 100-years war' (Paper given at the Institute of Historical Research, 31 Jan. 1992).

[9] Stoate (ed.), *Devon Lay Subsidy Rolls 1524-7*, p. iv (new assessments), and Schofield, 'Parliamentary lay taxation', p. 251 (exemptions).

[10] Lander, *Government and Community*, p. 148 (general); Barron, 'The later Middle Ages', p. 49 (London).

[11] J. Rosenthal, *The Purchase of Paradise* (London, 1972), p. 34.

[12] Thomson, 'Piety and charity', 182, with reference to Jordan, *Charities of London*, pp. 54–5.

ecclesiastical life.[13] At Norwich between 1490 and 1517, practically every testator made provisions for masses, gilds, and parish churches, and donations to the high altar or church fabric were the most common item in wills from all over the country, be it the South-West, Wiltshire, or towns like Bury St Edmunds.[14] It was this deliberate concentration of increased resources on the parish framework which explains the remarkable pre-Reformation boom in local initiatives. One or two of its best-known features deserve to be recalled.

In an effort which mirrored the feverish construction period between 1050 and 1150, parishioners turned the late Middle Ages into the great age of parish church rebuilding. In spite of a relatively stable population, 'there is no period at which money was lavished so freely on parish churches as in the fifteenth century'.[15] With thousands of projects undertaken at the same time, they now provide the main representatives of English Perpendicular building, which was 'normally the result of a concerted communal effort'.[16] There were always remarkable individual contributions,[17] but the surviving parish records show a 'large amount of corporate giving and fundraising quite apart from the generosity of exceptionally wealthy families'.[18] Both Louth (Lincs.) and Bodmin (Cornwall) provide outstanding examples: merchant initiative, voluntary work, Sunday collections, and contributions from parochial gilds all helped to pay for costs in excess of £300 for the 'house not made with hands' at Louth, while at Bodmin over £260 was raised by local

---

[13] See for example the choice of burial location (Chapter 3.3).

[14] Holt and Rosser (eds), *The English Medieval Town*, p. 13 (shift of gift giving in English towns); Whiting, *Blind Devotion*, appendix 2 (South-West); Brown, 'Late medieval Wiltshire', p. 265 (Wilts.); Tanner, *Church in Norwich*, pp. 222–3 (Norwich); Craig, 'Reformation, politics, and polemics', p. 75 (Bury). Percentages of bequests made in wills, of course, have to be treated with a great deal of caution (Burgess, 'Late medieval wills'), but this uniform picture does not look like a mere coincidence.

[15] Thompson, *English Clergy*, p. 128. Similar Lander, *Government and Community*, p. 148; Harvey, *Gothic England*, p. 107, speaks of a 'great period of prosperous parish life inaugurated … in 1471'. Owen, *Medieval Lincolnshire*, p. 97, refers to the time-span between 1360 and 1530 in general. For the tenth- and eleventh-century proliferation of parish churches built in stone: Morris, *Churches in the Landscape*, p. 147.

[16] Harper-Bill, *Pre-Reformation Church*, p. 72.

[17] The lord of Hungerford seems to have financed the new church at Farleigh Hungerford (Somerset) on his own, while Richard Darnell left £100 to the rebuilding at East Bergholt (Suffolk): French, 'Local identity', pp. 20, 264. Other notable benefactions included the £10 John Ford gave towards the rood loft at Ashburton (CWA, 1521–2), or the £90 of a Lord Mayor's widow at St Michael Cornhill, London (Newcourt (ed.), *Repertorium*, i. 479ff).

[18] MacCulloch, *Suffolk and the Tudors*, p. 140; the same point in Morris, *Churches in the Landscape*, p. 315.

fraternities, rates, and no less than 460 individual benefactors.[19] Even towns in precarious economic circumstances found means to invest in architectural work: almost all Chester churches underwent repair in the fifteenth century, and an increase in the commitment to the parish has also been identified at Winchester, a place which was clearly past its prime.[20]

The phenomenon is often explained as a consequence of pious devotion and seen as evidence for the English people's unbreakable allegiance to the old religion. And yet, while we can certainly speak of an increased involvement in ecclesiastical affairs, massive church building around 1500 was too widespread to supply any clues about future denominational allegiances. Brittany, Normandy, and the Champagne could be cited as examples from Catholic France,[21] but future protestant strongholds were involved in exactly the same kind of activity: in the last century before the Reformation, the balance of ecclesiastical building in Scotland 'swung from the greater to the lesser churches', and evidence from St Nicholas, Aberdeen, St Giles, Edinburgh, St Mary, Haddington, and countless other places suggests that this was just as much an 'age of the parish church' as south of the border.[22] In the rural territories of Zwingli's Zurich, too, no less than half of the churches were reconstructed or extended between 1470 and 1525, and a similar process can be observed in many regions of the Holy Roman Empire.[23] Italy, on the other hand, may have lagged somewhat behind: visitations routinely refer to the dilapidated state of buildings, and Italian travellers in Germany commented on the astonishing degree of construction activity there in comparison with their own country.[24] Religious motives alone can hardly explain this pattern.

The most recent study of England's ritual and ceremonial life, to move to another prominent area of late medieval lay activity, has concluded

---

[19] Dudding (ed.), *CWs Book of Louth*, p. xiv (quote) and passim; Wilkinson (ed.), *Bodmin Church*, pp. 42–9.

[20] Jones, *Church in Chester*, pp. 114–15; Rosser, 'Parish and guild', p. 48; Keene, *Medieval Winchester*, i. 116ff.

[21] Huard, 'Paroisse rurale', 21.

[22] Fawcett, *Scottish Medieval Churches*, p. 55.

[23] P. Jezler, *Der spätgotische Kirchenbau in der Zürcher Landschaft* (Wetzikon, 1988), p. 12; A. Knoepfli, *Die Kunstgeschichte des Bodenseeraums* (Sigmaringen, 1963), ii. 156.

[24] Hay, *Church in Italy*, pp. 56–7; P. Johanek, 'La Germania prima della Riforma' in P. Prodi and Johanek (eds), *Strutture ecclesiastiche in Italia e Germania prima della Riforma* (Bologna, 1984), p. 25, quotes Antonio de Beatis, who visited the country as secretary to a cardinal and wrote in 1517: 'tante [chiese] se ne edificano de nuovo, che considerando la cultura de le cose divine che se fa in Italia et quante povere ecclesie sono dilapidate et se ruinano, ho invidia ad queste parti non mediocre et mi doglio in fine a le viscere de la poca religione de noi altri italiani'.

that many of the customs practiced in the early sixteenth century 'had been either introduced or embellished only a few generations before or within living memory... . The evidence for accumulation of communal customs and for the elaboration of the ritual year in England between about 1350 and about 1520 is ... very strong', and consistent with the 'pattern of progressive physical embellishment of the churches with which many of these activities were associated'.[25] But again, religious motives cannot be the only cause; having weighed the potential influence of intangible fashions, socio-economic stimulants, and spiritual incentives, the author admits that there was 'no clear and obvious reason for the apparent greater investment in English seasonal ceremony during the later Middle Ages'. Now if his findings can be substantiated[26] (and the coincidence is too striking to be dismissed out of hand), it would seem obvious to suggest that the 'rise' of the parish supplies the missing cause. Reflecting exactly this mixture of contemporary taste, religion, and socio-economic fortunes, it provided the sort of framework within which an ever more confident and prosperous laity could add to (or at least participate in) the ritual life of the nation.

5.2 The relative size of parish resources

Moving to the less spectacular everyday activities, an idea of the actual size of the parishioners' investment can only emerge from a comparison with other demands made upon their collective resources. Lay taxation may provide a convenient starting point, as it involved claims made for another public purpose (secular rather than ecclesiastical) to all members of the local community. The 1377 Poll Tax, for instance, amounted to four pence for every adult, which – even allowing for inflation – was considerably less than the per-capita income of most parishes.[27] Two further experiments were made with somewhat higher quotas, but the idea was soon abandoned. A more regular and reliable guide is the tax on moveable goods, levied at the rate of a fifteenth in the countryside and a tenth in towns. Like churchwardens' accounts, it concerned a local community, albeit vills or townships rather than parishes. Table 5.1 compares the size of the two respective demands.

It goes without saying that an analysis of local taxation would deserve a study in its own right. The present figures can only be approximate for several reasons. For a start, it is often difficult to establish the precise

[25] Hutton, *Merry England*, pp. 61–2.
[26] See the note of caution sounded at the end of Chapter 3.2.
[27] Cf. Table 3.4.

Table 5.1 Pre-Reformation parish income compared to direct royal taxation (1334/1371/all fifteenths and tenths and lay subsidies)

Parish	Size/Type	1334 quota of 15th & 10th (1330s index: 106.7)	1334 adjusted to period of first 10 years of CWA (index)	A/v of first 10 years of CWA	Annual 15th & 10th level (collected c. once in 2 years) cf. to parish a/v	1371 subsidy adjusted to period of 1st CWA (and cf. to parish a/v; 1370s index: 130.8)	Total lay subsidy yield in CWA period (parish quota cf. to a/v parish income in %)[1]
Mary-at-Hill[2]	2/5 of ward	3024 d.	2673 d. (1470s: 94.3)	21409 d.	6.0%	1004 d. (5%)	£ 185 750 (2%)
Boxford	village	598	869 (1530s: 155.1)	3391	13.0%	1651 (49%)	1 278 666 (39%)
Yatton	village	1178	1112 (1440s: 100.7)	3925	14.0%	1072 (27%)	2 262 893 (9%)
Ashburton	town+manor	1123	1221 (1480s: 116.0)	3043	20.0%	1234 (41%)	1 986 493 (10%)
Botolph Aldersg.	4/5 of ward	1344	1311 (1460s: 104.1)	3232	20.5%	1108 (34%)	2 094 993 (7%)
Andrew Hubbard[2]	1/5 of ward	1512	1406 (1450s: 99.2)	2009	35.0%	1056 (53%)	2 169 493 (21%)
Edmund Salis.	1/3 of town	6001	5663 (1440s: 100.7)	4378	64.7%	1072 (24%)	2 286 893 (18%)
All Saints	1/18 of town	2933	3035 (1400s: 110.4)	2140	71.0%	1175 (55%)	3 108 493 (11%)
St Ewen's	1/18 of town	2933	2727 (1450s: 99.2)	1375	99.0%[3]	1056 (77%)	2 169 493 (37%)
Peterborough	town+members	6126	5977 (1460s: 104.1)	1537	194.5%	1108 (72%)	2 094 993 (17%)
Halesowen	town+vills	8918	9694 (1480s: 116.0)	1338	362.5%	1234 (92%)	1 963 493 (77%)
Prescot	town+vills	5220	7240 (1520s: 148.0)	980	369.5%[4]	1575 (161%)	1 430 235 (127%)

Sources: Glasscock, *Lay Subsidy 1334*, passim; Ormrod, 'Parish subsidy of 1371', 63; European State Finance Databaseormengd008.ssd (crown revenues from lay subsidies 1406–85); F. Dietz, *English Government Finance 1485–1558* (Illinois, 1921), pp. 225–6

Inflation adjustments based on Phelps-Brown/Hopkins index; a/v (average) level of 1377 subsidy: 116 s./parish

1. See text for details; CWA periods and a/v incomes are the same as in Appendix 3, table 'a' (Mary-at-Hill: 1477–92, 21409 d.; St Edmund, Salisbury: 1443–1560, 3259 d.).
2. Mary-at-Hill and Andrew Hubbard were both situated in Billingsgate ward and covered perhaps three fifths of its area.
3. Overestimate (smaller than a/v area)
4. Overestimate (1 separate chapel)

geographical relation between parishes and vills, or ecclesiastical and secular urban units. In the case of Bristol, the quota of the whole town has simply been divided by 18 (the number of parishes), which must overestimate the burden placed on a tiny area such as that of St Ewen's.[28] In London, Billingsgate ward contained both Andrew Hubbard and Mary-at-Hill, and – in the absence of more reliable clues – their share has been assumed to correspond to their respective topographical extent. For some vills, no taxation assessment survives,[29] for others, it is not absolutely clear whether they formed part of a parish in this sample.[30] To obtain precise data, the subsidy rolls of each locality would have to be consulted in detail, with all their variations and the reductions granted by the crown in the course of the later Middle Ages. The benefits of such a large-scale undertaking, however, would be limited: the figures might look somewhat different, but not the general trends.

All of the assessments in this study, to restate a very important point, are based on churchwardens' accounts alone. In other words, they represent a massive minimum of overall lay investment. The figures refer to communal activities only, and the resources of chantries, gilds, chapels, and incumbents (including all tithes and oblations) would have to be added to arrive at an overall estimate of expenditure for religious provision. But the general picture from Table 5.1 is clear enough. The third column contains an estimate of the level of fifteenths and tenths in each of the case studies and the fourth the adjusted equivalent for the first decade of surviving parish accounts.[31] Listed next is the average total income of the ten earliest years in the various communities, and the highlighted sixth column expresses the taxation level (halved to take account of the roughly biannual collection[32]) in percentages of parochial resources. The result is remarkable: in 9 out of 12 cases, the wardens raised more than the Exchequer officials, even at the relatively low level of this early documentation. Of the three cases which do not conform to this pattern, one can at least be partly explained by an overestimation of the taxation quota. Looking at the percentages in more detail, large

---

[28] All the relevant tax assessments are printed in Glasscock (ed.), *Lay Subsidy of 1334*.

[29] For example for Prescot proper in the multi-township parish of the same name, or for Lappall and Illey in Halesowen.

[30] Longthorpe and Eye in Peterborough.

[31] By means of the Phelps-Brown and Hopkins index in their 'Seven centuries of the prices of consumables'. The 1334-quota is divided by the average index for the 1330s (106.7) and multiplied by the average index of the decade with the first surviving parish account. This figure (entered in the fourth column) would have imposed as high a burden on contemporary parishioners as on those of 1334.

[32] Between 1337 and 1454 66.66 fifteenths and tenths were granted, afterwards the frequency declined markedly (I owe this information to Mark Ormrod).

market-town based parishes are again placed at the bottom of the table, while the ranking of the prosperous communities of Boxford and Yatton probably reflects the lower rate levied in the countryside. Apart from the extraordinarily wealthy Mary-at-Hill, most of the higher-taxed London and Bristol parishes appear in mid-table positions, with some possibly misplaced due to the uncertainties about the conversion of ward or city totals into parish-based quotas. All Saints, furthermore, is 'caught' at a very early stage of its development and a time when the 1334 assessments may still have had a closer bearing to economic realities than at the later date of most other case studies. The overall trend emerges even more strongly from a juxtaposition of parish revenue with the (adjusted) subsidy of 1371 in column seven. This is perhaps the most straightforward comparison, given that both referred to exactly the same unit. An average of £5 16s. had to be levied from each community,[33] which was well below the annual intake of all but one of the case studies. Not surprisingly, it is once more Prescot which trails all the others, with the structurally similar Halesowen next in line.

The figures in the last column, even more approximate than the others, attempt to relate the overall yield of direct taxation to the size of parochial incomes in the timespan covered by the respective churchwardens' accounts. The crown's gross revenue from all fifteenths and tenths and Tudor lay subsidies from the starting date of the parish reckonings to the cut-off date of 1560 is divided by 8000 (a very conservative estimate of the number of parishes) and the number of years in the period.[34] The method, of course, applies to an imaginary 'average' taxpaying community rather than the specific case study, but the resulting percentages are not dramatically different from those in the other columns. Mary-at-Hill tops the list again, followed by the other metropolitan and rural case studies and – as usual – Halesowen and Prescot at the end. Even though city centre areas paid much more than this average, it would have had to be (in the case of Mary-at-Hill) 50 times as much to match the parochial revenues.

But what was the situation once Henry VIII had closed tax loopholes and imposed a much heavier fiscal burden on the laity? Table 5.2 allows an assessment of the 1524 subsidy. Listed are a selection of case studies

---

[33] Individual parish quotas could be identified in the respective subsidy rolls, but again the emphasis is on the general trend. For details of this taxation experiment cf. Ormrod, 'Parish subsidy of 1371', and Chapter 2.3.1.

[34] Taxation yields (pre-1485) from European State Finance Database (\orm\engd008.ssd), and (post-1485) from Dietz, *English Government Finance*, pp. 225–6. The latter is now outdated in many respects (cf. for example, Schofield, 'Parliamentary lay taxation'), but still the most convenient published list. For starting dates and average incomes of CWA see Appendix 3 and Table 5.1, n. 1.

Table 5.2   Some 1524 lay subsidy payments compared to churchwardens' income

Parish	Type	Subsidy 1524	Nearest CWA		Subsidy in % of CWA	1524 source
[All Saints	part of ward	7794 d.	13229 d.	(1524–5)	59%	PRO, E179 113/192]
Ashburton	town+manor	10151	12506	(1524–5)	81%	Stoate, pp. 231–2
Botolph Alders.	part of ward	8336	9951¼	(1524–5)	84%	Sheail, vol. ii
Andrew Hubb.	part of ward	3404	2195	(1524–5)	155%	Sheail, vol. ii
Boxford	village	5640	3093	(1530–6)	182%	Harvey, pp. 13–15
Prescot	town+vills	2388	1016	(1524–5)	235%	Sheail, vol. ii
[St Ewen	part of ward	4144	1321	(1515–17)	314%	PRO, E179 113/192]
Halesowen	town+vills	1618	470	(1524)	344%	Sheail, vol. ii

[ ] = Only the roughest estimates are possible for Bristol, where it is impossible to allocate the ward-based figures to the various parishes with any degree of certainty. The Boxford CWA figure is the a/v for the years 1530–6.

with actual or estimated subsidy dues and the wardens' income in the nearest surviving accounts.[35] The percentages resulting from direct comparison are now higher, but the size of parochial revenues remains astonishing. All the more so, if it is taken into account that wardens raised similar amounts of money every year, while taxes were collected only when parliament made an explicit grant. The rhythm was irregular, with the occasional extra burden of multiple subsidies or fifteenths and tenths compensated by longer periods without any direct taxation whatsoever. The effective annual burden is difficult to quantify, but in the period 1515–40, for instance, 16 years saw no taxation grants, and the wardens' demands must have weighed more heavily on the parishioners.[36] Looking at the individual percentages scored, Halesowen and Prescot occupy their familiar places,[37] while St Ewen's lowly position has to be taken with a great deal of caution: the small area of the parish contained much public space ('Tolzey' house), and the rough-and-ready apportionment of the ward's tax burden may overestimate its actual share.[38] Boxford, meanwhile, fares considerably worse than in the previous table, probably due to the fact that the fresh assessments reflected its prosperity much more accurately than the 1334 quotas.[39] Confirmation of the substantial size of parochial turnovers even in humble rural communities comes from Morebath, where the village's subsidy assessment was just one fifth higher than the revenues of the main store of St George.[40]

Overall, it is safe to say that fifteenth- and early sixteenth-century English churchwardens raised more from their communities than the crown in direct lay taxation.[41] This, as recalled above, for what were

[35] The subsidy figures derive from PRO, E 179, the compilations in Sheail, 'Distribution of regional wealth', Harvey (ed.), *Suffolk in 1524*, and Stoate (ed.), *Devon Lay Subsidy Rolls 1524–7*; no detailed information has been found for Yatton or Peterborough.

[36] Taxation frequency from Dietz, *English Government Finance*, pp. 225–6.

[37] The high assessment for Nassaburgh hundred (over £280), of which Peterborough formed a substantial part, suggests that it would produce a similar percentage.

[38] The comparison with All Saints across the road reinforces this suspicion. As city-centre communities, both were certainly prosperous and heavily taxed, but subsidy totals exist for wards and streets only, and parish quotas have to be estimated on the basis of their territorial extent.

[39] Boxford was situated in a wealthy woollen cloth-making area: CWA, p. xii.

[40] 1240 d. (Stoate (ed.), *Devon Lay Subsidy Rolls 1524–7*, p. 52) compared to 1034½ d. (Binney (ed.), *Morebath*, CWA 1526).

[41] There were of course other state levies such as those on income, poll taxes on aliens, feudal aids, indirect taxes and so on, but they are all difficult to compare to the parish evidence. Not assessed communally, most would have only affected a fraction of the population, and with the exception of the charges on cloth and wool (export only) their overall size was negligible compared to the subsidies. I am grateful to Mark Ormrod for his information on fiscal revenues and procedures.

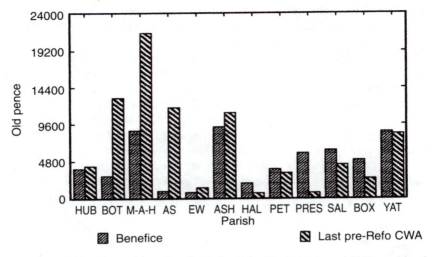

Figure 5.1 Benefice value (taken from the *Valor Ecclesiasticus*, 1535) compared to CWs' income (a/v of last pre-Reformation CWA) in 12 parishes (HUB = St Andrew Hubbard, London; BOT = St Botolph Aldersgate, London; M-A-H = Mary-at-Hill, London; AS = All Saints, Bristol; EW = St Ewen's, Bristol; ASH = Ashburton, Devon; HAL = Halesowen, Worcestershire; PET = Peterborough; PRES = Prescot, Lancashire; SAL = St Edmund, Salisbury; BOX = Boxford, Suffolk; YAT = Yatton, Somerset); unit: old pence (24,000 d. = £100)

essentially additional efforts on top of very many other commitments. But how do the figures compare to the payments made to the local incumbent? One way to answer this question is to juxtapose parish income with the valuation of benefices made in 1535.[42]

Figure 5.1 displays average parish income in the last few pre-Reformation accounts alongside the revenues of the respective incumbents.[43] The picture can only confirm the remarkable degree of investment recorded in the wardens' sources. In half of the cases, parish revenues exceed clerical income,[44] and at Mary-at-Hill, Botolph Aldersgate, and All Saints, the communal resources literally dwarf those

---

[42] Caley and Hunter (eds), *Valor Ecclesiasticus*, i. 187 (Yatton), 373 (Andrew Hubbard), 376 (Mary-at-Hill); ii. 88 (St Edmund, Salisbury), 364 (Ashburton); iii. 207 (Halesowen), 453–4 (Boxford); iv. 285 (Peterborough); v. 220 (Prescot). The Botolph Aldersgate figure refers to the valuation of the rectory in 1547 (Kitching (ed.), *Chantry Certificates*, p. 30); the Bristol estimates in Skeeters, *Community and Clergy*, p. 98.

[43] CWA-figures taken from the tables in Appendix 3, Mary-at-Hill CWA, 1477–92, and St Edmund Salisbury CWA, 1538–43.

[44] An ambiguous case was Morebath, where the vicarage was valued at £8 (Binney (ed.), *Morebath*, 'Introduction'), that is more than the normal income of the parish store of St George (*c.* £3–5), but less than the revenue of all the stocks taken together (*c.* £10).

of the rectors and vicars. From 1534, London tithe rates amounted to just 2 s. 9 d. for every pound paid in rent, and few parishioners will have contributed more: non-householders only paid 2 d. each on four offering days, and even merchant accommodation was available for £2–3 p.a.[45] In comparison, Mary-at-Hill's churchwardens raised 3 s. 6 d. per head of their congregation already in the late fifteenth century. On the other side of the spectrum, however, the modest communal resources at Halesowen and Prescot compare unfavourably with the income of their clergy.[46]

Moving to the secular field, parish revenues can also be compared to those of manors or courts. At Yatton, most of the parish was under the lordship of the see of Wells and contributed £62 2 s. 7 d. towards its income in 1537.[47] In the same year, the churchwardens accounted for £43 16 s. 3½ d. or almost two thirds of this figure, at a time when parish income had passed its prime.[48] Further south west in 1546, John Seyntclere paid the bishop of Exeter some £79 for the farm of the manor and borough of Ashburton, which was not quite twice as much as the parish average raised in the last few pre-Reformation years (£46 5 s. 4 d.).[49] In both of these places, the churchwardens' receipts amounted to over half of what the local communities paid to their secular lords in rents, fees, and fines. Even at Prescot, with its consistently low score in terms of parochial investment, the level of expenditure was somewhere in the region of local court leet revenues.[50]

Summing up, there cannot be any doubt that the sums entrusted to churchwardens were very substantial indeed. Running at a level comparable to royal taxation or the demands made by lords and rectors, they were one of the foremost financial engagements of the local community. Including payments for tithes, dues, gilds, and chapels, parochial life must have absorbed by far the biggest part of the limited resources available to most of its members.

---

[45] P. Hughes and J. Larkin, *Tudor Royal Proclamations* (3 vols, New Haven, 1964), i. 215–16 (tithe rate in London); Dyer, *Standards of Living*, p. 208 (rent levels). W. Hoskins, *The Age of Plunder* (London, 1976), p. 114, sees 5 s. as a typical urban rent.

[46] The comparison would look even more impressive if it was taken into account that due to inflationary and other pressures, many benefices were actually worth much less than their official valuation: see Carter, 'First fruits', 61.

[47] Valuation in Hobhouse (ed.), *CWA of Croscombe [etc.]*, p. 78.

[48] Yatton CWA, 1537–8.

[49] Ashburton CWA, 1541–6. John Seyntclere paid the farm between 1546 and 1551: H. Hanham, 'A tangle untangled', 444–5.

[50] Prescot Court Leet profit 1552: £4 11 s. 9 d. (D. Bailey, *Prescot Court Leet*, p. 13); expenditure in Prescot CWA, 1553–4 (the nearest complete evidence): £4 6 s. 1½ d.

5.3 Financial trends and their causes

As noted above, the upward trend in churchwardens' income was a temporary phenomenon. In light of what seems like wide-spread enthusiasm, it is intriguing that the momentum was not sustained further into the sixteenth century. Communal wealth could increase in importance compared to subparochial resources, and it held out longer than testamentary or life-time bequests, but even its size declined eventually.[51] It is tempting to relate this trend to changing religious priorities, but the available evidence is far from conclusive. A survey of recent scholarship leaves little doubt that evangelical beliefs did not start to take root in local communities before the mid-1530s, and that it was a long and slow process to build anything like a Protestant culture; the years between the break with Rome and 1570 were marked by uncertainty.[52] It would be very hard to posit reformed ideas as the decisive factor for all those places which saw their incomes decrease before 1530. Even where this happened later, there seems to be no straight connection. At Bristol, Hugh Latimer's sermons may have caused a great stir in 1533 and repercussions at the highest government level,[53] but there was a concerted clerical reaction in the city, and turnovers at All Saints, for instance, continued to rise for a few more years.[54] As for official attitudes, the first significant government interference in parochial practice dates from the injunctions of 1538, and truly dramatic changes cannot be observed before 1547.[55] In fact, conventional 'worship' took up roughly the same share of parochial budgets in the first as well as the last pre-Reformation accounts, and lights formed the single most important item in most places in the early 1540s. On the other hand, England was not free of heresy, and careful analysis of surviving Lollard evidence has shown that the movement survived well into the sixteenth century with a distinctive core of

---

[51] Cf. Chapter 4 (and the analysis of payments to priests and clerks) for the gradual shift away from the subparochial level, Chapter 3.3 for the development of the churchwardens' income, and Bittle and Lane, 'Inflation and philanthropy', 209, for W. K. Jordan's deflated data.

[52] A. Pettegree, 'Rewriting the English Reformation', *Nederlands Archief voor Kerkgeschiedenis*, 72 (1992), 47ff, and D. Palliser, 'Popular reactions to the Reformation during the years of uncertainty 1530–70' in F. Heal and R. O'Day (eds), *Church and Society in England* (London, 1977). The vigour of late medieval religion seems undiminished until the 1530s: Duffy, *Stripping of the Altars*, p. 479; Haigh, *English Reformations*, p. 38.

[53] Duffy, *Stripping of the Altars*, pp. 379–80.

[54] Skeeters, *Community and Clergy*, pp. 71, 149 (the conservative clergymen included St Ewen's rector), and support for the 'old ways' remained high until the late 1530s (p. 74).

[55] Hutton, 'Local impact', pp. 116, 120.

beliefs.[56] It has been described as an important 'spring-board' for Protestantism, and the possibility of significant pockets of nonconformity, at least in certain areas, should not be discounted.[57] At the same time, the movement could not prevent the late medieval boom in traditional religious activities, and it would be difficult to argue that it was suddenly strong enough to do so in the sixteenth century. Deprived of the backing of social elites after the Oldcastle rebellion and in the face of rigorous persecution, Lollards tended to keep their heads down. Historians cannot hope to see into people's souls, but judging from the evidence of parochial sources, Lollard ideas had very little effect on everyday communal life.[58]

With religious impulses appearing rather late or subdued, there may have been other, more prosaic reasons for decreasing parochial turnovers. After all, ecclesiastical expenditure was losing ground to spending on administrative and local government purposes. For these areas, at least, a better case can be made for the influence of the general socio-economic climate: a steady increase from the early fifteenth century, when conditions improved in both town and countryside, and decline at some point after 1520, when population and inflation started to rise.[59] The tightening land market triggered rent increases, and the purchasing power of wage earners was in decline. For average parishioners, standards of living were falling, famines once more a real threat, and poverty became the country's most pressing social problem.[60] Furthermore, it is not unreasonable to interpret large-scale investment in churches and intercessory institutions as conspicuous consumption. A beautiful rood loft in places like Yatton and Ashburton, scores of chantry priests at Mary-at-Hill, or a soaring spire as at Louth enhanced a parish's prestige. A church testified not only to the spiritual awareness of its congregation, but also to the material pride of the community.[61] In those places which relied predominantly on the 'living', the entertainment aspect of parochial activities such as May games, plays, and church ales

---

[56] M. Aston, *England's Iconoclasts* (vol. i, Oxford, 1988), and Plumb, 'Rural Lollardy'.

[57] Dickens, *English Reformation*, p. 36.

[58] Harper-Bill, *Pre-Reformation Church*, p. 82; for the later phase: Thomson, *The Later Lollards*. Even where links between Lollardy and parish events have been suggested, the argument focuses on probabilities rather than proofs: Aston, 'Iconoclasm', 550.

[59] Hatcher, *Population and the English Economy*, p. 65 (population); Outhwaite, *Inflation*, pp. 9ff.

[60] Dyer, *Standards of Living*, p. 277; C. Russell, *Crisis of Parliaments* (5th edn, Oxford, 1982), pp. 13ff (wage earners; cf. Phelps-Brown and Hopkins, 'Seven centuries of the prices of consumables', p. 302) and 20–1 (up to two thirds of sixteenth-century townspeople lived on the brink of poverty).

[61] Morris, *Churches in the Landscape*, p. 373.

was most likely to flourish in times of plenty and considerable spare resources. Perhaps it was here in the countryside that conditions started to deteriorate first. In the late fifteenth century, recently improved tenurial conditions came under seigneurial attack, while the conversion of much arable land into pasture added to the number of landless labourers. Enclosures reached a peak under Henry VII, and tensions between grazers and farmers were starting to put new strains on many village communities.[62] One example admittedly proves little, but it may be more than a coincidence that the Yatton accounts peak before 1500, much earlier than all the others. As long as basic pastoral provision was secured, there were now clearly more important things to do than to boost the revenues of the local church. All in all, the extraordinary spending spree at the close of the Middle Ages should be explained by favourable socio-economic circumstances as well as religious enthusiasm; the correlations are striking. Still, the fact that an ecclesiastical unit absorbed such a lot of money remains significant. Unpopular purposes would struggle to attract support even at the best of times.

The underlying reason for the strengthening of parochial institutions, independent of economic fortunes or religious enthusiasm, was the fact that the common people perceived communal organization as a key to greater self-government. Village assemblies, jury service, and collective resistance had familiarized the rural population with a broad range of responsibilities,[63] and in spite of the many strains put on to local society, the village community retained its coherence well into the fifteenth century and beyond.[64] At the same time, Bristol, York, Newcastle,

---

[62] Hilton, *Decline of Serfdom*, p. 58 (tenure); McIntosh, 'Local change', 220–1 (landless labourers); Russell, *Crisis of Parliaments*, p. 19 (enclosures); Dyer, 'Power and conflict', p. 31 (village tensions).

[63] There is evidence for non-manorial assemblies and legislation (for example at Framfield, Sussex in 1506: W. Ault, 'Village assemblies in medieval England' in *Album Helen Cam* (Louvin, 1960), p. 30). At Hemingford, Hunts., the local population farmed the rights and revenue of their manor from 1279 to 1533, which no doubt required considerable coordination (ibid., p. 22). Manorial juries consisted of substantial landholders, but could also include humbler members (R. Lennard, 'Early manorial juries', *EHR*, 77 (1962), 516ff; Dyer, *Lords and Peasants*, pp. 368–9). Peasants were called to serve on royal and county juries, too: Goheen, 'Peasant politics?', 46ff. The importance of collective resistance emerges strongly from the works of Rodney Hilton (for example, *A Medieval Society* (London, 1967), p. 166).

[64] Smith, ' "Modernization" ', pp. 156ff, for a convenient summary of the historiographical positions. E. Dewindt, *Land and People in Holywell-cum-Needingworth* (Toronto, 1972), pp. 263–75, and other representatives of the 'Toronto School' argue for

Norwich, and Lincoln all acquired the right to a common seal, tenure of land, and some legislative powers in what has been called 'the classic age of borough incorporations'.[65] From 1396, York's own sheriffs replaced county officers, aldermen exercised duties normally reserved to justices of the peace, and freemen had a say in the town assembly, a right they fought hard to defend.[66] The parish's growth benefited from, but at the same time enhanced, this existing competence: it is no coincidence that there is growing evidence for lay scribes and literacy in this period.[67] As in many Continental countries, the various and often overlapping local communities strengthened each other.[68] Quite apart from their spiritual dimensions, the parish and churchwardenship must have held a great deal of attraction for ordinary people. The office, if burdensome, carried a considerable degree of authority and power ranging from the allocation of jobs and ecclesiastical patronage to the screening of potential tenants for parish property. Eligibility for office holding was broadly defined and every householder expected to attend the parish assembly. The pre-Reformation parish offered a framework for the election of officials, considerable legislative power, and a room of manoeuvre as yet hardly restricted by seigneurial, ecclesiastical, or parliamentary guidelines.[69] This all added up to a degree of local prominence few individuals could have aspired to on their own. Parochial activities enhanced lay control, enriched local cultural life,[70] and guaranteed a steady flow of prayers for those too poor to establish intercessory institutions of their own. There was also often a reversal of

---

a post-1350 decline, which has been criticized by Zvi Razi as 'somewhat premature' ('Village community', 36). For Christopher Dyer, who provided the latest contribution to the debate ('The English medieval village', 429), the village community was still very much alive in the later Middle Ages; K. Wrightson, *English Society*, ch. 2, identifies the latter half of the sixteenth century as the crucial turning point.

[65] R. Horrox, 'Urban patronage in the fifteenth century' in R. Griffiths (ed.), *Patronage, the Crown, and the Provinces in Later Medieval England* (Gloucester, 1981), p. 146 (phrase from M. Weinbaum, *The Incorporation of Boroughs* (Manchester, 1937), ch. iv), and S. Reynolds, *An Introduction to the History of English Medieval Towns* (Oxford, 1977), pp. 113–14.

[66] Palliser, *Tudor York*, pp. 60ff: Reynolds, *Kingdoms and Communities*, p. 208 (continued participation as motivation for town rebellions).

[67] Reynolds, *English Medieval Towns*, p. 168; McIntosh, 'Local change', 227.

[68] Feine, 'Kirche und Gemeindebildung', p. 54, asserts 'dass sich kirchliche und städtisch-ländliche Gemeindebildung gegenseitig gefördert und vorangetrieben hat'; for further evidence see Chapter 2.3.

[69] Cf. the collective capacity discussed in Chapter 2.2.3 and the analysis of parish government in Chapter 6.2.

[70] Parish culture could be innovative and 'upwardly mobile': Robin Hood plays, for instance, started at the parish level, but were later performed at the royal court (Hutton, *Merry England*, p. 72).

social roles: Botolph Aldersgate listed both abbots and gentlemen among its tenants and proudly recorded a royal gift.[71] This was the sort of ground which produced the commonplace book of Robert Reynes of Acle. Compiled by a churchwarden in the late fifteenth century, its contents range from tax collection, court business, and manorial regulations to historiography, drama, and religion. Reynes was clearly a village authority with wide responsibilities, and almost half the entries in his manuscript can be said to concern his community life.[72] Far from being mere objects of anonymous socio-economic forces, people like him actively enhanced their role and widened their horizon. It is quite probable that contemporaries would have seen such officers as the personification of the parishes' gradual shift away from worship and fabric maintenance towards more secular and local government duties.[73] In town and countryside alike, churchwardens and parishes exemplified a habit of communal action which was to become an 'important legacy of the medieval church' to the secular world it preceded.[74]

---

[71] The abbot of Kirkstead owed an annual 4 s. to St Botolph, for example CWA 1493–4 (he was frequently in arrears, but at Peterborough the abbot regularly paid rent to the wardens without reservations: CWA 1539ff); the White Hart tenement in St Botolph's was let to Alexander Wryttyngton, gent., on 20 April 3 Edward VI (CWA 1548–9) for a period of 60 years. The royal gift in CWA 1509–10 (20 s. from Henry VII).

[72] Louis (ed.), *Robert Reynes*, passim and p. 114 (community life).

[73] In this sample, 'fabric' fell from 34 per cent in the first preserved CWA to 21 per cent during the last ten pre-Reformation years and 'worship' from 51 per cent to 48 per cent, but 'administration' increased its share from 11 per cent to 27 per cent in the same period (cf. the relevant pie graphs in Figure 3.6).

[74] Owen, *Medieval Lincolnshire*, pp. xxif.

CHAPTER SIX

Mid-Sixteenth-Century Change

Martin Luther's criticism of the late medieval Church provoked a fundamental redrawing of the religious, social, and political landscape in Central Europe. Somewhat belatedly, the new ideas swept across the channel and – in a modified form – helped to shape the complex process now referred to as the 'English Reformation'.[1] Many factual accounts of its impact on parish communities are now available, and in spite of local peculiarities, the overall impression is one of at least outward conformity to the long series of visitation articles, injunctions, royal proclamations, and acts of parliament enforced by the Tudor government machinery.[2] This cannot be the place to discuss the political background and theological motivation of all these changes, but some of the most important measures affecting the communal and financial organization of English parishes deserve to be recalled.

Henry VIII's manoeuvrings took a while to affect local religious life. The political decision to break with Rome led to the disappearance of 'Peter's pence' – payments from churchwardens' accounts, but major adjustments were not needed until September 1538, when royal injunctions demanded the provision of English bibles and the removal of all lights except those in front of the rood, high altar, and Easter sepulchre.[3] The local Reformation proper, however, is associated with the year 1547: a fresh set of injunctions, issued by the new Edwardian regime in July, reaffirmed those of 1538, additionally banned processions and images (in theory only those attracting pilgrimages or offerings, but none at all were tolerated from February 1548), and ordered the purchase of Erasmus' *Paraphrases*. An extensive royal visitation was set

---

[1] The latest summaries in Sheils, *Reformation*, and Haigh, *English Reformations*; for a historiographical survey: R. O'Day, *The Debate on the English Reformation* (London, 1986).

[2] This point emerges from all recent local and general studies: J. Bettey, *Bristol Parish Churches During the Reformation c.1530–60* (Bristol, 1979), p. 10, and 'The Reformation and the parish church', *The Historian*, 46 (Summer 1995), 11–14; Hutton, 'Local impact', pp. 137–8 (Reformation-related entries in CWA); Whiting, *Blind Devotion*, p. 265 (South-West); Gibbs, 'Parish finance', p. 205 (London), S. Yaxley, *The Reformation in Norfolk Parish Churches* (Dereham, 1990), p. 5, Duffy, *Stripping of the Altars*, p. 462 (attack on traditional ceremonial life).

[3] 25 Henry VIII, c. 21 (for parliamentary acts see the relevant volumes of *Statutes of the Realm*, in this case iii. 464–71; Peter's pence, however, was never a major item in parochial budgets); Frere and Kennedy (ed.), *Visitation articles*, i. 34–43 (injunctions).

up to enforce these changes, and at the end of the year, parliament approved communion in both kinds and dissolved all chantries and fraternities. The Chantries' Act rejected the whole concept of purgatory and transferred all endowments for superstitious purposes to the Court of Augmentations.[4] Parochial worship was redefined by the Act of Uniformity in January 1549, which prescribed the use of a new Prayer Book from the following Whit Sunday. With its ambiguous definition of Eucharistic doctrine and the modified but not fundamentally transformed liturgy, it represented a moderate approach to reform, but its most striking innovation for the laity was the use of English instead of Latin in divine service. More radical breaks with tradition followed with the removal of altars in 1550, the confiscation of now superfluous church plate by royal commissioners in 1552/3, and the theologically more radical second Prayer Book of 1552.[5] In its wake, parishes were left with not much more than a communion table, a surplice, a table cloth, a bell, and a communion cup, and the Church of England emerged with 'an unequivocally Protestant vernacular liturgy and an increasingly Calvinist theology'.[6] After Mary's accession in 1553, however, the country was told to re-equip its churches with ornaments and altars, only to see them disappear again in the reign of Elizabeth. A new and more enduring settlement was embodied in the Acts of Supremacy and Uniformity of April 1559. With a few exceptions, notably those concerning vestments and the wording used at Holy Communion, the Prayer Book of 1552 was reintroduced and – still in the same year – a fresh set of commissioners embarked on another 'draconian' visitation to finalize the new shape of the *Ecclesia Anglicana*.[7]

It would be futile to deny that the governments' religious policies and u-turns left traces on almost every page of parish manuscripts, but it is equally clear that the Reformation was not the only determining factor in the events of the mid-sixteenth century. It has been suggested that

---

[4] Ibid., 114–30 (1547 injunctions); 1 Edward VI, c. 1 (communion in both kinds) and c. 14 (Chantries Act). Drew (ed.), *Lambeth CWA*, p. xx (order in council on the removal of all images and lights).

[5] 2 & 3 Edward VI, c. 1 (first Act of Uniformity 1549); J. Dasent (ed.), *Acts of the Privy Council of England*, NS (vol. iii, London, 1891), pp. 168–9 (removal of altars); W. Page (ed.), *The Inventories of Church Goods for the Counties of York, Durham and Northumberland* (Durham, 1896), pp. 1–7 (appointment of commissioners for church plate inventory; there had been previous surveys in 1547 and 1549: Hutton, 'Local impact', p. 126, and Duffy, *Stripping of the Altars*, pp. 476–7); 5 & 6 Edward VI, c. 1 (second Act of Uniformity 1552); *The First and Second Prayer Books of Edward VI* (London, 1910).

[6] Duffy, *Stripping of the Altars*, p. 477 (parish ornaments); Sheils, *Reformation*, p. 46 (quote).

[7] 1 Mary, st. 2, c. 2 (first Act of Repeal); 1 Elizabeth, c. 1 and 2 (Acts of Supremacy and Uniformity); Duffy, *Stripping of the Altars*, p. 566 (1559 visitation).

socio-economic factors cannot be ignored in an assessment of the Tudor age, and a case could be made for many other influences.[8] This chapter will argue that parish finance and government underwent fundamental changes between the early and the late sixteenth century, but the exact causality of events must often remain obscure. Due to chronological coincidence and the nature of the source material, developments in the ecclesiastical field are highlighted here, but it must be kept in mind that the decisions of Tudor parishioners might well have been determined by a range of other, less well-documented factors.

Quite apart from the search for motives, it has recently been questioned whether the mid-sixteenth century should be associated with discontinuity at all. Influenced perhaps by the example of the 'Annales' school, historians now often point to structural continuities which are not affected by even the most hectic eruptions on the surface level of events and short-term variations.[9] David Palliser (with regard to parishes) and Richard Smith (for the village community) both refused to draw too stark a contrast between the Middle Ages and the early modern period. The parochial network remained largely intact, the office of churchwarden continued to be of crucial importance, and communal responsibilities existed before as well as after the Reformation.[10] In village life, external interference occurred in any period, and there were changes in intensity or degree, but hardly 'a major transformation in structure such as is implied by the "incorporationist" perspective, whereby local communities are seen to have been absorbed into a wider political entity'.[11] Long-term processes naturally need to be viewed in a differentiated fashion: the evidence is often ambiguous, and 'continuity and change' normally the most appropriate description; ultimately, the

---

[8] Even for something as unlikely as climatic change. Towards the end of the sixteenth century, atmospheric conditions in northern Europe deteriorated so dramatically that the period is now known as the 'Little Ice Age': see for example J. Grove, *The Little Ice Age* (London, 1988), p. 3. Long-term developments may have had a limited impact on all but certain sensitive areas, but short-term climatic fluctuations certainly affected standards of living (and therefore the availability of spare resources) in every pre-modern society (Dyer, *Standards of Living*, p. 261). 'In extreme marginal places [in the British Isles] the smallest change could have a dramatic effect upon the ecology of the community': G. Beresford, 'Climatic change' in C. Delano-Smith and M. Parry (eds), *Consequences of Climatic Change* (Nottingham, 1981), p. 30.

[9] The classic example remains: F. Braudel, *The Mediterranean and the Mediterranean World in the Age of Philipp II* (London, 1975), i. 25–354 ('The role of the environment').

[10] Palliser, 'The parish in perspective', pp. 12ff. Significantly, the survey is divided into two parts by the date 1350 rather than the Reformation.

[11] Smith, ' "Modernization" ', p. 177. The quote refers to the works of, for example, Keith Wrightson and the claim that the introspective nature of the medieval village community was changed fundamentally in the early modern period (ibid., pp. 144–6).

problem is one of definition and emphasis. On the basis of this sample, however, it would seem that the mid-Tudor years opened a completely new chapter in the history of the English parish. There can be little doubt that fifteenth-century churchwardens would have been puzzled by the way their communities were run in, say, 1600. To them, both parish accounts and government structure would have looked very different and distinctly 'early modern'. These two crucial areas need to be looked at in more detail.

6.1 Financial regimes

There is broad agreement that the Edwardian measures threw parochial budgets into disarray. Writing about Ashburton and the South-West, Robert Whiting observed a 'catastrophic' decline in revenues and a diversion of funds away from the church towards secular purposes.[12] The effects resulting from the Chantries Act of 1547 and the confiscations of church goods have been described as a 'disaster' for local religious life, turning the years 1536–53 into a period of unprecedented destruction and plunder in English history.[13] Parish administration was clearly in some turmoil, exemplified both by the small number of surviving records and their often sorry state.[14] However, the lack of quantitative work on churchwardens' accounts has made it impossible to proceed beyond general impressions about the financial impact of the changes. A closer analysis suggests that they were experienced quite differently in each locality, that they affected income and expenses in particular ways, and that they created a rather more complex overall picture than is generally assumed.

Taking average income growth in this sample as a first indication, the figure fell from 1.007 in the pre- to 0.995 in the post-Reformation period. Six out of the ten case studies experienced negative growth, and therefore a basically falling trend.[15] But Prescot, for instance, significantly improved its figure from 0.955 before 1547 to 1.206 after, and on the expenditure side, the average of all parishes increased marginally, too. Looking at fresh revenue only, that is disregarding

---

[12] Whiting, *Blind Devotion*, p. 96.

[13] Scarisbrick, *Reformation*, p. 85, and Duffy, *Stripping of the Altars*, p. 454 (quote), 477.

[14] There are no Edwardian accounts for Peterborough, and very limited evidence survives for Prescot; the records of Stogursey, Nettlecombe, and Trull 'all disintegrate or end' in the period (French, 'Local identity', p. 34), and there are only 18 sets of accounts which cover the period 1535–62 in full (Hutton, *Merry England*, p. 69).

[15] For the calculation and meaning of average growth cf. Chapter 3.3.

previous balances and arrears, the trend in absolute figures was not necessarily falling,[16] but problems resulted from the fact that expenditure (especially in the Marian years of restoration) either grew faster or decreased more slowly. As a consequence, Edwardian balances on the whole deteriorated by about 300 per cent compared to the immediate pre-Reformation years. At Ashburton, income was down by 40 per cent, but expenses only by 24. Having generated over £3 a year in the last phase of the old regime, the parish now made an average loss of over £2. Comparing the same periods, Halesowen marginally increased its fresh income by 4 per cent, but spent about a quarter more, and saw the deficit rise from a moderate annual 5 d. to over 11 s. In what was clearly a special case, Andrew Hubbard managed to boost revenues by 130 per cent under Edward VI due to the additional income from the benefice, but again expenditure grew faster and the churchwardens' balance deteriorated accordingly.[17] As everywhere, red figures were now a common phenomenon, although the impact was optically improved by injections from the church box. Under Edward, the average overall balance was negative only at Halesowen and Prescot. Still, there was cause for alarm. At Little Ilford in Essex, churchwarden Thomas Hutton complained about the level of his expenses in 1547 which 'the rest of the parisshe were faine to beare of their own proper cost for they never had no stock to the churche, therefore it hath been verie painefull'.[18]

This particular plight was due to the weak endowment basis of the community. Elsewhere, income-levels proved surprisingly resilient in spite of the fact that lights, chantries, and gilds had all disappeared. There were two redeeming features for parish finance. First, the most important pillar, rent revenue, could remain relatively unaffected. Landed endowments have attracted little scholarly attention, but where they did, the Reformation impact has been described in a rather stark and undifferentiated fashion. At Ashburton, for instance, rents were hardly down at all:[19] from £11 5s. 3d. between 1541 and 1546 to £10 19s. 11d. under Edward VI. As at All Saints, St Ewen's, and Botolph Aldersgate more than 85 per cent survived, while Peterborough, Mary-at-Hill, or Andrew Hubbard did indeed lose all or most of their endowments (see Figure 6.1: 'rents' continue in graphs (a) and (b), but disappear in the others). Clearly, not all parishes were affected in the

---

[16] In inflation-adjusted terms, however, revenues only increased at Prescot.

[17] For details of Andrew Hubbard's 'parsonage' accounts cf. Chapter 3.4.

[18] Quoted in Duffy, *Stripping of the Altars*, p. 486.

[19] Whiting, *Blind Devotion*, p. 97, lists rent decline due to confiscation as the first reason for the declining parish incomes. At Ashburton, however, only 22 s. of the slightly lower total rent income was considered 'superstitious' and passed on to the Crown in the post-Reformation CWA (CWA, p. ix and 1550ff).

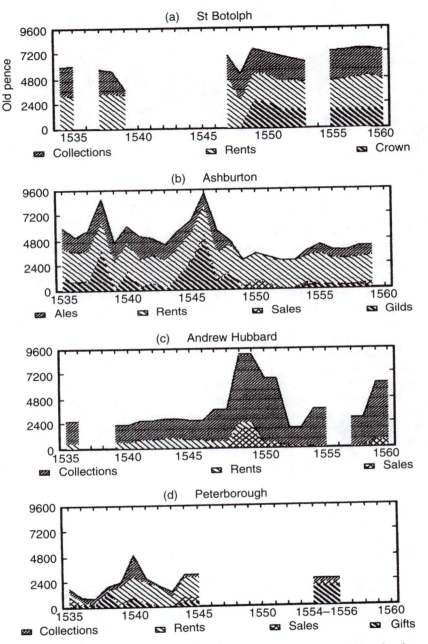

Figure 6.1   Reformation impact on parish income in four case studies: development of main items of revenue 1535–60; unit: absolute figures in old pence

same way, but what were the reasons for this divergence? There can be no doubt that the vast majority of lands and tenements were given in return for prayers, whether in the institutionalized form of chantries, anniversaries, or in the hope of inclusion in the parochial bede-roll: in 1417, to add just one more example to the cases discussed earlier, John Wilford left an acre of land, a garden, and appurtenances to John Melbury and Thomas Montague, wardens of St Kerrian, Exeter, 'on condition that the aforesaid wardens and their successors hold my anniversary in the aforesaid church'. After a period of 99 years, the tenements were to be sold to the best profit of the church.[20] This belief in the efficacy of intercession, however, was increasingly frowned upon by the crown, for financial as well as ideological reasons; at first sight, the high survival of 'superstitious' rents is certainly surprising.

And yet, there are a number of explanations. Crucially, perhaps, the government's attack on ecclesiastical property had left a few loopholes. When Henry VIII decided to stop the draining of his feudal revenues, parliament passed an act in 1532 which described enfeoffments for the benefit of parish churches and chapels as 'prejudicial' to the king and declared all those extending 'above the terme of xx yeres' to be void.[21] In legal practice, however, the time limit was applied to 'superstitious' purposes only (in particular the commission of prayers for the dead), while general needs of the church such as fabric maintenance could still be supported in the traditional way.[22] Four years later, the Statute of Uses introduced much more radical measures by transferring formal legal ownership of land held in use from the trustees to the *cestui que use*, upon whose death feudal incidents were payable by the heirs. Yet again, charitable purposes such as church maintenance were not affected.[23] Furthermore, Chancery continued to treat these causes with special 'tenderness', upholding trusts even 'despite the lack of capacity of the trustees to take legal title to the trust property, a difficulty which afflicted

---

[20] Will quoted in Ault, 'Village church', 211; for spiritual motives of benefactions in general see Burgess and Kümin, 'Penitential bequests', 613–14. As seen in Chapter 2.3.3, parishes also actively invested in lands, but this was still exceptional.

[21] 23 Henry VIII, c. 10. The land would thus escheat to the mesne lord: G. Jones, *History of the Law of Charity 1532–1827* (Cambridge, 1969), p. 11.

[22] F. W. Maitland, 'The unincorporate body' in his *Collected Papers*, iii. 284.

[23] 27 Henry VIII, c. 10. Partly because the machinery of the statute could not operate upon charitable uses. It executed the use by transferring legal title from the feoffees to the *cestui que use*, but in the case of a charitable use, there was no such beneficiary, for legal title could not be vested in a purpose (for example church repair). This was clear from the beginning and fully anticipated, but the strong resistance against the statute forced the crown to grant yet further concessions. Legislation passed in 1540 allowed, for the first time, the free devising by will of (certain categories of) lands: 32 Henry VIII, c. 1; Baker, *Introduction*, p. 293.

churchwardens in particular'.[24] By the time of the dissolution, therefore, common law had assumed an openly hostile attitude towards traditional kinds of religious bequests,[25] but churchwardens who made a plausible case that their endowments were intended for poor relief or general church maintenance had little to fear. The Tavistock 'feoffees to the uses of the parish church', for instance, survived well into the seventeenth century, even though benefactors were now very careful to specify acceptable purposes for their landed bequests.[26] But as far as pre-Reformation property was concerned, the donors' motives were difficult to disentangle, for even 'non-sensitive' gifts were in practice reciprocated by the prayers of the community. The situation with regard to landed parish property was thus rather complex and (at least in this respect) it would be misleading to speak of a full-scale spoliation of the local church. The royal commissioners who went round the country to supervise the implementation of royal policy would have encountered a rather 'mixed bag' of subparochial and communal endowments, and this must have been one of the reasons for the heterogeneous pattern of confiscation revealed by the sources.

Much may have depended on the attitude and energy of the officials involved.[27] At Ashburton, the crucial figure was John Prideaux, a local man who proved extremely conciliatory. The churchwardens managed to keep quiet about gilds and stipendiary priests and 'concocted a highly artificial set of accounts which purported to show that the only claim the crown had on the parish church was in respect of a number of rent-charges given to maintain obits and lamps'.[28] Even these were quoted at their original value and not the much higher level of the current accounts. The messuage and garden held by George Wyndeyate, for instance, appeared to yield just 5 s., while the churchwardens actually received no less than £3 1 s. 4 d.[29] A similarly 'modest' estimate had been

---

[24] N. Jones, 'Trusts: practice and doctrine, 1536–1660' (Ph.D. Cambridge, 1994), p. 194 (with a discussion of relevant late sixteenth-century cases pp. 194–8). I am grateful to Neil Jones for his help in these legal matters.

[25] See also the strong attack on superstitious beliefs in the preamble to the Chantries Act of 1547: 1 Edward VI, c. 14.

[26] 'Feoffees' appear for example still in 1656 (Worth (ed.), *Tavistock*, p. 100); a post-Reformation example of a gift to the parish for poor relief purposes is the grant made by Richard Williams 'ad solum opus usum & pfitum omn. pauperis de Tavystock' in 1552: ibid., p. 86.

[27] Some Edwardian commissioners are known to have failed to read the available evidence properly and they missed many an endowment: C. Kitching, 'The quest for concealed lands in the reign of Elizabeth I', *TRHS*, 5th Series, 24 (1974), 65.

[28] H. Hanham, 'Chantries in Ashburton', 118. The parish also tried to argue that the gild-market had not supported any superstitious uses, but here it was defeated: ibid., 119ff.

[29] Ibid., 119.

made for the lay subsidy. The 'feoffees' of the church were assessed at a mere £5 in 1544, while rent revenues yielded more than £11 in the last pre-Reformation accounts.[30] Here, and probably in many other places, it looks very much like a 'quick fix', with commissioners following the letter of the law rather than its spirit: clear-cut cases like the gild lands at Peterborough, the endowment for Juliana Fairhead's obit at Andrew Hubbard, or the chantry accounts of Mary-at-Hill disappeared.[31] Elsewhere though, the pattern was more complex. With a thoroughly misjudged sense of timing, almost £9 worth of new rents had accrued to Botolph Aldersgate in the last pre-Edwardian years. In 1548–9, this increase was more than wiped out by a loss of 10s. in quit rents ('as the seid quyte rentes ... ben grannted & assured to our seid sovereign lorde the kyng') and £8 16s. 4d. in other rents (transferred to Edward VI 'by vertue of the seid acte of parlyament wherby all channtrey lonndes wer ... assured to his highnes'[32]). On the other hand, the church house and the properties in Blackhorse Alley, where the wardens had actively invested in new property,[33] remained untouched, and the parish inherited the hall of the dissolved Trinity fraternity. A well-balanced solution was found for the house in Lambe Alley, which was to pay half of its rent to the wardens and half to the crown. Such arrangements confirm that there were many ambiguities and much room for compromise. Furthermore, as explicitly stated in the Chantries Act and suggested above, endowments could be preserved as long as they supported 'acceptable' uses of the commonwealth. Commissioners must have looked favourably upon fabric maintenance purposes,[34] especially in light of the loss of many other sources of parochial income. Some property was deliberately reallocated in accordance with the new political and religious priorities. The foundation or support of educational institutions was a possibility,[35] and at All Saints, the parish

---

[30] Stoate (ed.), *Devon Lay Subsidy 1543–5*, p. 192.

[31] H. Hanham, 'Chantries at Ashburton', 129 ('quick fix'); Peterborough and Andrew Hubbard CWA, post-1547 (the latter recovered part of this loss by renting out the parsonage during the period when it administered the benefice); Mary-at-Hill CWA, p. lxx: the chantry entries 'disappear wholly from the annual accounts'.

[32] Rent details and both quotes: Botolph CWA, 1548–9. Among the latter was the Saracen's Head, a tenement given to the rector and wardens by John Bath over one hundred years earlier to support a chantry. Now used as a brewery, it was sold to its tenant Richard Watters in 1548: Basing (ed.), *Fraternity Register*, pp. xix, xxvi.

[33] Botolph CWA, 1516–17; cf. Chapter 2.3.3.

[34] A statute of 1601, which became the basis for the later law of charity, was to include for example poor relief, education, and certain religious purposes among charitable uses.

[35] For the reassessment of society's need in the Tudor period and a positive interpretation of the educational impact of the Reformation: J. Simon, *Education and Society in Tudor England* (Cambridge, 1966). Examples of school foundations in Sheils, *Reformation*, pp.

managed to preserve some continuity for the endowment of the Spicer anniversary when it agreed 'that upon the xiiii[th] day of February the proctoures of the churche shall dystrybute amonge the presoners of Newgate the Lazar howsse & pore people in halfpeny and bred x[s] yerely'.[36]

Quite a lot of rent survival, however, was simply due to concealment. In contrast to their Henrician predecessors, who had visited every single monastery individually, Edwardian commissioners were content to summon representatives of a series of parishes to a regional centre. The records they were shown there were at best 'rough and ready', and it must have been possible to hide endowments from the crown.[37] The temptation was clearly difficult to resist: for generations, parishioners had profited from and participated in a ceremonial life built around the regular rhythm of obits and divine service endowed by their benefactors. They would be very reluctant to see it go, if not for religious, then certainly for financial reasons. Ashburton tampered with its evidence, and so did Botolph Aldersgate: as late as 1559–60, quit rents of £1 5s. vanished from the parish accounts, after someone had discovered that they were 'geven to the said church of S[t] Botulphe to the mantenance of Lampes Lightes & soch like there as by the search of thevidences thereof ... may appere. by reason whereof the same was geven to the late Kinge Edwarde the vj[th]'. The parish must have been aware of this all along (the relevant evidence was kept 'in the black [book?] in the custodie of the churwardens [sic]'), but had done nothing about it. The crown, of course, nurtured similar suspicions, and periodically initiated searches for concealed lands.[38] Detailed information on every single property would be needed to shed more light on this intricate process, but – to cut a long story short – 'rents' continued to be the backbone of parish finance under both Edward and Mary, losing no more than a third of

---

38–9 (Newark, Maidstone, Crediton). Cook, *Medieval Chantries*, pp. 76–7, argues that the crown's more immediate military and financial needs were given priority. At Ashburton, there was neither a particular zeal to found nor to destroy schools among the commissioners: H. Hanham, 'Chantries at Ashburton', 130.

[36] All Saints CWA, 1550–1; the obit for Thomas and Maud Spicer had always been held in mid-February, and it included alms of 3 s. to prisoners and the poor; overall costs in 1524–5 for example were 10 s. 4 d.

[37] Kitching, 'Quest for concealed lands', 64–5. The survival of so much church land at Bethersden may have been due to the lack of explicit reference to 'superstitious' uses in the CWA. Still, careful scrutiny would have revealed that one property at least was linked to an obit: Mercer (ed.), *CWA at Betrysden*, p. 32.

[38] Botolph CWA, 1559–60 (quotes); H. Hanham, 'Chantries at Ashburton', 119: some of the hidden evidence was closely inspected at Ashburton in 1564 and 1568; see also Kitching, 'Quest for concealed lands'.

their previous share of total revenues.[39] Endowments of cattle and livestock, the equivalent of lands in many rural surroundings, followed a similar pattern: at Bethersden, they were clearly linked to certain lights and disappeared gradually from 1538, but elsewhere, ideologically 'sound' bequests could survive the Reformation.[40] Overall, English parishioners managed to preserve an astonishing proportion of their material heritage, and some of the means they employed could hardly be described as religious 'conformity'. What was at stake here was not really doctrinal preference, but the livelihood of a community.

A similar point could be made about the second and more widely acknowledged redeeming factor of Edwardian budgets, the unprecedented sale of parish property. As seen in Chapter 3.3, churchwardens had always liquidated some of their assets, but for stock-clearing rather than fund-raising purposes, or in order to raise money for an extraordinary project. After 1547, however, sales emerge as the second most important item of revenue, rising from 4 per cent to some 20 per cent of fresh income.[41] The most striking case in this sample is the £47 raised from Boxford's mass silver in 1547–8, which appears somewhat indirectly as money lent out to parishioners. The wardens probably anticipated that their action would be frowned upon by a government constantly starved of cash and mentioned the profit only in a separate return, which went out of its way to detail the positive uses the money had been put to.[42] Judging from the interest and debt repayments recorded in post-Reformation sources, there must have been considerable demand for this local credit facility.[43] The same was true elsewhere: at Bethersden, the Edwardian commissioners discovered that the parish had sold at least 74 pounds of latten in Edward's reign without entering it into the accounts, and given the substantial amounts

---

[39] Cf. the stacks in appendix 4 (i): rents had scored 298 (out of max. 1000) percentage points in the last pre-Reformation years, but still reached 198 under Edward and 190 in Mary's reign. There is no Edwardian evidence for Peterborough, but the percentage score resulting from the other nine parishes has been increased by 10 per cent to allow direct comparison with the other periods.

[40] For bequests of livestock see Ault, 'Village church', 212ff, and Yatton or Halesowen in this sample. The Bethersden CWA include a memorandum that 'v kene' were given to the church by William Sander 'for to help and mayten certen lyghts' (Mercer (ed.), CWA at Betrysden, p. 60: 1512). Cows were sold from the late 1530s (for example p. 38) at 10 s. each. At Strood in the same county, however, cattle was still a pillar of parish revenue in the late sixteenth-century: H. Plomer (ed.), The CWA of Strood (Ashford, 1927), p. iv.

[41] Cf. the stacks in appendix 4 (i) (disregarding arrears and previous balances).

[42] Boxford CWA, p. xiv and 1547–8.

[43] Parochial banking services were of course not a Reformation innovation (see for example Peterborough CWA, 1475–7, or All Saints CWA, 1539–40: loan to vicar Thomas Yereth), but they became much more widespread from the late 1540s.

held by various debtors, it may have been an even bigger cover-up.[44] A contemporary petition by the parishioners of St Nicholas, Guildford, reveals another community with a guilty conscience:

> your orators not knowynge or conceyvynge any restraynt or com[and]ment not to sell the same plate (although an inventory was taken therof) which inve[ntory] your orators thought to [be] done only as a restraynt that churche wardens and others the parishioners [should] not imbesell the same to ther private uses … they … dyd sell ther saide churche plate partly to repayre reforme and alter ther sayd churche, and partly to put the overplus thereof into saf custody. … yf your orators sholde restore and make good [the proceeds of the sale] to the kynges majesti, it wolde be to ther utter undoynge.[45]

In Norfolk, Brisley did away with some £30 of plate to buy houses and tenements as more permanent church endowments, while the town of Aylesham raised no less than £102 for repairs to the local church, school, bridge, and almshouse.[46] In London parishes, sales of church property produced up to 20 per cent of total income in the 1550s and occurred more frequently 'than at any other time of the century'.[47]

Every locality may have had different reasons for the decision to part with much of its assets, ranging from sheer material greed to Protestant zeal, or even the hope of future restoration. The Cloptons of Long Melford bought parish plate in order to avoid profanation, and at Wakefield 25 alabaster images survived in the roof of a chapel. At Morebath in Devon, ornaments and vestments were distributed among the parishioners in 1547, and – as 'good catholyke men' – they returned whatever escaped the attention of the commissioners after 1553.[48] However, as in the case of parish rents, the fear of government appropriation of local resources and financial necessity must have been the most common motives. As early as 1539 and under the fresh

---

[44] Mercer (ed.), *CWA at Betrysden*, p. xii; the wardens accounted for a mysterious £8 4 s. 6 d. of 'chyrche mony' in 1547–8, and lent a total of some £24 in Edward's reign to various individuals at rates of between 6½–8½ per cent: ibid., pp. 87, 132. The interest was 10 per cent over at Strood: Plomer (ed.), *CWA of Strood*, p. iv.

[45] Roberts (ed.), 'Further Surrey inventories', 35 (the petition was addressed to the Edwardian commissioners).

[46] Both examples Scarisbrick, *Reformation*, p. 94. 69 out of the 90 parishes in Ronald Hutton's sample ('Local impact', p. 126) record sales after 1547, and so did Bury St Edmunds: Craig, 'Reformation, politics, and polemics', p. 68.

[47] Gibbs, 'Parish finance', p. 206. The examples confirming the trend in this sample are St Michael Cornhill and All Hallows Staining.

[48] All examples in Duffy, *Stripping of the Altars*, pp. 490–1, 498ff (the quote from Binney (ed.), *Morebath*, p. 185). 'There had been more resistance, concealment and evasion than has sometimes been supposed; more hesitation, more scruples about laying hands on sacred things': Scarisbrick, *Reformation*, p. 104.

impression of the dissolution of religious houses, Bristol parishes loaned some of their plate to the corporation, partly to prevent more royal plunder, but also to enable it to purchase pieces of former monastic property in the city.[49] Rumours of imminent confiscations of parish property had also circulated in the Pilgrimage of Grace in 1536, and how much more plausible were they in the face of royal agents repeatedly compiling inventories in the local church.[50] What happened in the reign of Edward was a 'stampede to prevent theft by the Crown' in a period of deteriorating economic circumstances and increased demands on local communities. Dykes, roads, and bridges had to be maintained, churches were always in need of repair, and the poor posed an ever greater challenge.[51] The development of government policy fully vindicated the churchwardens' fears: parish plate was confiscated in 1552–3, and almost £20000 worth of precious metals found their way into the royal mint.[52]

Of the traditional sources of parish revenue, church ales were worst affected. Under Edward, they fell from 15 to 5 per cent of fresh income, and recovered only marginally in the next reign.[53] At Boxford, for instance, ales and other entertainments had produced an annual average of £3 4s. 6d. in the accounts of 1540–1 to 1546–7, but disappeared almost immediately afterwards. At Yatton, where communal drinking and feasting had always dominated the wardens' reckoning, profits were down from £13 6d. (between 1540–1 and 1545–6) to £5 8s. 10d. (from 1547–8 to 1552–3). This general decline was the result of official attacks on a wide range of traditional popular customs, and a local environment increasingly fraught with inner-parochial tensions. 'Within eighteen months of its inception, the government of Protector Somerset had virtually demolished the seasonal rituals of the English Church.'[54] The

---

[49] Skeeters, *Community and Clergy*, p. 78. All Saints, for instance, delivered 96 ounces of plate, plus parcels of gilt and money to the city chamberlain, in return for the corporation's promise to make 'an oblygacyon ffor the payment afforsayd': CWA, 1539–40.

[50] M. Bowker, 'Lincolnshire 1536' in D. Baker (ed.), *Schism, Heresy, and Religious Protest* (Cambridge, 1972), pp. 198–9; inventories were ordered in 1547, 1549, and 1552. Confiscation fears prompted the constable of Davidstow (Cornwall) to advise the parishioners to sell their best chalice already in Henry VIII's reign: PRO, STAC 3/2/20 (I owe this reference to John Craig).

[51] Duffy, *Stripping of the Altars*, pp. 484 (quote) and 484ff (examples of sale out of financial need); similar Scarisbrick, *Reformation*, p. 95, and Whiting, *Blind Devotion*, p. 176. Some sales, however, were ordered by the commissioners themselves, for example at Yatton for the construction of a sluice: CWA 1549–50.

[52] Challis, *Tudor Coinage*, p. 165.

[53] Cf. Figure 6.1 for Ashburton, the stacks in Appendix 4 (i), Whiting, *Blind Devotion*, p. 98, and Hutton, 'Local impact', p. 123.

[54] Hutton, *Merry England*, p. 85.

holding of ales survived into the early modern period, periodically attacked as a puritan 'cause célèbre', but it never regained its previous importance.[55] Law and order concerns had always worried authorities, but from the sixteenth century opposition was growing, and after 1600 many places replaced ales with a system of parish rates.[56] The experience of St Andrew Holborn in London was symptomatic: churchwarden Thomas Bentley recorded in 1584 that church repairs had been financed by means of ales, plays, and other communal entertainments in previous times, while current regimes relied on assessments and benevolences of the rich.[57] Under Edward, however, ales were in sharp decline and other fundraising methods not yet established; this worst-case scenario was a reality for many parish communities.

So was the fact that the level of gift giving fell to an all-time low in the same period. Potential benefactors had every reason to be cautious: with confiscations looming, donations were not a wise move. Parishioners quickly regained their generosity under Mary, however, when bequests accounted for over 10 per cent of real parish income.[58] This may have reflected official incentives, but perhaps also genuine support for the re-equipment with traditional ornaments and ceremonies, for by the late sixteenth century, tables had turned again: less than 5 per cent of London testators made bequests to the church fabric, far fewer than in the pre-Reformation period.[59]

In spite of all these disruptions and fluctuations, the basic income regimes remained surprisingly unscathed. Calculating the share of the living and the dead for the Edwardian period, the figures and percentages have changed considerably, but not the underlying structure. Compared to the last pre-Reformation evidence, all the pie charts in Figure 6.2 retain their main feature.[60] Where rents had been important

---

[55] T. Barnes, 'County politics and a puritan cause célèbre', *TRHS*, 5th Series, 9 (1959), 103–22; five of 17 church ales survive in the sample of Hutton, 'Local impact', p. 123.

[56] Bennett, 'Conviviality', 36. Further evidence for medieval canonical legislation against the secular use of church and yard: Hutton, *Merry England*, p. 311, n. 7, but there was 'no general campaign' (ibid., p. 71).

[57] For Bentley's chronicle 'Some monuments of Antiquities' see Griffith, *Poor Rates*, (1831), pp. i–xlix, Barron and Roscoe, 'St Andrew Holborn', p. 31, and (with similar evidence from St Lawrence Jewry, and St Botolph Billingsgate) Archer, *Pursuit of Stability*, p. 94. Church courts evidence confirms the trend towards compulsory dues: R. Houlbrooke, *Church Courts and the People during the English Reformation* (Oxford, 1979), p. 154.

[58] That is, of total income minus balances; cf. the stacks in Appendix 4 (i).

[59] Archer, *Pursuit of Stability*, pp. 170–3; for the pre-Reformation evidence cf. Chapter 5.

[60] The same is true for other London examples, where there is generally a 'remarkable consistency in the sources of income': Gibbs, 'Parish finance', p. 214.

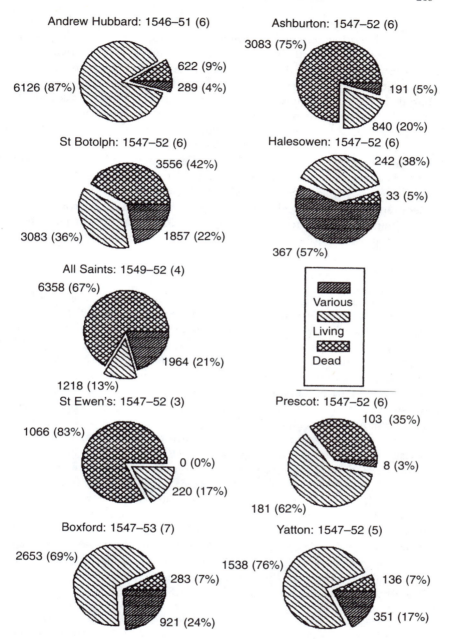

Figure 6.2 Income from the 'living' and the 'dead' in 9 case studies *t*. Edward VI, with dates and number of years analysed; unit: averages in old pence

and untainted by 'superstition' as in Bristol or St Botolph, the dead's share declined but retained its dominant position. At Ashburton, other parish activities seem to have come to a standstill, and the remaining rents actually contributed more to the Edwardian income, while Prescot increased its share of the dead quite literally, with growing fees from burials in the parish church. In London's Andrew Hubbard, the loss of the only landed endowment and the takeover of the benefice reinforced the parish's trend to rely on the living, just as in Edwardian Boxford, Peterborough, or Halesowen.[61] In spite of government policy and potential changes in popular religion, communal fundraising regimes withstood even a concerted wave of Reformation measures, confirming once more how much they depended on their social context. To change them required a wholescale redefinition of the parish's role from a self-governing community to a crown agent for local government purposes. The compulsory nationwide rates were to have a much greater impact, but these developments were still some way ahead.

The Reformation had a much more immediate effect on the spending priorities in churchwardens' accounts. Re-examining Figures 3.6 and 3.7, the Edwardian years emerge as a major turning point. Expenditure on 'fabric' remained relatively stable, but 'worship' declined significantly, and the trend towards 'administration' was reinforced. As for 'voluntary' and 'compulsory' spending, the tables had turned completely. Parishioners no longer allocated the majority of their resources on their own initiative, but on the basis of external directives. The Marian regime temporarily reversed the trend in terms of 'worship', but only by means of a further reduction in the 'voluntary' element of parish expenditure. As is evident from the stacks in Appendix 4 (ii), crown-related payments were the third biggest individual item in the reign of Edward VI with over 10 per cent of parish expenditure. Most of it related less to the traditional areas of subsidy collections and military duties, but primarily to the costly implementation of various Reformation measures such as the whitewashing of walls, removing of altars, and the provision of bibles. The dismantling of elaborate and heavy ornamentation often required paid labour, and the painting of scriptural texts, the acquisition of a communion table, or the purchase of new service books did not come cheaply either.[62]

---

[61] No evidence survives for Edwardian Peterborough, but the Marian CWA (1554–6) reveal the total loss of gild land revenues. Halesowen's 'various' category is boosted by a few substantial but unspecified entries, probably sales and therefore contributions by the living.

[62] Duffy, *Stripping of the Altars*, p. 485. 'Crown' accounted for over a quarter of Halesowen's expenses under Edward.

Figure 6.3 reflects the considerable financial consequences of this increased amount of contact with external authority.[63] In accordance with the definitions adopted for this study, all the 'crown' measures contained in acts of parliament, visitation articles, or royal injunctions have been classified as 'compulsory' spending.[64] This is admittedly a matter of interpretation, and potentially an underestimation of spontaneous local initiatives. However, churchwardens never elaborate on their community's attitude, and expenditure motives have to be reconstructed from indirect evidence. Every community was of course a special case; some responded early and exceeded their brief, others dragged their feet like the conservative vicar of Morebath who had to be summoned to Exeter no less than four times, but in the end few found an alternative to conformity.[65] The changes were enforced too quickly, too uniformly, too comprehensively, and also reversed too frequently to reflect genuine grass-roots developments. In fact, any divergent parochial initiative would have been stifled by the flood of meticulous guidelines and the intensive supervision.[66] As apparent from Figure 6.3 and the expenditure stacks in Appendix 4 (ii), parishes incurred considerable legal costs, and from the late 1530s an ever increasing part explicitly at visitations and ecclesiastical courts.[67] The psychological impact of such growing exposure to external authority cannot be quantified, but it is difficult to share the view that this was not a 'major transformation' and an absolutely crucial stage in the absorption of the parish into the wider entities of the Tudor state and the new *Ecclesia Anglicana*.[68] The catch

---

[63] Eleven-years averages of old pence. 'Legal costs' includes expenses incurred at visitations. Payments to the king's subsidy collectors explain the bump at All Saints in the 1520s.

[64] The composition of the categories is explained in Chapter 3.4 and Appendix 2.

[65] A few parishes witnessed anticlerical outbreaks and iconoclasm already in the early 1530s (Cross, *Church and People*, p. 78), while others like Halesowen were slow to give up the paschal candle or the ringing for the dead on the feast of All Saints (Hutton, *Merry England*, pp. 84–5); for a detailed account of Morebath see Duffy, *Stripping of the Altars*, pp. 497–502, and his forthcoming monograph on the same parish.

[66] Duffy, *Stripping of the Altars*, part II. 'The visitations had clearly been the principal force behind the changes', which 'left local people with no other choice than acquiescence or armed resistance': Hutton, *Merry England*, p. 87.

[67] Legal costs in this sample rose from 13 percentage points in the immediate pre-Reformation period to 58 under Edward. From the late 1530s, expenditure at visitations and in ecclesiastical courts started to dominate the category and was at its highest level ever in seven out of ten case studies. In a poor parish like Prescot (which may have also needed a lot of convincing), this could average almost 10 s. after 1550.

[68] The view advanced by Smith, ' "Modernization" ', p. 177, and quoted above. Supporting the case put forward here, the long-term analysis of London parishes in Gibbs, 'Parish finance', pp. 82–3, 355, also points to greater integration and closer external supervision (cf. Chapter 6.2 below). The events of the seventeenth century, however, show that there were limits to the degree of intrusion local society would tolerate.

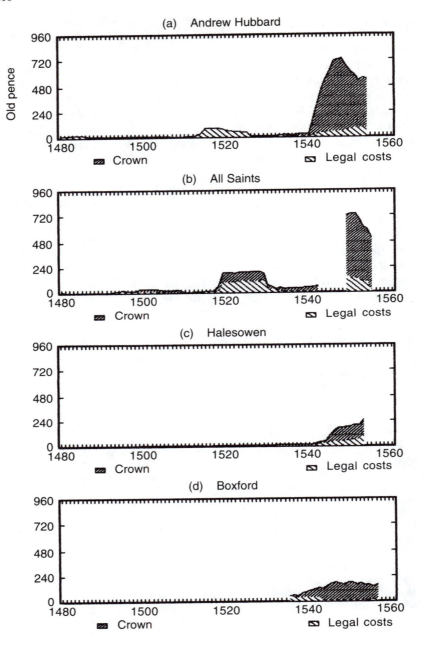

Figure 6.3 Contacts with external authority in four parishes (11-year averages of legal costs and crown-related expenses 1480–1560); unit: old pence

phrases for the post-Reformation period, in both Catholic and Protestant countries, were discipline, coercion, and order. As a potentially destabilizing factor, religious deviation could not be tolerated. With various degrees of success, princes used the Church as a means to increase their domestic power, and this was not the time for spontaneous parish initiatives.[69]

Turning to the individual categories of expenditure, many of the changes appear in sharper focus. The decline of 'worship', for instance, was the result of quite contradictory developments. The peak of investment for priests and clerks was more than wiped out by the slump in the importance of ornaments, lights, and the disappearance of anniversaries.[70] The first attack on lights before images in 1538 had immediate repercussions for some parishes like Botolph Aldersgate which spent much less on 'making lights', and sold the wax of those 'taken downe in the churche'.[71] On the other hand, there is a fair amount of evidence that many candles were simply transferred to the rood loft, where they were still tolerated, and most places recorded only marginally reduced costs up to the decisive injunctions of 1547. Afterwards, though, expenditure was down by 60 per cent, and just about covered the bare minimum of wax needed to light the church. There was no significant recovery under Mary either.[72] With saints falling from royal favour, the whole concept of intercession crumbled, and obits vanished from parish accounts. Some places made an effort to find appropriate alternative uses for their benefactors' endowments,[73] but most of the landed property now contributed to the parishes' livelihood without meeting the original stipulations, and it was also less carefully maintained. Rents had decreased by a third, but 'landlord' expenditure by 63 per cent. In line with government policy, ornaments suffered a 50 per cent fall under Edward, but returned to pre-Reformation levels in the next reign.

Some interesting changes occurred in the spending on ceremonial life. Rather surprisingly, it rose under Edward, but only as a result of a

---

[69] With the Reformation, 'religion became more dogmatic, it laid more emphasis on uniformity – on everyone in a kingdom or diocese or parish believing and doing the same, and it reduced variety': Orme, *Unity and Variety*, p. 70. For parallels in Continental and Catholic Europe: P. Collinson, 'The late medieval Church and its Reformation' in J. McManners (ed.), *The Oxford Illustrated History of Christianity* (Oxford, 1990), p. 266.

[70] See Chapter 3.4 (discussion of payments to clergymen) and Appendix 4 (ii).

[71] Botolph CWA, 1538–9 and 1539–40.

[72] It has recently been argued that – in line with a Christocentric trend throughout Catholic Europe – only a limited amount of images reappeared in Marian churches: Duffy, *Stripping of the Altars*, pp. 563–4 (p. 419 for the transfer of lights); at Ashburton, All Saints, Yatton, Andrew Hubbard, and Boxford the pre-1538 spending level on wax and lights was just 2 per cent higher than in the immediate pre-Reformation years.

[73] See for example the Spicer anniversary at All Saints, Bristol, discussed above.

redistribution of financial responsibilities between clergy and parishioners. In the pre-Reformation Church, the parson had been obliged to provide the bread and wine for communion himself,[74] but when Cranmer's new order of 1548 and the Prayer Book of 1549 approved the administering of wine to the laity, the increased costs necessitated a change in the system. This complex question still awaits detailed research, and the sources are far from unambiguous. Furthermore, there may have been considerable differences between official regulations and parochial practice, but the general development could be summarized as follows: the 1549 Prayer Book used the existing rota for the provision of the holy loaf as the basis for the new system. The 'pastor' still supplied the requisite elements for communion, but the parishioners were now ordered to 'offer euery Sonday, at the tyme of the Offertory, the iuste valour and price of the holy lofe … in suche ordre and course, as they were woont to fynde and pay the sayd holy lofe'. In other words, the head of the respective household, whose turn it was, now paid to the priest the same amount of money he would have spent on the holy bread, and he also received the sacrament on this occasion. For all other parishioners, annual communion remained the minimum requirement.[75] Some places, however, were unfamiliar with the custom (for example, Kirkby Malham in West Yorkshire), and the new system did not work. The second Prayer Book waived these explicit instructions and simply put the 'parish' in charge of the necessary payments.[76] The frequency of communion for every parishioner was increased to three times a year, and the administration of the sacrament was made conditional upon the participation of at least three or four communicants.[77]

On the whole, the sources reflect these changes fairly closely. Only Prescot made communal contributions in Henry's reign, otherwise incumbents seem to have been in charge. When Andrew Hubbard administered the benefice in 1549 and 1550, the wardens entered the

---

[74] G. Burnet, *The Holy Communion in the Reformed Church of Scotland* (Edinburgh, 1960), p. 32.

[75] *Prayer Books*, p. 230 (4th, 5th and 6th rubric after the order of Communion); Duffy, *Stripping of the Altars*, p. 464.

[76] The parishioners 'shalbe discharged of such summes of money, or other dueties, which hetherto they haue payde for the same, by order of theyr houses euery Sondaye' (*Prayer Books*, p. 392). J. Boulton, 'The limits of formal religion', *London Journal*, 10 (1984), 140, seems to interpret the passage as introducing house-to-house collections. For Kirkby Malham see Heath (ed.), *Clerical Accounts*, pp. 22–3 (weekly collection system rather than household rota).

[77] *Prayer Books*, p. 392, and Drew (ed.), *Lambeth CWA*, p. xxxviii. The system remained unchanged in 1559: J. Booty (ed.), *The Book of Common Prayer 1559* (Charlottesville, 1976), pp. 267–8.

payments for bread and wine into the accounts which dealt with the parson's responsibilities rather than their own reckonings. In return, they received 3 d. each on 97 offering days over two years for a total of £1 4 s. 3 d., no doubt as a result of the rotation required in the first Prayer Book.[78] From 1552 though, all churchwardens' accounts in the sample contain expenditure for this purpose, normally just a few shillings, but at St Botolph a considerable £1 for nine months and 1100 communicants.[79] Payments seem to become less frequent under Mary, possibly because of changes in administrative practice, and by the later sixteenth century there were many local varieties which are often inadequately covered by churchwardens' accounts.[80] In populous parishes, tri-annual communion remained impracticable and even around Easter a series of Sundays was needed to cater for all parishioners. To cover their costs for bread (and especially) wine, some communities levied weekly rates (All Hallows, London Wall), while others distributed tokens in return for the payment of annual dues (St Saviour, Southwark). But whatever the circumstances, churchwardens were fully aware of the financial importance of Easter communion, and went out of their way to ensure attendance even in otherwise poorly governed areas.[81]

In contrast, the first Reformation years brought little change in the share of building and maintenance costs. The 'great age of church rebuilding' with its accumulation of extraordinary efforts had been over for some time; in this new age, neither spare resources nor spiritual encouragements matched those of the later Middle Ages. But there was always something to mend or improve, as for instance at St Edmund, Salisbury, where the parish spent a great deal of money on the steeple in the midst of the Edwardian regime.[82] The contrast to the pre-Reformation boom was noticeable, but it should not be exaggerated. Protestant worship did not require the same sort of elaborate physical framework, and parish investment picked up as soon as official attitudes

---

[78] Prescot has (unexplained) payments for 'singing bread' or wafers since CWA 1534–5; Andrew Hubbard, parsonage account 1549 and 1550.

[79] Botolph CWA, 1553–4.

[80] Drew (ed.), *Lambeth CWA*, pp. xxxviif: the first relevant entries date from 1570. At Botolph Aldgate in London, only monthly communions (restricted to members of the vestry) appear in the parish accounts. At Easter, bread and wine was supplied by the farmer of the parsonage, and payments to him were entered in separate records: Boulton, 'Limits of formal religion', 142.

[81] Ibid., 140, 144; all dues to the clergy were payable at Easter: Booty (ed.), *Book of Common Prayer 1559*, p. 268.

[82] St Edmund CWA, 1550–1. This extraordinary effort pushed the Edwardian average of spending on the fabric to over £6 5 s., much higher than in the immediate pre-Reformation years; see Burgess, 'Fond thing', pp. 78–9, for the loss of spiritual motives.

seemed to allow or demand it. Under Mary, bells were given high priority in the re-equipment process, and 'the enthusiasm for rebuilding and refurbishing churches' increased again from the late sixteenth and early seventeenth centuries. Churchfounding on a large scale, however, only resumed in the nineteenth, when the inadequacies of the ecclesiastical network were finally tackled.[83]

6.2 Parish government

By 1560, a religious settlement had been found, and local society started to come to terms with it. This process is not readily quantifiable, but the emergence of new sources such as vestry minutes or overseers' accounts reinforces the impression that parish development entered a new stage. The accession of Elizabeth can thus serve as a convenient cut-off point for a study of churchwardens' accounts, since they no longer provide the same overall insight into communal affairs for the later part of the century.[84] Still, an analysis of parish government benefits from an extended chronological perspective. Medieval communal life appears in sharper focus when compared to the sort of administrative practices found around 1600. To illuminate the differences, this chapter will attempt to evaluate external influence and inner parochial structure both before and after the mid-sixteenth century.

6.2.1 Medieval parish government

The fact that the parish was not subjected to secular lordship, but run by elected officials of quite humble social status has caught the imagination of many historians. It has been seen as a particularly pure example of the medieval search for broad consensus,[85] or even as the one shining

---

[83] Morris, *Churches in the Landscape*, p. 399 (quote), references to post-Reformation activities on pp. 402, 404 and 424 (nineteenth century). For evidence of late sixteenth-century building see the contribution of A. Foster to the forthcoming volume of essays *The Parish in English Life 1400–1600*, edited by K. French, G. Gibbs, and B. Kümin. In Staffordshire, the first post-Reformation churches date from the 1630s: Palliser, *Staffordshire Landscape*, p. 99.

[84] A similar assessment in Boxford CWA, p. xii; for the diversification (and better survival) of parish records in the Tudor period: West, *Village Records*, pp. 73ff.

[85] For example Hobhouse (ed.), *CWA of Croscombe [etc.]*, p. xi; for the consensus culture in town government: Reynolds, *Kingdoms and Communities*, p. 190; in manorial courts: J. Beckerman, 'Customary law in English manorial courts in the thirteenth and fourteenth centuries' (Ph.D. London, 1972), pp. 241–7.

alternative to an otherwise oppressive feudal system.[86] There is indeed plenty of evidence for the strength of communal ties and the strive for inner-parochial harmony.

The first impulse was no doubt spiritual and derived from the recommended nature of Christian worship: 'synguler preyer of one persone is good in chambre & in oratorie, but it is better in holy chyrche with the comounte whan tyme is of comoun preyere & whanne men mon wel attendyn therto'.[87] The saints as the Church's role models also emphasized the importance of neighbourliness and cooperation. Miracles were often of strikingly communal character and a result of corporate invocation. To benefit from the intercessory powers of the holy company of heaven, parishioners had to prove that they were a genuine Christian community, and many places turned the festival of their patron saint into the core element of the ritual year.[88] The mass as the focal point of late medieval piety, multiplied by countless foundations of chantries, trentals, fraternities, or anniversaries, similarly demanded a congregation inspired by peace and charity. No one should take communion without being reconciled with God and the world.[89] After all, the elevation of the host was a most sacred moment, and parishioners knew that the priest 'was preparing to make God present'.[90] Even if communion did only take place at Easter, the laity regularly shared the Holy Loaf as a sign of brotherly love.

Communal worship was boosted further by the doctrine of purgatory. Parochial chantries for example 'neatly satisfied a desire to assist the soul at the same time as advancing the efficacy of the parish as a centre of worship, ministry, and instruction – as a centre, in short, facilitating salvation', and the 'penitential motive in action ensured considerable practical benefits for parish and parishioners alike'.[91] Late medieval communities thus not only included the living, but generations of ancestors, whom they recalled at every recitation of the bede-roll. Former parishioners depended on the living's prayers just as the latter needed the dead's intercession for the health of their souls. Individual support was welcome, but it was corporate remembrance that really mattered. Many wills and bequests explicitly benefit parish events, parish poor, and parish institutions, which makes sense only 'in a community which

---

[86] For Jessopp, 'Parish life', 47ff, the parish provided a 'means to lift people up'.

[87] P. Heath Barnum (ed.), *Dives and Pauper* (Oxford, 1976), p. 196.

[88] Duffy, *Stripping of the Altars*, chapter 'The Saints' (esp. pp. 161–2), and Bossy, *Christianity*, p. 73; Rosser, *Medieval Westminster*, p. 272 (St Margaret's day at Westminster).

[89] Brigden, *London and the Reformation*, p. 19.

[90] Bossy, *Christianity*, p. 68.

[91] Burgess, 'Fond thing', p. 73.

placed a special value on the religious dimensions of community, and which believed that the prayers of the parish assembled precisely as a parish, either in fact or in the person of its representatives, its priests, and wardens, were more powerful than the sum of its component parts'.[92]

Similar forces were at work on a more mundane level. The pre-Reformation parish offered a place for festivities, plays, meals, and common drinking. In spite of occasional troubles, such shared experiences reinforced inner-parochial ties, and contemporary moral philosophy put possible risks in perspective: 'The seven deadly sins were a system of community ethics making more excuse for the sins of concupiscence than for those of aversion. The sins of aversion destroy community, but without some flirtation with the sins of concupiscence there is unlikely to be a community at all.'[93] In much the same way, a sense of territorial unity was conveyed by the beating of parochial bounds in Rogation week processions. Exemplifying the delicate balance between 'official' and 'popular' religion, evil spirits were driven out of the parish on this occasion, and blessings invoked for the harvest and all members of the community.[94] Parochial documents went out of their way to underline the dignity of communally agreed rules of conduct. The ordinances of St Stephen, Bristol, for example, ended with the firm commitment that 'in witnesse whereof and performang perpetuall of these our seyd agrementis, consentis, and actys, ande penaltese, ande every of them, welle ande trewly to be observed, fulfylled, and kept, we the seyd parson, proctors and parishionars hathe put to our commyn seale the day ande yere above expresszd'.[95] Existing collective identity was reinforced in times of threat: whatever the religious preferences in 1549, the parishioners of Westminster assembled with bows and arrows to prevent attempts to use their church as a quarry for Somerset House.[96]

However, two factors undermined communal harmony. First, parishioners were a heterogeneous group with a wide variety of different interests and priorities. Second, local communities like the parish were never fully self-contained, but subject to the interference of secular and ecclesiastical authorities.[97] The following passages will assess the strength of external influences (clerical hierarchy, gentry, state) and the nature of inner-parochial relations, both at the beginning and at the end of the Tudor period, arguing that developments on all these levels combined to

---

[92] Duffy, *Stripping of the Altars*, p. 136.
[93] Bossy, *Christianity*, p. 35.
[94] Duffy, *Stripping of the Altars*, pp. 136ff; similar Dyer, *Lords and Peasants*, p. 360.
[95] Fox (ed.), 'St Stephen', 202.
[96] Rosser, *Medieval Westminster*, pp. 275–6.
[97] Smith, ' "Modernization" ', pp. 160, 178.

effect a fundamental change in the structure of parochial government.

An ambiguous position was taken up by the local priest. On the one hand, he was the foremost representative of outside authority, a man of the Church, set apart by holy orders, and entrusted with the cure of souls, *regimen*, and *jurisdictio* over his benefice.[98] Worldly possessions such as the glebe and claims to tithes, dues, and mortuary payments gave him something of seigneurial status.[99] In other respects, however, incumbents must have felt close to their parishioners. Many were of humble social origin, subject to local agrarian regulations, and dependent on voluntary contributions from their flock.[100] Some acted as parochial record keepers, and others advised their congregation in complicated legal matters.[101] Parish assemblies were often held in the parson's presence and many clerical appointments made with his consent. The possession of one of the keys to the parish chest gave rectors and vicars some leverage in controversial matters, but it is equally clear that they did not have the final say in communal affairs. Parish funds were kept strictly separate from those of the benefice, and the laity displayed a 'robust independence of mind'.[102] As long as their rights were not challenged, clergymen had little reason to stifle local communal life. Where they were absent from their cure (which was rather less common than on the Continent[103]), clerical interference decreased further. Some

---

[98] Fuhrmann, 'Kirche im Dorf', pp. 149–50.

[99] Ault, 'Village church', 197–8. In Warwickshire, for example, glebes were extensive and varied between 25 and 75 acres.

[100] Priests were bound to observe village by-laws: ibid., 203. The vast majority of clergymen came from (richer) peasant or yeomen families: Swanson, *Church and Society*, p. 38.

[101] Sir Christopher Trychay kept the records of Morebath: Binney (ed.), *Morebath*, 'Introduction'. Educational standards were better than often assumed: in the diocese of Lincoln, the graduate quota rose from 14 per cent in 1400 to 30 per cent in 1500 (*Lander, Government and Community*, p. 131; with further evidence). Recent quantitative work for some Continental areas points in the same direction: by 1500, 50 per cent of incumbents (and 30 per cent of deputies) in North Brabant had attended a university: Bijsterveld, *Kerk and wereld*, pp. 383–4.

[102] Mary-at-Hill's parson had to be called back from Stratford to attend the assembly in 1497–8 (CWA, p. 230); many references to the vicar in All Saints ordinances and audit memoranda (for example CWA, 1510–11). Further evidence for an administrative role of the priest in Marshall, *Catholic Priesthood*, p. 205 (the quote ibid., p. 204).

[103] Absenteeism affected for example 25 per cent of parishes in the diocese of Lincoln on the eve of the Reformation (Lander, *Government and Community*, p. 135), but 30–40 per cent in the bishopric of Rouen (Huard, 'Paroisse rurale', 19; late fifteenth century) and up to two thirds in some areas of Germany and the Netherlands: Hergemöller, 'Parrocchia', p. 164; Bijsterveld, *Kerk and wereld*, p. 385.

areas of friction remained, but English priests seem to have suffered much less anticlericalism than their Continental colleagues and on the whole enjoyed a more harmonious relationship with their parishioners.[104]

Moving up the ecclesiastical hierarchy, bishops had a range of opportunities to influence parochial life. They could order proclamations from the chancel, ordain local clergymen, or modify ecclesiastical boundaries. The most immediate contact, however, took place at visitations. On these occasions, the ordinary or his representative summoned all priests and a number of parishioners to a major church, where they were expected to answer a series of questions about their community. While lay representatives are simply referred to as *fidedigni* at the time of the earliest evidence in the thirteenth century, churchwardens normally played a very prominent part by the fifteenth.[105] Sometimes they attended alone, but sometimes in conjunction with specially selected 'sidesmen', *iurati*, or *viri probi*.[106] A visitation was a major local event, with a great array of secretaries, chaplains, notaries, and armed knights in the bishop's retinue. Some minor wrongs could be dealt with on the spot, while more complex issues were referred to an appropriate episcopal or archidiaconal court. If certain things were found to be generally wanting, a set of injunctions might follow the proceedings.[107]

In light of the scarcity of documentation, it is difficult to generalize about the impact of late medieval visitations. They could be fairly frequent as in Hampshire, where the bishop visited each autumn and the archdeacon each spring. Early sixteenth-century churchwardens' accounts record regular expenses for this purpose, and parishes were expected to submit half-yearly reports on their situation.[108] In general though, the rhythm of supervision seems to have been declining and the emphasis to have shifted to the procuration of fees.[109] From the earliest

---

[104] Cf. the discussion of anticlericalism in Chapter 3.4.

[105] Powicke and Cheney (eds), *Councils and Synods*, i. 254–5, 262, and Simpson, 'Visitations 1249–52', for example 10, 12, 24–5 (early evidence; no CW mentioned); for the fifteenth-century situation see Gibson (ed.), *Codex*, p. 960, Meade, *Medieval Church*, p. 41, W. Simpson (ed.), *Visitations of Churches Belonging to St Paul's in 1297 and 1458*, for example p. 79 (presence of CW at Heybridge in 1458), and Brown, 'Late medieval Wiltshire', p. 127 (CWs' oath at the visitation of the dean of Salisbury in 1480).

[106] 'Iurati' appeared before the commissary of the abbot of Whalley in the early sixteenth century: A. Cooke (ed.), *Act Book of the Ecclesiastical Court of Whalley 1510–38* (Manchester, 1901), p. 12; 'viri probi' were cited by prebendary John Clere at Stanwick in 1464: Fowler (ed.), *Acts of Ripon*, p. 219.

[107] For more detailed information about procedures see Wood-Legh (ed.), *Kentish Visitations*, pp. xviff, or R. Hill (ed.), *Visitations of Archbishop Melton*, pp. 2–3.

[108] Williams (ed.), *Early CWA of Hampshire*, pp. xliff.

[109] Swanson, *Church and Society*, p. 164.

evidence of 1249, the main areas of inquisition remained the same: the church fabric, the adequate provision of ornaments, the conscientious administration of sacraments, the moral shortcomings of all members of the community, and debts to the parish funds.[110]

The ordinary had no means to undertake his own investigations and depended on the cooperation of parish representatives. It was essentially up to local judgement to decide which offences or irregularities needed to be presented. In the case of Hampshire, few wardens seem to have made accusations against their fellow parishioners,[111] but elsewhere, absence from divine service, moral irregularities, Sunday work, and other types of offensive behaviour were presented quite frequently.[112] Financial dues to the parish church were always among the most conspicuous items brought to the visitor's attention.[113] Over one hundred such complaints came to light in the archdeaconry of Oxford in 1520, and some parishioners were also accused of withholding church goods.[114] At Chilham, where Richard Dryland had initiated a tithe strike, it was decided 'that the parisshones to defend the right of the parsone ley theire heddes togider and make a commen purse to striffe for thesaid tithes'.[115] But how effectively did ecclesiastical judges deal with such matters? *Acta* of subsequent proceedings by commissioners or officials survive only very rarely, but where they do, it looks as if wardens with a good case stood a fair chance of success. Many examples can be found among the records of the Kentish visitations of 1511: at St Dunstan, Canterbury, the wardens supported their claims for rents and dues in kind by means of documentary evidence, at Lydd, Thomas Robyn was ordered to pay his rent arrears of 12 d., while contributions to wages of parish employees were successfully enforced in several other places. Similarly, when

---

[110] Simpson (ed.), 'Visitations 1249–52', ixf (churches belonging to St Paul's in London). According to a statute of 1224, ordinaries had to ask for an inventory of church goods and to inquire into the state of the fabric: Powicke and Cheney (ed.), *Councils and Synods*, i. 128: Statutes of Winchester, c. 13.

[111] Williams (ed.), *Early CWA of Hampshire*, p. xliii.

[112] 'CWs' presentments', 75–117, or Cooke (ed.), *Act Book Whalley*, passim.

[113] A frequent cause of instance cases (ten were heard by the consistory court of Canterbury in 1482 alone), and 'in the majority of these suits the plaintiffs were churchwardens': B. Woodcock, *Medieval Ecclesiastical Courts in the Diocese of Canterbury* (Oxford, 1952), pp. 86 (quote), 105 (1482 cases).

[114] 'CWs presentments', passim; Leicestershire returns of 1518 similarly include presentments for withholding of customary payments, testamentary bequests, or parts of clerks' wages: A. Thompson (ed.), *Visitations of the Diocese of Lincoln 1517–31* (3 vols, Hereford, 1940–7), i. xli and lii. Cases about refusals to make normal contributions to candles, collections, and the provision of the holy bread are discussed in French, 'Local identity', pp. 258–9.

[115] Wood-Legh (ed.), *Kentish Visitations*, p. 176.

Thomas Fraunces of Hambleden was cited before the chapter of the archdeacon of Buckingham 'ad instanciam yconomorum ibidem in causa subtractionis juris ecclesiastici', he admitted owing 6 s. 8 d., paid on the spot, and was dismissed.[116]

Ecclesiastical justice could take its time, however, and parishioners needed persistency as well as considerable resources. In 1486, the wardens of St Dunstan, Canterbury, sued the executors of one William Belser in the consistory court for the recovery of three cows worth £3. An arbitration panel was established, but its activity soon lapsed. A new set of officers resumed the suit in 1490, and lavished expenses on proctors, commissaries, and court officials. Eventually, they recovered 30 s. from the executors as well as an award of 15 s. 8 d. for costs, but they had spent a total of 33 s. 2 d. in the process.[117] Still, legal action could be the last glimmer of hope: in 1473, the wardens of Linwood (diocese of Lincoln) made a moving appeal to ecclesiastical jurisdiction:

> It his to haue in mend that Thyrston fayreclogh has off the kyrke godys xxvjs viijd and has hadd many yerys and they chan newyr getyd howt of his handys, and god knowed they haue gret nede therto, wat for renewyng of the bellis, and also for a chalys, for they haue but oon that is but lityll worth and therfor at the reuerens of gode lett hym be sumown, for with owt my lordys help they gete it neauer.[118]

Another very concerned officer was the warden of Ruckinge in Kent, who implored the official of the archdeaconry of Canterbury that certain *comperta* presented at the last visitation needed urgent attention:

> Master Official I desire you to have in remembraunce that where I labored unto your mastershipp for reformacon of divers matters mysordered w^t in the parish of Rokyng, and [you] commandyd me to bryng it in wrytying at the corte; pleaseth it you to understand that whereas it was presented at the last visitation before you for the amendment of the churchyard ther it is not amendment, but all manner of bests come into hit dayly, so that the Curate and the parishons may not go in procession for dungyng of bests & misordering of other bests to. Item for paying of my baner which cost vjs vjd. I desire you to have in remembraunce thereof, it hath been in the parishes hondes by a yere and halff.[119]

---

[116] Ibid., pp. 56, 147; F. Ragg (ed.), 'Fragments of folio M.S. of archdeaconry courts of Buckinghamshire, 1491–5', *Records of Bucks.*, 11 (1920–6), 36–7 (chapter held at Great Wycombe, 1491).

[117] Woodcock, *Medieval Ecclesiastical Courts*, pp. 106–7; the costs amounted to about a quarter of their annual receipts.

[118] E. Peacock (ed.), 'Extracts from Lincoln episcopal visitations', *Archaeologia*, 48 (1885), 249–50.

[119] C. Woodruff (ed.), 'An archidiaconal visitation of 1502', *Archaeologia Cantiana*, 47 (1935), 53 (c.1502–7).

But sometimes, the ordinary's help was clearly insufficient, and parishes decided to take the matter to secular jurisdiction. At Rainham in 1511, for instance, the wardens were engaged in a suit before Chancery, while their colleagues at Wye proceeded to common law for the recovery of some landed bequests.[120]

Not all churchwardens were models of efficiency of course, but comparatively few abused their community's trust. Parish administration was criticized in just 12 of more than 200 Kentish parishes in 1511,[121] and a similar trickle of cases was recorded in the archdeaconry of Oxford in 1520. John Chacobbe had not rendered an account at Adwell for seven years, the Fritwell wardens 'minus juste differunt restitucionem' of altar hangings they had borrowed of their colleagues at Ardeley, ex-proctor Simon Gunne of Hanborough refused to reveal the whereabouts of 16 bushels of barley, and the *gardiani* of St Mary, Oxford, had 'ex negligencia eorundem' lost track of over £8 belonging to the provost of Oriel College and other parishioners.[122] In Canterbury courts, several parishes resorted to *ex officio promoto* actions to force negligent churchwardens to execute their duties,[123] while a Laurence Tailour, to cite a final example, perjured himself before an ecclesiastical official in the archdeaconry of Buckingham. Fellow warden John Hawkyns flatly denied Tailour's claim that certain repairs to the churchyard at Leckhampstead had been carried out, and the offender was sentenced to do public penance on each Sunday in Lent.[124]

Far more often, however, deficiencies in church buildings or furnishings had less to do with irresponsible office holders than with the fact that it was difficult to fulfil all the canonical requirements all the time; many a parson struggled with the same problems in his portion of

---

[120] Wood-Legh (ed.), *Kentish Visitations*, pp. 266 and 190; cf. the references to secular court action in Chapter 2.2.2, and French, 'Local identity', ch. 6.

[121] Eight officers did not render proper accounts, others owed the parish some money: Wood-Legh (ed.), *Kentish Visitations*, passim.

[122] 'CWs presentments', 79, 85, 97, 112. In total, nine irregularities involving parochial officers were reported, a roughly similar ratio as in Kent.

[123] This was a rare type of action, whereby a judge undertook a prosecution of someone at the promotion of a third party: for example Parishioners of Westwell *v.* William Edynton and John Rusyll (a petition by the community to force their elected wardens to fulfil their duties): Woodcock, *Medieval Ecclesiastical Courts*, p. 68. The Somerset parish of Nynehead Flory sought help in Chancery for the same purpose: French, 'Local identity', p. 250.

[124] The penance was adjourned until a final decision by the official after an intervention by 'many venerable persons': case cited in Harper-Bill, *Pre-Reformation Church*, p. 104 (1520).

the church.[125] The authorities normally reacted by issuing a deadline for the necessary repairs, purchases or improvements, with mixed success. At Rossendale (see Map 4.1) in April 1527, the recently built chapel was already in such a bad state that it rained on the altar. The inhabitants were told to repair it by Pentecost in the same year, then by the Translation of St Martin 1528, but the problem was still pending in May 1529. The records of 1530 at last contain a confident 'omnia bene', but new defects appeared the year after.[126] The wardens at Addington (Bucks.), in contrast, seem to have acted speedily: cited for not enclosing their cemetery, 'comparuerunt et allegant reparacionem, et dimissi sunt'.[127] Others had to be threatened with heavy fines, and some were actually excommunicated before they made amends.[128] It would be hazardous to try and quantify this evidence, but – together with financial matters – fabric repairs formed a very large part of complaints in any visitation. Parishioners were clearly not always as conscientious as their visitors would have wished, but the records do not show anything 'corrosive of the fabric of the church' in a wider sense, and 'no Augean stable to be cleansed'.[129] Indications of fundamental challenges such as heresy or witchcraft are few and far between.[130] On the whole, visitations seem to have provided the authorities with an opportunity to correct the most obvious failings of the cure of souls, and the parishioners with a chance to present those sorts of problems that they could not solve locally.[131]

As in most countries, noblemen kept their distance from everyday parish affairs,[132] but they could be approached for help and advice in particular circumstances. In this sample, the Earl of Derby was contacted by Prescot about land transfers, clerical appointments, dealings with rebellious chapels, or support for a free school.[133] The most immediate

---

[125] Only three parishes answered the visitors with 'omnia bene' in the archdeaconry of Oxford in 1520 ('CWs presentments', 110, 113, 115): the chancel for example needed repair at Easington (78).

[126] Cooke (ed.), *Act Book Whalley*, pp. 114, 117, 124, 131, 139.

[127] Ragg (ed.), 'Archdeaconry Courts of Bucks.', 149.

[128] In 1493/4, the wardens of Denham faced a fine of 10 s., while Thomas Nele, 'yconomus', was described as 'excommunicatus': ibid., 199, 323.

[129] C. Harper-Bill (ed.), 'The diocese of Norwich in 1499', *PSIA*, 34 (1980), 41.

[130] A mere two cases of idolatry/witchcraft surfaced in the archdeaconry of Oxford in 1520: 'CWs' presentments', 80, 95.

[131] The same point is made by McLane, 'Juror attitudes', p. 64, and Wrightson, 'Two concepts of order', p. 30, for the field of secular jurisdiction.

[132] Genicot, *Rural Communities*, p. 105.

[133] Prescot CWA, for example 1546–7, 1549–50, 1550–1, 1553–4, and 1555–6.

representatives of secular authority, however, were the local gentry families. Their wealth and political power set them apart from other parishioners, and many exerted a decisive influence in clerical or communal elections.[134] Local elites also provided the necessary leadership and resources for many a parish initiative. John Fanner, for instance, sparked a broad subscription campaign for assistant clergy in his Suffolk parish by supplying the financial basis himself,[135] and Stephen Jennings, merchant tailor and sometime mayor of London, paid the northern part of the great middle aisle of St Andrew Undershaft out of his own pocket.[136] At Long Melford, the Clopton family invited the whole parish to the manor house on a regular basis,[137] knowing that it would have been 'political suicide' to withdraw completely from such an important centre of political and social life.[138] But it is equally evident that many gentlemen had other priorities. Pious literature naturally played a much bigger part in the devotional practice of educated seigneurial classes, and it contributed to an increasing emphasis on introspection. Their presence in parish churches was often restricted to side chapels or family pews,[139] and many preferred to worship in private oratories.[140] Urban elites confirm this pattern: very few of the richest London merchants actively participated in parish organizations.[141] There were always exceptions to this rule, but the distinctive feature of late medieval English parish life was not the role of the gentry (which remained at best stable), but the increasingly active part of the common people. They all but monopolized the crucial office of churchwarden, and they appear alongside local dignitaries in the preambles of countless parish ordinances.[142] In many towns (and rural communities with divided secular lordship), gentry influence was further reduced. Even as justices of the peace, an office

---

[134] 'Memorandum that Mr Eccleston with the aduyse of the parysshe, elected and chose Rauf Holland of Prescote ... and Alexandre Roughley churche wardens of the parysshe churche of Alhallowes of Prescote' (1528; Sir John was lord of the manor of Eccleston-by-Knowsley: CWA, p. 11).

[135] Richmond, *John Hopton*, p. 176 (Eye).

[136] Newcourt (ed.), *Repertorium*, i. 266.

[137] Duffy, *Stripping of the Altars*, p. 137.

[138] C. Carpenter, 'The religion of the gentry of fifteenth-century England' in D. Williams (ed.), *England in the Fifteenth Century* (Woodbridge, 1987), p. 66.

[139] Harper-Bill, *Pre-Reformation Church*, p. 87.

[140] Richmond, 'English gentleman' and 'English gentry', p. 137: 'The whole tone (if not spirit) of fraternity life, as to my mind of parochial life also, is not gentlemanly.'

[141] Barron, 'Parish fraternities', p. 30.

[142] At Botolph Aldersgate, exchequer baron Nicholas Lathell signed all ordinances first, but clearly as a 'primus inter pares', supported by 'all the hole body of the paryssh' (CWA 1494–5).

which formed a 'necessary part' of their power base,[143] local elites had not yet been given supervisory functions over parochial affairs.

As for state influence, the ecclesiastical framework was occasionally used for purposes such as tax collection and the levying of troops, but details were left to the communities themselves.[144] Monarchs did not actively encourage parochial development, but simply acknowledged the existence of a nationwide network of local communities with administrative competence. Statutes of mortmain, jurisdiction over advowsons, and the influence over ecclesiastical appointments created further links with central government, but all had only an indirect effect on ordinary parishioners. At that time, public works, land management, and the increase of divine service did not need any state encouragement or legislation.

Summing up, there was remarkably little in terms of legal obligations or external supervision which interfered with the running of late medieval parish affairs. This autonomy and a favourable socio-economic climate combined to give the local laity an opportunity to model religious life to their own liking, and to assume control over an impressive amount of monetary and landed resources.

And yet, it would be misleading to conclude from this that communal life was necessarily 'harmonious' or even 'democratic'. Parish government reflected the heterogeneous nature of local society and its many inherent conflicts. Not all parishioners fulfilled their customary responsibilities all the time, and many insisted on the expression of social differences even in ceremonies of egalitarian character.[145] Clergymen could be faced by a violent or unruly congregation, and neighbours did not shy away from settling their scores during divine service. The evidence is not widespread, but sometimes drastic. Star Chamber heard about a 'most riotous' conflict at Yalding church in Kent on 26 December 1552, while parson Thomas Raulyn from Cornwall told Chancery in 1396 that a certain Alan Bugules had threatened 'de luy tuer

---

[143] G. R. Elton (ed.), *The Tudor Constitution* (Cambridge, 1962), p. 453.

[144] Cf. Chapter 2.3.1.

[145] Brown, 'Late medieval Wiltshire', p. 25 (refusal to supply the holy bread); parishioners could react nastily if they felt that they were not given their proper place in the sequence of those kissing the pax or receiving the holy bread: Craig, 'Reformation, politics, and polemics', p. 138.

deuaunt toutz le ditz parochiens', and had chased him out of the chancel window.[146]

In church, seats were allocated on the basis of rank, sex, and seniority, in spite of canon law objections.[147] Benches were originally introduced to accommodate the old and infirm, but once the whole nave had been fitted with seats (normally in urban parishes first), women tended to occupy the north and men the south side of the nave.[148] Pews were soon treated as status symbols. In London's Christopher-le-Stocks, a pew at the front of Trinity chapel cost 2 s. 4 d. a quarter, while 2 d. were sufficient for a seat in the nave.[149] This was no mere urban phenomenon: at Littleborough (Map 4.1) places were hereditary, and allocated according to the families' merits about the chapel, with three back rows reserved for 'maids to kneel on'.[150] Far from being a post-Reformation innovation, pew fees are a (modest) source of parish revenues from the early fifteenth century. At All Saints, Bristol, they occur from the earliest account of 1406, at St Ewen's and Ashburton from 1454 and 1483, while Halesowen, Prescot, and Yatton recorded charges from around 1550.[151] Further late medieval examples include Ashton-under-Lyme, St Michael, Bath, Yeovil, St Lawrence, Reading, and St Mary Woolchurch in London, where the wardens were told by the Lord Mayor in 1457 to seat rich and poor apart from each other.[152]

What mattered most in terms of parish government, though, was not gender, age, or wealth, but households. Contemporary literary evidence such as Richard Whitford's *A Werke for Householders* (1530) points to their crucial role in society as a whole, and the local ecclesiastical unit

---

[146] PRO, STAC 3/1/89 (I owe this reference to John Craig); Baildon (ed.), *Select Cases in Chancery*, pp. 23–5; at Ashburton, the bishop ordered an inquiry into a case of alleged bloodshed in the church in 1482 (defiled churches and yards had to be reconsecrated), but found that it had been a mere scuffle: Amery, 'Presidential address', 79ff.

[147] Powicke and Cheney (eds), *Councils and Synods*, ii. 1007 (Statutes of Winchester; 1287).

[148] There were of course many local varieties. See M. Aston, 'Segregation in church' in W. J. Sheils and D. Wood (eds), *Women in the Church* (Oxford, 1990), pp. 237–94, and French, 'Local identity', pp. 174–81 (with a seating plan for Bridgwater church).

[149] Ashby, 'Parish life in London', p. 193 (since 1524).

[150] Fishwick, *Rochdale*, p. 191.

[151] Yatton had fitted pews in the 1440s, but did not rent or sell them before the mid-sixteenth century.

[152] Hardy, 'Seat reservation', 98–9. The other examples ibid., 95ff. Once seats had become a general feature of Continental churches, segregation by sex and social standing was equally evident, but this did not occur until the Reformation period: J. Peters, 'Der Platz in der Kirche', *Jahrbuch für Volkskunde und Kulturgeschichte*, 28 (1985), 77–106. Post-Reformation English evidence in Craig, 'Reformation, politics, and polemics', p. 24, for example the separation by sex at Stowlangtoft, Suffolk, or the link with certain landed property at Winterslow in Wiltshire.

was no exception. As revealed by the communion rubrics in the first Prayer Book, the provision of holy bread was one duty which rotated among them. From as early as 1292, explicit references to the custom survive for Cuddesdon in Oxfordshire, Bristol, Coventry, Mells in Somerset, and Torksey in Lincolnshire.[153] The clerk's wages were also collected from property holders only: the regulations of the vestry of St Stephen, Bristol, stated in 1524 'that any manne of the sayde parishe or of any other parishe holdynge or kepynge any tenement or tenementis that hath beyne dwellynge housis in tymes past within the sayde parishe … shall paye the clerkes wagys and bere the church taske as wother men dothe'.[154] Householders only contributed to the 'tallage' or local rate at Bridgwater in Somerset, the same was true for wax-scot payments in most communities, and at St Mary at the Northgate, Canterbury, a complainant was freed from his duties 'because he did not possess a tenement in the parish'.[155] Certain religious or ceremonial occasions, however, were marked by offerings from all members of the congregation.[156]

Compulsory financial contributions were graded in accordance with social status. Canonical legislation had recommended to levy the members of the community 'secundum portionem terrae' and with reference to their 'possessiones et facultates'.[157] The last names in Mary-at-Hill's book of the clerk's wages appear without a specified amount, presumably because of the poverty of the respective individuals, but all the others were assessed at quarterly instalments of between 1 d. and 16

---

[153] *Prayer Books*, p. 230; the early evidence in N. Adams and C. Donahue Jr. (eds), *Select Cases from the Ecclesiastical Courts of the Province of Canterbury c.1200–1301* (London, 1981), p. 404; St Ewen's CWA, p. xxiii; Phythian-Adams, *Desolation of a City*, p. 167 (Coventry); French, 'Local identity', p. 258 (Mells, 1455). The custumal of Torksey stipulated 'item parochiani debent de dicto domo quando terminum suum venerit unum panem precio 1d. qui vocatur panis benedictus'.: Bateson (ed.), *Borough Customs*, ii. 212 (c. 1345).

[154] Fox, 'St Stephen', 200. Over at St Ewen's, testator John Mathew left 6 s. 8 d. yearly in 1521 to relieve poor householders of the clerk's wages (CWA, p. xxiii). In London's Mary-at-Hill, 76 names are listed in the 'booke of the clarkes wages' (CWA, pp. 126f: 1483–5), and there were 400 communicants in 1547 (Kitching (ed.), *Chantry Certificates*, p. 6), which – despite the chronological gap – fits quite well with the conventional estimate that an average household contained about five individuals.

[155] French, 'Local identity', p. 104; Owen, 'Two medieval parish books', pp. 121–2; Thomson, *Early Tudor Church*, p. 288.

[156] See for example the Easter collection at All Saints 'for dewte of them that were howseled' (CWA 1521–2).

[157] Statutes of the synod of Exeter (1287), c. 9: Powicke and Cheney (eds), *Councils and Synods*, pp. 1002–4; Drew, *Early Parochial Organisation*, pp. 12–13.

d.[158] At All Saints in 1488, all parishioners were required to attend the annual audit, on pain of a fine of one pound of wax for the wealthier members of the community and half a pound for all the others.[159] It would be quite wrong to assume that only the more prosperous households were taken into account. Again and again, the sources reveal obligations of very humble layers of local society: cottagers had to make a (reduced) contribution to the church ale at Elvaston in Derbyshire, as well as to the 'Peter's pence' at Morebath.[160] Servants, however, were in a different position: at Ashburton, they could make donations to the light at the high cross 'after ther devocyon, as schall plesse them and ther masteres'. The same applies to women, who were certainly required to attend church, but assumed full 'parishioner' status only as heads of independent households.[161]

'Dwellynge housis' were thus the main unit of parish finance, but what about communal government? Continental evidence suggests that 'the faithful wanted to be associated with the management of parochial institutions', yet it can rarely provide more detailed information.[162] The richer English archives led Bishop Hobhouse to conclude that 'the community was completely organized with a constitution which recognized the rights of the whole and of every adult member to a voice in self-government',[163] but in practice 'political rights' were linked to financial duties: the basis of parish government was an assembly of all householders.[164] This is spelt out in an ordinance passed at Botolph Aldersgate:

> Also hyt ys ordeynyd the viii day of marche in the yere of our lord god [1485] ... by the advyse of Nicholas Lathell Richard Cornyssh

---

[158] For example John Bircham 1 d. and 'Maister W. Remyngton' (alderman of Billingsgate ward) 16 d. (CWA, pp. 126–7). Similar amounts were due in neighbouring Andrew Hubbard: CWs tended to pay around 12 d. a quarter, which was a relatively high but not extraordinary figure. Other parish collections were organized on the same basis (CWA, 1521–2 or 1531–2).

[159] Burgess, 'Benefactions of mortality', p. 80.

[160] Carrington, 'Ancient ales', 193 (1 d. instead of 2 d.); Binney (ed.), Morebath, pp. 34–5 (¼ d. instead of ½ d.).

[161] Ashburton CWA, p. 192. Very exceptionally, servants contributed to the 'tallage' at Bridgwater, but – just like women – they were normally subsumed under their household: French, 'Local identity', p. 214, and ch. 5 on 'Gendering the parish'. As for church attendance of men and women, the official of the archdeacon of Buckingham told notorious church absentees in 1491 'quod de cetero veniant et audiant et eorum quilibet veniat et audiat divina, et eorum uxores omni die festo in ecclesia parochiali': Ragg (ed.), 'Archdeaconry Courts of Bucks.', 37–8.

[162] Genicot, Rural Communities, p. 102.

[163] Hobhouse (ed.), CWA of Croscombe [etc.], p. xi.

[164] For its powers see the section on 'legislation' in Chapter 2.2.3.

Gent' Alen Johnson Wylliam Woode William Webley William
Eustache John Jacob William Bampton and other many worshipfull
of the paryssh beyng at thys accompt determyned and endyd in the
fest of candylmas abovesayd that suche a persone or personys beyng
a parysshon and an householder in the same paryssh aftyr hyt ys
openly warnyd in the pulpyte that he that woll absent hym and wyll
not come to the yeldyng up of the accompt of the chyrch wardeyns
he and eny of theym so beyng absent w'out a resonable excuse shall
pay viiid or a lb of wex to the meynteynyng of the chyrch lyghte.
Roger Russell and John Frende beyng chyrch wardens at the tyme of
thys ordenance.[165]

The ordinance was repeated frequently, and later versions replaced 'other
many worshipfull' with 'all the worshypfull' (CWA 1489–90) or 'all the
hole body of the paryssh' (CWA 1494–5), which should not be
interpreted as an arbitrary choice of terminology, but as the result of a
successful enforcement campaign. Fourteen parishioners were listed as
absent in 1486–7 and fined 4 d., 8 d. or a pound of wax each. Even
latecomers and members of the absolute elite like Nicholas Lathell did
not escape punishment.[166] After 1497, no more amercements were
actually collected, but the heading (with an added 'nil') remained a part
of the churchwardens' reckoning. Whether this meant that every
parishioner did indeed attend every year, or whether the rule was
enforced with less vigour, is impossible to judge.

The holding of parish assemblies was by no means restricted to the big
cities. Morebath householders were regularly summoned to a 'day of
communication', as were those of Bethersden in Kent.[167] At Tavistock,
meetings took place 'vpon a monycion & warnyng of the vycar of the
seid Churche of Tavystoke openly in the pulpytte to the parisshens of the
same and [after] the most substancyall men of the same parische wer
warned by the warden of the seid Churche to assemble together'.[168] The
sources also reveal when the gatherings took place: St Stephen, Bristol,
held its annual audit at 8 a.m. on the Monday after the Purification of

---

[165] Botolph CWA, 1485–6. At St Ewen's, too, 'only householders' attended the parish
assembly (CWA, p. xxi).

[166] 'And byn amercyd': Master Peke, William Eustace [a signatory of the original
ordinance!], Thomas Wallesdon and nine others paid a pound of wax, John Brewet 4 d.,
and Richard Mathew 8 d. (CWA 1486–7). In 1487–8, the wardens noted: 'M Lathell in
amerciamente iiiid [8 d. crossed out and added] so muche lesse because he came nat at the
begynyg of the accompt', which shows that the list of absentees was compiled when
proceedings started. Sixteen others were fined with him, and 6 s. 8 d. was received in
1490–1 (for example of four brewers).

[167] Binney (ed.), *Morebath*, for example p. 84; Mercer (ed.), *CWA of Betrysden*, for
example pp. 19, 70, 131 (election of CWs).

[168] Leadam (ed.), *Court of Requests*, p. 21 (meeting held in Jan. 1519).

our Lady,[169] but a more common choice was the time after matins or morning prayer on a Sunday or feast day, when all parishioners would (or should) be in attendance anyway.[170] As seen at St Botolph or Tavistock, the meeting would be announced by the priest from the pulpit in good time, or by lay officers such as the wardens. The constable summoned the parishioners at Davidstow in Cornwall on at least one occasion,[171] and the sexton did so at Bethersden: the wardens noted in their accounts of 1524–5 that they had 'be councell of the parissh causyd the sexten to geve all the parissh a warenynge that the hole parissh sholde a pere to gether, the viii[th] daye of Januare the xvi[th] yere of kynge Herry the viii[th] that they might have a comynicacion of how many kene that where parteynynge to the cherche of Betrysden and also to have a parfet knowleg unther what maner a forme they where orden to the cherche'.[172]

There was always a strong attempt to reach unanimity, but communal approval could not be taken for granted. At Tavistock in 1519, 'the hole parisshens' agreed to buy a new cross 'excepte suche as were mooved to the contrary by Thomas Burges Rychard Langbrooke and John Cole with vj moo or thereaboutes of theyr affinite'. This opposition sufficed to defeat a prestigious, but not vital embellishment plan which had received the backing of the 'most substancyall' of the parish.[173] Majority decisions, however, were enforced if they concerned canonical duties and other unavoidable responsibilities. When Morebath voted on a settlement concerning the payment of the parish clerk, 'ther ware xxvj yn on parte' who were in favour, '& there was v menof y[e] other parte y[t] wolde not be orderyd by no man'. This may have sounded very emphatic, but ecclesiastical and manorial representatives put so much pressure on the minority to respect the 'moste parte of y[e] parysse' that, when they were 'demanndyd a gayn by name', a revised proposal was accepted without dissent.[174] Similarly, the wardens of All Saints were chosen by the 'most voice' of the parish, but whether here, too, all householders were asked to say 'yea', or – as documented at Yalding – whether one of the more prominent parishioners posed a general question ('that yf there were any manne not contente withe thordre aforesaid that they should speake ther myndes to the contrarye') is not recorded.[175]

---

[169] Fox (ed.), 'St Stephen', 199.

[170] 'Upon a holydaye betwyn matens & masse' at Tavistock, on the Sunday 'prima post Octabis Epiphanie' for the audit at Peterborough (CWA, 1477–8).

[171] PRO, STAC 3/2/20 (reign of Henry VIII).

[172] Mercer (ed.), CWA at Betrysden, pp. 60–1 (8 Jan. 1525 was a Sunday).

[173] Leadam (ed.), Court of Requests, p. 28.

[174] Binney (ed.), Morebath, pp. 82–6. 31 of the 33 householders of the parish were present and consulted at the assembly, quite literally the whole community.

[175] Burgess, 'Benefactions of mortality', p. 80; PRO STAC 3/1/89.

Continental evidence, if less explicit, points to similar institutional arrangements. The special financial obligations of householders appear in many French documents, and the existence of compulsory parish assemblies for election, audit, and other purposes is equally evident.[176] Examining the circumstances of a large number of parochial elections from various countries, Dietrich Kurze found no reason to question the validity of phrases such as 'universitas parochianorum' or 'the rich and the poor'.[177] The association of political rights with heads of households was a feature of pre-modern European society in general. It can be observed in parishes, town assemblies, court leets, English village communities, as well as the political organization of German peasants.[178] Fines for absentees from assemblies were no parochial peculiarity either.[179]

The special summonses for the 'most substancyall' parishioners, the naming of certain individuals in communal ordinances, and the differentiations in wealth and prestige have shown that it was common for some householders to be more 'equal' than others. Here again, the parallels to the social reality outside the parish are obvious. Certain families were clearly more powerful than others, had a bigger share in office holding, and generally assumed a more prominent profile in communal affairs.[180] In manors, juries of substantial peasants gradually assumed duties which had once been exercised by the whole body of suitors, and in towns access to municipal executives became more and more restricted.[181]

---

[176] See for example the emphasis on 'chacun feu tenant' in a regulation of duties from Burgundy (Aubrun, *Paroisse*, pp. 240–5), and the references to assemblies in Mousnier, *Institutions de la France*, pp. 429, 432–3 (village and parish assemblies overlap, and 'dans la plupart des communautés, l'assistance à l'assemblée était obligatoire sous peine d'amende' for all 'chefs de feux'), and Huard, 'Paroisse rurale', 16.

[177] Kurze, 'Wahlen im Niederkirchenbereich', p. 205.

[178] Gibbs, 'Parish finance', p. 73 (male householders attend London wardmotes); Bailey, *Prescot Court Leet*, pp. 20ff (Prescot: the rates are levied from larger holdings only, and offices as well as certain duties rotate among local householders); Reynolds, *Kingdoms and Communities*, p. 142, and Hilton, *Medieval Society*, p. 151 (English villages); P. Blickle, *Die Revolution von 1525* (2nd edn, Munich, 1983), p. 194 (Holy Roman Empire).

[179] See for example the normative evidence in Bateson (ed.), *Borough Customs*, ii. 50–5, and the fines imposed at Norwich from the fourteenth to the seventeenth century: W. Hudson (ed.), *Leet Jurisdiction in the City of Norwich* (London, 1892), pp. 63, 70, 97 (ranging from 4–12 d. in the early phase). The degree of involvement by the whole community in manorial or village assemblies varied of course from period to period and region to region: Genicot, *Rural Communities*, pp. 80–8.

[180] E. Britton, *The Community of the Vill* (Toronto, 1977), pp. 98, 104 (members of some families are more likely to hold offices or to be pledges for other villagers) and Olson, 'Jurors of the village court', 238 (local leaders tend to belong to long-established families).

[181] Beckerman, 'Customary law', p. 99 (manors); Thomson, *Transformation*, p. 52, and S. Rigby, 'Urban "oligarchies" in late medieval England' in J. Thomson (ed.), *Towns and Townspeople in the Fifteenth Century* (Gloucester, 1988), pp. 62ff (towns).

On the parish level, too, the bigger landholders certainly expected to be given an adequate say in the running of communal affairs. From the earliest evidence, a smaller elite of householders emerges as a distinct body. At St Mary, Oxford, in 1276, three wardens were elected with the rector's consent, who had to submit their accounts to certain 'discreet' parishioners and could be removed at the latter's will. The administrators of the fabric box at Reculver in 1296 were chosen by the whole parish, but accounted yearly to the vicar and only a number of parishioners.[182] These were early days in terms of the development of parochial institutions, and later arrangements normally included more extensive communal rights. Still, collective decisions must at all times have resulted from some kind of 'amorphous consensus in which we may guess that the richer and more senior ... took the leading part'.[183] We have seen that the 'chief of the parishioners' (quite literally the 'frontbenchers' of the assembly) presented to many a subparochial benefice, and from the latter part of the fifteenth century in particular, they assumed an ever more prominent role in many places. Two factors may have played an important part in this process.

First, there are indications that socio-economic change normally associated with the sixteenth century affected some areas already in the late fifteenth. Greater mobility, the creation of larger landholdings, and the emergence of new crafts reinforced existing social distinctions. Local communities began to differentiate between deserving poor and strangers or vagrants, while the more prosperous inhabitants suspected the less well-off of undermining social order. Parish elites started worrying about the consequences of sexual misbehaviour, and bylaws protecting their economic and social interests multiplied.[184]

Second, the steady accumulation of landed property meant that parish wardens dealt with ever greater financial resources, and that administrative efficiency called for more flexible instruments than a yearly assembly. Tenements needed to be maintained, documents had to be drawn up, and rent collection was a large-scale operation.[185] From 1488, the wardens of All Saints had to consult certain substantial parishioners in matters of property, and they were given strict spending

---

[182] Drew, *Early Parochial Organisation*, pp. 17 (Reculver) and 21 (Oxford).
[183] Reynolds, *Kingdoms and Communities*, p. 100.
[184] Elaborated by McIntosh, 'Local change'.
[185] In Bristol, parish-based 'service'-chantries multiplied at that time (Burgess, 'Strategies for eternity', p. 23); cf. the higher share of rent revenue in the stacks in Appendix 4 (i). The All Saints rent rolls give a good insight into the administration of property: BRO, P/AS/ChW/2. Even rural wardens were busy making 'covenants' with some of their tenants: Mercer (ed.), *CWA at Betrysden*, p. 64.

limits for some of their activities.[186] The same ordinance, however, made it clear that the annual audit and the election of wardens remained communal responsibilities. Over at St Stephen's, the vestry regulations of 1524 were passed by a body of 22 men, together with the parson and wardens,[187] and the same number of signatures appeared on a memorandum about salary levels for various parish employees at Botolph Aldersgate in 1534.[188] Exceptionally strong traces of an emerging parish hierarchy can be found in the accounts of St Mary-at-Hill, where property endowments had reached unrivalled levels: around 1500, burial fee ordinances, bell ringing arrangements, and even the passing of accounts or the election of wardens could be witnessed by a fairly limited amount of parishioners.[189]

By the sixteenth century, yet smaller 'parish councils' had emerged as a feature of communal government. Recruited from among the 'frontbenchers' of a community, they could be called 'masters', 'auditors', or 'feoffees', but all took care of some executive and supervisory duties over officers and parish property.[190] The body of the 'iiii [or v] men' at Morebath, which controlled the finances of the various stores, was officially approved by an ecclesiastical visitation in the 1530s (an ominous precedent for the establishment of select vestries in the later part of the century),[191] while the 'eight men' of Ashburton, responsible for the regulation of parish affairs and the fining of offenders, are first mentioned in 1484.[192] Councils, however, were not yet a universal phenomenon: in boroughs such as Wells or Newcastle-under-Lyme, the same function was fulfilled by municipal authorities,[193] and in 'living' regimes, there were generally fewer signs of oligarchical government. Church ales, collections, plays, and other entertainments depended on the active involvement of all parishioners,

---

[186] Nicholls and Taylor, *Bristol Past*, ii. 94; Botolph Aldersgate agreed at a later date that no warden could bestow more than 20 s. on the maintenance of church property without the consent of six 'honest & elderlie neighbours of the parishe' (CWA, 1551–2).

[187] Fox (ed.), 'St Stephen', 198–9.

[188] Botolph CWA, 1533–4.

[189] Mary-at-Hill CWA, 1522–3, 1501–2, 1498–9, and 1507–8.

[190] 'Auditors' at Andrew Hubbard (CWA 1527–8), 'masters' at All Saints (CWA 1519–20), 'eight men' at Ashburton (CWA, p. xviii), 'feoffees' at Tavistock (Worth (ed.), *Tavistock*, p. 85).

[191] Binney (ed.), *Morebath*, pp. 34, 83.

[192] CWA, p. xviii, and Amery, 'Presidential address', 67; 'four men' also existed at Lydeard St Lawrence in Somerset: French, 'Local identity', p. 73; cf. the 'auditors' discussed in Chapter 3.2. The 'four men' at Chagford, however, were identical with the churchwardens: Osborne (ed.), *CWA Chagford*, p. 130.

[193] French, 'Local identity', p. 74; Pape, *Newcastle-under-Lyme*, p. 20.

and there was much less landed property which required constant expert attention.[194]

A balanced view of early Tudor parish institutions must certainly acknowledge the existence of hierarchies. Everyday business, however, was in the hands of the middling sort rather than elites. The wardens as 'chief executives' worked in conjunction with the council, but had often more in common with humbler members of the community.[195] In inner-parochial conflicts they tended to remain neutral, to hope for arbitration, or to restrict their interventions to financial or procedural considerations.[196] The average parishioner continued to have a voice in elections, audits, or important communal decisions in accordance with local custom.[197] 'Frontbenchers' or councillors who forgot that they were looking after communal rather than private business could be reprimanded by their sovereign institution. When the Tavistock assembly refused to sanction a *fait accompli* by their elite, the warden John Gooscott reminded one of the feoffees that the community could not be bound by 'certen persons not hauyng the hoole power or auctorite ... without the assent of the hoole parisshe'.[198] This, without any doubt, was still more than just an empty phrase.

6.2.2 Early modern parish government

At the beginning of the seventeenth century, the structures of parish government looked rather different. There was no one single cause, and the degree of change varied from place to place, but a combination of external and internal factors had redefined the balance within the communities.

---

[194] Bennett, 'Conviviality', 39: church ales were attended predominantly by the middling sort; in this sample, there are few signs of oligarchy in a 'living' regime such as Yatton.

[195] The council was frequently, as at Morebath, the culmination of a 'cursus honorum' and the preserve of very substantial members of the community. For the (middling) status of CWs see McIntosh, 'Local change', 226, 231, and Chapter 2.2.2 above.

[196] Communal decision-making and the workings of parish government in times of conflict are explored in the author's forthcoming "By all the whole body of the paryssh" essay.

[197] Four of Ashburton's 'eight men' were elected by the town and four by the manor (in a parish without eminent gentry; CWA, pp. xix and 192–3). Andrew Hubbard's auditors are appointed by the parish (CWA, 1526–7). 'Crucial communal decisions' often included the leasing of parish property to new tenants (for example Botolph CWA, 1512–13).

[198] Leadam (ed.), *Court of Requests*, p. 19.

The clergy's position continued to be ambiguous. On the one hand, Reformation theology reduced both their sacramental power and their number. All that mattered now for the laity in the quest for salvation was faith and knowledge of the scriptures. In the wake of the dissolution, some parishes also managed to secure rights over patronage and the financial administration of benefices. At Ipswich, where most communities had always enjoyed considerable autonomy vis-à-vis their monastic patrons, the majority of livings became donatives of the parishioners, and the years between 1530 and 1570 saw a 'decline of clerical independence, and the growth of lay control' in Bristol parishes. Tithes or rates for ministers appeared in the post-Reformation churchwardens' accounts of St Andrew Hubbard and St Stephen Coleman Street in London, St Ewen's, Bristol, and several Chester parishes, to name but a few. At the same time, the municipal framework pushed ever more strongly into the ecclesiastical field. The best known example is the establishment of town lectureships in places such as Rye, Exeter, King's Lynn, or Ipswich, where the Elizabethan godly corporation even secured an act of parliament approving the levying of rates for the stipends of ministers.[199] Advowsons of livings at Norwich, King's Lynn, Stratford, or Leeds were also held by communal bodies and in London, some 13 vestries appointed their own incumbents by the 1630s.[200] On the other hand, this progress in terms of lay influence (if it was progress at all[201]) should be contrasted with the loss of the subparochial level of lights, chantries, and fraternities. Quite apart from the resulting pastoral problems, countless endowments had been removed from collective lay control, and many a parishioner had lost a position of local power and patronage. Anniversaries had also disappeared, and with them one of the prime incentives to endow parishes with lands or property. These intercession-related bequests had played a crucial part in the expansion of communal activities, and they

---

[199] For Reformation Ipswich: MacCulloch and Blatchly, 'Tudor Ipswich'; for Bristol: Skeeters, *Community and Clergy*, p. 149. Andrew Hubbard CWA, 1546ff; Gibbs, 'Parish finance', p. 214; St Ewen CWA, p. xxxviif; N. Alldridge, 'Loyalty and identity in Chester parishes 1540–1640' in Wright (ed.), *Parish, Church and People*, p. 92 (tithes and compulsory contributions). Ipswich was a particularly advanced 'model of the godly civic commonwealth': P. Collinson, *The Religion of Protestants* (Oxford, 1982), p. 170; other examples of town preachers: ibid., pp. 173–4.

[200] Ibid., pp. 141, 174, and Sheils, 'Religion in provincial towns', p. 161 (patronage). For London see Seaver, *Puritan Lectureships*, p. 138.

[201] Tithes had always been paid in one way or another, both communal patronage and the farming of benefices had existed in the pre-Reformation period, albeit on a smaller scale (cf. Chapter 2.2.3; Swanson, *Church and Society*, p. 218), and auxiliary clergy had also been supported frequently.

would have been an invaluable asset in a time of high inflation. The drastically reduced number of resident clergymen also intensified the problems of absenteeism, vacancies, and clerical negligence.[202] Congregations depended much more strongly on incumbents, whose position was further enhanced by the importance of instruction and preaching in Protestant worship. The increasing emphasis on university education may have widened the gap which separated clergymen from their flock, and the moral rigour of puritan values added to the potential for a new kind of clericalism in many communities.[203]

As seen earlier in this chapter (6.1), the frequency of visitations increased. There were two main reasons for the closer supervision of parochial life: first, the hectic pace of legislation on matters of doctrine and administration, and second, the crown's appointment of its own commissioners for the enforcement of religious policy.

As for the former, a few examples may suffice to illustrate the increasing intrusiveness of later sixteenth-century government. For a start, the various sets of articles and injunctions contained an astonishing amount of regulations about all aspects of communal worship. Throughout the late Middle Ages, the maintenance of the fabric and the provision of a certain number of ornaments had been the sole formal requirements, and there was considerable room for extra efforts or special local cults. Now certain options had been outlawed (lights, saints), others (puritan lectureships) displayed a marked doctrinal bias. The room for manoeuvre had become very tight indeed, and something like the proper choice of vestments could turn into an issue which called for international arbitration.[204]

Similar attempts were made to synchronize parish administration. Royal injunctions ordered the keeping of registers and the purchase of adequate parish chests.[205] From the later sixteenth century, ecclesiastical canons started to regulate matters such as the holding of parochial elections or the ideal length of term for local office holders. Even the churchwardens' range of duties was specified meticulously, although local custom had to be taken into account.[206] This last point emerges

---

[202] 11 Bristol parishes were vacant by 1563: Skeeters, *Community and Clergy*, p. 109.

[203] On the role and position of the post-Reformation clergy see for example Haigh, 'Anticlericalism', p. 74; Scarisbrick, *Reformation*, ch. 8; Collinson, 'The late medieval Church and its Reformation', p. 254; F. Heal and R. O'Day (eds), *Princes and Paupers in the English Church 1500–1800* (Leicester, 1981).

[204] Sheils, *Reformation*, p. 64.

[205] Frere and Kennedy (eds), *Visitation Articles*, ii. 34–43 (1538) and iii. 1–29 (1559).

[206] E. Cardwell (ed.), *Synodalia* (Oxford, 1842), i. 122–6 (canons of archbishop Parker 1571); Gibson (ed.), *Codex*, pp. 215–16 (extract of Bancroft's canons of 1604; a whole section dealt with matters of parish administration).

strongly from a look across the border into Wales, which had a similar legislative framework. Church court proceedings resulted from complaints about the place, date, or electorate involved in churchwardens' appointments, but if they corresponded to established custom, the election was normally upheld.[207] Ecclesiastical authorities continued to be unable to refuse a candidate whom the parishioners had thought fit to serve, and their powers over wardens' accounts were limited, too. Canon 89 of 1603 stipulated that reckonings had to be yielded within a month after the end of a term to a parish assembly or select vestry, but with the exception of fraud and major unauthorized expenditure, there was little chance of challenging individual items in the spiritual courts.[208] Even so, the mere fact that such suits were now brought and heard in large numbers is significant testimony to the increased outside involvement in parochial affairs.

As for parliamentary legislation, the Act of Uniformity of 1559 ordered wardens to levy 12 d. from those who absented themselves from church, and in spite of practical problems of enforcement, some prosecutions against negligent parish officers were actually brought.[209] Bishops, too, took an unprecedented interest in the details of parish administration and interfered with specific orders: the ordinary at Norwich complained about the nine years one Mr Wynter had served as warden of the parish of Barningham, and at Botolph Aldersgate the first direct evidence for episcopal directives dates from Mary's reign, when Larry Bedell was paid 2 s. ½ d. for writing 'the booke of the clerkes wages, the booke of all the names of the parishnirs and for wryting and setting up the names of the pewes at the byshops comanndment'.[210] Elizabethan churchwardens must have felt that their performance was under much closer scrutiny. Historians differ in their assessment of local support for the authorities,[211]

---

[207] W. T. Morgan, 'Disputes before the Consistory Courts of St Davids', *Journal of the Historical Society of the Church in Wales*, 3 (1953), 90–9.

[208] Gibson (ed.), *Codex*, p. 215 (elected candidate); W. T. Morgan, 'An Examination of Churchwardens' Accounts', *Journal of the Historical Society of the Church in Wales*, 8 (1958), 70–1.

[209] 1 Elizabeth, c. 2; prosecutions of churchwardens for example in Houlbrooke, *Church Courts*, pp. 247, 258, and M. Dwyer, 'Catholic Recusants in Essex c.1580–1600' (MA London, 1960), pp. 24–5.

[210] R. Houlbrooke (ed.), *The Letter Book of John Parkhurst* (Norwich, 1975), p. 259 (bishop Parkhurst, 1570s); Botolph CWA, 1555–6. In 1565, wardens in the diocese of Coventry and Lichfield were ordered to fine parishioners which still used beads: Duffy, *Stripping of the Altars*, p. 572, and Frere and Kennedy (eds), *Visitation Articles*, iii. 163–70.

[211] For a survey of contemporary and present-day views on the role and attitude of post-Reformation churchwardens: Craig, 'Reformation, politics, and polemics', pp. 32–44. The fact that there is such a debate is significant; no one would even think of labeling parish officers as instruments of a 'totalitarian regime' (A. Tindal-Hart, *The Man in the Pew* (London, 1966), p. 66) in the medieval period.

but there can be no doubt that the pressure on parish officers increased. The whole climate became more restrictive and ecclesiastical control intensified:[212] early modern wardens were reminded of their duties from the pulpit every Sunday and – on pain of excommunication – expected to make much more wide-ranging presentments than their medieval predecessors.[213] Nicholas Harpsfield's 1557 inspection of parochial religion in Kent has been described as the 'most searching visitation carried out in any diocese in the Tudor period', only to be followed a few years later by 'draconian' Elizabethan commissioners with completely different expectations.[214] No wonder that potential candidates became more hesitant to accept the office in the later sixteenth century.[215]

Due to the appointment of royal commissioners, visitations were not only more searching, but also more frequent. The years around 1550 were a particularly intensive period (see Figure 6.3) but as early as 1538, all wardens and sidesmen of the northern province were to swear 'oaths of fealty and obedience to the king, denouncing the pope and his jurisdiction'.[216] Overall, the English evidence hardly differs from the increasing intrusiveness of early modern government on the Continent.[217]

The beneficiaries of the sixteenth-century changes were crown and gentry rather than parish communities. To take patronage as an example, the king presented to less than 5 per cent of livings in the archdeaconries of Essex, Middlesex, and Colchester before the Reformation, but to over 17 per cent at the death of Mary. The laity (or more specifically the gentry) doubled its share of advowsons from just over a third in the early part of the century to 66 per cent under

---

[212] In the long run 'ecclesiastical authorities ... were able to oversee parochial life more thoroughly than had hitherto been possible': M. Ingram, *Church Courts, Sex, and Marriage in England 1570–1640* (Cambridge, 1987), p. 329.

[213] Frere and Kennedy (eds), *Visitation Articles*, iii. 268 (reminding of duties); Rodes, *Lay Authority*, pp. 138, 163.

[214] Duffy, *Stripping of the Altars*, pp. 524 and 566. In the capital, too, 'the authority of the hierarchy became increasingly intrusive', and local officials spent 'a great deal of time and effort answering the bishop or his officers': Gibbs, 'Parish finance', p. 317, and pp. 82–3.

[215] Gibbs, 'Parish finance', pp. 45–6, and Archer, *Pursuit of Stability*, p. 94 (candidates in later Elizabethan London); Craig, 'Reformation, politics, and polemics', p. 43 (increasing pressure on office holders at Mildenhall).

[216] C. Kitching (ed.), *The Royal Visitation of 1559* (Gateshead, 1975), p. xiv.

[217] Schröcker, *Kirchenpflegschaft*, pp. 141–6 (legislation by territorial princes in Germany); F. Rapp, 'Communautés rurales et paroisses en basse Alsace' in *Communautés rurales*, p. 468 (more frequent and thorough visitations).

Elizabeth.[218] Monastic property was distributed in a similar way. The crown never intended to keep this land and sold it to 'local landowners, often of gentry status, who wished to consolidate their estates'.[219] In Norfolk, for instance, no less than 174 manors were added to the possessions of well-established gentlemen, while the nobility's holdings increased by just 31, and yeomen had to content themselves with the purchase of smaller farms.[220] Parish property, too, found its way into gentry households: Sir William Stafford confiscated the bells from several Essex churches (at Hawkwell at least 'contrary to the myndys of the seyd paryshioners'), and much disappeared elsewhere.[221] This large-scale transfer of wealth reinforced the local power structure and enhanced the process of social differentiation which was under way in both town and countryside.

Other Reformation-related changes had the same effect. At Bristol, the powers of the leading citizens increased to an extent which allowed them to oversee their fellow townsmen 'from cradle to grave',[222] while public life in Elizabethan Coventry 'was characterised above all by a polarisation of society', and municipal ceremony assumed a distinctively different flavour, with aldermen 'proclaiming the status of the ruling oligarchy rather than the unity of the community as a whole'.[223] Parochial disputes which used to be dealt with by internal mediation were now often referred to external authority.[224] At the same time – according to many social historians – the gap between the upper and lower sections of village society widened. Yeomen had added substantial portions to their holdings and felt increasingly closer to the gentry than the local poor. Social control rather than 'social ethics' was now the order of the day.[225] The reinforcement of social divisions may or may not have been deliberate, but the practical effects of the Reformation were no doubt welcomed by local leaders after the somewhat destabilizing socio-economic developments of the later Middle Ages,[226]

---

[218] Oxley, *Essex*, pp. 263–4. Most advowsons were attached to manors in the hands of influential families like the Darcys. In Lancashire, the gentry presented to a third of the benefices in 1530 and to 47 per cent in 1560: Haigh, *Lancashire*, pp. 24, 142.

[219] Sheils, *Reformation*, pp. 28–9.

[220] Hoskins, *Age of Plunder*, p. 137.

[221] Duffy, *Stripping of the Altars*, pp. 488–9. The motive was not necessarily selfish; some gentlemen may have wanted to preserve church goods from profanation.

[222] Sacks, *Bristol and the Atlantic Economy*, pp. 162–3.

[223] Phythian-Adams, *Desolation of a City*, p. 271, and P. Clark and P. Slack, *English Towns in Transition 1500–1700* (Oxford, 1976), p. 131.

[224] For example at Andrew Holborn, London: Archer, *Pursuit of Stability*, p. 85.

[225] Russell, *Crisis of Parliaments*, pp. 16–17; Wrightson, *English Society*, pp. 140–2; Hill, *Society and Puritanism*, p. 432; Richmond, 'English gentry', p. 146 (social ethics).

[226] 'The struggle of local leaders in attempting to deal with community problems helps to explain their willingness to accept the firm authority offered by Henry Tudor and his successors': McIntosh, 'Local change', 219.

when vast amounts of land had been removed from their control and given to monasteries, cathedrals, and also to parishes. As a consequence, churchwardens emerged 'as irritating rivals wielding limited but telling authority over local property and populace'.[227] Sir Thomas Smith certainly spoke for many of his influential contemporaries when he emphasized that 'such lowe and base persons' should have no part in the running of the commonwealth, but grudgingly admitted that they had become used to doing so.[228] Even preachers expressed a latent fear that this trend would ultimately pose a serious threat to the established order. Some London benefactors went as far as making gifts to the poor dependent on the exclusion of the humbler parishioners from communal government.[229]

Consciously or not, the crown dispersed such worries by turning the parish into a closely monitored part of its local government structure. It is uniformly recognized that the Tudor state appropriated the existing parochial framework to tackle the ever increasing amount of social and administrative problems.[230] In many ways, this echoed the takeover of the village community by external authorities a few hundred years earlier. When lords or royal officials started to rely on the vill for the levying of contributions or the gathering of information, they appropriated a unit which had been developed by the local peasantry to deal with its own agricultural interests.[231] In the Tudor period, the process got under way in 1533 with an act for the destruction of 'Choughes, Crowes, and Rokes', which ordered parishes to keep crow nets for a period of ten years.[232] The legislation on 'thamendyng of Highe Wayes' of 1555 put parishes in charge of road repair, ordering constables and wardens to assemble the inhabitants for the election of 'surveyors', and to specify four days each year for labour services in accordance with the landed

---

[227] Burgess and Kümin, 'Penitential bequests', 628.

[228] Smith, *De republica Anglorum*, pp. 76–7.

[229] Craig, 'Reformation, politics, and polemics', pp. 2–3 (citing the 'homily against disobedience and wilful rebellion'); Archer, *Pursuit of Stability*, pp. 70–1 (bequest of Thomas Lane to St Mildred Poultry in 1594).

[230] Hobhouse (ed.), *CWA of Croscombe [etc.]*, p. xv; J. Redlich, *Die englische Lokalverwaltung* (Leipzig, 1901), p. 29; Jordan, *Philanthropy*, p. 82; West, *Village Records*, p. 66; having functioned very much outside the state system, the parish now changed its character: 'Aus einem grossen sozialen Gemeindewesen wurde es ein rechtlich anerkanntes und zu Staatslasten verpflichtetes Gemeinwesen' (J. Hatschek, *Englische Verfassungsgeschichte* (Munich, 1913), p. 473). The legislators realized that it was 'the one local organisation' capable of dealing with collective responsibilities: Drew (ed.), *Lambeth CWA*, p. xi.

[231] Dyer, 'Power and conflict', pp. 31–2, and elaborated in an unpublished manuscript 'Aufstieg und Niedergang der Gemeinde in England von 500–1700', pp. 5ff.

[232] 24 Henry VIII, c. 10; further (extended) legislation on vermin in 1565–6.

wealth of each member of the community.[233] The military use of the ecclesiastical network was institutionalized at the end of Mary's reign, when parishioners who were not individually liable to serve were charged with the provision and maintenance of weapons.[234] The most important new duty, however, was statutory poor relief.

In 1536, the act for the punishment of vagabonds and beggars called for collections in aid of the impotent poor and 'laid full responsibility for them on the parish'.[235] Every Sunday, money was to be gathered in common boxes on a voluntary basis and to be accounted for by special collectors, but the act eventually lapsed. The problem, however, did not go away, and the royal injunctions of 1547 ordered every parish to provide an alms chests, while places such as Norwich or York introduced compulsory town levies around 1550. An important step towards a national poor rate was taken by parliamentary legislation in 1552, which kept contributions voluntary, but introduced records of pledges by individual parishioners. Outstanding payments could now be reported to ecclesiastical courts, and this first shadow of compulsion was reinforced in 1563, when those who sturdily refused to contribute were to be admonished first by the ordinary and eventually faced imprisonment by the justices of the peace.[236] The latter became even more closely involved in the local communities with the act of 1572, which expected them to compile surveys of all impotent poor and to tax local inhabitants accordingly. The final Elizabethan Poor Law, however, defined the justices' role as one of supervision and appeal and placed the executive burden on to church wardens and overseers. In 1598, they were told to put the able-bodied to work, to find apprenticeships for suitable candidates, and to assess every parishioner according to the value of his landed wealth.[237]

Whatever the exact function of the gentlemen who looked over the parishioners' shoulders, the changing tone and character of parish records leaves no doubt that the days of relative autonomy had come to an end.[238] From the mid-Tudor years (and on top of ecclesiastical

---

[233] 2 & 3 Philip and Mary, c. 8.

[234] 4 & 5 Philip and Mary, c. 2.

[235] 27 Henry VIII, c. 25. This passage on the development of the poor law is based on Slack, *Poverty and Policy*, pp. 113–31 (quote: p. 118), Drew (ed.), *CWA of Lambeth*, pp. xl–xlv, G. Elton, *The Parliament of England 1559–81* (Cambridge, 1986), pp. 268–71, and McIntosh, 'Local responses to the poor'.

[236] 5 & 6 Edward VI, c. 2 (1552), and 5 Elizabeth I, c. 3. CWA start to record such contributions in the 1550s, even though the system still looks somewhat 'scattered' and 'haphazard': Slack, *Poverty and Policy*, p. 124.

[237] 14 Elizabeth I, c. 5 (1572), and 39 Elizabeth I, c. 3 (1598).

[238] Poor reckonings had to be submitted to a representative of secular authority (according to the acts of 1572 and 1598; Hill, *Society and Puritanism*, p. 429), overseers

directives), the churchwardens 'received through the justices of the peace, the itinerant justices of assize, and the local commissions of inquiry specially appointed, a continuous stream of orders issued from the Privy Council downwards'.[239] The government's presence in the community became very tangible: regular attendance of divine service was a statutory duty of any loyal subject of her Majesty, and the traditional religious ornaments in the local church had given way to the royal arms.[240]

French parishes, to point to a Continental parallel, experienced a similar integration into the secular government structure. The sixteenth and seventeenth centuries brought new military and poor relief duties, countless 'règlements d'Etat' about the administration of fabric funds, and reinforced the bureaucratization and state control of the local community.[241]

It would be wrong, of course, to claim that external supervision was now as extensive as to stifle every sort of local initiative, but the point is that it changed its character compared to the late medieval period. In the religious field, popular activities could no longer have the same 'communal' quality. The Reformation created or reinforced parochial divisions all over the country, and many a community was visibly 'scarred' by the years of controversy.[242] The sermons of puritan preachers, for instance, could hardly appeal to all parishioners, and churchwardens – now increasingly preoccupied with their secular duties – were less likely candidates for the organization or supervision of

were appointed by the justices, and the Elizabethan legislation 'leads to a striking change of emphasis in the accounts, which by the end of the period are largely taken up with the provision of relief to the poor, arrangements for the care of orphans and the sick, the training of soldiers and the provision and upkeep of their arms and armour': Ashburton CWA, p. x. The parish turned into an 'Instrument der Herrschaft von oben': C. Davies, 'Die bäuerliche Gemeinde in England 1400–1800' in W. Schulze (ed.), Aufstände, Revolten, Prozesse (Stuttgart, 1983), p. 55.

[239] Farmiloe and Nixseaman (ed.), Elizabethan CWA, p. xxix (Bedfords.).

[240] Craig, 'Reformation, politics, and polemics', p. 21; J. Cox and A. Harvey, English Church Furniture (London, 1907), pp. 351–6.

[241] Gaudement, 'Vie paroissiale', p. 83; Goujard, 'Fonds de fabriques', 100; Mousnier, Institutions de la France, pp. 433–4.

[242] For examples of 'scarred' communities: Duffy, Stripping of the Altars, p. 497; in the capital, 'the world of shared faith was broken … and the Christian community divided' (Brigden, London and the Reformation, p. 639); at Yatton, little was left of the 'corporate spirit' which had transformed a humble rural church into the 'Cathedral of the Moors' (Edwards, 'Yatton', 547); for the reinforcement of existing divisions: Cross, Church and People, p. 93.

religious initiatives.[243] As for secular affairs, poor relief and education did offer some room for manoeuvre for collective enterprise. By 1630, eight charities had been established in Chester parishes in addition to the statutory duties, and the first parochial library opened at Bury St Edmunds in the 1590s. School foundations at parish level continued, too, and every community devised some peculiar fundraising methods.[244] Such initiatives, however, lacked both the broad communal basis and innovative character of their medieval predecessors. The expansion into the secular field and the ever increasing accumulation of landed property had been developed without or even against instructions of outside authority.[245] The activities of early modern parochial communities, in contrast, concerned rather uncontroversial matters (many officially assigned to the parish anyway) and presented little challenge to local elites. New rents were earmarked for specific charitable purposes, and the allocation of any surplus no longer subject to scrutiny by the parish assembly. In the new religious climate, the poor became a mere burden without the chance of offering their prayers for the spiritual health of the community. The Bury library was primarily a clerical initiative (which received the support of certain parishioners), and when communities did try to express their peculiar identity, then they often chose symbols of order and hierarchy, a concern well in tune with the general atmosphere of the period.[246]

The perhaps most dramatic change in parish government was the emergence of select vestries. Householders retained their special role in

---

[243] The geographically defined parish lost in importance due to the marked shift towards other *foci* of religious life such as households and conventicles: Hill, *Society and Puritanism*, pp. 458, 491. 'The household was the basis of the organisation of Puritanism': R. Acheson, *Radical Puritans in England 1560–1660* (London, 1990), p. 30.

[244] Alldridge, 'Chester parishes', p. 104; Craig, 'Reformation, politics, and polemics', p. 106 (Bury); Archer, *Pursuit of Stability*, p. 85 (school at St Olave, Southwark); the argument for continuing parish 'vitality', however, becomes rather strained: 'the large measure of freedom [parishioners] enjoy for the devising of ways and means to meet the demands made upon them (though they have no option whatever in granting or withholding supplies) gives to the parish a vigorous entity and a certain autonomous life of its own': Ware, *Elizabethan Parish*, p. 91.

[245] The Church resented the creation of independent parish funds (cf. Chapter 2.1.2). The potential threat posed to established authority by independent communal institutions has been noted earlier in this chapter.

[246] Craig, 'Reformation, politics, and polemics', pp. 106 (Bury) and 54 (order and hierarchy at Mildenhall). The worsening socio-economic circumstances restricted the scope for broadly based communal initiatives further. Radical and controversial projects were of course embarked upon in this period, but they tended to be sponsored by individuals, gathered Churches, or municipal élites rather than parochial institutions (Kümin, 'Voluntary Religion').

terms of contributions and responsibilities,[247] but the years between 1530 and 1560 were to prove crucial for the development of more oligarchical communal regimes. This point is best illustrated by two Bristol ordinances from just before and just after this period:

> The regulations of the vestry of St Stephen in 1524, passed 'with all the whole assent ande consent' of the parishioners, emphasized that all members of the community were to attend the audit of the parish accounts, to choose a successor to the retiring churchwarden, and to come to the church whenever they were summoned. Less than forty years later, however, 'the proctors and major sort' of St Thomas reserved the appointment of churchwardens to a select vestry. The remaining parishioners had to be content with the 'publication thereof ... by the curate the same day' and were no longer required to attend the annual audit.[248]

Quite clearly, communal influence at St Thomas had been severely curtailed. In a similar development, the post-1530 accounts of Botolph Aldersgate no longer refer to fines imposed on absentees from the annual audit, and from 1551–2, wardens became answerable to a small body of dignitaries for any major financial investment. The timing does not look like a coincidence. The crown codified parochial responsibilities in this period and gradually shifted the emphasis from voluntary towards compulsory contributions. From the late 1550s, rates proliferated for a variety of purposes: the poor, ministers, fabric repairs, ornaments, county gaols, maimed soldiers, London prisons, public works, or the wine at communion,[249] and many were explicitly imposed from above: 'in the Middle Ages the bishop did not ... actually order a rate to be made; in the sixteenth and seventeenth centuries he was, through his Consistory and Archdeaconry Courts, continually doing so', with or without communal consent.[250] Examples are easy to find: at Lambeth in 1556,

---

[247] Archbishop Grindal, for instance, requested 'that the lay people of every parish ... and especially householders, having no lawful excuse to be absent shall ... resort with their children and servants to their parish church or chapel on the holy days': Frere and Kennedy (eds), *Visitation Articles*, iii. 266 (1571).

[248] Fox (ed.), 'St Stephen', 198–206, and Taylor (ed.), 'St Thomas', 193–8 (1563). Both parishes were of moderate size and located outside the city centre.

[249] For example Alldridge, 'Chester parishes', pp. 91–2 (ministers and repair); W. Hale, *Precedents in Causes of Office against Churchwardens* (London, 1841), p. 2 (communion cup; St George's Botolph Lane, London); Farmiloe and Nixseaman (eds), *Elizabethan CWA*, pp. xxxiif (gaol, soldiers, prison: on the basis of the statutes of 1572, 1592–3 and 1598; Bedfords.); Archer, *Pursuit of Stability*, p. 86 (public works: St Margaret Moses, London); Boulton, 'Limits of formal religion', 140 (wine: St Margaret Lothbury and All Hallows London Wall).

[250] Drew (ed.), *Lambeth CWA*, p. liii. When the necessity of a rate was proven in the eyes of the authorities, 'the ecclesiastical judge ... whether bishop, archdeacon, official, or surrogate, has power to authorize and command the churchwardens to call a meeting of

royal commissioners ordered a compulsory assessment of the parish for
essential church furniture, at Andover, the bishop imposed a rate in
1564, and the court of the archdeacon of St Alban's reminded the
wardens of Northaw in 1597 'to make a seasement of every parishener
according to their severall abilities and at the next court to bringe in that
seasement and then also to enforme the court who they be that refuse to
paye'. A London consistory court judge even specified the exact date and
place for the levying of rates at Hendon in 1613, and the trend continued
throughout the Laudian years.[251] This type of fundraising regime
required a much more elaborate bureaucratic machinery,[252] and annual
parish assemblies must have appeared increasingly inadequate and
cumbersome.[253]

After 1560, Bristol and London parishes reacted to these changes with
the introduction of select vestries, from 1590 increasingly with episcopal
backing.[254] By 1638, 59 out of 109 London vestries had become select.
The pioneering role of the big cities is no surprise, for it was here that
large scale property holding had led to an early administrative
sophistication and the first traces of a more exclusive form of parish
government (for instance at Mary-at-Hill). Urban centres also
experienced particularly pressing social problems and extraordinarily
high mobility.[255] The core of resident rate payers understandably sought
to secure a bigger say in the allocation of their contributions. The tone
of contemporary documents, however, leaves no doubt that the
establishment of select vestries was not simply the result of practical
considerations, but a deliberate act of self-conscious local elites. At
Martin Ludgate in 1592, it was argued that 'through the generall
admittance of all sortes of parishioners unto theire vestries theire falleth
out great hinderaunce to good proceedinges by the dissent of the
inferiour & late inhabitantes being for the most part the greater number
and more headye to crosse then either discreet or hable to further any

---

the parishioners, and at that meeting to make a rate, or cause it to be made, with or without
the consent of a majority of the parishioners': Hale, *Precedents*, p. viii.

[251] Drew (ed.), *Lambeth CWA*, p. 69; Houlbrooke, *Church Courts*, p. 169 (Andover);
Hale, *Precedents*, pp. 88 (Northaw) and 39 (Hendon). At Bangor in 1636, a levy for
ornaments and repairs had to be carried out without the consent of the parish by two
wardens nominated by the bishop: Hill, *Society and Puritanism*, pp. 430–1.

[252] Ibid., p. 432, and Ingram, *Church Courts*, p. 101.

[253] The same tendency can be observed in Wales: by the seventeenth century, most
traditional sources of income had dried up and revenues derived almost exclusively from
rates (Morgan, 'Examination of CWA', 59).

[254] Hill, *Society and Puritanism*, p. 433.

[255] Archer, *Pursuit of Stability*, p. 69 (vestry number); Russell, *Crisis of Parliaments*, pp.
20–1 (poverty in towns), and S. Rappaport, *Worlds Within Worlds* (Cambridge, 1989), ch.
3 (special city context).

good order for the benefitt of the church & parish'.[256] Even though certain post-Reformation ordinances still referred to the consent of 'general vestries' or the whole parish, three crucial areas were now normally removed from communal influence: the appointment of parochial 'executives', the choosing of wardens, and the formal auditing of parish accounts. Late medieval councils, such as the 'assessors' of the clerk's wages at All Saints or the 'auditors' at Andrew Hubbard, tended to have a clear mandate from the assembly.[257] From the 1560s, however, Bristol vestries became self-elected bodies, and at Botolph Aldgate, too, new members were 'to be chosen by the residue of the said vestrymen'.[258] After 1570, Ashburton's 'eight men' and 24 other parishioners assumed sole responsibility for the passing of the accounts, and by 1563, the vestry of St Thomas, Bristol, appointed the churchwardens 'in private'.[259]

Many local peculiarities remained: the records of St Andrew Holborn reveal that 'grave' business had been dealt with by a select body of 12 ancient inhabitants from time out of mind, but the accounts, at least, were always 'given up publicly before the whole parish'.[260] Elsewhere, a lengthy 'cursus honorum' opened the door to vestry membership for some humbler parishioners. There were many communal offices to fill, and the status of those who made the first step on the ladder did not differ dramatically from that of their late medieval predecessors. Independent initiative, however, was hampered by the fact that they were continually answerable to the parish elite and closely supervised by external authority. If at all, positions of real power were achieved only at an advanced age and after the candidates had proven their suitability.[261]

By the late sixteenth century, the trend towards oligarchical parish government had spread beyond London and provincial capitals: it was

---

[256] GL, MS 1311/1, f. 86, quoted in Archer, *Pursuit of Stability*, p. 70. The 'better sort' of Botolph Aldgate argued similarly that 'by reason of the ignorance and weakness of judgement ... of some parishioners' there had 'fallen out some unquietness and hindrance to good proceedings', so that they desired the appointment of 'xlviij [of the most sufficient men] ... continually to be vestrymen': Gibson (ed.), *Codex*, p. 1476. The same phraseology appeared in the petition of Botolph Aldersgate in 1605 (Staples, *Notes on St Botolph*, p. 13), where the gentry had secured a fixed quota on the vestry (Archer, *Pursuit of Stability*, p. 50).

[257] Nicholls and Taylor, *Bristol Past*, p. 93; Andrew Hubbard CWA, 1526–7.

[258] Taylor (ed.), 'St Thomas', 196 (Bristol); Gibson (ed.), *Codex*, p. 1477.

[259] Ashburton CWA, p. 193; Taylor (ed.), 'St Thomas', 194.

[260] Griffith, *Poor Rates*, pp. 68ff (1635). Other places also continued to refer particular items to a wider parish assembly (Archer, *Pursuit of Stability*, p. 69, or Ashburton CWA, p. 194), but institutionalized communal supervision was lost.

[261] Examples for a 'cursus honorum' in Chester (Alldridge, 'Chester parishes', pp. 105ff), Coventry (Phythian-Adams, *Desolation of a City*, p. 169) and London (Archer, *Pursuit of Stability*, pp. 63ff).

practised for instance at Lambeth, Southwark,[262] Prescot, or Pittington. The Prescot 'eight men' monopolized the crucial areas of rate assessments, audits, and elections, although they were elected 'by the major part' of a parish assembly. Even so, the gentry kept a close eye on this Lancashire community, and there was no explicit attendance requirement for all parishioners.[263] Occasionally, there was no takeover by local elites, but quite simply a surrender of communal rights out of exhaustion or complacency: the select vestry at Pittington was set up by a decision of the whole parish which agreed in 1584 to 'electe and chuse out of the same [parish] xij men to order and define all common causes pertaininge to the churche, as shall appertaine to the profit & commoditie of the same, without molestation or troublinge of the rest of the comon people'.[264] But not all English parish communities went down this road. Bethersden still recorded 'new churche wardens chosen by the holl consent of the holl paryshe' in the mid-1560s, and the best chances for the preservation of broad participation seem to have existed in parishes – such as Mildenhall in Suffolk – which ran their secular business on a communal basis, too.[265] Other smaller market towns or rural places also continued to exercise communal supervision through a meeting attended by an unspecified number of parishioners, but even they were not immune to the trends of increasing compulsion and external interference.[266]

By 1600, the Reformation, socio-economic developments, and an increasing self-consciousness of local elites had combined to reinforce a

---

[262] Drew (ed.), *Lambeth CWA*, pp. ix, xiii; Archer, *Pursuit of Stability*, pp. 71ff (Southwark).

[263] Bailey, 'CWA of Prescot', 176–9. Both Bailey and Haigh, *Lancashire*, p. 18, interpret the decree which established the eight men (1555) as the formal institutionalization of gentry control. For a contrasting view see Craig, 'Prescot', p. 55.

[264] M. Barmby (ed.), *CWA of Pittington* (Durham, 1888), pp. 12–13; the parishioners of St Bartholomew Exchange and St Margaret Lothbury in London seem to have had the opportunity to attend their vestry, but there were rarely more than 20 of them present: Archer, *Pursuit of Stability*, pp. 69–70.

[265] Mercer (ed.), *CWA at Betrysden*, p. 131 (1564–5); Craig, 'Reformation, politics, and polemics', p. 47. Twenty-four elected yeomen claimed jurisdiction over the whole of the parish of Mildenhall.

[266] At Northill in the archdeaconry of Bedford audits were conducted 'vigorously', and the CWA record bi-annual visitations: Farmiloe and Nixseaman (eds), *Elizabethan CWA*, pp. xii, 27. The 'increase of governance' plays an important part in the complex causality of social change in early modern local communities: K. Wrightson, 'The politics of the parish' in P. Griffith et al. (eds.), *The Experience of Authority in Early Modern England* (Basingstoke, forthcoming).

polarization in parochial life which had always existed, but been restrained in late medieval communities. With the loss of spiritual motives for parish harmony, increasing financial and outside pressures allowed the 'more honest' members of the community to monopolize decisions ever more clearly. In spite of unchanged boundaries and familiar institutional organization, Elizabethan parishioners must have had a strong sense of discontinuity about local ecclesiastical life.

Conclusion

Churchwardens' accounts have played an important part in the recent debate on the English Reformation, but the parish and its main source deserve to be studied in their own right. This book proposes a more comprehensive and less pronouncedly religious approach to the great wealth of surviving evidence. It attempts to provide a general rather than localized survey for the years between 1400 and 1560, and an account in which ecclesiastical matters are discussed alongside three more neglected themes: the structure, development, and dynamics of communal organization, the links between parish finance and socio-economic circumstances, and the importance of 'secular' aspects in everyday parochial life. The empirical core of the argument consists of a sample of ten case studies (selected to represent a wide range of different contexts) and supplementary evidence from a great number of other local communities. The subject matter suggested a somewhat impersonal and quantitative approach, but what did it all mean to the parishioners themselves? This summary cannot hope to cover the enormous range of different individual experiences, but it can point to the most important trends at the transitional stage between the medieval and early modern periods.

By the time the analysis opens (the evidence is too scarce to allow comparative scrutiny before the fifteenth century), both the parochial network and the main lay duties were firmly established. The canonical responsibilities about the church fabric and the provision of ornaments provided an important starting-point for mutual cooperation, but the 'shaping of the community' to its fully developed state was an achievement of the parishioners themselves. More and more parochial expenditure was absorbed by 'voluntary' activities without 'official' encouragement, and the coordination of these initiatives required more than ad-hoc organization. A particularly important incentive was the need to protect the growing number of landed bequests from clerical encroachments. From the late thirteenth century, churchwardens started to take care of internal parish affairs and to represent the parishioners to the outside world. Appointed in a customary way by their communities, officers from a broad range of backgrounds (but rarely from the very lowest or highest social groups) served terms of one or two years, after which they accounted to the parish's sovereign institution, an assembly of all householders. Many places gradually developed an executive body or council, but pre-Reformation communal government was no monopoly of social elites and offered the humbler members of society an unusual degree of influence and responsibility.

Informally, and by exploitation of legal devices such as enfeoffment to use, the community acquired quasi-corporate status and the capacity to legislate on important common concerns, to tax its members, and to arbitrate in their disputes. Quite in contrast to the conventional image of the waning of the Middle Ages, there is little sign of sterility or decline until about the third decade of the sixteenth century. Many communities recorded a dramatic increase in resources and a creative elaboration of their festive and ceremonial calendar up to the very eve of the Reformation. The size of churchwardens' income was astonishing and parishioners normally paid more to them than either to the royal Exchequer or their incumbent, even though tithes, customary dues, and investment in subparochial institutions are all not covered by churchwardens' accounts. There are few indications of religious discontent: this was the great age of parish church rebuilding, and expenditure on worship, additional clergy, and ornamentation ran at consistently impressive levels. And yet, the parish had become much more than an ecclesiastical unit, and a narrowly religious perspective will fail to do it justice. Parishioners played an active part in subsidy collections, military provision, or municipal government, and had expanded into public works and property management out of their own initiative. Directly or indirectly, the parish also served educational and poor relief purposes. In many places, it must have strengthened or superseded the existing secular community, and by the Tudor age it was the logical local government unit. The general trends in parish finance can be more easily linked to the socio-economic climate than religious developments: generous investment and conspicuous consumption occurred in times of plenty (for the large majority of the common people), and declining enthusiasm marked a period when inflation and population pressures had turned the tables.

The parishioners' experience depended heavily on the social context of their community. Wealthy city-centre locations and prosperous rural areas raised much more from their members than large, market-town based parishes. For various reasons, metropolitan communities developed financial regimes which relied more heavily on the 'dead' (particularly their endowments, but also investment for funerals and post-obit provision), while fundraising in other social contexts depended predominantly on active contributions by the 'living'. Churchwardens in the former were increasingly absorbed by estate management, in the latter they had to organize a continuous sequence of events to make ends meet. 'Dead'-orientated communities were characterized by a more commemorative emphasis, while 'living' regimes involved the parishioners in a series of rather merrier activities (church ales). Throughout the period and sometimes successfully, badly provided for villages attempted to bring the ecclesiastical network in line with their needs and convenience. If they failed to found new parishes, they often used chapels, gilds, or chantries to improve their pastoral services. Both here and in other contexts, such subparochial institutions catered for specific groups and additional religious needs, but they cooperated with the parish and posed no fundamental challenge to its towering position in local ecclesiastical life.

The various Tudor Reformations were the most obvious and best-documented changes affecting the parish in the mid-sixteenth century. The records leave no doubt of their disruptive and lasting influence, but the overall impact was quite complex. By 1600, no doubt, parish government and financial regimes had changed fundamentally, but there were continuities as well as discontinuities, winners as well as losers. The trend towards a secular use of the parish continued, albeit on a statutory basis and with increased outside supervision. The 'voluntary' dimension of parochial budgets, however, declined, and the subparochial level of chantries and fraternities disappeared. 'Lay control' was pushed to unprecedented levels, even though the beneficiaries were social elites rather than local communities. The gentry in particular increased their estates (by the purchase of former ecclesiastical property) and political power (advowsons, supervision of petty officers), while the crown had managed to subject the Church and to turn the parish into a local government unit. The casualties included the many 'good catholyke' people, the rich pre-Reformation ritual and ceremonial life, and the humbler householders who found it increasingly difficult to make themselves heard in now rather more oligarchical communities. Socio-economic change and the loss of spiritual incentives for parish harmony had reinforced existing internal polarization. There was, however, no full-scale spoliation of communal property. Many parishes prevented confiscation by selling their religious assets, and a surprising amount of lands and rents survived into the early modern period, in spite of their often clearly 'superstitious' origins. The basic income regimes proved quite resilient, with both living and dead orientated regimes retaining their main characteristics after the first Reformation impact.

Comparisons with Continental parish life are complicated by the vagaries of source survival. The English Church is unusually well documented both on the episcopal and parochial level, while impressions of everyday religious life elsewhere are often distorted by the prevalence of complaints literature or litigation records. Still, the canonical guidelines for parochial organization, the fossilization of ecclesiastical boundaries, and the problems of appropriations and clerical non-residence were, in various degrees, universal phenomena. Much depended on the respective secular framework. In areas with a strong hierarchy of lordship such as England, the potential for local Church control was limited, and the acquisition of patronage or tithes normally beyond the community's reach. If secular needs could be catered for by well-established corporate towns and villages, as in many parts of Central Europe, parishioners had fewer incentives to expand outside the ecclesiastical field. Wherever we look, however, there is evidence for substantial investment in local religious provision (the great age of parish church rebuilding was no English peculiarity), for a widespread belief in official sacramental teachings, for increasing lay control, for overlaps between secular and ecclesiastical activities, and a relatively broadly based autonomous parish government. Social differences and conflicting individual priorities ensured that parish life was never entirely 'harmonious', but the corporate nature of late medieval worship and the existence of common interests provided sufficient grounds to sustain communal institutions. The sixteenth century redefined all these parameters. Religious innovations, increasing outside interference, and the bureaucratization of parish government were experienced all across the Continent. For local society in England and elsewhere, the 'Reformation' of the parish must have come as a mixed blessing.

Epilogue: The Communalization of Late Medieval Society

There can be little doubt that communal action played an important part in medieval Europe. It emerged early and shaped a range of often overlapping territorial units such as villages, towns, and parishes.[1] Each provided a framework for the solution of problems which affected all members of local society, but transcended their individual powers. The trend intensified during the later Middle Ages, both in town and countryside. Out of the diversity of motives behind the peasant rising of 1381 'emerged ideas and actions hostile not just to serfdom and servile tenures, but also to the very existence of lordship, championing the realizable goal of independent and self-governing village communities'. The rebellion failed, of course, and the development of local elites soon started to put strains on the English vill, but the rise of the parish provided a strong alternative focus of communal activities.[2] For Central Europe with its network of corporate towns and villages, the term 'communalism' is now used alongside 'feudalism' to describe social reality between 1200 and 1800. This is not the place to elaborate on a controversial debate, but the concept is based on the observation that – from the thirteenth century – peasants and townspeople created similar communal structures to deal with their local affairs. Both developed assemblies with powers of legislation and jurisdiction, both chose office holders by means of elections, and both shared a set of values intended to further the 'common good'. 'Communalism' emphasizes the importance of horizontal ties in an age which is too often seen through the feudal and vertical perspective of lordship and subordination.[3] In its

---

[1] For a comparative discussion of these units between 900 and 1300 see Reynolds, *Kingdoms and Communities*.

[2] C. Dyer, 'The social and economic background to the rural revolt of 1381' in R. Hilton and T. Aston (eds), *The English Rising of 1381* (Cambridge, 1984), p. 42 (quote), and 'Power and conflict', p. 29 (the activities of churchwardens reinforced social ties). The idea is elaborated in his 'English medieval village'. The increasing autonomy of English towns is reflected in the growing amount of incorporations: Horrox, 'Urban patronage', p. 146.

[3] Peter Blickle proposed the concept in 1981 (the latest summary in his 'Kommunalismus'); see A. Holenstein, B. Kümin, and A. Würgler, 'Diskussionsbericht' in P. Blickle (ed.), *Landgemeinde und Stadtgemeinde in Mitteleuropa* (Munich, 1991), pp. 489–505, and R. Scribner, 'Communalism: universal category or ideological construct?', *Historical Journal*, 37 (1994), 199–207, for a summary of the main issues in the current debate.

present form, the concept is inextricably linked to the socio-economic circumstances of Central Europe,[4] but the study of other areas suggests that it contains elements of wider geographical and thematic significance. Antony Black, for instance, has argued 'that communalism is woven into the history of democracy ... as inextricably as are individual liberty and individual equality', and communal action can be found in Mediterranean villages as well as the English parish.[5] The common characteristics of the phenomenon could perhaps be subsumed under the heading of 'communalization' and be defined as a combination of:

1. A set of autonomously developed institutions to meet the specific needs of a territorial unit in town or countryside;
2. A government structure based on a sovereign assembly of householders with powers of legislation, taxation, and election of officials;
3. A tendency to expand into other areas of local concern; and
4. A system of shared values.

On the basis of the available evidence, it would appear that 'communalization' could have ecclesiastical as well as socio-economic roots. In the south-western corner of the Holy Roman empire, local political communities emerged in response to changing secular circumstances and gradually expanded on to the ecclesiastical field.[6] In England, on the other hand, religious initiative led to the development of parish institutions which tended to assume worldly responsibilities and local government duties. Here, the shared set of values included a spiritual dimension from the start,[7] while activities on the continent were motivated by a wish to supplement the more mundane 'common good' ideology of the local political community with similar 'sacral attributes'.[8]

---

[4] The term does not apply to all collective associations, but specifically to territorial *Gemeinden* with state functions, that is a degree of administrative and legal self-government, powers of enforcement over its members, and a representative function towards the outside world: P. Bierbrauer, 'Der Aufstieg der Gemeinde' in P. Blickle and J. Kunisch (eds), *Kommunalisierung und Christianisierung* (Berlin, 1989), pp. 30–1. The crucial economic factor in its development was the lasting change from demesne farming to independent peasant holdings: Blickle, 'Kommunalismus', pp. 22–3.

[5] I am grateful to Antony Black for allowing me to read his forthcoming 'Communal democracy and its history' (the quote on manuscript, p. 3); for Spain see Christian, *Local Religion*, p. 56.

[6] Fuhrmann, 'Kirche im Dorf', and von Rütte, 'Religionspraxis der Bauern', p. 40 (expansion in the rural context); K. Körber, *Die kirchenrechtliche Theorie von der Verwaltung und Verwendung der Kirchengüter* (Halle, 1912), p. 19, Schröcker, *Kirchenpflegschaft*, p. 107, and Frölich, 'Altarpfründen', 539 (urban context).

[7] Namely the belief in the efficacy of reciprocal intercession and good works.

[8] Blickle, 'Communal Reformation', 224.

Clearly, the leading role fell to the stronger of the two units, but both combined to reinforce communal identity and strove to control as much of their daily affairs as possible.[9]

Such local initiative had a considerable innovative potential. New social challenges such as poor relief became an issue for English parishioners long before parliament addressed the problem in 1495.[10] The management of landed property, the keeping of records, and the administration of large monetary resources all contributed to a degree of sophistication not normally associated with the humbler elements of society. The conventional concentration on central government, seigneurial classes, and intellectual movements cannot but miss out on other important factors in the historical process. Even as momentous a change as the Reformation may have owed as much to structural developments on the lowest ecclesiastical level as to theological argument, royal initiative, and doctrinal discontent:

> The activities of churchwardens, and lay control over much church wealth ... would foster ideas of lay control over the church in a wider sense. If this seemed increasingly 'natural', then attempts to extend it would not face strong lay opposition. As the churchwardens and others were responsible for many spiritualities, it was perhaps not unreasonable for the king to seek similar control over the church as a whole. The change in mental perspectives may be one of the most important reasons for the lack of effective opposition to Henry VIII's Reformation, when it came.[11]

Pushing the argument further, Continental historians have pointed out that the ecclesiology of the early reformers may have had similar late medieval roots. Huldrych Zwingli, for instance, came from the valley of Toggenburg, an area with strong communal traditions.[12] 'The idea that parishes should be empowered to elect their pastors and to decide questions of doctrine remained undisputed among the majority of reformers ... at least until the "Communal Reformation" turned into the "Revolution of the Common Man"' [in 1525].[13] In addition, the

---

[9] The parish compensated for the weakness of rural communities in France (R. Ganghofer, 'Rapport général' in *Communautés rurales*, pp. 48ff) and England (Hatschek, *Verfassungsgeschichte*, p. 261), while there was less need for such secular activities in Central Europe. English towns, however, could achieve a degree of control over ecclesiastical affairs which resembled that of imperial free cities: see for example Pape, *Newcastle-under-Lyme*, or Wood-Legh, *Perpetual Chantries*, pp. 165ff (York, Bristol).

[10] McIntosh, 'Local change', 228–9.

[11] Swanson, *Church and Society*, p. 250; for the increase of lay control on other levels of society: Harper-Bill, *Pre-Reformation Church*, pp. 9ff, and Thompson, 'Habendum et tenendum', pp. 232ff.

[12] Von Rütte, 'Religionspraxis der Bauern', pp. 41–2.

[13] Blickle, 'Communal Reformation', 227.

Zwinglian view of the Eucharist can be interpreted as a 'sacrament of communalism', as an oath 'by which the believer confessed himself publicly and bindingly to a *Gemeinde* that had committed itself to Christ, its Lord'; in other words, an engagement which created and sealed a sworn union not unlike the civic community.[14]

The precise relationship between communalism and Protestantism, however, is complex and controversial.[15] The English example suggests that the reality of the reformed Church brought disruption and interference rather than increased local autonomy. Furthermore, communal ecclesiastical structures were perfectly compatible with a traditional religious framework: canonists may have had their reservations, but the Catholic emphasis on corporate worship and reciprocal intercession provided natural incentives. Where sixteenth-century people had a genuine religious choice, the decision could go either way.[16] Doctrinal preference, after all, was but one of many variables in the complex equation to determine what was best for the local community. In the regions affected by the German Peasants' War, rampant anticlericalism and an explosive socio-economic situation made the Reformation look like an attractive revolutionary programme. In England, however, neither of these factors applied, and popular attitudes were more ambiguous.[17] The loss of so many popular traditional practices was clearly resented, but the prospect of increased lay control and parochial responsibilities may have appeared as a redeeming feature of the Reformation, even though – with hindsight – such hopes were not well-founded.

The appropriation of the parish by the Tudor state curtailed 'ecclesiastical communalism' in much the same way as German princes defused the potential of its 'socio-economic' variety. In England, though, the concept was to reemerge in the seventeenth century, and – characteristically for the period – not out of the parochial mainstream, but in the programme of a radical sectarian group. In protest against the erosion of local powers, the Levellers called for the parishioners' right to

---

[14] H. R. Schmidt, 'Die Häretisierung des Zwinglianismus im Reich seit 1525' in P. Blickle (ed.), *Zugänge zur bäuerlichen Reformation* (Zurich, 1987), pp. 230, 235.

[15] It forms an important link in Blickle's *Gemeindereformation* (Munich, 1985). For an insight into the debate on the concept of communal Reformation see his 'Wie begründet ist die Kritik an der "Gemeindereformation"?' in H. Guggisberg and G. Krodel (eds), *Die Reformation in Deutschland und Europa* (Gütersloh, 1993), pp. 159–73, and the critical questions in T. Scott, 'The Communal Reformation between town and country', ibid., pp. 175–92.

[16] Central Switzerland, a communal stronghold, stayed firmly Catholic: Guggisberg, 'The problem of failure'; Scott, 'Communal Reformation', p. 192.

[17] Blickle, *Die Revolution von 1525*; Clark and Slack, *English Towns*, p. 150 (less severe social tensions in England).

choose their ministers and to determine clerical income. Reform would not have stopped there, but was meant as 'the foundation for democracy not only in the church but also in the state'.[18] In this ideal world, the 'people' were to elect all public officers, approve all taxes, and render central executives and legislative bodies all but superfluous. As if to confirm the importance of a European perspective, Cromwell suspected that the Levellers 'wanted to break up England into a federation of self-governing cantons like Switzerland'.[19] Whatever the actual model, he certainly realized that the power of local communities was an important issue of his time, and one – we might add – which deserves its place in the analysis of any historical period.

---

[18] B. Manning, *The English People and the English Revolution* (2nd edn, London, 1991), p. 394. For an exploration of the communal roots of the Leveller movement see my 'Gemeinde und Revolution' in P. Blickle (ed.), *Gemeinde und Staat in Europa* (forthcoming).

[19] Manning, *English People*, pp. 410–11.

An alphabetical list of English churchwardens' accounts
c. 1300–1547

For all practical purposes, the most authoritative compilation is now Hutton, *Merry England*, pp. 263–93. This list is printed mainly for reference purposes and to substantiate the summary remarks on source survival made in Chapter 3.1. It has emerged in a pragmatic fashion and should be treated accordingly. Most discrepancies to the appendix of *Merry England* (accounted for by brief references) result from the less stringent definitions adopted for this study, but they do not affect the overall geographical and chronological pattern. Each entry lists locality, church dedication (where necessary), county, and the year of the first surviving evidence.

Amersham	Bucks.	1529	Bletchingley	Surrey	1546
Andover[1]	Hants.	1470	Bodmin[3]	Cornwall	1469
Antony	Cornwall	1538	Bolney	Sussex	1536
Arlington	Sussex	1455	Boxford	Suffolk	1530
Ashburton	Devon	1479	Braintree[4]	Essex	1522
Ashstead[2]	Surrey	1547	Bramley	Hants.	1523
Ashurst	Sussex	1522	Brede	Sussex	1546
			Brenzett	Kent	1546
Badsey	Worcs.	1525	Bridgwater	Somerset	1318
Baldock	Herts.	1540	Brightwalton	Berks.	1481
Banwell	Somerset	1515	Bristol		
Bardwell	Suffolk	1524	All Saints[5]	Bristol	1406
Bassingbourn	Cambs.	1497	Christ Church	Bristol	1531
Bath	Somerset	1349	Ewen	Bristol	1454
Bethersden	Kent	1515	John Baptist	Bristol	1532
Billingshurst	Sussex	1520	Nicholas	Bristol	1520
Bp's Stortford	Herts.	1431	Thomas	Bristol	1544

[1] Williams (ed.), *CWA of Hampshire*, pp. 1–9.

[2] *Surrey Archaeological Collections* 24 (1911), 2–3.

[3] Edited in *Camden Society Miscellany* 7, (1874).

[4] *East Anglian* 3 (1869), 78.

[5] BRO, P/AS/ChW/1.

Broadhempston	Devon	1517
Broomfield	Essex	1540
Brundish	Suffolk	1475
Bungay, Mary	Suffolk	1523
Calne	Wilts.	1527
Camborne	Cornwall	1538
Cambridge		
Great St Mary	Cambs.	1504
Holy Trinity	Cambs.	1504
Canterbury		
Andrew	Kent	1485
Dunstan	Kent	1484
Chagford	Devon	1480
Chedzoy[6]	Somerset	1508
Chester		
Holy Trinity	Cheshire	1532
Mary Hill	Cheshire	1536
Cheswardine	Shrops.	1544
Chevington[7]	Suffolk	1532
Clifton	Beds.	1543
Coventry[8]	Warw.	1452
Cowfold	Sussex	1460
Cranbrook	Kent	1509
Cratfield	Suffolk	1490
Crondall	Hants.	1543
Croscombe	Somerset	1474
Culworth	Northants.	1531
Dartington	Devon	1484
Dartmouth	Devon	1430
Dennington	Suffolk	1539
Denton	Norfolk	1507
Derby, All Saints	Derbys.	1465
Devizes, Mary	Wilts.	1499
Dover, Mary	Kent	1536
East Dereham	Norfolk	1413

Ecclesfield	Yorks.	1524
Ellingham	Hants.	1543
Exeter		
Holy Trinity	Devon	1415
John's Bow	Devon	1412
Mary Steps	Devon	1410
Petrock	Devon	1425
Folkestone[9]	Kent	1487
Fordwich[10]	Kent	1509
Glastonbury, John	Somerset	1366
Gloucester, Michael	Glos.	1545
Goathurst	Somerset	1545
Great Dunmow	Essex	1526
Gt Hallingbury	Essex	1526
Great Salkeld	Cumb.	1547
Gt Witchingham	Norfolk	1528
Great Yarmouth	Norfolk	1465
Grimsby, Mary	Lincs.	1411
Hadleigh[11]	Suffolk	1535
Hagworthing-ham[12]	Lincs.	1526
Halesowen	Worcs.	1487
Halse	Somerset	1540
Hawkhurst	Kent	1547
Hedon		
Augustine	Yorks.	1371
James	Yorks.	1350
Nicholas	Yorks.	1379
Henley	Oxon.	1521
Heybridge[13]	Essex	1508
Holywell	Hunts.	1547
Horham	Suffolk	1531

---

[6] French, 'Local identity', p. 39.
[7] Cambridge University Library, MSS Hangrave Hall, 17 (1).
[8] Blair, CWA, p. 5.
[9] Canterbury Cathedral Archives.
[10] Archaeologia Cantiana 18 (1889), 93.
[11] Among the town records in the Guildhall.
[12] Lincs. Notes and Queries 1 (1888–9), 7.
[13] Philips, 'List', 338.

Horley	Surrey	1507
Hythe	Kent	1412
Ilminster	Somerset	1543
Ingoldmells	Lincs.	1542
Kingston/Th.	Surrey	1497
Kirkby Stephen	Westm.	1485
Kirton-in-Lindsey[14]	Lincs.	1484
Lambeth, Mary	Surrey	1504
Launceston	Cornwall	1405
Leicester[15]		
Margaret	Leics.	1498
Martin	Leics.	1544
Mary Castro	Leics.	1490
Leverington	Cambs.	1494
Leverton	Lincs.	1492
Lewes		
Andrew	Sussex	1542
Andrew & Michael	Sussex	1546
London		
All Hall. Stain.	London	1491
All Hall. Wall	London	1455
Alphage Wall	London	1527
Andr. Holborn	London	1547
Andrew Hubb.	London	1454
Bot. Alders.	London	1466
Bot. Aldgate	London	1547
Christch. N. G.	London	1546
Dunstan East	London	1494
Dunstan West	London	1516
Lawrence P.	London	1530
Marg. Moses	London	1547
Marg. Patt.	London	1506
Martin Orgar	London	1471

Martin Outw.	London	1509
Mary M. Milk	London	1518
Mary Wool.	London	1539
Mary-at-Hill	London	1420
Matt. Friday	London	1547
Michael Corn.	London	1456
Mich. Querne	London	1514
Nich. Olave[16]	London	1529
Nich. Shamb.	London	1452
Peter Westch.	London	1441
Stephen Cole.	London	1486
Stephen Walb.	London	1474
Long Melford	Suffolk	1547
Long Sutton	Lincs.	1543
Louth, James	Lincs.	1500
Ludlow	Shrops.	1469
Lydd[17]	Kent	1524
Lydeard St L.[18]	Somerset	1524
March[19]	Cambs.	1542
Marston	Oxon.	1529
Masham	Yorks.	1542
Melton Mowbray[20]	Leics.	1547
Metfield	Suffolk	1486
Mickfield	Suffolk	1538
Mildenhall	Suffolk	1446
Morebath	Devon	1520
Nettlecombe	Somerset	1507
New Windsor	Berks.	1531
North Curry[21]	Somerset	1443
North Elmham	Norfolk	1538

[14] *Proceedings of the Society of Antiquaries*, 2nd Series **2** (1861–4), 383–9.
[15] Blair, *CWA*, p. 10.
[16] J. Malcolm (ed.), *Londinium Redivivum* (1807), iv. 548–51.
[17] Williams (ed.), *CWA of Hampshire*, p. lxvi.
[18] French, 'Local identity', p. 39.
[19] Imperfect transcript in County Record Office.
[20] *Leics. Architectural & Archaeological Society Transactions* **3** (1872), 180–206.
[21] French, 'Local identity', p. 39.

Nt Petherwin	Devon	1493
Okehampton	Devon	1543
Oxford		
Aldate	Oxon.	1440
Martin	Oxon.	1544
Mary Magd.	Oxon.	1404
Mary Virgin	Oxon.	1509
Michael	Oxon.	1404
Peter East	Oxon.	1440
Peterborough	Northants.	1467
Pilton	Somerset	1498
Plymouth, And.	Devon	1483
Poughill	Cornwall	1525
Prescot	Lancs.	1523
Rainham[22]	Kent	1517
Ramsey	Hunts.	1511
Reading		
Giles	Berks.	1518
Lawrence	Berks.	1432
Ripon	Yorks.	1354
Rotherfield	Sussex	1509
Rye	Sussex	1546
Saffron Walden	Essex	1439
St Breock	Cornwall	1529
Salisbury		
Edmund	Wilts.	1443
Thomas	Wilts.	1545
Sandwich[23]	Kent	1444
Sherborne	Dorset	1514
Shere[24]	Surrey	1502
Sheriff Hutton	Yorks.	1537
Shipdam	Norfolk	1511

Smarden	Kent	1536
Snettisham	Norfolk	1468
Solihull[25]	Warw.	1444
South Tawton	Devon	1524
Southwark,	Surrey	1444
Margaret		
Spelsbury	Oxon.	1526
Stafford	Staffs.	1528
Stanford[26]	Lincs.	1427
Steeple Ashton	Wilts.	1542
Steyning	Sussex	1519
Stogursey	Somerset	1502
Stoke Charity	Hants.	1541
Stoke Edith	Heref.	1532
Stratton	Cornwall	1512
Sutterton	Lincs.	1483
Swaffham	Norfolk	1505
Tavistock	Devon	1392
Thame	Oxon.	1442
Tilney	Norfolk	1443
Tintinhull	Somerset	1434
Trull[27]	Somerset	1524
Walberswick	Suffolk	1450
Walsall	Staffs.	1462
Waltham Abbey	Essex	1542
Wanborough[28]	Wilts.	1535
Wandsworth	Surrey	1545
Warwick[29]		
Mary	Warw.	1545
Nicholas	Warw.	1547
Wells[30], Cuth.	Somerset	1377

---

[22] *Archaeologia Cantiana* **15** (1882), 333.
[23] J. A. Ford (paper at the Institute of Historical Research, London, 31 May 1990).
[24] Williams (ed.), *CWA of Hampshire*, p. lxv.

[25] Ibid., p. lxiv.
[26] F. Peck (ed.), *Academia tertia Anglicana* (1727), lib. xiv, pp. 4–5.
[27] French, 'Local identity', p. 39.
[28] A. Brown, 'Lay piety', p. 21.
[29] In corporation accounts: *Journal of the Archaeological Association* NS **19** (1913), 265ff.
[30] Totals only in corporation records: French, 'Local identity', p. 39.

West Tarring	Sussex	1515	Worcester			
Westminster			Helen	Worcs.	1519	
Margaret	Middlesex	1460	Michael Bed.	Worcs.	1539	
Martin i-t-F.	Middlesex	1525	Worfield	Shrops.	1500	
Weyhill[31]	Hants.	1543	Worksop	Notts.	1546	
Wigtoft	Lincs.	1484	Worth	Sussex	1528	
Wimborne Min.	Dorset	1404	Wye[33]	Kent	1513	
Wing	Bucks.	1527	Wymondham	Norfolk	1544	
Winkfield[32]	Berks.	1521				
Winkleigh	Devon	1513	Yatton	Somerset	1445	
Winterslow	Wilts.	1542	Yeovil[34]	Somerset	1457	
Woodbury	Devon	1538	York, Mich. S.	Yorks.	1518	
Woodland	Devon	1527	Yoxall	Staffs.	1541	

[31] Williams (ed.), *CWA of Hampshire*, pp. 156–63.

[32] Johnston, 'Berkshire', p. 337.

[33] J. A. Ford (paper at the Institute of Historical Research, London, 31 May 1990).

[34] French, 'Local identity', p. 39.

Categories and definitions used in the figures and tables

The currency unit throughout is old pence. The purpose of the figures and tables is not to create an illusion of precision or mathematical accuracy for a source which can be incomplete and fragmentary, but to illustrate the argument put forward in the text.

Tables

All averages refer to a one-year period, and longer accounts have been split up accordingly. In Appendix 3, 'total' is the fresh calculation made of all individual items, 'wardens' total' the figure based on the officers' own entries. 'Number' lists the amount of times a category appears in the respective set (and in the case of 'total' gives the overall number of years analysed), 'per cent' expresses the average as a percentage of the 'total'. All tables marked (a) yield the overall picture, those styled (b) the respective yearly averages and percentages for the 'pre-Reformation' and 'post-Reformation' sources and the four periods 'first ever accounts', 'last pre-Reformation years', 'Edward VI', and 'Mary'. All averages (except those less than one) have been rounded to the nearest unit, which accounts for any discrepancies between 'totals' and the addition of all individual categories. Rarely (at Yatton, Pre-Reformation Andrew Hubbard, and Prescot) only the income or only the expenditure of a particular account has survived. In such cases, the average balance does not equal the subtraction of the average expenditure from the average income listed in the table. It is sometimes difficult to judge whether an account is incomplete, that is whether an item is missing, or whether indeed nothing was spent for the purpose. As a rule, whenever a year has been entered on the database, those categories which did not appear were given the value '0'. It is therefore possible that some averages are slightly too low. Dates refer to the years the accounts opened (that is 1476–7 = 1476).

Categories of income

The income has been divided into the following categories (listed with the respective abbreviations). Not all occur in every parish, and the tables include only financially significant categories.

Balance (Bal/Ba)	cash balance carried forward from last account and arrears due to the wardens
Collections (Coll/C)	for lights and customary purposes on various occasions, and extraordinary collections for special projects
Townships	regular contributions from hamlets and townships (Halesowen)
Waxsilver (Wax/W)	customary and often fixed payments for church wax and lights
Rates (Ra)	agreed sums raised by fixed portions from individuals or townships (Prescot)
Church box	income from unspecified 'boxes' (Prescot)
Pews	fees for the use of certain seats or pews in the church
Ales (A)	profit from church ales (at Boxford included in the category 'Entertainments', together with plays and May games)
Dancing	surplus from dancing entertainments (St Ewen's)
May money	May day games and entertainments (Peterborough)
Stalls	fees for market stalls in churchyards or at the church gate on certain days
Sales (S)	sale of church property, ornaments, raw material, surplus stocks, bequests
Hire	hiring out of players' costumes and church goods for events other than burials and obits
Church house	renting out of church house and appurtenances for ales and other social occasions
Money-lending (Lend/L)	interest for or repayment of loans given to clergy, towns, and parishioners
Fines	for non-attendance at the churchwardens' audit day (Botolph Aldersgate)
Rent (Re)	revenue from lands, houses, gardens, tenements and so on in possession of the parish
Lifestock	hiring out of animals such as sheep or cows (Halesowen, Yatton)
Burial rites (Bur)	fees for burial in the church and hiring of torches and ornaments for funerals and obits
Gilds	contributions from fraternities for various purposes

Relics	offerings to relics kept by the parish (Halesowen)
Gifts	bequests by living and past parishioners (in money or in kind)
Debt (D)	payment of arrears and debts (except those explicitly deriving from loans)
Various	unspecified and summary entries which cannot be placed elsewhere

Categories of expenditure

Building (Fab)	all building/repair costs (including labour) for the fabric (walls, roof, tower, seats)
Bells (Be)	purchase of new and maintenance of existing bells (including spare parts and labour)
Clock (Cl)	material and labour invested in parish clocks
Churchyard (Yar)	anything spent in or for the churchyard (wall, gate, trees, cross)
Candles/Wax	costs of wax and oil for candles, the paschal, and lighting in the church
Ceremonial life (Cer)	expenses for ceremonies: processions, Corpus Christi, watching the sepulchre
Social life	maintenance and purchase of players' costumes; organization of parish events
Priests, Clerks (Pr)	payments to the clerk(s) and any clergymen in higher orders active in the parish
Ornaments (Orn)	any costs incurred for ceremonial items (altars, images, vestments, stained glass, books, font, pax, pyx, candlesticks, hearse cloths, washing of church clothes and so on)
Obits (Ob)	payments for anniversaries of past parishioners and those attending them (clergy, mayors, clerk)
Organs (Org)	anything spent on repair or purchase of organs
Ringing	ringers on special occasions (knells for the dying, arrival of monarchs and bishops)
Cathedral	customary payments to the mother church of a diocese
Peter's pence	the annual contributions from English parishes to the Church in Rome (Boxford)
Accounting (Acc)	expenses for paper and scribes needed for bookkeeping; audit dinners
Wages (Wag)	wages of parish employees not (normally) in

	holy orders: scavengers, sextons, conducts
Crown (Cr)	any costs triggered by the crown: subsidies, armour, Reformation enforcement
Public works (Pub)	upkeep of bridges, streets, river banks, sluices and so on
Poor relief (Po)	payments to the poor, orphans, and widows (excluding those made at obits)
Legal costs (Leg)	expenses at various secular and ecclesiastical courts (fines, attorneys, visitations)
Landlord (Lan)	maintenance of and investment in landed property; quit rents; vacations
Potations	food and drink given to clergymen, town officers, or parishioners
Allowance	allowances to the wardens for debts (Botolph) or chantry deficits (All Saints)
Other ales	contributions made to ales held by other parishes (Yatton)
Various	unspecified expenditure or summary items

Figures

The units used in Figures 3.3(a), 3.6, 3.7, and the Appendices 4(i) and (ii) are percentage points (that is an addition of all the percentage points an item scores in the ten parishes during the relevant time span; maximum 1000, that is 100 per cent in every case study), in Figures 3.3(b)/(c), 4.1, 4.2, 5.1, 6.1, and 6.2 absolute figures or averages, in Figure 3.2, 3.4, 3.5, and 6.3 11-years moving averages (the y-value of any year expresses the average of the 11-year period of which this particular year forms the centre; this helps to reduce the distorting effect of extraordinary accounting periods).

The summarizing categories shown in the pie charts are composed of the following items:

| Living | active fundraising by the living parishioners: collections, townships, rates, stalls, ales, entertainments, sales, fines, money-lending, pews, dancing, may money, box, church house, waxsilver |
| Dead | revenue from property bequeathed by former parishioners or rites and institutions invoking |

prayers for the dead: rents, lifestock, burial
rites, relics, contributions from gilds, knells

The chequered section of the pies denotes the share of the 'dead', the lighter slice that of the 'living' (darker slice: various).

Fabric	building, churchyard, bells, clock
Worship	ornaments, lights/wax, organs, ceremonial life, priests (including clerks and conducts), obits, ringing, cathedral, Peter's pence, social life (religious plays)
Administration	wages, accounting, legal costs, crown, poor, public works, landlord, other ales
Compulsory	official ecclesiastical or secular duties: building, churchyard, bells, clerk, bread and wine (from 1548), ornaments, crown, accounting, cathedral/Peter's pence, visitations
Voluntary	clock, organ, lights, ceremonial life, priests, obits, social life, ringing, poor, public works (the Tudor legislation on the latter two areas only started at the very end of the period under scrutiny), landlord, legal costs, potations, other ales
Various	all items which cannot be placed in any of the above categories

Detailed income/expenditure analysis for the case studies in the sample

See Appendix 2 for notes and definitions; currency unit: old pence.

Andrew Hubbard, London: income analysis 1454–1560

(a) Overall

	First entry	Last entry	Average	Number	Per cent	Highest entry	Year	Lowest entry	Year
Balance	1454	1559	362	70	12.3	1892	1545	0.5	1485
Collections	1454	1559	1669	94	56.9	6688	1548	469	1465
Rates	1517	1517	5	1	0.2	470	1517	470	1517
Stalls	1457	1477	3	14	0.1	24	1469	3	1458
Sales	1454	1559	106	46	3.6	1894	1548	2	1458
Rents	1454	1559	481	90	16.4	1400	1465	12	1486
Burial rites	1454	1559	151	84	5.1	492	1457	12	1525
Gifts	1454	1555	118	54	4	1458	1521	3	1520
Debts	1472	1558	10	17	0.3	228	1507	9	1554
Various	1460	1559	30	29	1	401	1468	1	1535
Total	1454	1559	2934	94	100	10 409	1548	1169	1466
Wardens' total	1454	1559	2891	92	98.5	10 409	1548	1169	1466

(b) Development over time

	Pre-Refo 1454–1546	Per cent	Post-Refo 1546–1559	Per cent	First CWA 1454–1459	Per cent	Last pre-Refo CWA 1541–1546	Per cent	Edward 1546–1551	Per cent	Mary 1552–1558	Per cent
Balance	369	14.9	320	5.7	558	23.5	1210	28.9	436	5.8	261	7.6
Collections	1220	49.4	4238	75.8	617	26	1839	44	5331	71.3	2706	79
Rates	6	0.2	0	0	0	0	0	0	0	0	0	0
Stalls	3	0.1	0	0	2	0.1	0	0	0	0	0	0
Sales	48	1.9	435	7.8	107	4.5	818	19.6	796	10.7	25	0.7
Rents	533	21.6	185	3.3	800	33.7	152	3.6	367	4.9	48	1.4
Burial rites	146	5.9	174	3.1	190	8	151	3.6	255	3.4	127	3.7
Gifts	113	4.6	142	2.5	100	4.2			200	2.7	132	3.9
Debts	9	0.4	15	0.3	0	0	0	0	18	0.2	16	0.5
Various	21	0.9	84	1.5	0	0	13	0.3	72	1	111	3.2
Total	2469	100	5593	100	2374	100	4183	100	7473	100	3427	100
Wardens' total	2419	98	5593	100	2374	100	4183	100	7473	100	3427	100

Andrew Hubbard: expenses 1454–1560

(a) Overall

	First entry	Last entry	Average	Number	Per cent	Highest entry	Year	Lowest entry	Year
Building	1454	1559	312	96	12	2518	1522	5	1457
Bells	1454	1559	42	82	1.6	1328	1521	2	1504
Clock	1458	1559	20	63	0.8	102	1472	1	1480
Churchyard	1458	1558	13	59	0.5	245	1520	1	1491
Candles/Wax	1454	1559	192	97	7.4	383	1546	2	1550
Ceremonial life	1454	1559	46	96	1.8	141	1550	1	1454
Priests, clerks	1454	1559	984	97	37.9	4920	1548	15	1466
Ornaments	1454	1559	433	97	16.7	2776	1554	12	1517
Obits	1454	1547	110	81	4.2	206	1505	60	1504
Organs	1526	1559	12	25	0.5	326	1557	6	1533
Ringing	1454	1559	6	68	0.2	20	1528	2	1460
Accounting	1454	1559	25	88	1	146	1550	1	1528
Wages	1460	1559	74	86	2.8	696	1510	2	1465
Crown	1539	1559	81	16	3.1	1110	1548	19	1543
Public works	1454	1532	7	9	0.3	192	1454	2	1466
Poor relief	1545	1559	2	10	0.1	50	1546	5	1545
Legal costs	1466	1559	32	54	1.2	567	1468	1	1476
Landlord	1454	1559	112	83	4.3	430	1468	12	1552
Various	1460	1559	96	79	3.7	1476	1507	1	1509
Total	1454	1559	2597	97	100	10 806	1548	750	1517
Wardens' total	1454	1559	2602	97	100.2	10 806	1548	750	1517
Balance	1454	1559	388	97	14.9	2528	1517	–913	1522

(b) Development over time

	Pre-Refo 1454–1546	Per cent	Post-Refo 1546–1559	Per cent	First CWA 1454–1459	Per cent	Last pre-Refo CWA 1541–1546	Per cent	Edward 1546–1551	Per cent	Mary 1552–1558	Per cent
Building	242	11.5	727	13.2	418	21.4	174	6	1091	15	370	10.8
Bells	48	2.3	5	0.1	63	3.2	43	1.5	4	0.1	7	0.2
Clock	20	1	23	0.4	2	0.1	44	1.5	42	0.6	9	0.3
Churchyard	10	0.5	30	0.5	2	0.1	7	0.2	36	0.5	35	1
Candles/Wax	203	9.6	125	2.3	268	13.7	290	9.9	51	0.7	223	6.5
Ceremonial life	37	1.8	96	1.7	9	0.5	81	2.8	91	1.3	97	2.8
Priests, clerks	729	34.6	2491	45.2	628	32.2	1087	37.2	3832	52.6	733	21.5
Ornaments	381	18.1	737	13.4	259	13.3	663	22.7	303	4.2	1373	40.2
Obits	125	5.9	22	0.4	104	5.3	149	5.1	50	0.7	0	0
Organs	5	0.2	57	1	0	0	13	0.4	11	0.2	109	3.2
Ringing	6	0.3	6	0.1	6	0.3	11	0.4	7	0.1	5	0.1
Accounting	12	0.6	101	1.8	13	0.7	48	1.6	107	1.5	98	2.9
Wages	65	3.1	129	2.3	0	0	73	2.5	287	3.9	10	0.3
Crown	2	0.1	553	10	0	0	6	0.2	876	12	64	1.9
Public works	8	0.4	0	0	77	3.9	0	0	0	0	0	0
Poor relief	0	0	10	0.2	0	0	2	0.1	19	0.3	1	0
Legal costs	23	1.1	82	1.5	0	0	24	0.8	80	1.1	84	2.5
Landlord	127	6	25	0.5	106	5.4	192	6.6	42	0.6	12	0.4
Various	62	2.9	295	5.4	0	0	16	0.5	350	4.8	184	5.4
Total	2105	100	5513	100	1953	100	2920	100	7279	100	3412	100
Wardens' total	2113	100.4	5505	99.9	1944	99.5	2920	100	7279	100	3412	100
Balance	440	20.9	80	1.5	421	21.6	1263	43.3	195	2.7	15	0.4

Botolph Aldersgate, London: income analysis 1468–1560

(a) Overall

	First entry	Last entry	Average	Number	Per cent	Highest entry	Year	Lowest entry	Year
Balance	1468	1559	3816	64	41.7	9661	1516	1	1468
Collections	1468	1559	1754	67	19.2	9772	1486	354	1505
Stalls	1490	1550	4	11	0.1	64	1528	4	1490
Sales	1468	1559	292	25	3.2	3607	1534	3	1501
Fines	1487	1497	2	3	0.1	80	1490	12	1487
Rents	1468	1559	2241	67	24.5	4822	1547	466	1470
Burial rites	1468	1559	371	66	4.1	1032	1487	8	1534
Gifts	1468	1548	187	24	2	3520	1534	8	1495
Debts	1485	1551	32	8	0.3	1600	1551	6	1497
Crown	1549	1559	276	10	3	2520	1549	1680	1551
Various	1470	1559	187	16	2	2880	1556	8	1504
Total	1468	1559	9159	67	100	19 286	1534	2548	1491
Wardens' total	1468	1559	9158	67	100	19 286	1534	2548	1491

(b) Development over time

	Pre-Refo 1468–1539	Per cent	Post-Refo 1547–1559	Per cent	First CWA 1468–1481	Per cent	Last pre-Refo CWA 1533–1539	Per cent	Edward 1547–1552	Per cent	Mary 1553–1558	Per cent
Balance	3355	42.4	5929	39.9	495	19.3	5684	43.7	5613	39.8	5817	38.9
Collections	1615	20.4	2390	16.1	497	19.4	2190	16.8	2226	15.8	2523	16.9
Stalls	3	0.1	7	0.1	0	0	10	0.1	13	0.1	0	0
Sales	182	2.3	795	5.3	199	7.8	653	5	844	6	480	3.2
Fines	2	0.1	0	0	0	0	0	0	0	0	0	0
Rents	2063	26.1	3056	20.5	997	38.8	3243	24.9	3085	21.9	3035	20.3
Burial rites	328	4.1	567	3.8	271	10.6	257	2	471	3.3	606	4.1
Gifts	210	2.7	80	0.5	39	1.5	960	7.4	160	1.1	0	0
Debts	6	0.1	147	1	0	0	7	0.1	293	2.1	0	0
Crown	0	0	1540	10.4	0	0	0	0	1400	9.9	1680	11.2
Various	149	1.9	363	2.4	69	2.7	12	0.1	3	0.1	820	5.5
Total	7913	100	14 873	100	2567	100	13 016	100	14 109	100	14 961	100
Wardens' total	7907	99.9	14 893	100.1	2567	100	13 013	100	14 109	100	14 961	100

Botolph Aldersgate: expenses 1468–1560

(a) Overall

	First entry	Last entry	Average	Number	Per cent	Highest entry	Year	Lowest entry	Year
Building	1468	1559	776	66	14.2	9234.5	1534	2	1491
Bells	1468	1559	50	54	0.9	440	1553	2	1484
Clock	1538	1559	42	13	0.8	570	1538	72	1539
Churchyard	1468	1558	48	23	0.9	1189	1511	2	1468
Candles/Wax	1468	1558	533	62	9.8	2432	1508	6	1518
Ceremonial life	1468	1559	44	61	0.8	735	1553	2	1470
Priests, clerks	1482	1559	1054	42	19.3	5200	1557	80	1510
Ornaments	1468	1559	656	67	12	7844	1486	53	1484
Obits	1468	1547	109	56	2	448	1547	34	1491
Organs	1470	1559	97	36	1.8	320	1482	8	1506
Ringing	1468	1558	16	53	0.3	66	1487	4	1538
Accounting	1471	1559	54	62	1	180	1559	24	1471
Wages	1493	1559	200	51	3.7	1480	1559	12	1493
Crown	1497	1559	210	15	3.9	3404	1555	8	1497
Public works	1502	1557	81	9	1.5	1700	1557	4	1539
Poor relief	1539	1550	8	4	0.1	264	1550	2	1539
Legal costs	1468	1559	86	64	1.6	727	1552	2	1484
Landlord	1471	1559	1125	64	20.6	9884	1528	49	1485
Allow. (debts)	1485	1558	72	18	1.3	657	1551	12	1485
Various	1468	1555	189	28	3.5	2814	1516	3	1514
Total	1468	1559	5452	67	100	14 093	1486	1192	1510
Wardens' total	1468	1559	5453	67	100	14 093	1486	1192	1510
Balance	1468	1559	3708	67	68	9661	1515	–323	1493

(b) Development over time

	Pre-Refo 1468–1539	Per cent	Post-Refo 1547–1559	Per cent	First CWA 1468–1481	Per cent	Last Pre-Refo CWA 1533–1539	Per cent	Edward 1547–1552	Per cent	Mary 1553–1558	Per cent
Building	724	15.4	1012	11.5	496	25.3	1775	23.5	847	10.1	381	4.5
Bells	49	1	55	0.6	19	1	55	0.7	2	0.1	129	1.5
Clock	12	0.3	178	2	0	0	107	1.4	179	2.1	175	2.1
Churchyard	57	1.2	7	0.1	114	5.8	0.5	0.1	13	0.2	1	0.1
Candles/Wax	614	13	164	1.9	665	34	738	9.8	54	0.6	329	3.9
Ceremonial life	15	0.3	178	2	0	0.1	18	0.2	80	1	330	3.9
Priests, clerks	648	13.7	2915	33	100	0	987	13.1	2792	33.2	3390	40.5
Ornaments	727	15.4	332	3.8	55	5.1	368	4.9	469	5.6	218	2.6
Obits	126	2.7	37	0.4	97	2.8	391	5.2	75	0.9	0	0
Organs	109	2.3	42	0.5	11	5	0	0	49	0.6	37	0.4
Ringing	17	0.4	11	0.1	14	0.6	11	0.1	3	0.1	22	0.3
Accounting	45	1	95	1.1	0	0.7	43	0.6	81	1	95	1.1
Wages	82	1.7	742	8.4	0	0	527	7	697	8.3	648	7.7
Crown	3	0.1	1162	13.2	0	0	22	0.3	749	8.9	1639	19.6
Public works	31	0.7	311	3.5	0	0	90	1.2	338	4	340	4.1
Poor relief	0.1	0.1	47	0.5	0	0	0.5	0.1	94	1.1	0	0
Legal costs	58	1.2	216	2.4	162	8.3	43	0.6	207	2.5	230	2.7
Landlord	1136	24.1	1078	12.2	221	11.3	2220	29.4	1385	16.5	189	2.3
Allow. (debts)	69	1.5	85	1	0	0	61	0.8	110	1.3	72	0.9
Various	196	4.2	158	1.8	3	0.2	89	1.2	193	2.3	149	1.8
Total	4716	100	8823	100	1958	100	7547	100	8414	100	8374	100
Wardens' total	4717	100.1	8828	100.1	1958	100	7547	100	8414	100	8385	100.1
Balance	3196	67.8	6050	68.6	609	31.1	5470	72.5	5695	67.7	6587	78.7

All Saints, Bristol: income analysis 1406–1560

(a) Overall

	First entry	Last entry	Average	Number	Per cent	Highest entry	Year	Lowest entry	Year
Balance	1463	1559	433	36	8	5854	1551	59	1526
Collections	1406	1559	392	104	7.2	2585	1472	96	1475
Ales	1457	1463	37	2	0.7	2872	1457	1024	1463
Pews	1406	1558	33	79	0.6	134	1453	4	1518
Sales	1408	1559	187	54	3.4	3500	1524	4	1444
Money lending	1487	1557	155	25	2.9	2400	1505	240	1488
Rents	1406	1559	3596	105	66.2	7416	1524	660	1443
Gilds	1509	1530	66	20	1.2	735	1519	120	1529
Burial rites	1406	1558	127	81	2.3	812	1450	6	1428
Gifts	1406	1558	179	44	3.3	2616	1530	4	1439
Debts	1463	1558	69	11	1.3	1920	1536	12	1480
Various	1420	1553	151	25	2.8	4800	1523	4	1515
Total	1406	1559	5425	105	100	19 173	1530	1051	1451
Wardens' total	1406	1559	5417	105	99.9	19 173	1530	1051	1451

(b) Development over time

	Pre-Refo 1406–1542	Per cent	Post-Refo 1549–1559	Per cent	First CWA 1406–1409	Per cent	Last Pre-Refo CWA 1538–1542	Per cent	Edward 1549–1552	Per cent	Mary 1553–1558	Per cent
Balance	302	6.1	1674	16.5	0	0	1945	16.5	2644	21.7	931	10.7
Collections	378	7.7	522	5.2	221	9.6	966	8.2	488	4	547	6.3
Ales	41	0.8	0	0	0	0	0	0	0	0	0	0
Pews	35	0.7	12	0.1	11	0.5	26	0.2	0	0	24	0.3
Sales	185	3.8	207	2	74	3.2	607	5.2	415	3.4	13	0.1
Money lending	137	2.8	322	3.2	0	0	780	6.6	315	2.6	392	4.5
Rents	3304	67	6373	63	1350	58.6	7340	62.3	6278	51.5	6426	73.7
Gilds	73	1.5	0	0	0	0	0	0	0	0	0	0
Burial rites	128	2.6	123	1.2	235	10.2	26	0.2	80	0.7	183	2.1
Gifts	194	3.9	41	0.4	414	18	0	0	80	0.7	18	0.2
Debts	37	0.8	373	3.7	0	0	80	0.7	720	5.9	170	1.9
Various	117	2.4	476	4.7	0	0	10	0.1	1164	9.6	20	0.2
Total	4931	100	10 123	100	2304	100	11 780	100	12 183	100	8724	100
Wardens' total	4926	99.9	10 082	99.6	2307	100.1	11 772	99.9	12 183	100	8652	99.2

All Saints: expenses 1406–1560

(a) Overall

	First entry	Last entry	Average	Number	Per cent	Highest entry	Year	Lowest entry	Year
Building	1406	1559	280	105	6.6	3926	1549	3	1481
Bells	1406	1558	58	66	1.4	1918	1533	2	1413
Churchyard	1406	1559	24	38	0.6	701	1475	1	1473
Candles/Wax	1406	1559	408	105	9.6	928	1519	2	1551
Ceremonial life	1406	1559	58	102	1.4	183	1436	6	1406
Priests, clerks	1444	1559	572	72	13.4	3770	1559	8	1450
Ornaments	1406	1559	463	104	10.8	4332	1552	2	1467
Obits	1407	1559	356	99	8.3	946	1541	29	1408
Organs	1489	1558	13	18	0.3	881	1519	1	1536
Ringing	1448	1558	1	11	0.1	26	1555	2	1541
Cathedral	1406	1535	11	83	0.3	28	1413	8	1476
Accounting	1408	1559	110	76	2.6	1586	1551	1	1426
Wages	1406	1559	156	89	3.7	1580	1549	1	1433
Crown	1504	1559	59	15	1.4	2021	1553	1	1541
Landlord	1427	1559	1244	92	29.1	7433	1524	3	1454
Poor relief	1538	1558	24	6	0.6	1260	1551	4	1538
Legal costs	1406	1559	65	53	1.5	832	1549	1	1436
Potations	1421	1559	37	73	0.9	161	1479	2	1446
Allow. (chantry)	1514	1551	174	14	4.1	7252	1530	70	1521
Various	1407	1559	159	42	3.7	4800	1530	2	1439
Total	1406	1559	4272	105	100	19 114	1530	439	1410
Wardens' total	1406	1559	4250	104	99.5	19 114	1530	439	1410
Balance	1406	1559	1153	105	27	5854	1550	-1385	1524

(b) Development over time

	Pre-Refo 1406–1542	Per cent	Post-Refo 1549–1559	Per cent	First CWA 1406–1409	Per cent	Last Pre-Refo CWA 1538–1542	Per cent	Edward 1549–1552	Per cent	Mary 1553–1558	Per cent
Building	245	6.4	612	7.3	225	14.8	205	2.4	1187	11.7	221	3.1
Bells	60	1.6	36	0.4	40	2.6	6	0.1	7	0.1	66	0.9
Churchyard	25	0.7	22	0.3	77	5.1	1	0.1		0.5	3	0.1
Candles/Wax	440	11.5	101	1.2	359	23.6	431	5	10	0.1	146	2.1
Ceremonial life	58	1.5	59	0.7	13	0.9	100	1.2	12	0.1	106	1.5
Priests, clerks	367	9.6	2520	30	0	0	1505	17.4	2091	20.5	2612	36.8
Ornaments	420	10.9	868	10.3	707	46.4	176	2	1142	11.2	809	11.4
Obits	377	9.8	156	1.9	34	2.2	882	10.2	0	0	240	3.4
Organs	14	0.4	4	0.1	0	0	10	0.1	2	0.1	6	0.1
Ringing	1	0.1	3	0.1	0	0	1	0.1	0	0	6	0.1
Cathedral	12	0.3	0	0	22	1.4	0	0	0	0	0	0
Accounting	42	1.1	752	8.9	2	0.1	400	4.6	1159	11.4	461	6.5
Wages	61	1.6	1058	12.6	5	0.3	696	8.1	1264	12.4	938	13.2
Crown	13	0.3	495	5.9	0	0	60	0.7	266	2.6	707	10
Landlord	1273	33.2	975	11.6	0	0	3190	37	1427	14	656	9.2
Poor relief	0.1	0.1	250	3	0	0	1	0.1	549	5.4	62	0.9
Legal costs	62	1.6	99	1.2	4	0.3	15	0.2	210	2.1	21	0.3
Potations	40	1	2	0.1	0	0	75	0.9	0	0	1	0.1
Allow. (chantry)	177	4.6	144	1.7	0	0	699	8.1	360	3.5	0	0
Various	149	3.9	250	3	36	2.4	176	2	506	5	42	0.6
Total	3837	100	8403	100	1523	100	8628	100	10 192	100	7103	100
Wardens' total	3813	99.4	8400	100	1529	100.4	8627	100	10 192	100	7096	99.9
Balance	1094	28.5	1720	20.5	781	51.3	3151	36.5	1992	19.5	1621	22.8

St Ewen's, Bristol: income analysis 1454–1560

(a) Overall

	First entry	Last entry	Average	Number	Per cent	Highest entry	Year	Lowest entry	Year
Balance	1454	1554	148	5	8.8	2854	1554	201	1457
Collections	1454	1559	89	49	5.3	179	1455	17	1516
Ales	1454	1492	86	10	5.1	998.5	1466	88	1456
Pews	1454	1554	23	43	1.4	83	1485	4	1487
Sales	1454	1552	28	19	1.7	602.5	1547	4	1465
Dancing	1455	1467	5	3	0.3	167	1464	28	1455
Rents	1454	1559	936	52	55.8	1758.5	1559	460	1458
Burial rites	1456	1547	22	20	1.3	172	1497	2	1456
Gifts	1454	1500	195	25	1	4138	1473	8	1468
Debts	1456	1514	27	12	1.6	612	1483	20	1514
Various	1454	1514	121	10	7.2	4320	1492	1	1477
Total	1454	1559	1678	52	100	8655	1492	595	1458
Wardens' total	1454	1559	1694	52	101	8871	1492	595	1458

(b) Development over time

	Pre-Refo 1454–1517	Per cent	Post-Refo 1547–1559	Per cent	First CWA 1454–1456	Per cent	Last Pre-Refo CWA 1515–1517	Per cent	Edward 1547–1552	Per cent	Mary 1554	Per cent
Balance	44	2.8	1120	45.5	365	15.9	0	0	915	41.6	2854	73.6
Collections	97	6.1	22	0.9	173	7.5	36	2.7	0	0	36	0.9
Ales	95	6	0	0	391	17	0	0	0	0	0	0
Pews	24	1.5	6	0.2	29	1.3	27	2	0	0	28	0.7
Sales	17	1.1	132	5.4	26	1.1	7	0.5	220	10	0	0
Dancing	5	0.3	0	0	9	0.4	0	0	0	0	0	0
Rents	910	57.1	1178	47.8	503	21.9	1198	90.7	1058	48	958	24.7
Burial rites	24	1.5	5	0.2	1	0.1	53	4	8	0.4	0	0
Gifts	216	13.5	0	0	709	30.8	0	0	0	0	0	0
Debts	30	1.9	0	0	93	4	0	0	0	0	0	0
Various	134	8.4	0	0	1	0.1	0	0	0	0	0	0
Total	1595	100	2462	100	2300	100	1321	100	2202	100	3876	100
Wardens' total	1613	101.1	2456	99.8	2300	100	1543	116.8	2194	99.6	3876	100

St Ewen's: expenses 1454–1560

(a) Overall

	First entry	Last entry	Average	Number	Per cent	Highest entry	Year	Lowest entry	Year
Building	1454	1559	117	52	8.7	2115	1477	1	1492
Bells	1456	1547	3	13	0.2	87	1491	1	1497
Churchyard	1457	1547	28	18	2.1	621	1464	1	1547
Candles/Wax	1454	1559	193	51	14.4	452	1485	2	1559
Ceremonial life	1454	1559	35	52	2.6	66	1547	3	1455
Priests, clerks	1455	1559	88	27	6.6	954	1554	1	1483
Ornaments	1454	1554	331	51	24.7	7324	1473	12	1552
Obits	1454	1547	56	48	4.2	228	1547	27	1455
Cathedral	1454	1497	5	39	0.4	8	1457	4	1474
Accounting	1455	1559	17	11	1.3	336	1551	2	1472
Wages	1484	1552	4	4	0.3	132	1551	7	1484
Crown	1497	1559	17	6	1.3	306	1547	4	1551
Poor relief	1547	1547	1	1	0.1	28	1547	28	1547
Legal costs	1455	1559	69	23	5.1	1251	1463	1	1480
Landlord	1454	1559	364	46	27.1	10 327	1492	7	1464
Potations	1460	1554	3	26	0.2	72	1552	1	1475
Various	1455	1559	13	12	1	360	1497	1	1489
Total	1454	1559	1342	52	100	10 722	1492	357	1484
Wardens' total	1454	1559	1337	52	9.6	10 638	1492	357	1484
Balance	1454	1559	336	52	25	3664	1454	–2067	1492

(b) Development over time

	Pre-Refo 1454–1517	Per cent	Post-Refo 1547–1559	Per cent	First CWA 1454–1456	Per cent	Last Pre-Refo CWA 1515–1517	Per cent	Edward 1547–1552	Per cent	Mary 1554	Per cent
Building	124	9.4	51	3.2	14	1.9	42	4.1	33	1.9	125	6.2
Bells	3	0.2	1	0.1	2	0.3	7	0.7	1	0.1	0	0
Churchyard	31	2.4	0.2	0.1	0	0	0	0	0.3	0.1	0	0
Candles/Wax	198	15	140	8.8	109	15	248	24.5	118	6.7	346	17.2
Ceremonial life	36	2.7	34	2.1	6	0.8	40	3.9	33	1.9	52	2.6
Priests, clerks	27	2.1	661	41.8	2	0.3	41	4	669	38	954	47.6
Ornaments	360	27.3	59	3.7	420	57.6	118	11.6	59	3.3	116	5.8
Obits	57	4.3	46	2.9	28	3.8	91	9	76	4.3	0	0
Cathedral	5	0.4	0	0	6	0.8	0	0	0	0	0	0
Accounting	1	0.1	166	10.5	5	0.7	0	0	230	13.1	100	5
Wages	0.1	0.1	36	2.3	0	0	0	0	60	3.4	0	0
Crown	2	0.2	162	10.2	0	0	0	0	150	8.5	301	15
Poor relief	0	0	6	0.4	0	0	0	0	9	0.5	0	0
Legal costs	59	4.5	163	10.3	16	2.2	1	0.1	249	14.1	4	0.2
Landlord	399	30.3	34	2.1	110	15.1	410	40.4	49	2.8	0	0
Potations	2	0.2	16	1	0	0	0.3	0.1	24	1.4	8	0.4
Various	13	1	6	0.4	11	1.5	16	1.6	0	0	0	0
Total	1317	100	1582	100	729	100	1014	100	1762	100	2006	100
Wardens' total	1311	99.5	1578	99.7	729	100	1023	100.9	1758	99.8	2005	100
Balance	278	21.1	881	55.7	1571	216	308	30.4	440	25	1871	93.3

Ashburton, Devon: income analysis 1479–1560

(a) Overall

	First entry	Last entry	Average	Number	Per cent	Highest entry	Year	Lowest entry	Year
Arrears	1479	1559	2327	73	33.1	7156	1528	7	1552
Collections	1482	1559	58	69	0.8	746	1559	5	1546
Ales	1479	1559	1500	74	21.3	2577	1534	376	1479
Waxsilver	1482	1559	290	70	4.1	1066	1559	240	1541
Stalls	1491	1556	2	16	0	24	1491	3	1508
Church house	1486	1559	62	71	0.8	120	1553	19	1509
Pews	1483	1558	42	66	0.6	136	1551	4	1509
Sales	1479	1559	146	67	2.1	4808	1529	1	1505
Rents	1482	1559	1514	78	21.5	2958	1555	136	1483
Gilds	1487	1558	737	46	10.4	6240	1525	48	1493
Burial rites	1482	1558	110	69	1.6	378	1530	2	1488
Gifts	1479	1559	165	76	2.3	2495	1521	4	1498
Various	1486	1559	74	39	1.1	640	1549	2	1506
Total	1479	1559	7028	79	100	16 100	1525	1446	1479
Wardens' total	1479	1559	6900	77	98.2	16 100	1525	1446	1479

(b) Development over time

	Pre-Refo 1479–1546	Per cent	Post-Refo 1547–1559	Per cent	First CWA 1479–1486	Per cent	Last Pre-Refo CWA 1541–1546	Per cent	Edward 1547–1552	Per cent	Mary 1553–1558	Per cent
Arrears	2607	35.8	906	15.8	1355	44.4	4259	38.4	1725	29.5	195	3.5
Collections	35	0.5	174	3	21	0.7	17	0.2	17	0.3	235	4.2
Ales	1683	23.1	571	9.9	1110	36.4	1561	14.1	420	7.2	669	12.1
Waxsilver	262	3.6	432	7.5	215	7.1	271	2.4	0	0	759	13.7
Stalls	2	0.1	4	0.1	0	0	3	0.1	4	0.1	6	0.1
Church house	62	0.9	63	1.1	13	0.4	59	0.5	62	1.1	58	1
Pews	39	0.5	60	1	8	0.3	50	0.5	52	0.9	78	1.4
Sales	136	1.9	201	3.5	25	0.8	175	1.6	285	4.9	65	1.2
Rents	1287	17.7	2663	46.4	177	5.8	2703	24.3	2639	45.2	2691	48.6
Gilds	826	11.3	283	4.9	0	0	1602	14.4	378	6.5	235	4.2
Burial rites	118	1.6	71	1.2	59	2	155	1.4	65	1.1	90	1.6
Gifts	180	2.5	90	1.6	62	2	185	1.7	46	0.8	132	2.4
Various	45	0.6	226	3.9	5	0.2	65	0.6	145	2.5	323	5.8
Total	7281	100	5745	100	3049	100	11 104	100	5839	100	5536	100
Wardens' total	7126	97.9	5754	100.2	3029	99.3	11 113	100.1	5866	100.5	5528	99.9

Ashburton: expenses 1479–1560

(a) Overall

	First entry	Last entry	Average	Number	Per cent	Highest entry	Year	Lowest entry	Year
Building	1479	1559	822	79	17.7	5732	1524	13	1529
Bells	1479	1559	271	78	5.8	2118	1503	2	1495
Clock	1479	1559	48	27	1	2745	1536	1	1522
Churchyard	1482	1558	40	28	0.9	1236	1546	1	1558
Candles/Wax	1479	1559	384	78	8.3	1330	1508	3	1552
Ceremonial life	1483	1559	17	19	0.4	222	1557	1	1487
Social life	1489	1559	50	41	1.1	573	1556	4	1554
Priests, clerks	1482	1559	537	72	11.6	2240	1545	4	1483
Ornaments	1479	1558	773	78	16.6	8083	1528	12	1553
Obits	1482	1547	75	63	1.6	200	1538	13	1482
Organs	1483	1558	106	23	2.3	3606	1540	2	1557
Accounting	1482	1559	52	76	1.1	85	1558	12	1482
Wages	1479	1559	186	69	4	580	1538	4	1507
Crown	1483	1559	155	21	3.3	1630	1545	20	1539
Public works	1540	1549	15	6	0.3	800	1548	44	1549
Poor relief	1543	1555	81	12	1.7	1304	1548	120	1555
Legal costs	1482	1559	297	68	6.4	3015	1525	1	1509
Landlord	1479	1559	604	79	13	3605	1517	24	1479
Various	1482	1559	136	46	2.9	1856	1497	2	1528
Total	1479	1559	4649	79	100	13 351	1525	1073	1482
Wardens' total	1479	1559	4544	78	97.7	13 046	1525	1053	1482
Balance	1479	1559	2379	79	51.2	7157	1527	-1046	1487

(b) Development over time

	Pre-Refo 1479–1546	Per cent	Post-Refo 1547–1559	Per cent	First CWA 1479–1486	Per cent	Last Pre-Refo CWA 1541–1546	Per cent	Edward 1547–1552	Per cent	Mary 1553–1558	Per cent
Building	864	18.9	608	12.1	650	34	758	12.5	618	13.4	639	11.8
Bells	260	5.7	328	6.5	43	2.3	726	11.9	68	1.5	632	11.7
Clock	50	1.1	42	0.8	3	0.2	27	0.4	16	0.3	64	1.2
Churchyard	42	0.9	28	0.6	5	0.3	242	4	48	1	12	0.2
Candles/Wax	403	8.8	287	5.7	226	11.8	322	5.3	87	1.9	529	9.8
Ceremonial life	9	0.2	56	1.1	10	0.5	0	0	17	0.4	90	1.7
Social life	37	0.8	119	2.4	0	0	91	1.5	49	1.1	202	3.7
Priests, clerks	469	10.3	879	17.4	5	0.3	1320	21.7	720	15.6	864	16
Ornaments	879	19.2	235	4.7	506	26.5	175	2.9	164	3.6	346	6.4
Obits	88	1.9	12	0.2	12	0.6	161	2.6	26	0.6	0	0
Organs	123	2.7	22	0.4	7	0.4	22	0.4	0	0	48	0.9
Accounting	47	1	81	1.6	14	0.7	77	1.3	80	1.7	81	1.5
Wages	181	4	212	4.2	82	4.3	414	6.8	284	6.2	135	2.5
Crown	53	1.2	673	13.3	33	1.7	523	8.6	362	7.9	855	15.8
Public works	5	0.1	65	1.3	0	0	49	0.8	141	3.1	0	0
Poor relief	13	0.3	427	8.5	0	0	138	2.3	805	17.5	120	2.2
Legal costs	310	6.8	231	4.6	119	6.2	337	5.5	260	5.6	175	3.2
Landlord	637	13.9	439	8.7	190	10	693	11.4	352	7.6	492	9.1
Various	104	2.3	300	5.9	6	0.3	14	0.2	514	11.1	135	2.5
Total	4572	100	5043	100	1909	100	6088	100	4611	100	5418	100
Wardens' total	4525	99	4638	92	1917	100.4	6053	99.4	4628	100.4	4522	83.5
Balance	2709	59.3	702	13.9	1140	59.7	5016	82.4	1228	26.6	118	2.2

Halesowen, Worcestershire: income analysis 1487–1560

(a) Overall

	First entry	Last entry	Average	Number	Per cent	Highest entry	Year	Lowest entry	Year
Balance	1487	1548	262	41	25	2258	1532	2	1518
Collections	1487	1558	263	56	25	438	1501	14	1554
Townships	1487	1558	28	53	2.7	496	1558	7	1487
Rates	1517	1529	2	2	0.2	74	1517	72	1529
Ales	1502	1543	241	16	23	2240	1533	225	1517
Pews	1548	1553	3	3	0.3	108	1548	12	1551
Sales	1496	1552	63	22	6	978	1537	4	1516
Rents	1487	1558	44	60	4.2	262	1496	9	1549
Lifestock	1487	1555	23	52	2.2	120	1502	16	1532
Gilds	1522	1522	2	1	0.2	96	1522	96	1522
Burial rites	1500	1549	35	27	3.3	400	1531	6	1514
Relics	1504	1536	6	32	0.6	18	1510	7	1507
Gifts	1487	1558	28	25	2.7	440	1525	2	1505
Various	1487	1558	51	15	4.9	920	1550	6	1516
Total	1487	1558	1050	62	100	4663	1533	85	1553
Wardens' total	1487	1558	1059	49	100.9	4643	1533	85	1553

(b) Development over time

	Pre-Refo 1487–1545	Per cent	Post-Refo 1547–1558	Per cent	First CWA 1487–1499	Per cent	Last Pre-Refo CWA 1540–1545	Per cent	Edward 1547–1552	Per cent	Mary 1553–1555	Per cent
Balance	307	26.9	23	4	855	61.5	24	3.8	38	5.6	0	0
Collections	306	26.8	40	7	280	20.1	244	38.1	49	7.2	9	4.1
Townships	24	2.1	52	9.1	22	1.6	27	4.2	4	0.6	0	0
Rates	3	0.3	0	0	0	0	0	0	0	0	0	0
Ales	288	25.2	0	0	0	0	187	29.2	0	0	0	0
Pews	0	0	16	2.8	0	0	0	0	20	2.9	0	0
Sales	56	4.9	102	17.9	27	1.9	30	4.7	170	25	12	5.4
Rents	50	4.4	16	2.8	122	8.8	28	4.4	15	2.2	0	0
Lifestock	26	2.3	11	1.9	44	3.2	16	2.5	11	1.6	9	4.1
Gilds	2	0.2	0	0	0	0	0	0	0	0	16	7.2
Burial rites	41	3.6	4	0.7	0	0	47	7.3	7	1	0	0
Relics	7	0.6	0	0	0	0	0	0	0	0	0	0
Gifts	33	2.9	2	0.4	30	2.2	37	5.8	2	0.3	0	0
Various	2	0.2	305	53.4	9	0.6	0	0	365	53.6	176	79.3
Total	1142	100	571	100	1391	100	640	100	681	100	222	100
Wardens' total	1184	103.7	571	100	1404	100.9	681	106.4	681	100	222	100

Halesowen: expenses 1487–1560

(a) Overall

	First entry	Last entry	Average	Number	Per cent	Highest entry	Year	Lowest entry	Year
Building	1487	1558	237	59	29.2	3772	1533	1	1517
Bells	1487	1558	67	61	8.3	908	1522	2	1488
Clock	1488	1558	7	28	0.9	99	1516	1	1526
Churchyard	1487	1558	8	31	1	116	1548	1	1498
Candles/Wax	1487	1558	198	61	24.4	368	1522	1	1552
Ceremonial life	1487	1552	3	10	0.4	146	1552	1	1535
Social life	1505	1505	1	1	0.1	26	1505	26	1505
Priests, clerks	1502	1558	7	33	0.9	24	1532	1	1548
Ornaments	1487	1558	133	60	16.4	896	1503	7	1553
Organs	1503	1555	45	14	5.5	1475	1530	1	1554
Ringing	1500	1548	2	27	0.2	4	1510	3	1500
Cathedral	1545	1548	1	3	0.1	24	1545	24	1545
Accounting	1487	1558	9	61	1.1	30	1558	4	1507
Crown	1537	1539	24	8	3	456	1550	6	1553
Public works	1539	1552	1	1	0.1	80	1539	80	1539
Poor relief	1548	1558	1	3	0.1	48	1552	6	1550
Legal costs	1496	1555	22	50	2.7	423	1558	1	1512
Landlord	1499	1555	25	6	3.1	1141	1538	2	1554
Various	1497	1551	19	22	2.3	477	1497	1	1514
Total	1487	1558	812	62	100	4293	1533	153	1521
Wardens' total	1487	1558	835	49	102.8	4292	1533	189	1507
Balance	1487	1558	239	62	29.4	2009	1531	−629	1558

(b) Development over time

	Pre-Refo 1487–1545	Per cent	Post-Refo 1547–1558	Per cent	First CWA 1487–1499	Per cent	Last Pre-Refo CWA 1540–1545	Per cent	Edward 1547–1552	Per cent	Mary 1553–1555	Per cent
Building	258	31.2	128	17.5	29	5	125	20.1	169	21.6	69	19.8
Bells	64	7.7	87	11.9	22	3.8	66	10.6	58	7.4	121	34.8
Clock	8	1	6	0.8	15	2.6	11	1.8	7	0.9	3	0.9
Churchyard	5	0.6	26	3.6	7	1.2	1	0.2	38	4.9	1	0.3
Candles/Wax	223	27	65	8.9	255	44	163	26.2	57	7.3	69	19.8
Ceremonial life	1	0.1	15	2	5	0.9	0	0	24	3.1	0	0
Social life	1	0.1	0	0	0	0	0	0	0	0	0	0
Priests, clerks	8	1	3	0.4	0	0	12	1.9	0	0	1	0.3
Ornaments	133	16.1	134	18.3	129	22.2	190	30.6	104	13.3	27	7.8
Organs	54	6.5	1	0.1	0	0	0	0	1	0.1	1	0.3
Ringing	2	0.2	0.5	0.1	0	0	3	0.5	1	0.1	0	0
Cathedral	1	0.1	5	0.7	0	0	4	0.6	8	1	0	0
Accounting	8	1	12	1.6	9	1.6	12	1.9	11	1.4	8	2.3
Crown	3	0.4	135	18.4	0	0	0	0	203	26	2	0.6
Public works	2	0.2	0	0	0	0	0	0	0	0	0	0
Poor relief	0	0	9	1.2	0	0	0	0	14	1.8	0	0
Legal costs	7	0.8	99	13.5	2	0.3	11	1.8	72	9.2	44	12.6
Landlord	30	3.6	0.5	0.1	27	4.7	0	0	0	0	1	0.3
Various	21	2.5	8	1.1	81	14	23	3.7	13	1.7	0	0
Total	827	100	732	100	580	100	621	100	781	100	348	100
Wardens' total	862	104.2	730	99.7	573	98.8	661	106.4	778	99.6	348	100
Balance	315	38.1	-161	-22	811	139.8	19	3.1	-100	-12.8	-126	-36.2

Peterborough: income analysis 1467–1556

(a) Overall

	First entry	Last entry	Average	Number	Per cent	Highest entry	Year	Lowest entry	Year
Arrears	1475	1556	2701	59	67.9	6756	1536	198	1544
Collections	1467	1556	502	67	12.6	2144	1540	260	1495
Money lending	1475	1494	5	6	0.1	120	1485	10	1475
Sales	1467	1556	102	36	2.6	1080	1534	2	1484
Hire	1467	1514	3	5	0.1	80	1514	10	1469
May money	1531	1532	8	2	0.2	245	1531	245	1531
Rents	1467	1545	318	59	8	1972	1540	12	1467
Gilds	1534	1535	5	2	0.1	159	1534	159	1534
Burial rites	1467	1556	55	61	1.4	198	1506	4	1539
Gifts	1467	1556	237	60	6	1835	1554	10	1485
Various	1468	1543	41	22	1	918	1543	3	1475
Total	1467	1556	3978	69	100	7747	1536	709	1473
Wardens' total	1467	1556	4094	59	102.9	7759	1536	732	1501

(b) Development over time

	Pre-Refo 1467–1545	Per cent	Post-Refo	Per cent	First CWA 1467–1469	Per cent	Last Pre-Refo CWA 1543–1545	Per cent	Edward	Per cent	Mary 1554–1556	Per cent
Arrears	2840	70	cf. Mary		0	0	427	13.1	no evidence		−125	−5.3
Collections	512	12.6			1288	83.8	265	8.1			291	12.4
Money lending	5	0.1			0	0	0	0			0	0
Sales	91	2.2			61	4	332	10.2			336	14.3
Hire	3	0.1			21	1.4	0	0			0	0
May money	8	0.2			0	0	0	0			0	0
Rents	334	8.2			37	2.4	1612	49.5			0	0
Gilds	5	0.1			0	0	0	0			0	0
Burial rites	57	1.4			12	0.8	21	0.6			11	0.5
Gifts	159	3.9			89	5.8	295	9.1			1835	78.2
Various	43	1.1			28	1.8	306	9.4			0	0
Total	4058	100			1537	100	3257	100			2347	100
Wardens' total	4196	103.4			1537	100	3262	100.2			2347	100

Peterborough: expenses 1467–1560

(a) Overall

	First entry	Last entry	Average	Number	Per cent	Highest entry	Year	Lowest entry	Year
Building	1467	1556	289	64	24.1	2485	1506	2	1542
Bells	1467	1556	173	64	14.4	2865	1540	8	1494
Clock	1472	1556	33	46	2.8	413	1533	1	1486
Churchyard	1468	1556	32	45	2.7	732	1533	1	1468
Candles/wax	1468	1556	13	39	1.1	108	1544	1	1475
Ceremonial life	1477	1545	1	15	0.1	16	1539	2	1482
Social life	1479	1483	0.5	2	0.1	20	1479	5	1483
Priests, clerks	1468	1545	169	49	14.1	2040	1537	12	1475
Ornaments	1467	1556	239	65	19.9	1072	1515	15	1486
Obits	1467	1556	16	58	1.3	77	1533	7	1472
Organs	1467	1545	21	24	1.8	288	1540	1	1472
Ringing	1469	1556	4	24	0.3	40	1554	1	1469
Accounting	1467	1545	5	37	0.4	40	1493	2	1515
Wages	1467	1556	71	53	5.9	328	1544	8	1513
Crown	1506	1556	36	10	3	544	1554	7	1538
Public works	1475	1556	9	8	0.8	242	1533	12	1544
Legal costs	1475	1545	9	16	0.8	172	1542	1	1479
Landlord	1480	1545	72	21	6	1076	1537	2	1480
Various	1467	1556	7	25	0.6	164	1541	1	1494
Total	1467	1556	1199	69	100	4276	1506	136	1534
Wardens' total	1467	1556	1265	62	105.5	4273	1506	136	1534
Balance	1467	1556	2779	69	232	6876	1535	-662	1473

(b) Development over time

	Pre-Refo 1467–1545	Per cent	Post-Refo	Per cent	First CWA 1467–1469	Per cent	Last Pre-Refo CWA 1543–1545	Per cent	Edward	Per cent	Mary 1554–1556	Per cent
Building	275	24.3	cf. Mary		871	73.6	311	15.3	no evidence		581	22.4
Bells	149	13.2			100	8.5	76	3.7			646	24.9
Clock	33	2.9			0	0	75	3.7			32	1.2
Churchyard	33	2.9			1	0.1	121	6			2	0.1
Candles/wax	13	1.2			2	0.2	103	5.1			28	1.1
Ceremonial life	1	0.1			0	0	3	0.1			0	0
Social life	0.5	0.1			0	0	0	0			0	0
Priests, clerks	177	15.7			39	3.3	100	4.9			0	0
Ornaments	218	19.3			91	7.7	344	17			655	25.3
Obits	16	1.4			8	0.7	14	0.7			17	0.7
Organs	22	1.9			14	1.2	59	2.9			0	0
Ringing	2	0.2			0.5	0.1	0	0			40	1.5
Accounting	5	0.4			12	1	4	0.2			0	0
Wages	74	6.5			42	3.6	259	12.8			20	0.8
Crown	11	1			0	0	154	7.6			544	21
Public works	8	0.7			0	0	8	0.4			27	1
Legal costs	9	0.8			0	0	1	0.1			0	0
Landlord	76	6.7			0	0	398	19.6			0	0
Various	7	0.6			2	0.2	1	0.1			2	0.1
Total	1130	100			1183	100	2029	100			2593	100
Wardens' total	1192	105.4			1183	100	2619	129			2594	100
Balance	2928	259.1			354	29.9	1228	60.5			–246	–9.5

Prescot, Lancashire: income analysis 1523–60

(a) Overall

	First entry	Last entry	Average	Number	Per cent	Highest entry	Year	Lowest entry	Year
Balance	1523	1558	51	3	5.5	773	1529	312	1558
Collections	1523	1559	178	20	19.4	438	1537	84	1559
Rates	1523	1559	366	12	39.9	3638	1555	79	1538
Waxsilver	1523	1558	149	13	16.2	419	1537	80	1523
Pews	1547	1547	0.5	1	0.1	12	1547	12	1547
Sales	1523	1558	31	10	3.3	480	1548	12	1558
Church box	1525	1558	21	6	2.2	192	1554	14	1550
Burial rites	1523	1559	114	19	12.4	660	1557	24	1530
Gifts	1524	1559	4	6	0.5	45	1547	1	1549
Various	1534	1557	4	3	0.4	49	1557	20	1534
Total	1523	1559	916	26	100	4274	1555	0	1552
Wardens' total	1523	1559	928	20	101.3	4380	1555	0	1552

(b) Development over time

	Pre-Refo 1523–1546	Per cent	Post-Refo 1547–1559	Per cent	First CWA 1523–1530	Per cent	Last Pre-Refo CWA 1537–1546	Per cent	Edward 1547–1552	Per cent	Mary 1553–1557	Per cent
Balance	72	8.2	24	2.5	192	16.2	0	0	0	0	0	0
Collections	268	30.4	66	6.9	323	27.2	143	19.9	16	5.5	112	7.8
Rates	317	35.9	425	44.4	530	44.6	315	43.8	0	0	728	50.5
Waxsilver	130	14.7	172	18	13	1.1	201	27.9	74	25.3	305	21.2
Pews	0	0	1	0.1	0	0	0	0	2	0.7	0	0
Sales	22	2.5	41	4.3	40	3.4	2	0.3	86	29.5	0	0
Church box	4	0.5	42	4.4	10	0.8	0	0	2	0.7	72	5
Burial rites	61	6.9	180	18.8	78	6.6	48	6.7	103	35.3	214	14.9
Gifts	5	0.6	4	0.4	2	0.2	11	1.5	8	2.7	0	0
Various	4	0.5	4	0.4	0	0	0	0	0	0	10	0.7
Total	883	100	958	100	1188	100	720	100	292	100	1441	100
Wardens' total	878	99.4	982	102.5	1156	97.3	625	86.8	290	99.3	1755	121.7

Prescot: expenses 1523–60

(a) Overall

	First entry	Last entry	Average	Number	Per cent	Highest entry	Year	Lowest entry	Year
Building	1523	1559	216	24	22.5	2025	1555	1	1547
Bells	1523	1559	183	25	19	2136	1558	3	1555
Clock	1523	1555	1	2	0.1	12	1523	3	1555
Churchyard	1523	1559	7	9	0.7	55	1523	2	1529
Candles/wax	1523	1558	267	23	27.8	786	1556	4	1553
Ceremonial life	1534	1559	42	14	4.4	163	1547	19	1555
Priests, clerks	1555	1555	1	1	0.1	20	1555	20	1555
Ornaments	1523	1558	137	27	14.2	1746	1555	1	1554
Organs	1549	1549	0.5	1	0.1	7	1549	7	1549
Accounting	1523	1559	14	17	1.5	187	1556	1	1529
Crown	1548	1559	11	5	1.1	134	1550	1	1548
Legal costs	1523	1559	51	20	5.3	698	1553	2	1534
Various	1523	1559	33	14	3.4	316	1523	1	1537
Total	1523	1559	962	28	100	4423	1555	0	1552
Wardens' total	1523	1559	981	17	102	4311	1555	0	1552
Balance	1523	1559	−75	28	−7.8	618	1529	−2827	1556

(b) Development over time

	Pre-Refo 1523–1546	Per cent	Post-Refo 1547–1559	Per cent	First CWA 1523–1530	Per cent	Last Pre-Refo CWA 1538–1546	Per cent	Edward 1547–1552	Per cent	Mary 1553–1557	Per cent
Building	232	30.6	195	15.9	446	41.4	204	36.8	16	4.6	430	20.6
Bells	58	7.7	345	28.1	120	11.1	20	3.6	24	6.9	432	20.7
Clock	1	0.1	0.5	0.1	2	0.2	0	0	0	0	1	0.1
Churchyard	7	0.9	7	0.6	10	0.9	8	1.4	4	1.1	10	0.5
Candles/wax	285	37.6	244	19.9	269	25	185	33.4	85	24.4	428	20.5
Ceremonial life	35	4.6	50	4.1	0	0	46	8.3	78	22.3	19	0.9
Priests, clerks	0	0	2	0.2	0	0	0	0	0	0	4	0.2
Ornaments	71	9.4	224	18.2	80	7.4	53	9.6	33	9.5	537	25.7
Organs	0	0	1	0.1	0	0	0	0	1	0.3	0	0
Accounting	5	0.7	26	2.1	3	0.3	7	1.3	4	1.1	45	2.2
Crown	0	0	26	2.1	0	0	0	0	45	12.9	1	0.1
Legal costs	24	3.2	85	6.9	57	5.3	6	1.1	44	12.6	162	7.8
Various	41	5.4	23	1.9	88	8.2	25	4.5	16	4.6	18	0.9
Total	758	100	1229	100	1077	100	554	100	349	100	2086	100
Wardens' total	927	122.3	1029	83.7	1064	98.8	688	124.2	257	73.6	2674	128.2
Balance	74	9.8	-271	-22.1	115	10.7	1	0.2	-57	-16.3	-646	-31

Boxford, Suffolk: income analysis 1530–60

(a) Overall

	First entry	Last entry	Average	Number	Per cent	Highest entry	Year	Lowest entry	Year
Balance	1530	1559	977	29	29.8	2476	1547	7	1535
Collections	1530	1553	51	16	1.6	296	1553	18	1543
Money lending	1544	1559	229	15	7	924	1551	72	1547
Entertainments	1530	1549	746	19	22.8	5735	1535	135	1549
Sales	1532	1554	464	9	14.2	12 539	1547	7	1532
Rents	1530	1559	410	30	12.5	978	1546	114	1553
Burial rites	1542	1542	3	1	0.1	80	1542	80	1542
Gifts	1531	1553	154	5	4.7	4080	1537	4	1531
Debts	1531	1556	217	9	6.6	3597	1547	24	1531
Various	1531	1559	26	5	0.8	456	1550	10	1551
Total	1530	1559	3277	30	100	19 427	1547	1150	1553
Wardens' total	1530	1559	3270	30	99.8	19 427	1547	1102	1553

(b) Development over time

	Pre-Refo 1530–1546	Per cent	Post-Refo 1547–1559	Per cent	First CWA 1530–1536	Per cent	Last Pre-Refo CWA 1540–1546	Per cent	Edward 1547–1553	Per cent	Mary 1554–1558	Per cent
Balance	872	28.6	1115	31.2	718	23.2	1041	40.7	975	20.2	1313	61
Collections	38	1.2	67	1.9	69	2.2	12	0.5	124	2.6	0	0
Money lending	27	0.9	494	13.8	0	0	66	2.6	570	11.8	400	18.6
Entertainments	1286	42.2	39	1.1	1751	56.6	774	30.2	72	1.5	0	0
Sales	33	1.1	1029	28.8	14	0.5	62	2.4	1887	39.1	32	1.5
Rents	494	16.2	300	8.4	443	14.3	561	21.9	283	5.9	341	15.8
Burial rites	5	0.2	0	0	0	0	11	0.4	0	0	0	0
Gifts	268	8.8	4	0.1	69	2.2	0	0	7	0.1	0	0
Debts	15	0.5	482	13.5	3	0.1	33	1.3	848	17.5	67	3.1
Various	11	0.4	47	1.3	26	0.8	0	0	67	1.4	0	0
Total	3049	100	3575	100	3093	100	2559	100	4832	100	2153	100
Wardens' total	3042	99.8	3569	99.8	3077	99.5	2559	100	4822	99.8	2151	99.9

Boxford: expenses 1530–60

(a) Overall

	First entry	Last entry	Average	Number	Per cent	Highest entry	Year	Lowest entry	Year
Building	1530	1559	611	28	33.6	6134	1537	2	1546
Bells	1530	1559	73	28	4	342	1556	5	1540
Clock	1530	1559	33	17	1.8	324	1549	1	1534
Churchyard	1531	1557	18	12	1	316	1534	2	1532
Candles/wax	1530	1558	97	19	5.3	355	1532	2	1558
Ceremonial life	1552	1552	0.5	1	0.1	13	1552	13	1552
Social life	1530	1535	18	4	1	540	1535	3	1532
Priests, clerks	1530	1558	211	26	11.6	640	1551	24	1558
Ornaments	1530	1559	120	29	6.6	529	1534	8	1558
Organs	1530	1541	16	5	0.9	319	1530	7	1533
Peter's pence	1530	1532	2	3	0.1	24	1530	24	1530
Accounting	1530	1530	0.5	1	0.1	13	1530	13	1530
Wages	1530	1559	218	30	12	294	1546	160	1548
Crown	1538	1559	94	18	5.2	350	1554	2	1542
Public works	1531	1556	39	9	2.1	486	1543	1	1554
Poor relief	1547	1558	142	12	7.8	892	1550	4	1547
Legal costs	1530	1559	27	16	1.5	368	1537	2	1546
Landlord	1530	1558	58	25	3.2	434	1548	1	1554
Various	1530	1555	43	5	2.4	474	1540	1	1541
Total	1530	1559	1821	30	100	7260	1537	447	1558
Wardens' total	1530	1559	1837	30	100.9	7260	1537	447	1558
Balance	1530	1559	1456	30	80	16 625	1547	−414	1539

(b) Development over time

	Pre-Refo 1530–1546	Per cent	Post-Refo 1547–1559	Per cent	First CWA 1530–1536	Per cent	Last Pre-Refo CWA 1540–1546	Per cent	Edward 1547–1553	Per cent	Mary 1554–1558	Per cent
Building	948	46.3	171	11.2	949	42.9	125	11.2	267	13.8	69	6.5
Bells	61	3	89	5.8	57	2.6	52	4.7	41	2.1	137	12.9
Clock	29	1.4	37	2.4	33	1.5	19	1.7	60	3.1	10	0.9
Churchyard	24	1.2	10	0.7	49	2.2	8	0.7	1	0.1	24	2.3
Candles/wax	163	8	10	0.7	220	10	95	8.5	19	1	0.5	0.1
Ceremonial life	0	0	1	0.1	0	0	0	0	2	0.1	0	0
Social life	32	1.6	0	0	79	3.6	0	0	0	0	0	0
Priests, clerks	143	7	301	19.7	140	6.3	161	14.5	520	26.8	55	5.2
Ornaments	149	7.3	81	5.3	188	8.5	123	11	48	2.5	116	10.9
Organs	28	1.4	0	0	60	2.7	9	0.8	0	0	0	0
Peter's pence	4	0.2	0	0	10	0.5	0	0	0	0	0	0
Accounting	1	0.1	0	0	2	0.1	0	0	0	0	0	0
Wages	235	11.5	195	12.8	227	10.3	240	21.5	182	9.4	200	18.8
Crown	48	2.3	155	10.2	0	0	114	10.2	140	7.2	153	14.4
Public works	47	2.3	27	1.8	45	2	70	6.3	32	1.6	24	2.3
Poor relief	0	0	328	21.5	0	0	0	0	466	24	201	18.9
Legal costs	37	1.8	15	1	28	1.3	8	0.7	7	0.4	12	1.1
Landlord	53	2.6	65	4.3	89	4	24	2.2	120	6.2	1	0.1
Various	43	2.1	42	2.8	38	1.7	68	6.1	34	1.8	62	5.8
Total	2046	100	1527	100	2214	100	1114	100	1940	100	1064	100
Wardens' total	2068	101.1	1536	100.6	2227	100.6	1148	103.1	1954	100.7	1067	100.3
Balance	1003	49	2048	134.1	880	39.7	1445	129.7	2892	149.1	1090	102.4

Yatton, Somerset: income analysis 1445–1559

(a) Overall

	First entry	Last entry	Average	Number	Per cent	Highest entry	Year	Lowest entry	Year
Balance	1445	1559	3851	106	55.8	12 840	1534	11	1457
Collections	1445	1558	83	100	1.2	725	1543	63	1449
Church house	1474	1555	27	60	0.4	136	1486	1	1555
Ales	1445	1559	2499	102	36.2	4388	1533	600	1550
Pews	1550	1550	1	1	0.1	80	1550	80	1550
Sales	1445	1554	98	92	1.4	662	1461	1	1470
Rents	1552	1554	2	2	0.1	80	1552	80	1552
Lifestock	1445	1445	1	1	0.1	48	1445	48	1445
Burial rites	1446	1559	37	30	0.5	420	1538	4	1558
Gifts	1445	1558	216	98	3.1	1993	1492	12	1449
Debts	1453	1556	32	18	0.5	464	1529	20	1536
Various	1445	1556	55	20	0.8	1306	1445	1	1470
Total	1445	1559	6900	106	100	18 004	1534	1870	1552
Wardens' total	1445	1559	6292	61	91.2	19 573	1524	1870	1552

(b) Development over time

	Pre-Refo 1445–1545	Per cent	Post-Refo 1547–1559	Per cent	First CWA 1445–1451	Per cent	Last Pre-Refo CWA 1540–1545	Per cent	Edward 1547–1552	Per cent	Mary 1554–1558	Per cent
Balance	4078	56.2	1895	49.5	1001	25.5	4586	55.2	2266	52.8	1612	49.5
Collections	86	1.2	58	1.5	138	3.5	203	2.4	29	0.7	98	3
Church house	29	0.4	6	0.2	0	0	11	0.1	12	0.3	0	0
Ales	2626	36.2	1402	36.6	1760	44.8	3126	37.7	1306	30.4	1257	38.6
Pews	0	0	7	0.2	0	0	0	0	16	0.4	0	0
Sales	95	1.3	119	3.1	200	5.1	36	0.4	175	4.1	87	2.7
Rents	0	0	15	0.4	0	0	0	0	16	0.4	16	0.5
Lifestock	1	0	0	0	10	0.3	0	0	0	0	0	0
Burial rites	29	0.4	104	2.7	3	0.1	48	0.6	120	2.8	46	1.4
Gifts	234	3.2	63	1.6	123	3.1	220	2.6	96	2.2	43	1.3
Debts	29	0.4	56	1.5	0	0	72	0.9	52	1.2	72	2.2
Various	49	0.7	104	2.7	689	17.6	0	0	203	4.7	26	0.8
Total	7256	100	3829	100	3925	100	8302	100	4291	100	3257	100
Wardens' total	6834	94.2	3830	100	4216	107.4	7867	94.8	4291	100	3259	100.1

(a) Overall

Yatton: expenses 1445–1560

	First entry	Last entry	Average	Number	Per cent	Highest entry	Year	Lowest entry	Year
Building	1445	1559	636	105	22	4023	1490	1	1476
Bells	1445	1559	211	102	7.3	1901	1452	2	1535
Clock	1532	1559	23	16	0.8	1331	1538	1	1536
Churchyard	1450	1547	22	23	0.8	866	1525	1	1450
Candles/wax	1445	1559	712	105	24.6	2892	1478	1	1550
Ceremonial life	1466	1557	3	31	0.1	155	1554	0.5	1522
Social life	1445	1559	27	25	0.9	948	1545	2	1507
Priests, clerks	1450	1547	75	25	2.6	1680	1543	1	1455
Ornaments	1445	1559	692	106	23.9	9465	1534	1	1550
Obits	1446	1467	0.5	14	0	4	1458	1	1448
Organs	1461	1559	54	15	1.9	4068	1527	1	1531
Accounting	1445	1559	7	65	0.2	48	1543	0.5	1467
Wages	1446	1559	39	101	1.3	108	1547	18	1466
Crown	1538	1559	28	17	1	652	1548	10	1558
Public works	1522	1559	8	13	0.3	280	1522	12	1557
Poor relief	1445	1559	4	4	0.1	186	1558	16	1559
Legal costs	1450	1559	84	45	2.9	2016	1485	1	1534
Landlord	1470	1559	120	59	4.1	4776	1473	3	1492
Other ales	1446	1543	4	28	0.1	96	1537	4	1446
Various	1445	1559	143	75	4.9	3240	1501	1	1455
Total	1445	1559	2892	107	100	12 305	1534	132	1476
Wardens' total	1445	1559	2750	76	95.1	9369	1482	466	1553
Balance	1445	1559	4047	105	140	12 976	1533	89	1473

(b) Development over time

	Pre-Refo 1445–1545	Per cent	Post-Refo 1547–1559	Per cent	First CWA 1445–1450	Per cent	Last Pre-Refo CWA 1541–1545	Per cent	Edward 1547–1552	Per cent	Mary 1553–1558	Per cent
Building	661	21.9	438	23.7	442	16.3	465	11.4	623	34.2	315	16.5
Bells	204	6.7	262	14.2	134	4.9	195	4.8	59	3.2	417	21.8
Clock	24	0.8	18	0.8	0	0	9	0.2	4	0.2	30	1.6
Churchyard	25	0.8	1	0.1	1	0.1	1	0.1	1	0.1	0	0
Candles/wax	780	25.8	168	9.1	284	10.5	1030	25.4	204	11.2	141	7.4
Ceremonial life	1	0.1	18	1	0	0	0	0	0	0	0	1.8
Social life	25	0.8	45	2.4	5	0.2	274	6.7	32	1.8	35	1.8
Priests, clerks	83	2.7	17	0.9	1	0.1	893	22	40	2.2	23	1.2
Ornaments	738	24.4	327	17.7	1464	54	541	13.3	116	6.4	539	28.2
Obits	1	0.1	0	0	1	0.1	0	0	0	0	0	0
Organs	58	1.9	20	1.1	0	0	64	1.6	0	0	0	0
Accounting	6	0.2	14	0.8	4	0.1	18	0.4	8	0.4	23	1.2
Wages	35	1.2	66	3.6	12	0.4	88	2.2	58	3.2	74	3.9
Crown	6	0.2	203	11	0	0	92	2.3	254	13.9	188	9.8
Public works	4	0.1	43	2.3	0	0	12	0.3	20	1.1	50	2.6
Poor relief	1	0.1	31	1.7	11	0.4	0	0	34	1.9	31	1.6
Legal costs	89	2.9	51	2.8	1	0.1	41	1	88	4.8	27	1.4
Landlord	134	4.4	3	0.2	0	0	4	0.1	2	0.1	4	0.2
Other ales	4	0.1	0	0	2	0.1	13	0.3	0	0	0	0
Various	145	4.8	128	6.9	354	13	324	7.8	281	15.4	17	0.9
Total	3023	100	1851	100	2715	100	4063	100	1823	100	1913	100
Wardens' total	2882	95.3	1994	107.7	2998	110.4	4063	100	2226	122.1	1901	99.4
Balance	4327	143	1849	99.9	1227	45.2	4398	108.2	2472	135.6	1179	61.6

Sources of revenue (i) and expenditure (ii) in ten parishes

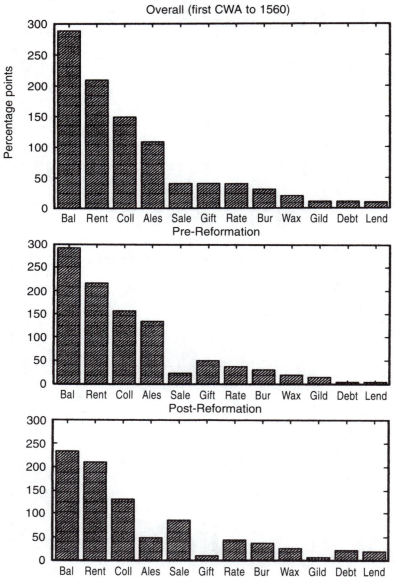

Figure A4(i) Sources of revenue in 10 parishes (9 parishes *t*. Edward VI; for categories and abbreviations see Appendix 2); unit: percentage points scored in the sample (cf. n. 39 in Chapter 6)

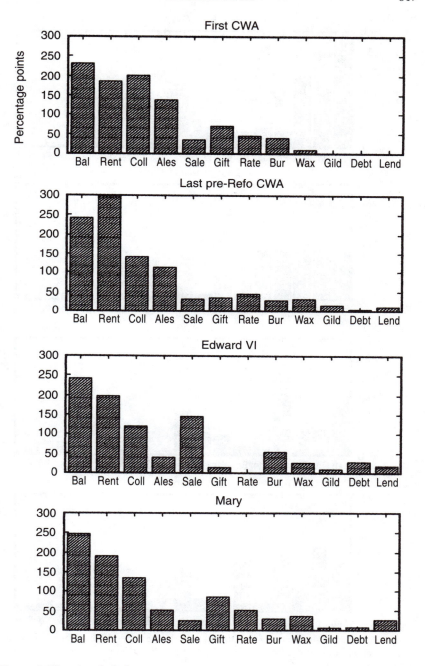

Figure A4(i) *concluded*

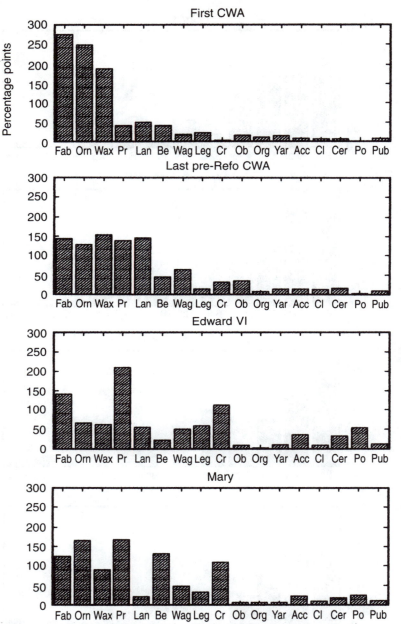

Figure A4(ii)   Main items of expenditure in 10 parishes (9 parishes *t*. Edward VI; for categories and abbreviations see Appendix 2); unit: percentage points scored in the sample (cf. n. 39 in Chapter 6)

Bibliography

Manuscript sources

Bristol Record Office
P/AS/ChW/ 1: 1406/7–1481/2   Church Book of All Saints, Bristol
       3: 1485/6–1559/60   CWA of All Saints, Bristol
P/AS/ChW/2   Rent Rolls of the Parish of All Saints, Bristol
P/AS/C/1   Halleway Chantry Accounts (All Saints, Bristol)

London: Guildhall Library
MS 1279/1: 1454/6–1522/3   CWA of St Andrew Hubbard, London
       2: 1524/5–1558/60
MS 1278/1   Parish Registers of St Andrew Hubbard, London
MS 1454, rolls 1 (1466/8)–65   CWA of St Botolph Aldersgate, London
(1559/60)
MS 9531/4   Register of Robert Fitzhugh, Bishop of London
MS 9531/5   Register of William Gray, Bishop of London
MS 9531/6   Register of Robert Gilbert, Bishop of London

London: Public Record Office
C 1   Early Chancery Proceedings
E 179 113/192   Lay Subsidy Roll 14–15 Henry VIII (Bristol)
STAC 3   Star Chamber Proceedings, Edward VI

Taunton: Somerset Record Office
D/P/yat/4/1/1: 1445/6–1521/2   CWA of Yatton, Somerset
       2: 1523/4–1539/40
       3: 1540/1–1559/60

Printed sources

Adams, N., and Donahue, C. Jr (eds), *Select Cases from the Ecclesiastical Courts of the Province of Canterbury c.1200–1301*, Selden Society vc (London, 1981)

Atchley, E. G. C. F. (ed.), 'Some documents relating to the parish of All Saints', *Archaeological Journal*, NS 8 (1901), 147–81

Baildon, W. P. (ed.), *Select Cases in Chancery 1364–1471*, Selden Society x (London, 1896)

Bailey, F. A. (ed.), *A Selection from the Prescot Court Leet and Other Records 1447–1600*, The RS for the Publication of Original Documents Relating to Lancashire and Cheshire lxxxix (Preston, 1937)

—— (ed.), *The CWA of Prescot, Lancashire 1523–1607*, The RS for the Publication of Original Documents Relating to Lancashire and Cheshire civ (Preston, 1953)

Baker, J. H. (ed.), *The Reports of Sir John Spelman*, Selden Society xciv (vol. ii, London, 1978)

Bannister, A. T. (ed.), 'Visitation returns of the diocese of Hereford in 1397', *EHR*, **44** (1929), 279–89, 444–53, and **45** (1930), 92–101, 444–63

Barmby, M. (ed.), *CWA of Pittington and Other Parishes in the Diocese of Durham from 1580–1700*, Surtees Society lxxxiv (Durham, 1888)

Basing, P. (ed.), *Parish Fraternity Register: The Fraternity of the Holy Trinity and SS Fabian and Sebastian in the Parish of St Botolph without Aldersgate*, London RS Publications xviii (London, 1982)

Bateson, M. (ed.), *Borough Customs*, Selden Society xviii and xxi (2 vols, London, 1904–6)

Bickley, F. B. (ed.), *The Little Red Book of Bristol* (2 vols, Bristol/London, 1900)

Binney, J. E. (ed.), *The Accounts of the Wardens of the Parish of Morebath 1520–73* (Exeter, 1904)

Booty, J. E. (ed.), *The Book of Common Prayer 1559: The Elizabethan Prayer Book* (Charlottesville, 1976)

Bramble, J. R. (ed.), 'From the records of St Nicholas church', *Proceedings of the Clifton Antiquarian Club*, 1 (1884–8), 142–50

Burgess, C. (ed.), *The Pre-Reformation Records of All Saints, Bristol* (3 vols, forthcoming)

Caley, J., and Hunter, J. (eds), *Valor Ecclesiasticus 1535* (6 vols, London, 1810–34)

Cardwell, E. (ed.), *Synodalia* (Oxford, 1842)

Chitty, H. (ed.), *Registra Stephani Gardiner et Johannis Poynet episcoporum Wintoniensium*, Canterbury and York Society xxxvii (Oxford, 1930)

'Churchwardens' presentments, 1520', *Reports of the Oxfordshire Archaeological Society*, **70** (1925), 75–117

Clark, A. (ed.), *Lincoln Diocese Documents 1450–1544*, Early English Text Society, OS cxlix (London, 1914)

Coke, Sir E., *The First Part of the Institutes of the Laws of England, or a Commentarie upon Littleton* (8th edn, London, 1670)

Cooke, A. M. (ed.), *Act Book of the Ecclesiastical Court of Whalley 1510-38*, Chetham Society, NS xliv (Manchester, 1901)

Dasent, J. R. (ed.), *Acts of the Privy Council of England*, NS iii: 1550–2 (London, 1891).

Dilks, T. B. (ed.), *Bridgwater Borough Archives 1200–1485*, Somerset RS xlviii, liii, lviii, lx, lxx (5 vols, Frome/London, 1933–1971)

Doree, S. G. (ed.), *The Early CWA of Bishop's Stortford*, Hertfordshire Record Publications x (Hitchin, 1994)

Drew, C. (ed.), *Lambeth CWA 1504–1645 and Vestry Book*, Surrey RS xviii (London, 1941)

Dudding, R. C. (ed.), *The First Churchwardens' Book of Louth 1500–24* (Oxford, 1941)

Elton, G. R. (ed.), *The Tudor Constitution: Documents and Commentary* (Cambridge, 1962)

Farmiloe, J. E., and Nixseaman, R. (eds), *Elizabethan CWA*, Publications of the Bedfordshire Historical RS xxxiii (Streatley, 1953)

Fishwick, H. (ed.), *Pleadings and Depositions in the Duchy Court of Lancaster*, RS for the Publication of Original Documents Relating to Lancashire and Cheshire xl (vol. iii, Manchester, 1896)

Fowler, J. T. (ed.), *Acts of Chapter of the Collegiate Church of Ripon 1452–1506*, Surtees Society lxiv (Durham, 1875)

Fox, F. F. (ed.), 'Regulations of the vestry of St Stephen, 1524', *Proceedings of the Clifton Antiquarian Club*, **1** (1884–1888), 198–206

Frere, W. H., and Kennedy, W. P. M. (eds), *Visitation Articles and Injunctions of the Reformation Period*, Alcuin Club xiv–xvi (3 vols, London, 1910)

Freshfield, E. (ed.), 'Some remarks upon the book of records and history of the parish of St Stephen Coleman Street', *Archaeologia*, **50** (1887), 17–57

Gibson, E. (ed.), *Codex iuris ecclesiastici Anglicani: or the Statutes, Constitutions, Canons, Rubricks and Articles of the Church of England ... with a Commentary, Historical and Juridical* (2nd edn, Oxford, 1761) [reprinted 1969]

Glass, D. V. (ed.), *London Inhabitants Within the Walls 1695*, London RS (London, 1967)

Glasscock, J. L. (ed.), *The Records of St Michael's Parish Church,*

Bishop's Stortford (London, 1882)

Glasscock, R. E. (ed.), *The Lay Subsidy of 1334*, Records of Social and Economic History, NS ii (Oxford, 1975)

Greatrex, J. (ed.), *The Account Rolls of the Obedientiaries of Peterborough*, Northamptonshire RS xxxiii (Wellingborough, 1984)

Green, E. (ed.), *The Survey and Rental of the Chantries, Colleges and Free Chapels in Somerset 1548*, Somerset RS ii (London/Frome, 1888)

Gross, C. (ed.), *Select Cases from the Coroners' Rolls 1265–1413*, Selden Society ix (London, 1895)

Hanham, A. (ed.), *CWA of Ashburton 1479–1580*, Devon and Cornwall RS, NS xv (Torquay, 1970)

Harper-Bill, C. (ed.), 'A late medieval visitation: the diocese of Norwich in 1499', *PSIA*, **34** (1980), 35–47

Harvey, P. D. A. (ed.), *Manorial Records of Cuxham 1200–1359*, Historical MSS Commission, Joint Publications xxiii (London, 1976)

Harvey, S. H. A. (ed.), *Suffolk in 1524, Being the Return for a Subsidy Granted in 1523*, Suffolk Green Books x (Woodbridge, 1910)

Heath, P. (ed.), *Medieval Clerical Accounts*, Borthwick Institute of Historical Research: St Anthony's Hall Publications xxvi (York, 1964)

Heath Barnum, P. (ed.), *Dives and Pauper*, Early English Text Society, OS cclxxv (Oxford, 1976)

Helmholz, R. H. (ed.), *Select Cases of Defamation to 1600*, Selden Society ci (London, 1985)

Hennessy, G. (ed.), *Novum repertorium parochiale Londinense* (London, 1898)

Hill, R. M. T. (ed.), *The Labourer in the Vineyard: The Visitations of Archbishop Melton in the Archdeaconry of Richmond*, Borthwick Papers xxxv (York, 1968)

Hobhouse, E. (ed.), *CWA of Croscombe, Pilton, Yatton, Tintinhull, Morebath and St Michael, Bath*, Somerset RS iv (London, 1890)

Hockey, S. F. (ed.), *The Account Book of Beaulieu Abbey*, Royal Historical Society: Camden 4th Series xvi (London, 1975)

Houlbrooke, R. (ed.), *The Letter Book of John Parkhurst, Bishop of Norwich, Compiled During the Years 1571–1575*, Norfolk RS xliii (Norwich, 1975)

Howard, A. J., and Stoate, T. L. (eds), *Devon Muster Rolls for 1569* (Bristol, 1977)

Hudson, W. (ed.), *Leet Jurisdiction in the City of Norwich During the Thirteenth and Fourteenth Centuries*, Selden Society v (London, 1892)

Hughes, P., and Larkin, J. F. (eds), *Tudor Royal Proclamations* (3 vols, New Haven, 1964–9)

Hussey, A. (ed.), *Kent Chantries*, Kent Records xii (Ashford, 1936)

——— (ed.), *Kent Obit and Lamp Rents*, Kent Records xiv (Ashford, 1936)

Irvine, W. F. (ed.), *A List of Clergy in Eleven Deaneries of the Diocese of Chester 1541/2*, RS for the Publication of Original Documents Relating to Lancashire and Cheshire xxxiii (Manchester, 1896)

Kitching, C. (ed.), *London and Middlesex Chantry Certificates 1548*, London RS xvi (London, 1980)

——— (ed.), *The Royal Visitation of 1559*, Surtees Society clxxxvii (Gateshead, 1975)

Lambarde, W., *The Dueties of Constables, Borsholders, Tythingmen and Such Other Lowe and Lay Ministers of the Peace* (London, 1602)

Leadam, I. S. (ed.), *Select Cases in the Court of Requests 1497–1569*, Selden Society xii (London, 1898)

——— (ed.), *Select Cases before the King's Council in the Star Chamber*, Selden Society xvi and xxv (2 vols, London, 1903–11)

Littlehales, H. (ed.), *The Medieval Records of a London City Church, St Mary at Hill 1420–1559*, Early English Text Society, OS cxxv and cxxviii (London, 1904/5)

Loengard, J. S. (ed.), *London Viewers and their Certificates 1508–58*, London RS xxvi (London, 1989)

Louis, C. (ed.), *The Commonplace Book of Robert Reynes of Acle: An Edition of Tanner MS 407*, Garland Medieval Texts i (New York/London, 1980)

Lyndwood, W., *Provinciale seu constitutiones Angliae* (Oxford, 1679)

Maclean, J. (ed.), 'Chantry certificates, Gloucestershire', *TBGAS*, 8 (1883/4), 232–51

Maitland, F. W. (ed.), *Select Pleas in Manorial Courts*, Selden Society ii (London, 1889)

Masters, B. R., and Ralph, E. (eds), *The Church Book of St Ewen's, Bristol 1454–1584*, Publications of the Bristol and Gloucestershire Archaeological Society: Records Section vi (Bristol, 1967)

Maxwell–Lyte, H. (ed.), *The Registers of Oliver King and Hadrian de Castello, Bishops of Bath and Wells*, Somerset RS liv (London, 1939)

Mellows, W. T. (ed.), *Peterborough Local Administration: Parochial Government Before the Reformation: CWA 1467–1573, with Supplementary Documents 1107–1488*, Publications of the Northamptonshire RS ix (Kettering, 1939)

Mercer, F. R. (ed.), *CWA at Betrysden 1515–73*, Kent Records v/2 (Ashford, 1928)

Moore, A. P. (ed.), 'Proceedings of the ecclesiastical courts in the archdeaconry of Leicester 1516–35', *Associated Architectural Society Reports and Papers*, 28 (1905/6), 117–220, 593–662

Myatt-Price, E. M. (ed.), 'Cromwell household accounts 1417–76' in

Littleton and Yamey, *History of Accounting*, pp. 99–113

Myers, A. R. (ed.), *English Historical Documents* (vol. iv, London, 1969)

Nash, T. R. (ed.), *Collections for the History of Worcestershire* (vol. i, London, 1781)

Newcourt, R. (ed.), *Repertorium ecclesiasticum parochiale Londinense* (2 vols, London, 1708-10)

Northeast, P. (ed.), *Boxford CWA 1530–61*, Suffolk RS xxiii (Woodbridge, 1982)

Osborne, F. M. (ed.), *The CWA of St Michael's Church, Chagford 1480–1600* (Chagford, 1979)

Overall, W. H. (ed.), *The Accounts of the CWs of the Parish of St Michael Cornhill* (London, 1871)

Page, W. (ed.), *The Certificates of the Commissioners Appointed to Survey the Chantries, Guilds, Hospitals etc. in the County of York*, Surtees Society xci and xcii (2 vols, Durham, 1892/3)

———— (ed.), *The Inventories of Church Goods for the Counties of York, Durham and Northumberland*, Surtees Society xcvii (Durham, 1896)

Palmer, W. M. (ed.), 'Fifteenth-century visitation records of the deanery of Wisbech', *Proceedings of the Cambridge Antiquarian Society*, 39 (1938–9), 69–75

Peacock, E. (ed.), 'Extracts from Lincoln episcopal visitations of the fifteenth, sixteenth and seventeenth centuries', *Archaeologia*, 48 (1885), 249–69

Pearson, C. B. (ed.), 'The CWA of the church and parish of St Michael without the North Gate, Bath 1349–1575', *Somersetshire Archaeological and Natural History Society Proceedings*, 23 (1877), i-xxiii, 1–28; 24 (1878), 29–52; 25 (1879), 53–100; 26 (1880), 101–38

Plomer, H. R. (ed.), *The CWA of St Nicholas, Strood*, Kent Records v (Ashford, 1927)

Powicke, F. M., and Cheney, C. R. (eds), *Councils and Synods with Other Documents Relating to the English Church*, part ii (2 vols, Oxford, 1964)

The First and Second Prayer Books of Edward VI, Everyman's Library cdxlviii (London/New York, 1910)

Ragg, F. W. (ed.), 'Fragments of folio M.S. of archdeaconry courts of Buckinghamshire, 1491–5', *Records of Buckinghamshire*, 11 (1920–6), 27–47, 59–76, 145–56, 199–207, 315–42

Raines, F. R. (ed.), *A History of the Chantries within the County Palatine of Lancaster*, Chetham Society lix and lx (2 vols, Manchester, 1862)

Redstone, V. B. (ed.), 'Chapels, chantries and gilds in Suffolk', *PSIA*, 12 (1906), 1–87

Roberts, R. (ed.), 'Further inventories of goods and ornaments of the churches of Surrey *t.* Edward VI', *Surrey Archeaological Collections*, 24 (1911), 1–39

Rolle, H., *Un abridgement des plusieurs cases et resolutions del common ley* (London, 1668)

Schiess, T. (ed.), *Quellenwerk zur Entstehung der Schweizerischen Eidgenossenschaft*, Abteilung 1 (vol. i, Aarau, 1933)

Sharpe, R. R. (ed.), *Calendar of Wills Proved and Enrolled in the Court of Hustings, London 1258–1688* (vol. ii, London, 1890)

Simpson, W. S. (ed.), 'Visitations of churches belonging to St Paul's cathedral in 1249–52', *Camden Miscellany*, 9 (1895), iii–38

────── (ed.), *Visitations of Churches Belonging to St Paul's Cathedral in 1297 and 1458*, Camden Society, NS lv (London, 1895)

Smith, D. M. (ed.), *A Calendar of the Register of Robert Waldby, Archbishop of York 1397*, Borthwick Texts and Calendars: Records of the Northern Province ii (York, 1974)

Smith, L. T. (ed.), *English Gilds: Original Ordinances of More Than 100 Early English Gilds of the Fourteenth and Fifteenth Centuries*, Early English Text Society, OS xl (London, 1870) [reprint 1924]

Smith, T. , *De republica Anglorum*, ed. M. Dewar (Cambridge, 1982)

Snell, L. S. (ed.), *The Chantry Certificates for Devon and the City of Exeter* (Exeter, 1961)

Somers, F. (ed.), *Halesowen CWA 1487–1582*, Worcestershire Historical Society (London, 1952–3)

Stallard, A. D. (ed.), *Transcript of the CWA of Tilney All Saints 1443–1583* (London, 1922)

Statutes of the Realm (vols iii and iv, London, 1817–19) [reprint 1963]

Stoate, T. L. (ed.), *Devon Lay Subsidy Rolls 1524–7* (Bristol, 1979)

────── (ed.), *Devon Lay Subsidy Rolls 1543–5* (Bristol, 1986)

Storey, R. L. (ed.), *The Register of Thomas Langley, Bishop of Durham 1406–37*, Surtees Society clxvi (vol. ii, Durham/London, 1957)

Swayne, H. J. F. (ed.), *CWA of St Edmund and St Thomas, Sarum 1443–1702*, Wiltshire RS (Salisbury, 1896)

Taylor, C. S. (ed.), 'Regulations of the vestry of St Thomas, Bristol, 1563', *Proceedings of the Clifton Antiquarian Club*, 1 (1884–8), 193–8

Thomas, A. H. (ed.), *Calendar of Plea and Memoranda Rolls Preserved Among the Archives of the Corporation of the City of London 1413–37* (Cambridge, 1943)

Thomassinus, L., *Vetus et nova ecclesiae disciplina circa beneficia et beneficiarios* (Venice, 1766)

Thompson, A. H. (ed.), *Visitations of the Diocese of Lincoln 1517–31*, Lincoln RS xxxiii, xxxv, xxxvii (3 vols, Hereford, 1940–7)

—— (ed.), 'Chantry certificates for Northamptonshire', *Associated Architectural Society Reports and Papers*, 31 (1911), 87–178

Topham, J, Morant, P. and Astle, T. (eds), *Rotuli parliamentorum* (6 vols, London, 1767–83)

Twemlow, J. A. (ed.), *Calendar of Papal Letters*, Calendar of Entries in the Papal Registers Relating to Great Britain and Ireland (vols ix and xiii, London, 1912 and 1955)

Veale, E. (ed.), *The Great Red Book of Bristol*, Bristol RS ii (Bristol, 1931)

Wasson, J. M. (ed.), *Devon*, Records of Early English Drama (Toronto, 1986)

Wilkinson, J. J. (ed.), *Receipts and Expenses in the Building of Bodmin Church 1469–72*, Camden Miscellany vii (London, 1874)

Williams, J. F. (ed.), *The Early CWA of Hampshire* (Winchester/London, 1913)

Wood–Legh, K. L. (ed.), *Kentish Visitations of Archbishop William Warham and his Deputies 1511–2*, Kent Records xxiv (Maidstone, 1984)

Woodruff, C. E. (ed.), 'An archidiaconal visitation of 1502', *Archaeologia Cantiana*, 47 (1935), 13–54

Worth, R. N. (ed.), *Calendar of Tavistock Parish Records* (Plymouth, 1887)

Yale, D. E. C. (ed.), *Sir Matthew Hale's 'The Prerogatives of the King'*, Selden Society xcii (London, 1976)

Zutshi, P. N. R. (ed.), *Original Papal Letters in England 1305–1415*, Index actorum Romanorum pontificium ab Innocentio III ad Martinum V electum v (Vatican City, 1990)

Secondary works

Acheson, R. J., *Radical Puritans in England 1560–1660* (London/New York, 1990)

Addleshaw, G. W. O., *The Development of the Parochial System from Charlemagne (768–814) to Urban II (1088–99)*, St Anthony's Hall Publications vi (London, 1954)

—— *Rectors, Vicars and Patrons in Twelfth and Early Thirteenth-Century Canon Law*, St Anthony's Hall Publications ix (York, 1956)

Addy, S. O., *Church and Manor: A Study in English Economic History* (London, 1913)

Alldridge, N., 'Loyalty and identity in Chester parishes 1540–1640' in S. J. Wright (ed.), *Parish, Church and People*, pp. 85–124

Amery, J. S., 'Presidential address', *Reports and Transactions of the Devonshire Association*, 56 (1925), 43–102

Archer, I. W., *The Pursuit of Stability: Social Relations in Elizabethan London*, Cambridge Studies in Early Modern British History (Cambridge, 1991)

Aston, M., *England's Iconoclasts* (vol. i, Oxford, 1988)

———— 'Iconoclasm at Rickmansworth 1522: troubles of churchwardens', *JEH*, 40 (1989), 524–52

———— 'Segregation in church' in W. J. Sheils and D. Wood (eds), *Women in the Church*, SCH xxvii (Oxford, 1990), pp. 237–94

Atchley, E. G. C. F., 'On the parish records of All Saints', *TBGAS*, 27 (1904), 221–74

Aubrun, M., *La paroisse en France des origines au XVe siècle* (Paris, 1986)

Ault, W. O., 'Village assemblies in medieval England' in *Album Helen Cam*, Studies Presented to the International Commission for the History of Representative and Parliamentary Institutions xxiii (Louvain/Paris, 1960), pp. 13–35

———— 'Manor court and parish church in fifteenth-century England: a study of village by-laws', *Speculum*, 42 (1967), 53–67

———— 'The village church and the village community in medieval England', *Speculum*, 45 (1970), 197–215

Bader, K. S., *Dorfgenossenschaft und Dorfgemeinde*, Studien zur Rechtsgeschichte des mittelalterlichen Dorfes ii (Cologne/Graz, 1962)

Bailey, D., *Prescot Court Leet* (Prescot, no date)

Bailey, F. A., 'The CWA of Prescot 1523–1607', *Transactions of the Historical Society of Lancashire and Cheshire*, 92 (1940), 133–201

Baillie, H., 'A London church in early Tudor times', *Music & Letters*, 36 (1955), 55–64

Baker, J. H., *An Introduction to English Legal History* (3rd edn, London, 1990)

Barnes, T. G., 'County politics and a puritan cause célèbre: Somerset church ales 1633', *TRHS*, 5th Series 9 (1959), 103–22

Barron, C. M., 'The parish fraternities of medieval London' in C. M. Barron and C. Harper-Bill (eds), *The Church in Pre-Reformation Society: Essays in Honour of F. R. H. Du Boulay* (Woodbridge, 1985), pp. 13–37

———— 'The later middle ages 1270–1520' in M. D. Lobel (ed.), *City of London*, British Atlas of Historic Towns iii (Oxford, 1989), pp. 42–56

Barron, C. M. and Roscoe, J., 'The medieval parish church of St Andrew Holborn' in A. L. Saunders (ed.), *London Topographical Record xxiv*, London Topographical Society Publications cxxiii (London, 1980), pp. 31–60

Barton, J. L., 'The medieval use', *Law Quarterly Review*, 81 (1965), 562–77

Bateson, M., 'Borough of Peterborough' in *VCH Northampton* (vol. ii, reprint London, 1970), pp. 421–60

Benedict, P., *Rouen during the French Wars of Religion* (Cambridge, 1981)

Bennett, J. M., 'Conviviality and charity in medieval and early modern England', *PaP*, **134** (1992), 19–41

Beresford, G., 'Climatic change and its effects upon the settlement and desertion of medieval villages in Britain' in C. Delano-Smith and M. Parry (eds), *Consequences of Climatic Change* (Nottingham, 1981), pp. 30–9

Bettey, J. H., *Bristol Parish Churches during the Reformation, c. 1530–60*, Bristol Branch of the Historical Association: Local History Pamphlets xlv (Bristol, 1979)

—— *Church and Community in Bristol during the Sixteenth Century*, Bristol RS (Bristol, 1983)

—— *Church and Parish: An Introduction for Local Historians*, Batsford Local History Series (London, 1987)

—— 'The Reformation and the parish church: local responses to national directives', *The Historian*, **46** (Summer 1995), 11–14

Bierbrauer, P., 'Der Aufstieg der Gemeinde: die Entfeudalisierung der Gesellschaft im späten Mittelalter' in P. Blickle and J. Kunisch (eds), *Kommunalisierung und Christianisierung: Voraussetzungen und Folgen der Reformation 1400–1600*, Beiheft 9 der Zeitschrift für Historische Forschung (Berlin, 1989), 29–55

Bijsterveld, A. J. A., *Laverend tussen Kerk en wereld: De pastoors in Noord-Brabant 1400–1570* (Amsterdam, 1993)

Bittle, W. G., and Lane, R. T., 'Inflation and philanthropy in England: a re-assessment of W. K. Jordan's data', *EcHR*, 2nd Series **29** (1976), 203–10

Blair, J., 'Introduction: from minster to parish church' in J. Blair (ed.), *Minsters and Parish Churches: The Local Church in Transition 950–1200*, Oxford University Committee for Archaeology: Monograph xvii (Oxford, 1988), pp. 1–19

—— and Sharpe, R. (eds), *Pastoral Care Before the Parish* (Leicester, 1992)

Blair, L., *A List of CWA* (Ann Arbor, 1939)

Blickle, P., *Die Revolution von 1525* (2nd edn, Munich, 1983) [English: Baltimore/London, 1981]

—— *Gemeindereformation: Die Menschen des 16. Jahrhunderts auf dem Weg zum Heil* (Munich, 1985) [English: Atlantic Highlands/ London, 1992]

—— 'Bauer und Reformation: Positionsbestimmungen' in his *Zugänge zur bäuerlichen Reformation*, Bauer und Reformation i

(Zurich, 1987), pp. 9–20

—— 'Communal Reformation and peasant piety: the peasant Reformation and its late medieval origins', *Central European History*, **20** (1987), 216–28

—— 'Kommunalismus: Begriffsbildung in heuristischer Absicht' in his *Landgemeinde und Stadtgemeinde in Mitteleuropa* (Munich, 1991), pp. 5–38

—— 'Eidgenossenschaften in reformatorischer Absicht, oder: Wie begründet ist die Kritik an der "Gemeindereformation"?' in H. R. Guggisberg and G. G. Krodel (eds), *Die Reformation in Deutschland und Europa*, Archiv für Reformationsgeschichte: Sonderband (Gütersloh, 1993), pp. 159–73

Bonfield, L., and Poos, L. R., 'The development of the deathbed transfer in medieval English manor courts', *Cambridge Law Journal*, **47** (1988), 403–27

Bossy, J., 'The Counter-Reformation and the people of Catholic Europe', *PaP*, **47** (1970), 51–70

—— 'Essai de sociographie de la messe 1200–1700', *Annales*, **36** (1981), 44–70 [English: *PaP*, **100** (1983)]

—— *Christianity in the West 1400–1700* (Oxford, 1985)

Du Boulay, F. R. H., *An Age of Ambition: English Society in the Later Middle Ages* (London, 1970)

Boulton, J. P., 'The limits of formal religion: the administration of holy communion in late Elizabethan and early Stuart London', *London Journal*, **10** (1984), 135–54

Bowker, M., *The Secular Clergy in the Diocese of Lincoln 1495–1520*, Cambridge Studies in Medieval Life and Thought, NS xii (Cambridge, 1968)

—— 'The commons supplication against the ordinaries (1532) in the light of some archidiaconal acta', *TRHS*, 5th Series **21** (1971), 61–77

—— 'Lincolnshire 1536: heresy, schism or religious discontent' in D. Baker (ed.), *Schism, Heresy and Religious Protest*, SCH ix (Cambridge, 1972), pp. 195–212

Braudel, F., *The Mediterranean and the Mediterranean World in the Age of Philipp II* (vol. i, London, 1975) [French: Paris, 1949]

Bridbury, A. R., 'The farming out of manors', *EcHR*, 2nd Series **31** (1978), 503–20

Brigden, S., 'Tithe controversy in Reformation London', *JEH*, **32** (1981), 285–301

—— *London and the Reformation* (Oxford, 1989)

Britton, E., *The Community of the Vill: A Study in the History of the Family and Village Life in Fourteenth-Century England* (Toronto, 1977)

Brooke, C. N. L., 'The missionary at home: the church in the towns 1000–1250' in G. J. Cuming (ed.), *The Mission of the Church and the Propagation of the Faith*, SCH vi (Cambridge, 1970), pp. 59–83

———— 'The churches of medieval Cambridge' in D. Beales and G. Best (eds), *History, Society and the Churches* (Cambridge 1985), pp. 49–76

Brooke, C. N. L. and Keir, G., *London 800-1216: The Shaping of a City*, History of London (London, 1975)

Brown, A. D., *Popular Piety in Late Medieval England: The Diocese of Salisbury 1250–1550*, Oxford Historical Monographs (Oxford, 1995)

Brushfield, T. N., 'The church of All Saints, East Budleigh, part ii', *Reports and Transactions of the Devonshire Association*, **24** (1892), 334–57

Burgess, C., ' "For the increase of divine service": chantries in the parish in late medieval Bristol', *JEH*, **36** (1985), 46–65

———— 'A service for the dead: the form and function of the anniversary in late medieval Bristol', *TBGAS*, **105** (1987), 183–211

———— ' "A fond thing vainly invented": an essay on purgatory and pious motive in later medieval England' in Wright (ed.), *Parish, Church and People*, pp. 56–84

———— 'Late medieval wills and pious convention: testamentary evidence reconsidered' in M. A. Hicks (ed.), *Profit, Piety and the Professions in Later Medieval England* (Gloucester, 1990), pp. 14–33

———— 'The benefactions of mortality: the lay response in the late medieval urban parish' in D. Smith (ed.), *Studies in Clergy and Ministry in Medieval England*, Borthwick Studies in History i (York, 1991), pp. 65–86

———— 'Strategies for eternity: perpetual chantry foundation in late medieval Bristol' in C. Harper-Bill (ed.), *Religious Belief and Ecclesiastical Careers in Late Medieval England*, Studies in the History of Medieval Religion iii (Woodbridge, 1991), pp. 1–33

Burgess, C. and Kümin, B., 'Penitential bequests and parish regimes in late medieval England', *JEH*, **44** (1993), 610–30

Burnet, G. B., *The Holy Communion in the Reformed Church of Scotland 1560–1960* (Edinburgh/London, 1960)

Butcher, J. H., *The Parish of Ashburton in the Fifteenth and Sixteenth Centuries as it Appears from Extracts from the CWA, with Notes and Comments* (London, 1870)

Cam, H. M., 'The community of the vill' in V. Ruffer and A. J. Taylor (eds), *Medieval Studies Presented to Rose Graham* (Oxford, 1950), pp. 1–14

Cannan, E., *The History of Local Rates in England* (London, 1912)

Carnwath, J., 'The CWA of Thame, Oxfordshire, c.1443–1524' in D. J. Clayton, R. G. Davies and P. McNiven (eds), Trade, Devotion and Governance: Papers in Later Medieval History (Stroud, 1994), pp. 177–97

Carpenter, C., 'The religion of the gentry of fifteenth-century England' in D. Williams (ed.), England in the Fifteenth Century, Proceedings of the 1986 Harlaxton Symposium (Woodbridge, 1987), pp. 53–74

—— 'Gentry and community in medieval England', Journal of British Studies, 33 (1994), 340–80

Carrington, F. A., 'Ancient ales in the county of Wiltshire', Wiltshire Archaeological and Natural History Magazine, 2 (1855), 191–204

Carter, P., 'The records of the court of first fruits and tenths 1540–54', Archives, 21 (1994), 57–66

Carus–Wilson, E. M., 'Bristol: the fourteenth and fifteenth centuries' in M. D. Lobel (ed.), Atlas of Historic Towns (vol. ii, London, 1975), pp. 10–14

Challis, C. E., The Tudor Coinage (Manchester, 1978)

Chew, H. M., 'Mortmain in medieval London', EHR, 60 (1945), 1–15

Christian, W. A. Jr, Local Religion in Sixteenth-Century Spain (Princeton, 1981)

Clark, P., English Provincial Society from the Reformation to the Revolution: Religion, Politics and Society in Kent 1500–1640 (Hassocks, 1977)

Clark, P. and Slack, P., English Towns in Transition 1500–1700 (Oxford, 1976)

Clément, M., 'Recherches sur les paroisses et les fabriques au commencement du XIIIᵉ siècle d'après les registres des Papes', Mélanges d'Archéologie et d'Histoire, 15 (1895), 387–418

Cohn, H., 'Reformatorische Bewegung und Antiklerikalismus in Deutschland und England' in W. J. Mommsen (ed.), Stadtbürgertum und Adel in der Reformation (London, 1979), pp. 303–30

Collinson, P., The Religion of Protestants: The Church in English Society 1559–1625 (Oxford, 1982)

—— 'Shepherds, sheepdogs, and hirelings: the pastoral ministry in post-Reformation England' in W. J. Sheils and D. Wood (eds), The Ministry: Clerical and Lay, SCH xxvi (Oxford, 1989), pp. 185–220

——, De Republica Anglorum or, History with the Politics Put Back, Inaugural Lecture 9 November 1989 (Cambridge, 1990)

—— 'The late medieval Church and its Reformation, 1400–1600' in J. McManners (ed.), The Oxford Illustrated History of Christianity (Oxford, 1990), pp. 233–66

Communautés rurales, vol. iv: Europe occidentale, Recueils de la société Jean Bodin xliii (Paris, 1984)

Constable, G., 'Resistance to tithes in the middle ages', *JEH*, **13** (1962), 172–85

Constant, G., 'Une source trop négligée de l'histoire paroissiale: les registres de marguilliers', *Revue d'Histoire de l'Eglise de France*, **24** (1938), 170–83

——— 'Une source négligée de l'histoire ecclésiastique locale: les registres anciens de marguilliers. Etude d'un de ces registres du XVIe siècle', *Revue d'Histoire Ecclésiastique*, **34** (1938), 504–41

Cook, G. H., *The English Medieval Parish Church* (London, 1954)

——— *Medieval Chantries and Chantry Chapels* (London, 1963)

Copinger, W. A., *The Manors of Suffolk: Notes on their History and Devolution* (vol. i, London, 1905)

Cornwall, J., *The Revolt of the Peasantry 1549* (London/Henley/Boston, 1977)

Coulton, G. G., *Ten Medieval Studies* (Cambridge, 1930)

Cowley, P., *The Church Houses: Their Religious and Social Significance* (London, 1970)

Cox, J. C., *CWA from the Fourteenth Century to the Close of the Seventeenth Century* (London, 1913)

Cox, J. C. and Ford, C. B., *Parish Churches* (London, 1934) [1961 edition]

Cox, J. C. and Harvey, A., *English Church Furniture* (London, 1907)

Craig, J. S., 'Elizabethan CWs and parish accounts', *Social History*, **18** (1993), 357–80

Cressy, D., *Bonfires and Bells: National Memory and the Protestant Calendar in Elizabethan and Stuart England* (London, 1989)

Cross, C., *Church and People 1450–1660: The Triumph of the Laity in the English Church*, Fontana Library of English History ii (Hassocks, 1976)

——— 'Communal piety in sixteenth-century Boston', *Lincolnshire History and Archaeology*, **25** (1990), 33–8

Cutts, E., *Parish Priests and their People in the Middle Ages in England*, Society for the Promotion of Christian Knowledge (London, 1898)

CWA of Parishes Within the City of London: a Handlist (2nd edn, London, 1969)

Davies, C. S. L., 'Die bäuerliche Gemeinde in England 1400–1800' in W. Schulze (ed.), *Aufstände, Revolten, Prozesse: Beiträge zu bäuerlichen Widerstandsbewegungen im frühneuzeitlichen Europa*, Geschichte und Gesellschaft: Bochumer Historische Studien xxvii (Stuttgart, 1983), pp. 41–59

Davies, R. G., 'Lollardy and locality', *TRHS*, 6th Series **1** (1991), 191–212

Delumeau, J., *Catholicism between Luther and Voltaire* (London, 1977)

Denholm–Young, N., *Seignorial Administration in England*, Oxford Historical Series (Oxford, 1937)

Dewindt, E. B., *Land and People in Holywell-cum-Needingworth: Structures of Tenure and Patterns of Social Organization in an East Midlands Village 1252–1457*, Pontifical Institute of Mediaeval Studies, Studies and Texts xxii (Toronto, 1972)

Dickens, A. G., *The English Reformation* (London, 1964) [quoted from 1968 edition; 2nd edn, 1989]

—— 'The early expansion of Protestantism in England 1520–58', *Archive for Reformation History*, **78** (1987), 187–222

Dietz, F., *English Government Finance 1485–1558*, Illinois University Studies in the Social Sciences ix (Illinois, 1921)

Dinn, R., ' "Monuments answerable to men's worth": burial patterns, social status and gender in late medieval Bury St Edmunds', *JEH*, **46** (1995), 237–55

Dobson, R. B., 'Urban decline in late medieval England' in Holt and Rosser (eds), *The English Medieval Town*, pp. 265–86 [originally: *TRHS*, 5th Series **27** (1977), 1–22]

Drew, C. E. S., *Early Parochial Organisation in England: The Origins of the Office of Churchwarden*, Borthwick Institute of Historical Research: St Anthony's Hall Publications vii (London, 1954)

Duffy, E., *The Stripping of the Altars: Traditional Religion in England 1400–1580* (New Haven/London, 1992)

Dyer, C., *Lords and Peasants in a Changing Society: The Estates of the Bishopric of Worcester 680–1540* (Cambridge, 1980)

—— 'The social and economic background to the rural revolt of 1381' in R. Hilton and T. H. Aston (eds), *The English Rising of 1381* (Cambridge, 1984), pp. 9–42

—— 'Power and conflict in the medieval English village' in D. Hooke (ed.), *Medieval Villages: A Review of Current Work*, Oxford University Committee for Archaeology: Monograph v (Oxford, 1985), pp. 27–32

—— *Standards of Living in the Later Middle Ages: Social Change in England c.1200–1520*, Cambridge Medieval Textbooks (Cambridge, 1989)

—— 'The English medieval village community and its decline', *Journal of British Studies*, **33** (1994), 407–29

Dykema, P. A., and Oberman, H. A. (eds), *Anticlericalism in Late Medieval and Early Modern Europe*, Studies in Medieval and Reformation Thought li (Leiden/New York/Cologne, 1993)

Dymond, R., 'The history of the parish of St Petrock, Exeter', *Reports and Transactions of the Devonshire Association*, **14** (1882), 402–92

Edwards, A. C., 'The medieval CWA of St Mary, Yatton', *Notes and*

Queries for Somerset and Dorset, **32** (1986), 536–47

Elton, G. R., *The Parliament of England 1559–81* (Cambridge, 1986)

Engen, J. Van, 'The Christian Middle Ages as an historiographical problem', *American Historical Review*, **91** (1986), 519–52

Farmer, D. L., 'Prices and wages 1350–1500' in E. Miller (ed.), *The Agricultural History of England and Wales* (vol. iii, Cambridge, 1991), pp. 431–525

Farrer, W., and Brownbill, J., 'Prescot', *VCH Lancaster* (vol. iii, reprint London, 1966), pp. 341–413

Fawcett, R., *Scottish Medieval Churches: An Introduction to the Ecclesiastical Architecture of the 12th to 16th Centuries* (Edinburgh, 1985)

Feine, H. E., 'Die genossenschaftliche Gemeindekirche im germanischen Recht', *Mitteilungen des Instituts für österreichische Geschichtsforschung*, **68** (1960), 171–96

———— 'Kirche und Gemeindebildung' in T. Mayer (ed.), *Die Anfänge der Landgemeinde und ihr Wesen*, Vorträge und Forschungen vii (Stuttgart, 1964), pp. 53–77

Finlay, R., *Population and Metropolis: The Demography of London 1580–1650* (Cambridge, 1981)

Fishwick, H., *The History of the Parish of Rochdale* (Rochdale/London, 1889)

Flower, C. T., *Public Works in Medieval Law*, Selden Society xxxiii, xl (2 vols, London, 1915–23)

Frankforter, A. D., 'The Reformation and the register: episcopal administration of parishes in late medieval England', *Catholic History Review*, **63** (1977), 204–24

Franklin, M., 'The cathedral as parish church: the case of southern England' in D. Abulafia, M. Franklin and M. Rubin (eds), *Church and City 1000–1500: Essays in Honour of Christopher Brooke* (Cambridge, 1992), pp. 173–98

Freytag, H. J., 'Zur Geschichte der Reformation in Plön', *Jahrbuch Plön*, **20** (1990), 32–5

Frölich, K., 'Die Rechtsformen der mittelalterlichen Altarpfründen', *Zeitschrift der Savigny-Stiftung für Rechtsgeschichte: Kanonische Abteilung*, **20** (1931), 457–544

Fuhrmann, R., 'Die Kirche im Dorf: kommunale Initiativen zur Organisation von Seelsorge vor der Reformation' in P. Blickle (ed.), *Zugänge zur bäuerlichen Reformation*, Bauer und Reformation i (Zurich, 1987), pp. 147–86

———— 'Dorfgemeinde und Pfründstiftung vor der Reformation: kommunale Selbstbestimmungschancen zwischen Religion und Recht' in P. Blickle and J. Kunisch (eds), *Kommunalisierung und*

Christianisierung, Beiheft 9 der Zeitschrift für Historische Forschung (Berlin, 1989), 77–112

―――― *Kirche und Dorf: Religiöse Bedürfnisse und kirchliche Stiftung auf dem Lande vor der Reformation*, Quellen und Forschungen zur Agrargeschichte xl (Stuttgart/Jena/New York, 1995)

Galpern, A. N., *The Religions of the People in Sixteenth-Century Champagne*, Harvard Historical Studies xcii (Cambridge Mass., 1976)

Ganghofer, R., 'Les communautés rurales en Europe occidentale et centrale (non méridionale) depuis le moyen âge: rapport général' in *Communautés rurales*, pp. 39–64

Gasquet, F. A., *Parish Life in Medieval England* (London, 1906)

Gaudemet, J., 'La vie paroissiale en occident au moyen âge et dans les temps modernes' in *Communautés rurales*, pp. 65–86

Genicot, L., *Rural Communities in the Medieval West*, John Hopkins Symposia in Comparative History xviii (Baltimore/London, 1990)

Gneist, R., *Geschichte und heutige Gestalt der englischen Communalverfassung* (vol. i, Berlin, 1863)

Goering, J. W., 'The changing face of the village parish, ii: the thirteenth century' in J. A. Raftis (ed.), *Pathways to Medieval Peasants*, Papers in Medieval Studies ii (Toronto, 1981), pp. 323–33

Goheen, R. B., 'Peasant politics? Village communities and the crown in fifteenth-century England', *American Historical Review*, 96 (1991), 42–62

Goujard, P., 'Les fonds de fabriques paroissiales: une source d'histoire religieuse méconnue', *Revue d'Histoire de l'Eglise de France*, 68 (1982), 99–111

Graves, E. B., *Oxford Bibliography of British History: to 1485* (Oxford, 1975)

Gray, I., and Ralph, E. (eds), *Guide to the parish records of Bristol*, Publications of the Bristol and Gloucestershire Archaeological Society: Records Section vi (Bristol, 1963)

Green, A.S., *Town Life in the Fifteenth Century* (2 vols, London/New York, 1894)

Griffith, E., *Cases of Supposed Exemption from Poor Rates ... with a Preliminary Sketch of the History of St Andrew Holborn* (London, 1831)

Grove, J. M., *The Little Ice Age* (London/New York, 1988)

Guggisberg, H. R., 'Einführung [to 'Bäuerliche Frömmigkeit und kommunale Reformation']', *Itinera*, 8 (1988), 5–13

―――― 'The problem of "failure" in the Swiss Reformation: some preliminary reflections', reprinted in his *Zusammenhänge in historischer Vielfalt*, Basler Beiträge zur Geschichtswissenschaft clxiv

(Basel/Frankfurt a.M., 1994), pp. 115–33

Gurevich, A., *Medieval Popular Culture: Problems of Belief and Perception*, Cambridge Studies in Oral and Literate Culture xiv (Cambridge, 1988)

Guth, D. J., *Late Medieval England 1377–1485*, Conference on British Studies: Bibliographical Handbooks (Cambridge, 1976)

Haigh, C., *Reformation and Resistance in Tudor Lancashire* (Cambridge, 1975)

―――― 'The recent historiography of the English Reformation', *Historical Journal*, **25** (1982), 995–1007

―――― 'Anticlericalism and the English Reformation' in Haigh (ed.), *The English Reformation Revised*, pp. 56–74 [first published *History*, **68** (1983)]

―――― (ed.), *The English Reformation Revised* (Cambridge, 1987)

―――― *English Reformations: Religion, Politics, and Society Under the Tudors* (Oxford, 1993)

Hale, W., *Precedents in Causes of Office Against Churchwardens and Others* (London, 1841)

Hanham, H., 'A tangle untangled: the lordship of the manor and borough of Ashburton', *Reports and Transactions of the Devonshire Association*, **94** (1962), 440–57

―――― 'The suppression of the chantries at Ashburton', *Reports and Transactions of the Devonshire Association*, **99** (1967), 111–37

Harding, A., *The Law Courts of Medieval England*, Historical Problems: Studies and Documents xviii (London/New York, 1973)

Harding, V., 'Burial choice and burial location in late medieval London' in S. Bassett (ed.), *Death in the Towns: Urban Responses to the Dying and the Dead 100–1600* (Leicester/London/New York, 1992), pp. 119–35

Hardy, W. J., 'Remarks on the history of seat-reservation in churches', *Archaeologia*, **53** (1892), 95–106

Harper-Bill, C., *The Pre-Reformation Church in England 1400-1530*, Seminar Studies in History (London/New York, 1989)

Harrison, F., 'The repertory of an English parish church in the early sixteenth century' in J. Robijns (ed.), *Renaissance-Muziek, 1400–1600*, Musicologica Lovaniensia i (Louvain, 1969) pp. 143–7

Harrod, H., 'Some particulars relating to the abbey church of Wymondham in Norfolk', *Archaeologia*, **43** (1880), 264–72

Hartridge, R. A. R., *A History of Vicarages in the Middle Ages*, Cambridge Studies in Medieval Life and Thought (Cambridge, 1930)

Harvey, J., *Gothic England: A Survey of National Culture 1300–1550* (2nd edn, London/Toronto/New York/Sydney, 1948)

Harvey, P. D. A., 'Initiative and authority in settlement change' in M.

Aston, D. Austin and C. Dyer (eds), *The Rural Settlements of Medieval England: Studies Dedicated to M. Beresford and J. Hurst* (Oxford, 1989), pp. 31–43

Hashagen, J., 'Laieneinfluss auf das Kirchengut vor der Reformation: ein Beitrag zu ihrer Vorgeschichte', *Historische Zeitschrift*, **126** (1922), 377–409

Haslam, J., 'Parishes, wards and gates in eastern London' in J. Blair (ed.), *Minsters and Parish Churches* (Oxford, 1988), pp. 35–43

Hatcher, J., *Plague, Population and the English Economy 1348–1530*, Studies in Economic and Social History (London/Basingstoke, 1977)

Hatschek, J., *Englische Verfassungsgeschichte*, Handbuch der mittelalterlichen und neueren Geschichte, Abteilung iii (Munich/Berlin, 1913)

Häusler, F., 'Von der Stadtgründung bis zur Reformation' in P. Meyer (ed.), *Berner – Deine Geschichte*, Illustrierte Berner Enzyklopädie (Wabern/Berne, 1981), pp. 51–106

Hay, D., *The Church in Italy in the Fifteenth Century: The Birkbeck Lectures 1971* (Cambridge, 1977)

—— 'Il contributo italiano alla riforma istituzionale della Chiesa' in P. Prodi and P. Johanek (eds), *Strutture ecclesiastiche in Italia e in Germania prima della Riforma*, Annali dell'Istituto Italo-Germanico xvi (Bologna, 1984), pp. 39–49

Heal, F., and O'Day, R. (eds), *Princes and Paupers in the English Church 1500–1800* (Leicester, 1981)

Heath, P., *The English Parish Clergy on the Eve of the Reformation*, Studies in Social History (London/Toronto, 1969)

—— 'Urban piety in the later middle ages: the evidence of Hull wills' in R. B. Dobson (ed.), *The Church, Politics and Patronage in the Fifteenth Century* (Gloucester, 1984), pp. 209–34

Henrey, T. S., *St Botolph without Aldersgate: Its Church and Parish Records* (London, 1895)

Hergemöller, B.-U., 'Parrocchia, parroco e cura d'anime nelle città anseatiche del basso medioevo' in P. Prodi and P. Johanek (eds), *Strutture ecclesiastiche in Italia e in Germania prima della Riforma*, Annali dell'Istituto Storico Italo-Germanico xvi (Bologna, 1984), pp. 135–69

Hill, C., *Society and Puritanism in Pre-Revolutionary England* (London, 1964)

Hilton, R. H., *A Medieval Society: The West Midlands at the End of the Thirteenth Century* (London, 1967)

—— *The Decline of Serfdom in Medieval England*, Studies in Economic History (London/Basingstoke, 1969)

—— *The English Peasantry in the Later Middle Ages: The Ford*

Lectures of 1973 and Related Studies (Oxford, 1975)

Holenstein, A., Kümin, B., and Würgler, A., 'Diskussionsbericht' in P. Blickle (ed.), *Landgemeinde und Stadtgemeinde in Mitteleuropa* (Munich, 1991), pp. 489–505

Holt, R., and Rosser, G. (eds), *The English Medieval Town: A Reader in English Urban History 1200–1540* (London/New York, 1990)

Horrox, R., 'Urban patronage in the fifteenth century' in R. A. Griffiths (ed.), *Patronage, The Crown and the Provinces in Later Medieval England* (Gloucester, 1981), pp. 145–66

Hoskins, W. G., *Devon*, A New Survey of England (Newton Abbot, 1972)

—— *The Age of Plunder: King Henry's England 1500–47*, Social and Economic History of England (London, 1976)

Houlbrooke, R., *Church Courts and the People during the English Reformation 1520–70*, Oxford Historical Monographs (Oxford, 1979)

Huard, G., 'Considérations sur l'histoire de la paroisse rurale des origines à la fin du moyen âge', *Revue de l'Histoire de l'Eglise de France*, 24 (1938), 5–22

Hudson, A., *The Premature Reformation: Wycliffite Texts and Lollard History* (Oxford, 1988)

Hughes, P., *The Reformation in England* (vol. i, London, 1950)

Hunt, W., *Growth and Development of the English Parish* (London, 1932)

Hutton, R., 'The local impact of the Tudor Reformations' in Haigh (ed.), *The English Reformation Revised*, pp. 114–38

—— *The Rise and Fall of Merry England: The Ritual Year 1400–1700* (Oxford, 1994)

Ingram, M., *Church Courts, Sex and Marriage in England 1570–1640*, PaP Publications (Cambridge, 1987)

Jacqueline, B., 'Les paroisses rurales en Normandie au moyen âge' in *Communautés rurales*, pp. 411–26

Jessopp, A., 'Parish life in England before the great pillage', *Nineteenth Century*, 43 (1898), 47–60, 431–47

Jewell, H. M., *English Local Administration in the Middle Ages* (Newton Abbot, 1972)

Jezler, P., *Der spätgotische Kirchenbau in der Zürcher Landschaft: Die Geschichte eines "Baubooms" am Ende des Mittelalters* (Wetzikon, 1988)

Johanek, P., 'La Germania prima della Riforma' in P. Prodi and Johanek (eds), *Strutture ecclesiastiche in Italia e in Germania prima della Riforma*, Annali dell'Istituto storico Italo-Germanico xvi (Bologna, 1984), pp. 19–38

Johnston, A. F., 'Parish entertainments in Berkshire' in J. A. Raftis (ed.), *Pathways to Medieval Peasants*, Papers in Medieval Studies ii (Toronto, 1981), pp. 335–8

—— 'The plays of the religious guilds of York: the Creed Play and the Pater Noster Play', *Speculum*, 50 (1975), 55–90

Jones, D. H., *The Church in Chester 1300–1540*, Remains Historical and Literary Connected with the Palatine Counties of Lancaster and Chester, 3rd Series vii (Manchester, 1957)

Jones, G. H., *History of the Law of Charity 1532–1827* (Cambridge, 1969)

Jordan, W. K., *Philanthropy in England 1480–1660: A Study of the Changing Pattern of English Social Aspirations* (London, 1959)

—— *The Charities of London* (London, 1960)

Jungmann, J. A., *The Mass of the Roman Rite: Its Origin and Development* (2 vols, New York, 1951–5)

Keene, D., *Survey of Medieval Winchester*, Winchester Studies ii (2 vols, Oxford, 1985)

Keily, G., *A Guide to the Parish Church of St Mary the Virgin, Yatton* (Yatton, no date)

Kettle, A. J., 'City and close: Lichfield in the century before the Reformation' in C. M. Barron and C. Harper-Bill (eds), *The Church in Pre-Reformation Society* (Woodbridge, 1985), pp. 158–69

Kirn, P., 'Der mittelalterliche Staat und das Geistliche Gericht', *Zeitschrift der Savigny-Stiftung für Rechtsgeschichte: Kanonische Abteilung*, 15 (1926), 162–99

Kitching, C., 'The quest for concealed lands in the reign of Elizabeth I', *TRHS*, 5th Series 24 (1974), 63–78

—— 'Church and chapelry in sixteenth-century England' in D. Baker (ed.), *The Church in Town and Countryside*, SCH xvi (Oxford, 1979), pp. 279–90

Kloczowski, J., 'Communautés rurales et communautés paroissiales en Europe médiévale et moderne' in *Communautés rurales*, pp. 87–106

Knoepfli, A., *Die Kunstgeschichte des Bodenseeraums* (vol. ii, Sigmaringen, 1963)

Körber, K., *Die kirchenrechtliche Theorie von der Verwaltung und Verwendung der Kirchengüter und die mittelalterliche Praxis* (Halle, 1912)

Kowaleski, M., 'Introduction' (to 'Vill, guild, and gentry: forces of community in later medieval England'), *Journal of British Studies*, 33 (1994), 337–9

Kreider, A., *English Chantries: The Road to Dissolution*, Harvard Historical Studies xcvii (Cambridge Mass., 1979)

Kümin, B. A., 'Parish finance and the early Tudor clergy' in A. Pettegree

—— (ed.), *The Reformation of the Parishes: The Ministry and the Reformation in Town and Country* (Manchester, 1993), pp. 43–62

—— 'Voluntary religion' in P. Collinson and J. Craig (eds), *The Reformation in English Towns* (Basingstoke, forthcoming)

—— 'The English parish in its European context' in K. L. French, G. G. Gibbs and B. A. Kümin (eds), *The Parish in English Life 1400–1600* (Manchester, forthcoming)

—— 'Gemeinde und Revolution – Die Kommunale Prägung der englischen Levellers' in P. Blickle (ed.) *Gemeinde und Staat in Europa*

Künstle, F. X., *Die deutsche Pfarrei und ihr Recht zu Ausgang des Mittelalters*, Kirchenrechtliche Abhandlungen, xx (Stuttgart, 1905)

Kurze, D., *Pfarrerwahlen im Mittelalter: Ein Beitrag zur Geschichte der Gemeinde und des Niederkirchenwesens*, Forschungen zur kirchlichen Rechtsgeschichte vi (Cologne/Graz, 1966)

—— 'Hoch- und spätmittelalterliche Wahlen im Niederkirchenbereich' in R. Schneider and H. Zimmermann (eds), *Wahlen und Wählen im Mittelalter*, Vorträge und Forschungen xxxvii (Sigmaringen, 1990), pp. 197–225

Lancashire, I., *Dramatic Texts and Records of Britain: A Chronological Topography to 1558* (Cambridge, 1984)

Lander, J. R., *Government and Community: England 1450–1509*, The New History of England i (London, 1980)

Lennard, R., 'Early manorial juries', *EHR*, 77 (1962), 511–18

Light, H. M., 'Halesowen', *VCH Worcester* (vol. iii, reprint London, 1971), pp. 136–53

Little, A. G., 'Personal tithes', *EHR*, 60 (1945), 67–88

Littleton, A. C., and Yamey, B. S. (eds), *Studies in the History of Accounting* (London, 1956)

Lobel, M. D., *Atlas of Historic Towns* (vol. ii, London, 1975)

—— *The City of London from Prehistoric Times to c.1520*, Atlas of Historic Towns iii (Oxford, 1989)

Luxton, I., 'The Reformation and popular culture' in F. Heal and R. O'Day (eds), *Church and Society in England: Henry VIII to James I*, Problems in Focus Series (London/Basingstoke, 1977), pp. 57–77

MacCulloch, D., *Suffolk and the Tudors* (Oxford, 1986)

MacCulloch, D. and Blatchly, J., 'Pastoral provision in the parishes of Tudor Ipswich', *Sixteenth Century Journal*, 22 (1991), 457–74

Macfarlane, A., *The Origins of English Individualism* (Oxford, 1978)

Maclean, J., 'Notes on the accounts of the procurators or CWs of the parish of St Ewen's, Bristol', *TBGAS*, 15 (1890/1), 139–82, 254–96

Maitland, F. W., 'The survival of archaic communities' in H. A. L. Fisher (ed.), *The Collected Papers of F. W. Maitland* (3 vols, Cambridge, 1911), ii. 313–65

————— 'The unincorporate body', ibid., iii. 271–84

Manaton, J., *Hatherleigh History in Brief*, Devonshire Association for the Advancement of Science, Literature and Art: Parochial History Section vi (Exeter, 1951)

Manning, B., *The English People and the English Revolution* (2nd edn, London, 1991)

Marshall, P., *The Catholic Priesthood and the English Reformation*, Oxford Historical Monographs (Oxford, 1994)

Mason, E., 'The role of the English parishioner 1100–1500', *JEH*, 27 (1976), 17–29

McFarlane, K. B., *John Wycliffe and the Beginnings of English Nonconformity* (3rd edn, London, 1972)

McIntosh, M. K., 'Local change and community control in England 1465–1500', *Huntington Library Quarterly*, 49 (1986), 219–42

————— *Autonomy and Community: The Royal Manor of Havering 1200-1500*, Cambridge Studies in Medieval Life and Thought (Cambridge, 1986)

————— 'Local responses to the poor in late medieval and Tudor England', *Continuity and Change*, 3 (1988), 209–45

McLane, B. W., 'Juror attitudes toward local disorder: the evidence of the 1328 Trailbaston proceedings' in J. S. Cockburn and T. A. Green (eds), *Twelve Good Men and True* (Princeton, 1988), pp. 36–64

Meade, D., *The Medieval Church in England* (Worthing, 1988)

Moorman, J. R. H., *Church Life in England in the Thirteenth Century* (Cambridge, 1945)

Morgan, W. T., 'Disputes before the consistory courts of St Davids', *Journal of the Historical Society of the Church in Wales*, 3 (1953), 90–9

————— 'An examination of CWA and of some disputes concerning them before the consistory court of St Davids', ibid., 8 (1958), 58–81

Morrill, J., 'The Church in England, 1642–9' in his *Reactions to the English Civil War 1642–9* (London, 1982), pp. 89–114

Morris, R., *Churches in the Landscape* (London, 1989)

Mousnier, R., *Les institutions de la France sous la monarchie absolue 1598–1789*, Histoire des institutions (vol. i, Paris, 1974)

Müller, W., 'Der Beitrag der Pfarreigeschichte zur Stadtgeschichte', *Historisches Jahrbuch*, 94 (1974), 69–88

Mullins, E. L. C., *Texts and Calendars: An Analytical Guide to Serial Publications* (2 vols, London, 1958–83)

Newbigging, T., *History of the Forest of Rossendale* (Rawtenstall, 1893)

Nicholls, J. F., and Taylor, J., *Bristol Past and Present* (vol. ii, Bristol, 1881)

O'Day, R., *The Debate on the English Reformation* (London/New York,

1986)

Olson, S., 'Jurors of the village court: local leadership before and after the plague in Ellington', *Journal of British Studies*, **30** (1991), 237–56

Oman, C., 'Security in English churches 1000–1548', *Archaeological Journal*, **136** (1979), 90–8

Orme, N. I., 'The medieval parishes of Devon', *Devon Historian*, **33** (1986), 3–9

———— *Unity and Variety: A History of the Church in Devon and Cornwall*, Exeter Studies in History xxix (Exeter, 1991)

Ormrod, W. M., 'An experiment in taxation: the English parish subsidy of 1371', *Speculum*, **63** (1988), 58–82

Oschinsky, D., 'Medieval treatises on estate accounting' in Littleton and Yamey (eds), *History of Accounting*, pp. 91–8

Outhwaite, R. B., *Inflation in Tudor and Early Stuart England*, Studies in Economic History (London/Melbourne/Toronto, 1969)

Owen, D. M., *Church and Society in Medieval Lincolnshire*, History of Lincolnshire v (Lincoln, 1971)

———— 'Chapelries and rural settlement: an examination of some of the Kesteven evidence' in P. H. Sawyer (ed.), *Medieval Settlement: Continuity and Change* (London, 1976), pp. 66–71

———— 'Two medieval parish books from the diocese of Ely: New College MS. 98 and Wisbech Museum MS. 1' in M. Barber, P. McNulty and P. Noble (eds), *East Anglian and Other Studies presented to Barbara Dodwell*, Reading Medieval Studies xi (Reading, 1985), pp. 121–31

Owst, G. R., *Preaching in Medieval England* (Cambridge, 1926)

Oxley, J. E., *The Reformation in Essex to the Death of Mary* (Manchester, 1965)

Palliser, D. M., 'The sources' in M. W. Barley (ed.), *The Plans and Topography of Medieval Towns in England and Wales*, Council for British Archaeology: Research Report xiv (Leamington, 1976), pp. 1–7

———— *The Staffordshire Landscape*, The Making of the English Landscape (London/Sydney/Auckland/Toronto, 1976)

———— 'Popular reactions to the Reformation during the years of uncertainty 1530–70' in F. Heal and R. O'Day (eds), *Church and Society in England: Henry VIII to James I*, Problems in Focus Series (London/Basingstoke, 1977), pp. 35–56

———— *Tudor York*, Oxford Historical Monographs (Oxford, 1979)

———— 'Introduction: the parish in perspective' in Wright (ed.), *Parish, Church and People*, pp. 5–28

———— 'Urban decay revisited' in J. A. F. Thomson (ed.), *Towns and Townspeople in the Fifteenth Century* (Gloucester, 1988), pp. 1–21

Pantin, W. A., *The English Church in the Fourteenth Century* (Cambridge, 1955)

Pape, T., *Newcastle-under-Lyme in Tudor and Early Stuart Times*, University of Manchester Publications: Historical Series lxxv (Manchester, 1938)

Pasche, V., *"Pour le salut de mon âme": Les Lausannois face à la mort (XIVᵉ siècle)*, Cahiers Lausannois d'histoire médiévale ii (Lausanne, 1989)

Peters, J., 'Der Platz in der Kirche: Über soziales Rangdenken im Spätfeudalismus', *Jahrbuch für Volkskunde und Kulturgeschichte*, **28** (1985), 77–106

Pettegree, A., 'Rewriting the English Reformation', *Nederlands Archief voor Kerkgeschiedenis*, **72** (1992), 37–58

Pfaff, C., 'Pfarrei und Pfarreileben: ein Beitrag zur spätmittelalterlichen Kirchengeschichte' in Historischer Verein der V Orte (ed.), *Innerschweiz und frühe Eidgenossenschaft* (2 vols, Olten, 1990), i. 203–82

Phelps-Brown, E. H., and Hopkins, S. V., 'Seven centuries of the prices of consumables, compared with builders' wage-rates', *Economica*, **23** (1956), 296–315

Philipps, E., 'A list of printed CWA', *EHR*, **15** (1900), 335–41

Phythian-Adams, C., 'Ceremony and the citizen: the communal year at Coventry 1450–1550' in P. Clark and P. Slack (eds), *Crisis and Order in English Towns 1500–1700* (London, 1972), pp. 57–85

———— 'Urban decay in late medieval England' in P. Abrams and E. A. Wrigley (eds), *Towns in Societies: Essays in Economic History and Historical Sociology* (Cambridge, 1978), pp. 159–85

———— *Desolation of a City: Coventry and the Urban Crisis of the Late Middle Ages*, PaP Publications (Cambridge, 1979)

Pievi e parrocchie in Italia nel basso medioevo (sec. XIII–XV): Atti del VI convegno di storia della Chiesa in Italia, Italia sacra: Studi e documenti di storia ecclesiastica xxxv (2 vols, Rome, 1984)

Platt, C., *The Parish Churches of Medieval England* (London, 1981)

Plumb, D., 'The social and economic spread of rural Lollardy: a reappraisal' in W. J. Sheils and D. Wood (eds), *Voluntary Religion*, SCH xxiii (Oxford, 1986), pp. 111–29

Pollock, F., and Maitland, F. W., *The History of English Law before the Time of Edward I* (2 vols, 2nd edn, Cambridge, 1968)

Poos, L. R., *A Rural Society after the Black Death: Essex 1350–1525*, Cambridge Studies in Population, Economy and Society in Past Time xviii (Cambridge, 1991)

Post, J. B., 'Jury lists and juries in the late fourteenth century' in J. S. Cockburn and T. A. Green (eds), *Twelve Good Men and True*

(Princeton, 1988), pp. 65–77

Powell, E., 'Jury trial at gaol delivery in the late Middle Ages: the Midland circuit 1400–29', ibid., pp. 78–116

Powicke, M. R., *Military Obligation in Medieval England* (Oxford, 1962)

Raftis, J. A., *Tenure and Mobility: Studies in the Social History of the Mediaeval English Village* (Toronto, 1964)

Rapp, F., 'Communautés rurales et paroisses en basse Alsace jusqu'à la fin du XVIᵉ siècle' in *Communautés rurales*, pp. 459–70

Rappaport, S., *Worlds Within Worlds: Structures of Life in Sixteenth-Century London* (Cambridge, 1989)

Razi, Z., 'Family, land and the village community in later medieval England', *PaP*, **93** (1981), 3–36

Redlich, J., *Die englische Lokalverwaltung* (Leipzig, 1901)

Redworth, G., 'Whatever happened to the English Reformation?', *History Today*, **37/10** (1987), 29–36

Reichel, O. J., *The Rise of the Parochial System in England* (Exeter, 1905)

——— *The Origin and Growth of the English Parish Illustrated by Material Taken from the Exeter Episcopal Registers*, The Society of SS Peter and Paul: Year Books xxxii (London, 1921)

Reynolds, S., *An Introduction to the History of English Medieval Towns* (Oxford, 1977)

——— *Kingdoms and Communities in Western Europe 900–1300* (Oxford, 1984)

Richmond, C., *John Hopton: A Fifteenth-Century Suffolk Gentleman* (Cambridge, 1981)

——— 'Religion and the fifteenth-century English gentleman' in R. B. Dobson (ed.), *Church, Politics and Patronage in the Fifteenth Century* (Gloucester, 1984), pp. 193–208

——— 'The English gentry and religion, *c.*1500' in C. Harper-Bill (ed.), *Religious Belief and Ecclesiastical Careers in Late Medieval England*, Studies in the History of Medieval Religion iii (Woodbridge, 1991), pp. 121–50

Rigby, S., 'Urban "oligarchies" in late medieval England' in J. A. F. Thomson (ed.), *Towns and Townspeople in the Fifteenth Century* (Gloucester, 1988), pp. 62–86

Robinson, D., *Pastors, Parishes and People in Surrey*, Surrey History: Extra Volume i (Chichester, 1989)

Rodes, R. E. Jr, *Ecclesiastical Administration in Medieval England: The Anglo-Saxons to the Reformation* (Notre Dame/London, 1977)

——— *Lay Authority and Reformation in the English Church: Edward I to the Civil War* (Notre Dame/London, 1982)

Roover, R. de, 'The development of accounting prior to Luca Pacioli' in Littleton and Yamey (eds), *History of Accounting*, pp. 114–74

Rosenthal, J. T., *The Purchase of Paradise: Gift Giving and the Aristocracy 1307–1485*, Studies in Social History (London/Toronto, 1972)

Rosser, G., 'Communities of parish and guild in the late middle ages' in Wright (ed.), *Parish, Church and People*, pp. 29–55

——— 'The Anglo-Saxon gilds' in J. Blair (ed.), *Minsters and Parish Churches*, Oxford University Committee for Archaeology: Monograph xvii (Oxford, 1988), pp. 31–4

——— *Medieval Westminster* (Oxford, 1989)

——— 'Parochial conformity and voluntary religion in late medieval England', *TRHS*, 6th Series 1 (1991), 173–89

——— 'Going to the fraternity feast: commensality and social relations in late medieval England', *Journal of British Studies*, 33 (1994), 430–45

Rubin, M., *Charity and Community in Medieval Cambridge*, Cambridge Studies in Medieval Life and Thought, 4th Series iv (Cambridge, 1987)

——— 'Small groups: identity and solidarity in the late Middle Ages' in J. Kermode (ed.), *Enterprise and Individuals in Fifteenth-Century England* (Stroud, 1991), pp. 132–50

——— 'Religious culture in town and country: reflections on a great divide' in D. Abulafia, M. Franklin, and M. Rubin (eds), *Church and City 1000-1500: Essays in Honour of Christopher Brooke* (Cambridge, 1992), pp. 3–22

Russell, C., *Crisis of Parliaments: English History 1509–1660* (5th edn, Oxford, 1982)

Rütte, H. von, 'Bäuerliche Reformation am Beispiel der Pfarrei Marbach im Sanktgallischen Rheintal' in P. Blickle (ed.), *Zugänge zur bäuerlichen Reformation*, Bauer und Reformation i (Zurich, 1987), pp. 55–84

——— 'Von der spätmittelalterlichen Frömmigkeit zum reformierten Glauben: Kontinuität und Bruch in der Religionspraxis der Bauern', *Itinera*, 8 (1988), 33–44

Sablonier, R., 'Innerschweizer Gesellschaft im 14. Jahrhundert: Sozialstruktur und Wirtschaft' in Historischer Verein der V Orte (ed.), *Innerschweiz und frühe Eidgenossenschaft* (2 vols, Olten, 1990), ii. 11–233

Sacks, D. H., *The Widening Gate: Bristol and the Atlantic Economy 1450-1700*, The New Historicism xv (Berkeley/Los Angeles/Oxford, 1991)

Scarisbrick, J. J., *The Reformation and the English People* (Oxford,

1984)

Schmidt, H. R., 'Die Häretisierung des Zwinglianismus im Reich seit 1525' in P. Blickle (ed.), *Zugänge zur bäuerlichen Reformation*, Bauer und Reformation i (Zurich, 1987), pp. 219–36

Schofield, R. S., 'The geographical distribution of wealth in England 1334–1649' in R. Floud (ed.), *Essays in Quantitative Economic History* (Oxford, 1974), pp. 79–106 [first published in *EcHR*, **18** (1965), 483–510]

Schöller, W., *Die rechtliche Organisation des Kirchenbaues im Mittelalter, vornehmlich des Kathedralbaues: Baulast – Bauherrenschaft – Baufinanzierung* (Vienna/Cologne, 1989)

Schröcker, S., *Die Kirchenpflegschaft: Die Verwaltung des Niederkirchenvermögens durch Laien seit dem ausgehenden Mittelalter*, Görres Gesellschaft zur Pflege der Wissenschaften im katholischen Deutschland: Veröffentlichungen der Sektion für Rechts- und Staatswissenschaft lxvii (Paderborn, 1934)

Schuler, P.-J., 'Das Anniversar: Zu Mentalität und Familienbewusstsein im Spätmittelalter' in his *Die Familie als sozialer und historischer Verband: Untersuchungen zum Spätmittelalter und zur frühen Neuzeit* (Sigmaringen, 1987), pp. 67–117

Scott, T., 'The Communal Reformation between town and country' in H. R. Guggisberg and G. G. Krodel (eds), *Die Reformation in Deutschland und Europa*, Archiv für Reformationsgeschichte: Sonderband (Gütersloh, 1993), pp. 175–92

Scribner, R. W., 'Ritual and popular religion in Catholic Germany at the time of the Reformation' in his *Popular Culture and Popular Movements in Reformation Germany* (London/Ronceverte, 1987), pp. 17–47

—— 'Anticlericalism and the German Reformation' in ibid., pp. 243–56

—— 'Paradigms of urban reform: *Gemeindereformation* or Erastian Reformation?' in L. Grane and K. Hørby (eds), *The Danish Reformation Against its International Background* (Göttingen, 1990), pp. 111–28

—— 'Communalism: universal category or ideological construct? A debate in the historiography of early modern Germany and Switzerland', *Historical Journal*, **37** (1994), 199–207

Seaver, P. S., *The Puritan Lectureships: The Politics of Religious Dissent 1560–1662* (Stanford, 1970)

Segesser, A. P. von, *Rechtsgeschichte der Stadt und Republik Luzern* (Luzern, 1850)

Sheils, W. J., 'Religion in provincial towns: innovation and tradition' in F. Heal and R. O'Day (eds), *Church and Society in England: Henry*

VIII to James I, Problems in Focus Series (London/Basingstoke, 1977), pp. 156–76

———— *The English Reformation 1530–70*, Seminar Studies in History (London/New York, 1989)

Simon, J., *Education and Society in Tudor England* (Cambridge, 1966)

Simpson, W. S., *Chapters in the History of Old St Paul's* (London, 1881)

Skeeters, M. C., *Community and Clergy: Bristol and the Reformation c.1530–c.1570* (Oxford, 1993)

Slack, P., *Poverty and Policy in Tudor and Stuart England*, Themes in British Social History (London/New York, 1988)

Slavin, A. J., 'Upstairs, downstairs: or the roots of Reformation', *Huntington Library Quarterly*, **49** (1986), 243–60

Smith, H. M., *Pre-Reformation England* (London, 1963) [first edn 1938]

Smith, J. T., *The Parish: Its Powers and Obligations at Law* (London, 1854)

Smith, R. M., '"Modernization" and the corporate village community in England: some sceptical reflections' in A. H. R. Baker and D. Gregory (eds), *Explorations in Historical Geography*, Cambridge Studies in Historical Geography v (Cambridge, 1984), pp. 140–79

Soil De Mariané, E., *L'église Saint-Brice* (Tournai, 1908)

Southern, W., *Western Society and the Church in the Middle Ages* (London, 1970)

Spufford, P., *Money and its Use in Medieval Europe* (Cambridge, 1988)

Staples, J., *Notes on St Botolph without Aldersgate* (London, 1881)

Swanson, R. N., *Church and Society in Late Medieval England* (Oxford, 1989)

———— 'Standards of livings: parochial revenues in pre-Reformation England' in C. Harper-Bill (ed.), *Religious Belief and Ecclesiastical Careers in Late Medieval England*, Studies in the History of Medieval Religion iii (Woodbridge, 1991), pp. 151–96

Tanner, N., *The Church in Late Medieval Norwich 1370–1532*, Pontifical Institute of Mediaeval Studies: Studies and Texts lxvi (Toronto, 1984)

Tate, W. E., *His Worship the Mayor: The Story of English Local Government in County and Borough* (London, 1943)

———— *The Parish Chest: A Study of the Records of Parochial Administration in England* (3rd edn, Cambridge, 1969)

Thomas, K., *Religion and the Decline of Magic: Studies in Popular Beliefs in Sixteenth and Seventeenth-Century England* (2nd edn, London, 1971)

———— 'Numeracy in early modern England: the Prothero lecture', *TRHS*, 5th Series 37 (1987), 103–32

Thompson, A. H., *The English Clergy and their Organization in the*

Later Middle Ages (Oxford, 1947)

Thompson, B., 'Habendum et tenendum: lay and ecclesiastical attitudes to the property of the church' in C. Harper-Bill (ed.), *Religious Belief and Ecclesiastical Careers in Late Medieval England* (Woodbridge, 1991), pp. 197–238

Thomson, J. A. F., 'Tithe disputes in later medieval London', *EHR*, **78** (1963), 1–17

——— 'Piety and charity in late medieval London', *JEH*, **16** (1965), 178–95

——— *The Later Lollards 1414–1520*, Oxford Historical Series, 2nd Series (Oxford, 1965)

——— *The Transformation of Medieval England 1370–1529*, Foundations of Modern Britain (London/New York, 1983)

——— *The Early Tudor Church and Society 1485-1529* (London/New York, 1993)

Tindal-Hart, A., *The Man in the Pew* (London, 1966)

Tupling, G. H., 'The pre-Reformation parishes and chapelries of Lancashire', *Transactions of the Lancashire and Cheshire Antiquarian Society*, **67** (1957), 1–16

Turner, R. V., 'The origin of the medieval English jury: Frankish, English or Scandinavian', *Journal of British Studies*, **7** (1968), 1–10

Vauchez, A., *Les laïcs au moyen âge: pratiques et expériences religieuses* (Paris, 1987)

Violante, C., 'Sistemi organizzativi della cura d'anime in Italia fra medioevo e rinascimento: discorso introduttivo' in *Pievi e parrocchie in Italia*, pp. 3–41

Wake, J., 'Communitas villae', *EHR*, **37** (1922), 406–13

Walters, H. B., *London Churches at the Reformation* (London, 1939)

Ware, S. L., *The Elizabethan Parish in its Ecclesiastical and Financial Aspects*, John Hopkins University Studies in History and Political Science xxvi/7–8 (Baltimore, 1908)

Webb, S. and B., *English Local Government from the Revolution to the Municipal Corporations Act: The Parish and the County* (London, 1906)

Weiss, U., *Die frommen Bürger von Erfurt: Die Stadt und ihre Kirche im Spätmittelalter und in der Reformationszeit*, Regionalgeschichtliche Forschungen im Verlag Böhlau (Weimar, 1988)

West, J., *Village Records* (Plymouth, 1982)

Westlake, H. F., *The Parish Gilds of Medieval England* (London, 1919)

Whitaker, T. D., *An History of the Original Parish of Whalley and Honour of Clitheroe* (2 vols, Manchester, 1872–6)

Whiting, R., 'Abominable idols: images and image-breaking under Henry VIII', *JEH*, **33** (1982), 30–47

—————— '"For the health of my soul": prayers for the dead in the Tudor South-West', *Southern History*, 5 (1983), 68–94

—————— *The Blind Devotion of the People: Popular Religion and the English Reformation*, Cambridge Studies in Early Modern British History (Cambridge, 1989)

Williams, E. E., *The Chantries of William Canynges in St Mary Redcliffe, Bristol* (Bristol, 1950)

Williamson, T., 'Parish boundaries and early fields: continuity and discontinuity', *Journal of Historical Geography*, 12 (1986), 241–8

Willson, A. N., *A History of Collyer's School* (London, 1965)

Wolf, E. R., *Peasants*, Foundations of Modern Anthropology Series (14th edn, Englewood Cliffs, 1966)

Wood-Legh, K. L., *Perpetual Chantries in Britain* (Cambridge, 1965)

Woodcock, B. L., *Medieval Ecclesiastical Courts in the Diocese of Canterbury* (Oxford, 1952)

Woolf, A. H., *A Short History of Accountants and Accountancy* (London, 1912)

Wright, S. J. (ed.), *Parish, Church and People: Local Studies in Lay Religion 1350–1700* (London/Melbourne/Auckland/Johannesburg, 1988)

Wrightson, K., 'Two concepts of order: justices, constables and jurymen in seventeenth-century England' in J. Brewer and J. Styles (eds), *An Ungovernable People: The English and their Law in the Seventeenth and Eighteenth Centuries* (London, 1980), pp. 21–46

—————— *English Society 1580–1680* (London/Boston/Sydney/Wellington, 1982)

—————— 'The politics of the parish' in P. Griffiths, A. Fox and S. Hindle (eds), *The Experience of Authority in Early Modern England*, Themes in Focus Series (Basingstoke, forthcoming)

Wrigley, E. A., and Schofield, R. S., *The Population History of England 1541–1871* (paperback edn, Cambridge, 1989) [1st edn, London, 1981]

Yaxley, S., *The Reformation in Norfolk Parish Churches* (Dereham, 1990)

Yeldham, F. A., *The Story of Reckoning in the Middle Ages* (London/Calcutta/Sydney, 1926)

Unpublished dissertations

Ashby, E. G., 'Some aspects of parish life in the city of London 1429–1529' (MA London, 1950)

Bainbridge, V. R., 'Gild and parish in late medieval Cambridgeshire *c.* 1350–1558' (Ph.D. London, 1994; forthcoming as *Gilds in the*

Medieval Countryside in 1996)

Beckerman, J. S., 'Customary law in English manorial courts in the thirteenth and fourteenth centuries' (Ph.D. London, 1972)

Brown, A., 'Lay piety in late medieval Wiltshire' (D.Phil. Oxford, 1990)

Craig, J. S., 'Ecclesiastical policy and local community: the parish of Prescot 1558–1603' (MA Ottawa, 1988)

────── 'Reformation, politics, and polemics in sixteenth-century East Anglian market towns' (Ph.D. Cambridge, 1992)

French, K. L., 'Lay piety in the medieval parish of Bridgwater' (MA Minnesota, 1988)

────── 'Local identity and the late medieval parish: the communities of Bath and Wells' (Ph.D. Minnesota, 1993)

Fuhrmann, R., 'Pfarrei und Kaplanei: Pfründstiftungen ländlicher Gemeinden innerhalb des Pfarrbannes von 1400–1525 als Chance und Grundlage zur Verwirklichung von "Gemeindekirche"' (Diss.phil. Berne, 1991)

Gibbs, G. G., 'Parish finance and the urban community in London 1450–1620' (Ph.D. Virginia, 1990)

Jones, N. G., 'Trusts: practice and doctrine, 1536–1660' (Ph.D. Cambridge, 1994)

Kümin, B. A., 'The late medieval English parish *c*.1400–1560' (Ph.D. Cambridge, 1992)

Mullins, E. L. C., 'The effects of the Marian and Elizabethan religious settlements upon the clergy of London 1553–64' (MA London, 1948)

Schofield, R. S., 'Parliamentary lay taxation 1485–1547' (Ph.D. Cambridge, 1963)

Sheail, J., 'The distribution of regional wealth in England as indicated in the lay subsidy returns of 1524/5' (Ph.D. London, 1968; revisions to gazetteer 1980)

Smith, P. M., 'The churchwardens of Mickfield and their accounts 1538–50' (Cambridge Certificate in Local History, 1994)

Index

Due to pressures of space, indexing has had to observe certain priorities. Given the book's emphasis on themes and general trends, there are no entries for individual CWs or parishioners. Place-names and authors from the main text only have been included here, with locations outside England subsumed under the respective countries. Individual members of the ecclesiastical hierarchy appear under 'popes' or 'bishops', aldermen and mayors under 'town officials', and parishes and gilds under the respective towns and villages. A page number succeeded by 'n' denotes a reference to a footnote.